# Educational Ministry
# in the Logic of the Spirit

*James E. Loder circa 1990*

# Educational Ministry in the Logic of the Spirit

James E. Loder Jr.

*Edited and with a Preface by* **Dana R. Wright**

*Forewords by* **Andrew Root** *and* **Ajit A. Prasadam**

CASCADE *Books* · Eugene, Oregon

Cascade Books
An Imprint of Wipf and Stock Publishers
199 W. 8th Ave., Suite 3
Eugene, OR 97401

www.wipfandstock.com

PAPERBACK ISBN: 978-1-5326-3185-6
HARDCOVER ISBN: 978-1-5326-3187-0
EBOOK ISBN: 978-1-5326-3186-3

*Cataloging-in-Publication data:*

Names: Loder, James E. (James Edwin), 1931–2001, author. | Wright, Dana R., editor. | Root, Andrew, 1974– foreword. | Prasadam, Ajit A., foreword.

Title: Educational ministry in the logic of the spirit / James E. Loder Jr. ; edited and with a preface by Dana R. Wright ; forewords by Andrew Root and Ajit A. Prasadam.

Description: Eugene, OR: Cascade Books, 2018. | Includes bibliographical references.

Identifiers: ISBN: 978-1-5326-3185-6 (paperback). | ISBN: 978-1-5326-3187-0 (hardcover). | ISBN: 978-1-5326-3186-3 (ebook).

Subjects: LCSH: Christian education (theory). | Christian education practice. | Holy Spirit.

Classification: BV4571.3 W33 2018 (print). | BV4571.3 (epub).

Manufactured in the U.S.A.                                    07/19/18

*To those around the world, in every
destitute place, who bear
witness to the gospel of Jesus Christ
in the power of the Spirit*

*Once you wise up to the presence of the Spirit, you can't wise down.*

—James E. Loder Jr.

# Contents

**Section IV: Human Participation in Divine Action
—The Claims of the Theory**

# Permissions

I WISH TO THANK the following persons, executors, or institutions for granting permission to use copyrighted materials: CS Lewis © copyright CS Lewis Pte Ltd., for permission to quote from *C. S. Lewis: A Biography*, by R. L. Green and W. Hooper (Harcourt Brace Jovanovich, 1974). Used by permission. Margaret A. Krych for permission to quote from her dissertation "Communicating 'Justification' to Elementary-Aged Children: A Study in Tillich's Correlation Method and Transformational Narrative for Christian Education," Princeton Theological Seminary, 1985. All rights reserved. Used by permission. John McClure for permission to quote from his dissertation "Preaching and the Pragmatics of Human/Divine Communication in the Liturgy of the Word in the Western Church: A Semiotic and Practical Theological Study," Princeton Theological Seminary, 1984. All rights reserved. Used by permission. Ellis S. Nelson, executor of the estate of C. Ellis Nelson for permission to quote from *Where Faith Begins*, Richmond, VA: John Knox, 1976. Used by permission. All rights reserved. Sharon Daloz Parks for permission to quote from her book *The Critical Years: Young Adults and the Search for Meaning, Faith, and Commitment*, (1980), re-released as *Big Questions, Worthy Dreams: Mentoring Young Adults in Their Search for Meaning, Purpose, and Faith*. San Francisco: Jossey-Bass, 2011. Used by permission. All rights reserved. Princeton Theological Seminary for permission to reprint a photo of James E. Loder Jr. All rights reserved. Used by permission.

I gratefully acknowledge permission to use materials from the following sources.

From *The Bible in Human Transformation*, by Walter Wink (1973), Augsburg/Fortress. Used by permission. All rights reserved. From *Word and Faith*, by Gerhard Ebeling (1963), Augsburg/Fortress. Used by permission.

# Illustrations, Photos, Diagrams, Puzzles

## TABLE

# Foreword (United States)

THE FIRST TIME THAT I heard the name James Loder was around the year 2000. I can't remember exactly when, but what I'm sure of is that those words "James Loder" were connected to another word: "genius." My professor at a seminary across the country from Princeton told me in no uncertain terms that his respect for Loder couldn't be higher—"Loder," he told me, "was a tower of creativity and insight."

In the summer of 2001, I started to prepare my application for Princeton's PhD program. The whole department was swimming with fascinating people, and Loder was at the center. Yet, in a few short weeks the world would change, and following it, the practical theology department at Princeton. On the eleventh day of September, 2001, the Twin Towers fell, and in November of the same year, so did Loder, gone before I could arrive (he died on November 9th).

Yet, from the day I stepped on campus in summer 2002 I was haunted by his ghost. Not literally of course, but the cloud of witnesses to his impact was everywhere. Like those in the early church who were converted by the people who knew Jesus telling stories about him, so it was for me with Loder. To push the analogy too far, I was more of a Paul than a Peter. I met James Loder vicariously in a seminar with his former students and colleagues.

We read nearly everything Loder wrote, including an early version of this book you now hold in your hands. My 2002 version is nothing like your fully edited book. I was given it only a chapter at a time, piece by piece, like it was contraband. And it was, in a sense. This was it—the book Loder was working on when he died. According to the community of scholars and former students, this was the book they were eagerly anticipating, because this was the book that would turn Loder's deep, at times esoteric, thought, to the practical. *Educational Ministry in the Logic of Spirit* would finally give practical flesh to all his theoretical work around theology, developmental

theory, physics, and philosophy. Finally, we'd have in print how Loder imagined people lived out the logic of the Spirit in the church.

When I first read these pages, photocopied, with Loder's marks still in
them, two things jumped out at me, (both of which made no sense at the
time). First, I thought, *Man, does this guy love Einstein! Why?* And second, I
thought, *I don't buy his justification that theory is actually practical.* I had the
greatest respect for Loder's mind, but felt like this argument was trying to
stack the deck in his favor, freeing him from the difficulty of actually *being*
practical and getting his hands dirty in practice. It seemed odd to me that
here we all wanted so badly to read Loder's practical contribution on what
Christian education looks like in the church, and yet he starts by claiming
that theory, the thing he's good at, is actually practical. It felt like a ruse,
but one I was willing to go along with because of how good all that theory
construction was.

Ironically, it's taken over fifteen years both for this book to be published
and for me to begin to see Loder's point. I'll admit I'm finally convinced, a
decade and half later, that he might be right; indeed, theory might indeed be
practical. But I only got to this point because I too fell in love with Einstein.

The connection between Loder and Einstein seems divergent, until
you realize that they lived on the same street. Both their houses sat on Mercer Street, Einstein's a much smaller white house, about eight houses down
from Loder's large yellow mansion on the seminary campus. They'd never
directly overlap on Mercer Street, Einstein dying in 1955 and Loder starting
his teaching career in 1962. But just as Loder was my ghost, Einstein was his.
Einstein was known for walking Mercer at least a few times a day, searching
high and low on those walks for his unified theory, pacing back and forth
in front of what would one day be Loder's house. What Einstein was specifically searching for was the connection that would bring his theory of relativity into union with Niels Bohr's quantum mechanics. Poor Einstein died
in Princeton never finding that theory on Mercer Street (or anywhere else).

After a car accident in 1970, when his life was transformed by the
Spirit, Loder entered his own journey. The book *The Transforming Moment*
chronicles this voyage. Dr. Loder was actually far from Mercer Street, somewhere on the New York Turnpike, being a Good Samaritan, when his life
was transformed. As he changed the tire for some stranded travelers, a semi
truck veered from its lane, hitting the car Loder was working on, the car
pinning him to the pavement as it pushed his powerless body toward its
demise. Yet, in the very moment when his human spirit was about to leave
his body, Loder experienced the overwhelming energy of the Holy Spirit,
feeling a rush of energy into his broken body and a deep love for everyone
around him.

Loder survived, and the next decades on Mercer Street would lead him to search for his own unified theory—not that would unite relativity and quantum theory but rather the Holy Spirit and the human spirit. Dr. Loder sensed, and would then sketch out in his books, *The Transforming Moment, The Knight's Move,* and mostly in *The Logic of Spirit,* that the human spirit was made for the Holy Spirit. And if one could just look at natural phenomena in a new way, perceiving it as four-dimensional, as Einstein had with space and time, then we could see a deep interaction between the divine and the human, just as Einstein did with space and time.

Loder often talked of four-dimensional reality. Drawing from the sciences and Kierkegaard, he claimed that the human spirit is Lived World, Self, Holy, and Void. On those walks on Mercer Street, Einstein too held that reality was four-dimensional—the three dimensions of space, plus time. Einstein showed that space and time were so interconnected that they are relative to one another. Space and time are not constant but respond to the sole constant of the natural universe—light. And it was a flood of light experienced as love that Loder felt as he lay dying on that roadside hill, when he felt the Holy Spirit meet him.

Light, then, was a tricky thing, a mystery with which Loder begins the first pages of this book. Einstein's hero, the faithful Presbyterian (like Loder himself) James Clark Maxwell, had calculated the speed of light, unpacking its mysteries. Einstein, long before living on Mercer Street, was known for skipping class to read Maxwell. Not only had Maxwell discovered the speed of light, but he had also shown that it came in waves, as electric fields.

Decades later the scientist Max Planck theorized that light did more than this. Oddly, he believed, light not only moved in waves but also as dots, as small quanta. But his idea languished as just an unsubstantiated idea, until the unknown Einstein in 1905 proved it with a paper. The universe was open to divergent realities, like waves and quanta, being united but not confused, in light. The creeds of Nicene and Chalcedon had witnessed to this relationality sixteen hundred years earlier, as Loder never tired of reminding his readers. The universe is made for the union of divergent realities; just as light can be wave and quanta, so divine and human nature can correlate in Jesus, and the human spirit finds its rest in the Holy Spirit. As light was made through paradox so too the human spirit, Loder would so vividly show me back in 2002. It is the reality of the void (death), that promises a union of new life. The void written into the human spirit (at every life stage) paradoxically reveals that we are made for more than death, that our spirits are open for the Holy Spirit.

But this leads us back to theory as practical. Planck had intuited a structure of reality: that indeed light came also as quanta. He had no way of proving this, but the eccentric Einstein did. Einstein would prove Planck's *feel* not by empirically showing it or practically demonstrating it—like you might in chemistry. Rather, Einstein found verification of Planck's idea through theory. Einstein theorized, but not as a disconnected robot doing pure mathematics. Instead Einstein became an imaginative child, letting his mind race into thought experiences about trains, riding light beams, and throwing objects from boats.

Even when he was walking Mercer Street, Einstein would feel his way into the universe through thought experiments like imagining what it would be like to ride a light beam and then look at yourself in a mirror. These thought experiments had no footing in reality. There was no way that Einstein could *do* any of these thought experiments, somehow repeating them a dozen times to check his calculations. But what these childish games did for Einstein was allow him to enter into the structures of reality, feeling himself deep within them, so that he could theorize about them.

So theory for Einstein wasn't disconnected from reality, but was the vehicle of feeling parts of reality that without imagination escape us, but somehow live within us. Theory is a way of painting a beautiful picture of the shape of reality. To understand what Loder means by theory being practical, you have to hear him speaking not as social scientist or philosopher, but as physicist. Because reality is structured and trustworthy, a physicist can trust that her theory is practical because she seeks to unveil the very reality we live within—what could be more practical than that?

When Einstein was asked what would happen if his theory of relativity was shown to be untrue, he responded as only he could. He said, "I would forgive God." Elaborating, Einstein said, he just couldn't imagine that relativity wasn't true, not because he had proved it in a laboratory, but because it was just too beautiful to not be true. Einstein's theory was so practical it was beautiful!

I believe that this is exactly what Loder means. If the Holy Spirit moves in the universe, bringing life out of the void of death, then this will never be empirically proven. It will never be defused into twenty-five bullet points, as practical as the manual for your blender. But if the call of the Christian minister is to testify to God's action in the world, witnessing to how death is turned into life, how a lost human spirit finds rest in the Spirit of God, then beautiful pictures will be the only way to see it, theoretical thought experiments its canvas. And nothing could be more practical than seeing this beautiful structure, for in seeing it is you will be changed—transformed—by it, as Loder always knew.

As you turn the page and step into Loder's last thought experiment, let his pictures of reality soak over you. Don't get discouraged. Just as reading

Einstein takes patience with esoteric mathematics, so reading Loder takes endurance. But if you hang in, you'll be changed because you'll begin to see reality differently. You'll see a picture of the logic of the Spirit.

Andrew Root
The Carrie Olson Baalson Associate Professor
of Youth and Family Ministry
Luther Seminary
St. Paul, Minnesota

# Foreword (India)

THIS BOOK, *EDUCATIONAL MINISTRY in the Logic of the Spirit* (henceforth *EMLOS*) is an altogether remarkable and path-breaking work in Christian education. It is highly readable despite difficult concepts, even for first-time readers of the author, James E. Loder, made plain through a constant ebb and flow of stories and parables. It invites readers into the study of the "object," Christian education, under investigation from within to disclose its hidden structure, dynamics, functions, and to unravel the deeper hidden orders of meaning through a process of transformation, in all areas of human action. In all his writings Loder is after the deep hidden orders of meaning in the Creator and in the created order—a passion he had from his undergraduate days driving him to diverse fields of study.

James E. Loder Jr., a polymath and theologian, was one of the rare creative thinkers in the second half of the twentieth century. I discovered his creativity through my association with him beginning in 1993 as a ThM student and later as a PhD candidate at Princeton Theological Seminary. It was great joy to have him as a guest in India in 1997, traveling with him to five cities where he gave his classic lecture series on transformation. On the sidelines we visited important sites. He was powerfully impacted by the visit to Mother Teresa's mission where people from around the world cared for the dying. This experience finds a place in his writings on identity formation in his book on human development. He was enthralled by the Taj and stood gazing at the mausoleum created to express love for one's beloved. He always engaged in deep reflection at the sites and over meals. The days with him, at Princeton Seminary and in India, helped me see a scientist at work from close quarters. Always in wonderment as he beheld the Creator and the created order, his eyes often brimmed over with tears of gratitude for what he could comprehend. He thought both from below (i.e., the sciences) and from above (i.e., theology). He saw theology as a science, in line with T. F. Torrance.

Loder, in all his books, has related theology to the sciences in accordance with a christomorphic pattern, Divine and human, in an asymmetrical relational unity, which at the same time maintains the two qualitatively distinctive entities, like the Mobius band. He thus overcame dualism to see things whole and has contributed to the healing of culture, society, nature, and persons. In *EMLOS*, as the title suggests, Loder brings his theology of the Holy Spirit in relation to the human spirit and education, into dialogue, in accordance with the same christomorphic pattern. His development of the relationality of the Holy Spirit and human spirit, qualitatively distinct, and the transformational dynamics of both the Holy Spirit and human spirit, which are akin, is a unique contribution to the doctrine of the Spirit in a Trinitarian understanding of God. In a praxis-oriented culture, Loder sets forth an explicit theoretical perspective in which praxis ever remains in reciprocal relationship to theory. Such an approach to the study of Christian education discloses the hidden order where the notion of what *Christian* means and the notion of what *education* means are in contradiction. He sees the far-reaching challenge education gives Christianity and similarly the Christian challenge to education. This mutual challenge, he says, is the crux of Christian education.

He enhances his discussion by critically drawing on Talcott Parsons's theory of general action, in which Parsons discusses why there is order and not disorder. Parsons calls this conservative force socialization, one that gives rise to order rather than disorder by maintaining the status quo in a "tension-reduction, pattern-maintenance" manner. Loder told me a week before he died that he had tinkered with the idea of change and transformation for forty years, an idea he incorporated into the neo-Parsonian model. Thus, he brought theology into dialogue with Parsons's scientific model, in a christomorphic pattern. In other words, Loder, though he refines Parsons's theory of action, is both faithful to Parsons and goes beyond Parsons by introducing transformation into the model.

Loder showed that not only is socialization operative in all fields of human action—biological, psychological, social, and cultural—but there is also another force called natural transformation operative as well. Transformation is basically a disruptive force that reveals hidden orders of meaning in all areas of human action. Because of the human penchant for order, socialization generally trumps transformation in order to reduce tension in the systems. Theologically transformed, however, socialization should be in the service of transformation. Loder draws upon theology to discuss the redemptive transformation of human experience by showing how through the mediation of Christ and the dynamics of the divine Spirit, the divine intersects the human plane, impacting the human spirit to bring about deep structural changes, in all areas of human action.

These changes reflect the values of sacrificial love given with integrity, power in the service of people, freedom, and justice. Enroute to this understanding he shows the inability of socialization to give rise to these values and to bring healing into the human situation. For when socialization is the dominant force in education, it gives rise to one of the following lifestyles: (1) achievement orientation with its obsession; (2) authoritarianism with its preoccupation with power and control; (3) oppressedness with its low self-esteem and latent anger against an unidentified oppressor, and with its inability to name reality and imaginatively take initiative to liberate oneself; and (4) proteanism with its perpetual identity crisis.

Historically, education has tended to be a handmaiden of socialization. The word *Christian* in Christian education is transformational in nature. Thus, the two forces, socialization and transformation, are at play in Christian education. When socialization dominates, the practice of Christian education tries to teach Christianity, which Loder says cannot be taught. Christian faith has to be discovered through a transformational process and engagement with the Word within a four-dimensional understanding of reality—the Self; the Lived World that we create through our interaction with the world; the Void, which we experience on the existential plane as negation; and the Holy, which we encounter in the midst of the Void. Four-dimensional transformation happens primarily as an act of the Spirit, in a Spirit-to-spirit relation revealed paradigmatically in worship.

This form of Christian education gives rise to the Christian style of life, characterized (1) by sacrificial love given with integrity as the ego defenses are transformed and a dialectical identity is formed with Christ; (2) by the experience of *koinonia*—fellowship in the Spirit where roles become reversible; (3) by freedom in the imageless spiritual presence of Christ through whom master images of culture give way to the divine; and (4) by the desire to see justice done in the world when intelligence is transformed turning knowledge (*scientia*) into wisdom (*sapientia*). As a result, Christians living in the Spirit become the bearers of the Word, fired into the world with a velocity not their own.

Christian education theorists, who have supported religious instruction, faith community, and spiritual formation, have tended to err on the side of socialization. Theorists who have emphasized liberation and interpretation have given transformation the upper hand, especially Paulo Freire and Thomas Groome. Loder critically draws upon Paulo Freire and sees liberation as the first step to four-dimensional transformation. He sees Groome's work as falling short of transformational Christian education as

Groome fails to recognize how the power of socialization typically dominates the power of critical reflection.

Loder's work has helped us in India develop a Christian education curriculum, *Windows to Encounter*, which is in use in India, Malaysia, the Gulf countries, and Sri Lanka. We have also developed teacher-training modules based on transformational Christian education, and so far delivered them in India, Myanmar, and Sri Lanka. I think his is cutting-edge work that goes beyond what Christian education theorists have developed in the twentieth century. It even goes beyond John Dewey's work that misses the crucial role of intuition and imagination in the leap of insight one gets working through a conflict, as Dewey's understanding of the process of knowing is unwittingly mired in the Enlightenment thinking of objectivism in the study of any field. We in India have also started exploring the use of Loder's transformational approach to education for the teaching of core subjects, taught in schools, with the help of the creative arts.

I am convinced that the book you hold in your hands has value and relevance not only for the educators and Christian educators in the West, but for all of us in the two-thirds world as well who care about education in general and Christian education in particular as we seek to see transformation at work in all areas of human action.

You need to read this remarkable book—extremely well-written for a serious reader of books—to see why we in India consider it of great significance for Christian education, education, and practical theology. I intend to use *EMLOS* for graduate and postgraduate classes I teach.

Dr. Ajit A. Prasadam
General Secretary, India Sunday School Union
Director of the St. Andrew Centre
for Human Resource Development & Counselling
Coonoor, Tamil Nadu, India

# Preface

THE RECENT ATTACKS IN New York City and Washington DC on September 11 were intended to be violent strikes against the political, economic, and military core of American pride and power. However, from a theological vantage, the attackers missed the point that lies at the heart of America's institutional power—the human spirit. In point of fact, these attacks may ultimately result in a new release of the spirit that underlies America's true strength, especially manifest through the latter part of the twentieth century in the civil rights movement and other such humanizing initiatives. Thus, we may discover through these horrific events a deeper appreciation than ever before for human values of love, faithfulness, compassion, responsibility, and accountability, etc.—values that make any culture flourish. Perhaps also the church will awaken to the depths of her own participation in God's Spirit and thereby to her own responsibility to witness to the gospel of Jesus Christ in a way that advocates a true transvaluation of values toward the renewal and transformation of our nation for the good of the world. Perhaps![1]

The cultural significance of imagining such a radical transvaluation of values is that it appears at a time when so-called postmodernism is supposed to have taken charge of the contemporary ethos. In 1905 Albert Einstein published his radical paper on special relativity. Since that time nonscientific culture has absolutized relativity as the key to postmodern mentality.

1. Editor's Note: This opening paragraph in Loder's preface contained a sentence that included unsubstantiated claims about the positive impact 9/11 had on the public life of America. Had he found a publisher, I feel quite sure that these statements would have been edited out. Thus, I emended the last part this first paragraph in a way that eliminated these untoward claims and placed Loder's reflections about the impact of 9/11 in a more subjunctive mood, using the verb "may" and the adverb "perhaps" twice. I am sure that had Loder lived longer into America's actual response to 9/11, he would have been quite dismayed by much of what has actually transpired. I say this with confidence based on the actual contents of this present volume. Loder would insist that nations, like persons and the church, must choose for or against the awakening of spirit in times of crisis.

As sociologist Neil Postman once remarked, "Einstein has made everything relative." Postman's remark, of course, is profoundly incorrect. Surely many things we thought were absolute were made relative by Einstein's view of the universe. However, Einstein's theory made everything in the universe relative to the speed of light in a vacuum, not absolutely relativistic. Indeed, the speed of light was for him a universal constant or absolute. Although some scientists challenge this Einsteinian axiom in physics, its actual truth lies very far from the sophisticated relativism that cultural artisans such as Derrida, Foucault, and their followers have tried to appropriate for philosophy and which ubiquitously and tragically infuses itself into the cultural consciousness at the popular level in the form of a casual "whatever-ism."

Ever since Newton, the hard sciences have set the criteria for cultural legitimacy. But this postmodern relativistic mentality has profoundly misunderstood the scientific claims involved in postmodern science. Not only that, but ontological and epistemological relativism has also been revealed to be an impotent and superficial bulwark in a post–September 11 world in which the human spirit must absorb far more sustenance than can be provided by an endlessly interplaying diet of words and images, "full of sound and fury [and feigned profundity] but signifying nothing."

On the theological landscape one response to this condition in human culture is a rising appreciation for what some have called "radical orthodoxy." Such a faith stance makes the basic claim that those who cried out, "Oh, my God!" as they watched the towers fall in New York City were not just emotionally overwhelmed and verbally vacuous in what they were saying. Their cry was a prayer! Their prayer was offered to the one and only reality they knew who was infinitely greater than the terror they felt. Postmodern relativism was and is ridiculously weak and irrelevant when such death-infused circumstances threaten to undo us. Of course, radical orthodoxy I have in mind here is not a regression to fundamentalism with its authoritarian absolutes based on fear.[2] The perfect love of God casts out fear. The radical orthodoxy affirmed in this study is that which knows deep down in one's spirit that God is more real than anything we can create with our hands, more real than any cultural or even theological construction related to God we create with our minds. God is reality, deeply personal, who

---

2. Editor's Note: Loder's emphasis on "postmodern relativism" in his preface overrides his trenchant critique of authoritarianism with its tribalistic responses to relativism. This volume says a great deal about the authoritarian temptation rampant in our world today. Had Loder written his preface today, he might have elaborated what he meant by this one sentence on fundamentalism. This volume actually addresses four postmodern lifestyles that destroy the integrity of human life: a lifestyle of protean relativism, a lifestyle of achievement obsession, an authoritarian lifestyle, and an oppressive lifestyle. See chapter 3.

undergirds our institutional life and all our thinking, even as God cannot be grasped or domesticated by any institutional or theoretical construct.

More personally and pointedly, God addresses us Spirit-to-spirit, and proves again and again that God is not only the definitive reality, more real than any human creation, but also more just than whatever punishments we can devise for evil. Deep justice is in the hands of God, more profound than our limited vision will let us see. This intuition in itself is a call for our repentance in the context of all the great world orders we seek to construct and control.

Furthermore, radical orthodoxy, as it is understood in this volume, bears some resemblance to, but is finally distinct from, the John Milbank school.[3] Radical orthodoxy in this volume does not negate science, neither the hard sciences nor the human sciences, in the way Milbank tends to do. In this volume I want to affirm an orthodoxy that seeks to use and transform scientific methods, claims, and insights theologically in the service of the Spirit of Christ. Thus, this book takes seriously the sciences and the essential but limited insight and control they try to exert over human life from the organic and personal to the cultural and philosophical. But it argues that these scientific forms of human understanding are finally too weak to make the crucial differences we need unless and until their insights are affirmed, negated, and empowered and redirected by the Spirit of God as revealed in Jesus Christ.

Thus, I want to place the self-revealed divine reality in Jesus Christ at the center of our thinking in this book, especially as we contemplate educating the upcoming generation in the redemptive power of God's transforming work as redeemer of all creation. The argument here sets the two great powers of human experience, socialization and transformation, understood scientifically, in relation to the redemptive transformational power of the Spirit of Christ, as understood in theological science.[4] In the Spirit, human

3. Editor's Note: John Milbank is a British Anglican theologian whose 1990 book *Theology and Social Theory* offered a neo-Augustinian integration with critical postmodern thought that gave rise to a "radical orthodox" approach to theology. See also Milbank, et al., eds., *Radical Orthodoxy*. Loder distinguished his own neo-Chalcedonian thought from Milbank's because he wanted to give a fuller play to the contribution of postmodern science in interdisciplinary practical theology than he felt Milbank and others did.

4. Editor's Note: Loder's "theological science" is set forth in his interdisciplinary trilogy: *Transforming Moment*, which makes a case for the scientific study of convictional experiences; *Knight's Move*, which elaborates the complementary relationality between Chalcedonian Christology and the natural and human sciences; and *Logic of the Spirit*, his comprehensive study of human development in the Spirit discerned through this Chalcedonian lens. These three works as well as two papers written later in his life— "Normativity" and "Place of Science"—provide readers with the core articulation of

action dynamically replicates the divine relationality in the Chalcedonian understanding of Christ, resulting in theological transformation of every realm of human action. In light of this transforming interaction, this book seeks a christomorphic view of education in and for the church in the power of the Spirit, a catalyst for the redemptive transformation of individual and communal life and for enabling the church's witness in and to the world.

The overall argument of this book, then, attempts to establish the logic of the Spirit, both human and divine, as the speed-of-light equivalent for human affairs and so the true norm for our educational perspectives and practices in the life of the church. The need for such a realignment of congregational existence through the Spirit comes at a time when the massive forces of historical events are dissolving postmodernism and the supposed scientific basis for radical relativism is being revealed to be little more than a contrived fiction.

James E. Loder Jr.
Princeton, New Jersey
November 2001

---

Loder's forty-year project to both bear witness to Christ in a scientific world and to enter into dialogue with that world in light of Christ. This present work draws upon all of this research and renders it accessible as a comprehensive theoretical guide for congregational transformation and much more.

# Editor's Preface

On November 2, 2001, I dined with Dr. James Loder at one of Princeton, New Jersey's landmark eateries, the Yankee Doodle Tap Room, located in the basement of the famed Nassau Inn. Beneath Norman Rockwell's rollicking mural of the dandy wannabe Doodle, feather in hat, parading on a tiny horse in front of bemused townspeople, excitable dogs, mischievous children, and several British soldiers doubled over with laughter, Dr. Loder and I "talked shop." Our conversation focused in particular on the manuscript he had given me a week prior, *Educational Ministry in the Logic of the Spirit* (henceforth *EMLOS*). The contents were familiar to me because the book was based on his popular and oft-repeated ED 105 lectures "Education Ministry." I had served as TA for this course on a number of occasions. Dr. Loder wanted feedback from me and other students and colleagues on the book before he submitted it to a publisher.[5] I remember only bits and pieces of the conversation. I did voice some concern about the preface he had written, which I had never seen before. His opening reflections on the impact of 9/11 on American culture seemed to me curiously overstated and unsubstantiated.[6]

More important, I do remember that Dr. Loder did not look well. During the course of our conversation he excused himself at least twice. Sadly, this engagement proved to be our last supper together. The following Monday he collapsed at a local bank, asked for prayer, and slipped into a coma. Several colleagues and students visited him in the hospital the next day, taking turns to be with him, our eyes bathed in tears of deep sadness mixed with feelings of great joy for the grace of having known him. Later that

5. I do not know if he had submitted this manuscript to a publisher at this point.

6. Dr. Loder made statements about prayer returning to schools and divorce rates plummeting. These statements could not have been based on serious research, since 9/11 had taken place a little over a month before our meeting. As I mentioned above in a note to Loder's preface, I feel confident that Dr. Loder would have omitted these comments from his opening paragraph had he lived to see this book published.

evening we surrounded him at his bedside. We softly sang joyous hymns of praise to God and eulogized God's beloved servant before saying our collective goodbye. On Friday, November 9, a week after our dinner, he was gone.[7]

*EMLOS* was not published. And to the consternation of many of us who wanted this particular book made available, it languished in obscurity for many years. Some attempts were made to make it accessible to scholars. I helped Loder's longtime secretary, Kay Vogen, place copies of several different iterations of the manuscript in the Loder archive of the seminary library sometime in 2002. I had hoped the manuscript would find the light of day shortly after the Loder Festschrift, *Redemptive Transformation in Practical Theology*, came out in 2004. Indeed, in anticipation of its publication we added a summary of *EMLOS* to the Festschrift itself to whet appetites for what we were sure would soon follow.[8] But publication did not follow. About six or seven years later a partial copy of the book became available online at a website associated with Wheaton College in Illinois.[9] Then, in 2014, I coedited a critical engagement with Loder's work by former students in dialogue with scholars from the Child Theology Movement. We had met at Princeton Theological Seminary in March of 2012 to discuss several papers on aspects of Loder's thought. Revisions of these papers were published in a book titled *The Logic of the Spirit in Human Thought and Experience*.[10] Fearing again that *EMLOS* would never get published, I wrote a comprehensive summary of it contents along with my understanding of its significance for inclusion in that book.[11]

Finally, after over fifteen years of waiting and substituting summarizations for the real thing, Loder's gift was given. *EMLOS* is his only book on Christian education per se, a discipline he taught for forty years at Princeton Theological Seminary. Now that the book is available, we sincerely hope that Loder's theory of Christian education will finally get the attention it deserves. Let me offer several reasons why I believe *EMLOS* still bears, after these many years, so much promise for Christian educators, practical

---

7. Those unfamiliar with James Loder and his work would benefit from reading any of my three introductions to his life and scholarship. See Wright, "Are You There?," 1–40; Wright, "*Homo Testans*," 1–30; and Wright, "James E. Loder Jr."

8. Haitch, "Summary," 298–324.

9. This resource no longer exists to my knowledge.

10. The Child Theology Movement is an international organization of scholars and practitioners who have joined together to advocate for a more humble and humane yet bold witness from the church in the world. The name of this organization alludes to Jesus's enacted parable about true greatness in Matt 18:1–5.

11. Wright, "*Educational Ministry*," 155–201. I have chosen not to include an introduction to this book that outlines its contents, since the two summaries mentioned (from Haitch and Wright) provide adequate overviews.

theologians, and all those concerned about the integrity and credibility of the church's spirit and witness in these perilous times.

*First,* Loder's book offers a bold, even scandalous, <u>christological</u> concentration that grounds his practical theology of divine and human interrelations wholly in the revealed God-human structure of reality. At the same time, and for that very reason, Loder critically and comprehensively engages the human sciences in a way that preserves the integrity of their contributions to knowing Christ. Loder offers here an exemplary model for doing critical confessional and interdisciplinary practical theology expansively and with integrity from within a major theological tradition called to witness to the gospel of Jesus Christ in a scientific world. The bold christological concentration of Loder's Reformed theological imagination at work here integrates the church's *kerygmatic* concern to proclaim Christ *to* culture and its *apologetic* concern to engage in dialogue *with* culture. But the integration itself is *thoroughly christological* and therefore quite scandalous in our pluralistic age.[12]

By *thoroughly christological* I mean that (1) the *witness* of the book (i.e., testifying to Christ crucified, raised, and reigning through the Spirit in our contemporary world), (2) the *contents* of the book (i.e., explicating how Christ takes hold of human experience through the logic of the Spirit), and (3) the *method* of the book (i.e., demonstrating the christological basis upon which Loder integrates theology with the human sciences to shape practical theological theory and practice in our postmodern context) all cohere. Loder mines the depth of the Christian tradition's understanding of the God-Human, Jesus Christ, mediated to us through the Holy Spirit. He not only draws upon the witness of seminal figures in the tradition, like the Gospel writers, Paul, the theologians of <u>Chalcedon</u>, Luther, Calvin, Kierkegaard,[13] Barth, <u>Torrance</u>, Pannenberg, and so forth, to make his case. He also draws on the stories of common people transformed by the

---

12. James Fowler recognized Loder's extraordinary christological concentration in their 1982 debate at Michigan State University sponsored by the Religious Education Association. See their joint follow-up essay: Fowler and Loder, "Conversations," 133–48.

13. The Kierkegaardian depth of Loder's project was recognized at the end of Root and Dean, *Theological Turn*. Root, who wrote one of the forewords to this volume, devised a <u>taxonomy</u> of emerging theological and interdisciplinary theories of youth ministry in a postscript to that book (218–36). He located his own work in what he called the Kierkegaardian category and pointed to Loder's work as also representative of this perspective. I think Loder would have joyfully—i.e., in an ironic Kierkegaardian way—accepted <u>Root</u>'s categorization, since Kierkegaard remained his primary interlocutor for scholarship throughout his life. Kierkegaard's thought was, as Loder often said, "language for my head."

presence of Christ—including on his own experience—to argue that Jesus Christ in his bipolar nature is indeed the Lord of Christian education's witness, content, and method, both in theory and practice, throughout history and now.[14]

*Second,* Loder's pneumatological STUDY OF THE HOLY SPIRIT understanding of transformation by the Spirit in all four dimensions of human action—organic, psychic, social, and cultural—is unique and holds enormous promise for guiding future reflection on this once neglected but now increasingly important and essential concern for practical theology.[15] In particular Loder specifies the Spirit's redemptive transformation of three core constructs of the human spirit: the psychic core (ego), the social core (role), and the cultural core (language and symbol), to demonstrate how the Spirit realigns human beings and communities according to the spiritual nature of Christ. We note here that Loder, by his own admission, did not fully attend to *bodily* transformation here so that this dimension remained primarily implicit in the book.

Loder's use of the adjective *redemptive* in relation to transformation—i.e., *redemptive* transformation—illuminates the radicalness of his pneumatology. Loder believed the signifier *transformation* had become a buzzword in practical theology (and throughout academic and popular discourse as well) meaning little more than a positive outcome or a positive movement in thought or action brought about by human perspicacity or creativity. Therefore, any practical theology that was truly Christian had to define and use the word *transformation* theologically if it was to speak with integrity of the Holy Spirit's *alien* involvement in human experience.[16] "*Redemptive* transformation" in Loder's thinking is thus shorthand for the divine transformation of all human transformations initiated and realized through

---

14. Loder had written extensively of how this God-Human relational reality finds theoretical analogy in the relation of theology to the human and natural sciences and existential analogy in the relation of the Holy Spirit to the human spirit in human experience. This volume sets forth Loder's expansive grasp of both the Reformed tradition and our scientific context and focuses attention on the implications of the living Christ for understanding and practicing the redemptive transformation of congregations in the emerging postmodern world.

15. Edward Farley drew attention to the lack of serious pneumatology in Christian education in the early 1960s with his controversial articles "Does Christian Education" in the journal *Religious Education.* Loder's work can be understood as one very important response to Farley's indictment. See chapter 2, 54–6 and chapter 5 of this book.

16. When I asked Dr. Loder what he wanted to title his Festschrift, he answered, *Redemptive Transformation in Practical Theology,* and he shared with me his concern about the careless and nontheological use of the word *transformation.* See Wright, *Redemptive,* 9n11. If one wants to understand Loder's distinctive contribution to practical theology, one has to understand the difference he articulates between transformation and *redemptive* transformation.

the power of the Holy Spirit. Human experience becomes redemptively or theologically transformative only when the human spirit participates in the eschatological power of God's reign acting in human history according to "the logic of the Spirit."

*Third,* Loder's scientific account of the redemptive transformation of human experience or action in Christian education also generates profound insights into how we read our own culture theologically, both affirmatively and critically. Loder organized *Educational Ministry in the Logic of the Spirit* in large part around his imaginative, theological rendering of Talcott Parsons's classic but nonetheless controversial action theory.[17] Loder studied at Harvard when Parsons held the floor in sociology there, and he absorbed and indwelt his action theory. Years later he reenvisioned it theologically through his neo-Chalcedonian lens. In doing so, Loder offers a way to see more than Parsons saw about the significance of the conforming and domesticating power of socialization, devising a profoundly simple (not simplistic!) explanatory dialectic of socialization and transformation with incredible interpretative power in all realms of human experience and history. Indeed, at the outset of *Educational Ministry in the Logic of the Spirit,* Loder himself writes, "the tacit agenda [of this book] to be made explicit at the conclusion is *to use this study of Christian education as a basis for articulating a comprehensive theory of practical theology embracing the whole field of human action in the light of God's power to transform that field through the presence and power of the Holy Spirit.*"[18] Loder himself believed that his particular theory of Christian education carried metatheoretical explanatory power beyond church education and the other practical concerns of academic practical theology—preaching, counseling, pastoral care, congregational studies—into every department in the seminary and beyond the seminary into the so-called secular academy as well. Loder wanted nothing less than to read all reality theologically through the lens of the God-Human Jesus Christ.[19]

17. For a helpful introduction to Parsons's complex thought, see Hamilton, *Parsons.*

18. See chapter 1, 3 (italics added). There is good evidence that Loder planned to write this comprehensive work for practical theology. In the Loder archive is a detailed table of contents for a work he intended to write, including a eighty-page chapter on Piaget that was found among Loder's papers. We can only guess at this point if he had written any other chapters for this mammoth work that were not recovered.

19. Indeed, so expansive is Loder's understanding of the practical range of his theological science that this book touches on diachronic as well as synchronic dimensions of human existence. For example, chapter 2 is an extraordinarily suggestive proposal for reading history itself christologically and pneumatologically—past, present, and future—a Christian theological theory of history in a nutshell.

My hope, therefore, is that this book might generate discussions in every seminary department—biblical, historical, systematic, and practical—as well as in universities where the full scope of human thought and experience should include a range of specific theological frameworks seriously considered and appropriately articulated. Loder longed to place theology into the larger cultural conversations required by a scientific culture where the voice of Christ could be heard clearly and articulately.[20]

*Fourth*, Loder's emphasis on the nature of the knower as a crucial epistemological factor brings theology and postmodern science together in a mutually illuminating way. Loder argued throughout his oeuvres that the nature of the knower determines how anything is known, especially at the depth of ultimate meaning. This concern for the nature of the knower again brings together Loder's *kerygmatic* concern to witness with boldness to Christ in a scientific culture and his *apologetic* concern to dialogue with culture with integrity and humility. From this standpoint we may discern that *Educational Ministry in the Logic of the Spirit* articulates what happens to human beings and communities when the Spirit of Christ works redemptively to transform the horizons of human consciousness and creativity at the level of spirit. Several implications can be drawn from this emphasis on the ontological transformation of the knower through the Spirit.[21]

First, the longing to know becomes, in the Spirit, an act of worship and an act of service for others across all boundaries that would divide the human community. Loder testified to and embodied this transformational reality in his life and scholarship. He testified to the proper grounding of life and scholarship in worship, following the tradition *lex orandi, lex credendi*. We pray (worship); therefore we know. We know as an act of prayer (worship). Worship is indeed the legitimate epistemological lens through which to view life at its most profound level. Loder possessed a palpable sense that human beings, individually and corporately, awaken to and embody their ontological vocation through worshipful participation in the Trinitarian life

---

20. From Loder's first major work, *Transforming Moment*, one of his goals has been to legitimate the study of convictional experiences in a scientific world. Loder's apologetic concern has been to give the Christian church a credible witness in a scientific culture that is generally reluctant to consider overt theological thought to be legitimate. In a pluralistic world, Christian theology should have a place at the academic scientific table to consider its ontological and epistemological claims. Loder sought to engage the best scientific thought in his other two major works—the human sciences in *Logic of the Spirit* and the physical sciences in *Knight's Move*.

21. Loder held the kerygmatic and the apologetic concerns of the gospel in the same christomorphic relational tension that permeates all his neo-Chalcedonian thought. The apologetic horizon always points beyond itself to its kerygmatic meaning while the kerygmatic meaning resides latently in the apologetic horizon.

of God. In Loder, prayer expanded the scope of scholarship, and scholarship informed the content of prayer—with neither prayer nor scholarship diminished in any way. There was a kind of *perichoretic* sensibility in the dance of Loder's prayerfulness and exemplary scholarship, such that his scholarship called out for worship and his prayers called out for deeper understanding and expression in scholarship. In Loder's own person, academic integrity became part of the liturgy, and the liturgy infused and enhanced academic integrity. Dedicated scholarship reached out to others as pastoral care, and pastoral care embraced us in scholarly reach. The intellect served worship, and worship became the context for exercising the intellect.[22]

Even those who did not know Loder or attend his classes or receive his counsel may, I believe, perceive on every page of this scholarly exposition evidence of Loder's own sanctified life and scholarship. In this book, scholarly erudition becomes evangelical appeal and evangelical appeal communicates itself through scholarly erudition. Loder profoundly communicates the urgency of Christ's calling to abandon our wayward ways and our half-truths and our false hopes for his way, his truth, and his life (John 14). But Loder also communicates what he called "the divine courtesy" of Christ, whose presence never manipulates, condescends, or pressures. Loder believed our essential natures needed to be redemptively transformed through the Spirit of Christ so that we could know divine-human relationality in the medium of Spirit-to-spirit dynamics. But for him, *the process of redemptive transformation was as sacred as the goal and result!* He wedded the urgency of the gospel to the finesse of the Spirit, preserving both the ultimate claims that the gospel presents to us and our human freedom to choose for or against redemptive transformation.

Second, the knowers reading this book under the influence of the Spirit of Christ risk becoming more fully aware of the profound crisis the cross of Christ poses for their existence and vocation. The pedagogical movement of the Holy Spirit in human experience agitates and disrupts all so-called normal states to generate new life and new thought. My guess is that reading this work will indeed cause profound disquiet, in the same way that the Word made flesh always brought disquiet into the world in order to heal and restore.[23] (*"Repent and believe, for the kingdom of heaven is at hand."*)

---

22. The last chapter of this book makes this ultimate concern for worship explicit in Loder's theory.

23. Loder himself faced this trauma after his experience of the Spirit in a 1970 accident. He told me in a personal interview that this experience caused him to reconsider his life and vocation as a theologian, and it disrupted several relationships with other scholars. See Wright and Kuentzel, *Redemptive*, 15.

*Educational Ministry in the Logic of the Spirit* encourages readers to take risks that they may not want to take, but which the gospel of Christ calls us to take if we are to know this love that will not let us go. Loder's thinking allows us to become more keenly self-aware of our resistance to the Spirit as the Spirit draws near. In one story Loder liked to tell in ED105 (indeed, it shows up in this volume!), a young man came to him after a class on the Spirit and asked Loder to pray for him to receive God's power. But right after Loder began to pray, the traumatized student shouted out, "Wait! Stop! I'm not ready for this!" Indeed, let readers beware!

The third implication for knowing in the Spirit is the call to know holistically, not narrowly. This book will encourage readers to overcome Enlightenment tendencies to dichotomize and isolate knowing into insular categories that destroy our ability to "think and know things whole" in light of Christ. This dichotomized, objectivist thinking is the hallmark of Enlightenment existence that alienates us from our intrinsically relational birthright bestowed on us through being created in the image of God. We tend to split spirituality from the body, subjectivist spiritual devotion from objectivist hard thinking, hard thinking from emotions, sacred from secular, and so forth, just as we split ourselves from others and put everything and everyone into separate and discrete categories in an effort to exert control over others—or to resist others' control over us. These assumptions are all based on false dichotomies that plague the church and the modern world in which we live. Such detached and disenchanted epistemic assumptions are corrected in the Spirit of Christ, whom John Calvin called the "inner Teacher" of our wholeness.

Thus, when the Spirit is active, we embody the epistemology of "faith seeking understanding" that vivifies in us a longing to *know* holistically so that we can *be* whole. Loder never tired of saying that the Spirit always puts us into the world, into the body, into the fullness of our creaturehood, all the while connecting us relationally to the vast expanse that included "the big infinity" (cosmology) and the "little infinity" (quantum worlds) and even the "infinity of nothingness" (Void) that haunts us. For Loder, the hidden intelligibility behind all of this vastness is revealed in Jesus Christ through the Spirit.[24]

In light of these convictions about the profundity of *EMLOS*, I believe this book serves as the best introduction to Loder's complex thought now available.[25] My hope, and the hope of many who knew James Loder and

---

24. My own judgment about Loder and his work can be summarized in the Latin neologism *homo testans*. Dr. Loder's primary concern was to bear witness to Christ in a scientific world through the power of the Spirit. See Wright, *"Homo Testans,"* 1–30.

25. I am grateful to my friend Rev. Mark Koonz for offering this suggestion.

his thought, is that this volume becomes a regular source of instruction, interaction, and inspiration in the things of the Spirit for many in varied academic and ecclesial settings, across denominational lines, and especially for those working in the realm of interdisciplinary practical theology in a scientific world, where the concern for the integrity of the relation of Christ to every dimension of culture continues to call out for insight and courage.[26]

Finally, I hope a bit of the existential joy and passion Loder so vividly displayed in his lectures seeps through this more academic iteration of his ideas. I cannot read this work apart from hearing Christ echoed in his voice and experiencing again the Spirit's mediation of the "divine courtesy." Loder presented and embodied Christ's "nonpossessive delight in the particularity of each one of us," as Loder loved to say. May God bless you, the readers, as you undertake to indwell this book in the spirit in which it was given, so as to discover anew the Spirit that ever wants to breathe new life into all of us for the sanctification of God's creation. Amen.

~

Let me offer some brief remarks about my editing of this volume. My original thought was to offer the manuscript Loder gave me in 2001 simply as it was, virtually untouched, with minimal editing. My hope was that this untouched version would capture something of the vividness of Loder's lectures and would let his spirit shine through. Loder's lectures were dotted with vivid stories that he told with humor and perfect timing. He was an excellent raconteur of the gospel experience, and I didn't want to lose the sanctified charm of his lectures to academic necessity.

But alongside this sensibility was my conviction that Loder never released anything into the public domain that was not thoroughly and academically sound and credible. He stated to me on many occasions that he wanted his theory to address a scientific culture with integrity, and he took great care with all of his published endeavors. As I read through the

---

26. I think this book could serve as a textbook for seminary courses in practical theology (Christian education, preaching, counseling, congregational spirituality, and so forth), across the denominational spectrum (Reformed, Lutheran, Methodist, evangelical, Catholic, charismatic, Pentecostal, and liberationist and beyond). But in addition, this book might stimulate scholars to take the Spirit more seriously in ways that inform the church's theological engagement with economic and political theories, culture criticism, cross-cultural and interreligious engagement, ideology critique, and all disciplines that might inform the church's understanding and practice of its mission in the world. Loder's focus on living and thinking in the creative *dynamics* of Spirit-to-spirit relationality and not out of the sedimented *products* of that creativity bears universal application in our globalized world in ways the church has not yet fully contemplated.

manuscript several times and finally, with the help of my secretary Janet Kelly and Rev. Mark Koonz, retyped the whole thing, I became more fully convinced that the manuscript needed a stronger editorial oversight.

First of all, the manuscript version of *Educational Ministry in the Logic of the Spirit* that Loder gave me in November, 2001 was really not yet ready for publication. That is, as it was given to me, it did not measure up to Loder's own academic standards. The movement from lectures to transcribed lectures to publishable manuscript was never quite accomplished.[27] For example, sometimes the readers of the manuscript continued to be addressed as auditors of a lecture. As a reader, I found this inconsistency of audience distracting. Second, many of Loder's passively constructed sentences seemed to me to weaken the power of his argument. I reworked many of these passive constructions with active verbs to bring more force to his presentation. Third, I possessed another manuscript and several iterations of transcribed class notes from ED105 that I used for comparison with the manuscript Loder gave me. On a very few occasions the manuscript Loder gave me did not seem to me as good at certain points as the comparative documents. I wanted the edited version to be the best possible version. So I substituted sentences or parts of paragraphs from these other sources when it seemed warranted.

Fourth, the manuscript often failed to identify, or misidentified, the sources Loder used. Sometimes he remembered sources wrongly or did not identify the particular edition of a source he was using. Sometimes he got the publisher wrong, and sometimes the title he noted was inaccurate. I sometimes had to trust my memory of his library to guess which source he was using. I hope my memory serves this edited version well. Fifth, Loder also sometimes referenced persons or events he wanted to use as examples in his discussions without being specific as to the place or time of the reference. I was concerned that these references might be inaccurate and misrepresent the persons or events cited. I want again to thank persons cited in the acknowledgements of this volume for their skills in research, and persons I directly contacted to verify Loder's intent. Verification proved difficult at times after so many years had lapsed between the original manuscript and this edited version.

---

27. Some of us who worked closely with Dr. Loder toward the very end of the last century suspected that his health was failing and that the rigorous demands of scholarship were taking their toll on his life in general. As I prepared this manuscript for publication, I tried to imagine how he might have wanted it edited to match his own high standards of scholarship, especially because this book represents his only full theoretical treatment on the practice of Christian education. He wanted this book placed on the same shelf with other major academic proposals in the field.

In light of these and other concerns for accuracy, let me alert readers to three general rules for reading footnotes.

(1) If the footnote appears without any editorial comment, that note is Loder's own citation unchanged or with minimal emendation.

(2) If I supplied a significant elaboration to Loder's quote, or footnoted a source that he did not provide but which seemed to warrant a footnote, I identified that elaboration or footnote by the tag, "Editor's Note."

(3) Sometimes I added an "Editor's Note" after Loder's notation to clarify or expand upon a point he made, or to direct readers to other discussions of the topic, either in Loder's works or in the works of others.

Beyond footnoting, I also often emended Loder's text to add clarity or consistency to a sentence or paragraph that seemed unclear. For example, Loder frequently did not provide a specific reference to a previous statement he had made, simply using the word "this" to continue his thought. This practice often left the actual reference (what the "this" referred to!) ambiguous. I tried to clarify his references as much as I could.

More significantly, I made some unilateral changes to the structure of the book's outline, especially in relation to the book's division into sections, subsections, or chapters, in order to bring more clarity or consistency to the flow of the text. I footnoted some of these changes, but not all of them. Since I worked from more than one manuscript, I saw how Loder sometimes changed titles and subtitles over time. I made educated guesses at times to judge what title best served a given section, always with the interest of bringing coherence and consistency to the book as a whole. I quite often added a section or subsection title that was not in the manuscript, to make his argument flow more smoothly. And at times I added a short conclusion to a chapter where one did not exist, in order to help make the text more readable and consistent and to provide a transition to the next section or chapter. On occasion I rearranged the order of sentences if those changes seemed to bring more clarity to what Loder was discussing. I also amplified Loder's description of the movie *Babette's Feast* so that readers not familiar with the movie might better understand the significance of Loder's discussion.

I should also draw attention to one significant change I made to the content of the manuscript. Loder cited Alfred North Whitehead's *Aims of Education* twice in this volume, using the exact same quote in two places—in chapters 10 and 11—to support different arguments. I found no indication from the manuscripts I possessed or from my own class notes that Loder either intended or was aware of this exact duplication. When I looked at the first use of this quote, which was given in chapter 10 in reference to Sharon Daloz Parks's book *The Critical Years* regarding mentoring young adults in college, Parks herself does not refer to *The Aims of Education* there. She actually quotes from a different book by Whitehead, *Symbolism: Its Meaning and Effect*, to make her argument. Parks's use of the quotation seemed to me more relevant to Loder's discussion of Parks than the quote Loder himself cited there from Whitehead's *Aims of Education*. So I decided to substitute the *Symbolism* quote that Parks used for Loder's quote. I even contacted Dr. Daloz Parks herself, who had studied with Loder and who knows his early work, to see if what I proposed made sense to her. She agreed with my decision, and so I went with the change. This change and rationale is duly laid out in a footnote.

Dana R. Wright
December 1, 2017,
Seattle, Washington

# Acknowledgments

As THE EDITOR OF this volume, I wish to thank many people—and first of all, the family of James E. Loder Jr., for giving their permission to make this work available. I also offer a special thanks to two wonderful friends who supported me throughout this editorial process. Rev. Mark Koonz of the Emmanuel Lutheran Church, Walla Walla, Washington, who retyped many of the chapters and provided encouragement and many helpful suggestions along the way, even driving to Seattle on several occasions to "talk Loder." Rev. Alan B. Beasley, retired pastor, chaplain, and educator who has encouraged me in many significant ways to help make Dr. Loder's work available to a wider audience. Two academic friends also need to be singled out for recognition. First, Andrew Root, who wrote the American foreword. Andrew took my Loder seminar at Princeton in 2003, and I suspected then that his vital mind and inquisitive spirit would lead him to blossom one day into one of the leading practical theologians in the United States. I just didn't think he'd get there so fast! Second, to Ajit Prasadam, who wrote the Indian foreword. Ajit is the general secretary of the India Sunday School Union and the director of the St. Andrew Centre for Human Resource Development & Counselling in Coonoor, India. I thank him for his long-standing friendship and his groundbreaking educational work in India, both of which have encouraged me immensely through the years. Ajit has taken Dr. Loder's work more seriously than anyone I know.

I also thank Rev. Dr. Alan Dorway, pastor of the First Presbyterian Church, Everett, Washington, and the wonderful people who make up that congregation. They have allowed me great flexibility in my schedule so as to engage in academic pursuits over the past ten years. Janet Kelly, longtime church secretary, retyped chapter 1 for me when I was just getting started.

Many people helped me with my research to document the sources Dr. Loder used, which was not always easy after so many years had passed between his 2001 unedited manuscript and this fully edited version. Lynn

Gray, whose inspiring work in New York City for the Urban Coalition is celebrated in this book, helped verify the accuracy of Loder's reporting of his (Gray's) efforts. I hope this manuscript gives Lynn a good reason to dive back into Loder's thought. Many librarians helped me track down sources in the manuscript that were incomplete, inaccurate, or missing. Steve Perisho, Theological Librarian at Seattle Pacific University, helped me find things I didn't even know I needed to find. Others on the Seattle Pacific University library staff, especially Cynthia Strong, also assisted me with enthusiasm. The library staffs at the University of Washington and Seattle University also offered me great service. I'm so thankful for having these world-class facilities in my backyard. Finally, thanks to Kate Skebutanis, Research Librarian at Speer Library, Princeton Theological Seminary, and her staff who serve Christ by serving scholarship. If Kate and her staff can't find it, it doesn't exist.

Thanks to Brian Palmer, Matthew Wimer, Jeremy Funk, Ian Creeger, and RaeAnne Harris of Cascade Books, who guided me with expertise and patience all along the way of this project. Thanks also to my friend Tonja Gabryshak, owner of heARTnSOUL art studio in Everett, Washington, for the wonderful work she did on the graphics for this book.

Finally, I am so grateful for two special people in my life. First, for Judy, my lovely and supportive wife of forty years, who keeps me attentive to the day-to-day matters essential to navigating our complex world. And second, for the one who kept us both worried and in stitches while she lived with us during the time this project took off, granddaughter Angelina (a.k.a. "Looney" or "Boop"). Angelina named me "Bacca" and bit my nose when she was a very small person, giving me my permanent geriatric identity. I served proudly as "Uber Bacca" for her and her friends as I watched her grow into a compassionate and beautiful young woman.

# Abbreviations

| | |
|---|---|
| 1 Sam | First Samuel |
| 2 Cor | Second Epistle to the Corinthians |
| Acts | Acts of the Apostles |
| *CD* | Karl Barth, *Church Dogmatics* |
| Col | Epistle to the Colossians |
| *EMLOS* | *Education Ministry in the Logic of the Spirit* |
| Gen | Genesis |
| Heb | Epistle to the Hebrews |
| *HTR* | *Harvard Theological Review* |
| LCC | Library of Christian Classics |
| *JSOT* | Journal of the Study of the Old Testament |
| Matt | Gospel of Matthew |
| Num | Numbers |
| OBT | Overtures to Biblical Theology |
| OTL | Old Testament Library |
| Phil | Epistle to the Philippians |
| Ps | Psalms |
| Rom | Epistle to the Romans |
| RSV | Revised Standard Version of the Bible |
| SNTSMS | Society for New Testament Studies Monograph Series |

# SECTION I

# Introductory Dilemmas and a Critical Perspective[1]

---

1. Editor's Note: In the original manuscript, section I started with chapter 2, and chapter 1 functioned as a kind of introduction to three following sections. I chose to make the first chapter of the original manuscript into section I of this edited version in order to highlight Loder's stated purpose to privilege the place of theory in his practical theology of Christian education. Thus, section I in this edited text contains chapter 1, followed by three more sections numbered II, III, and IV. I came up with this section I title by dividing Loder's original first chapter, "Introductory Dilemmas and a Critical Perspective: The Crux of Christian Education," in two. I used the original chapter title as the new title for section I. I used the original chapter subtitle as the title for chapter 1. Thus, this edited version of the manuscript is divided into four rather than three sections.

# 1

# The Crux of Christian Education

## (I) INTRODUCTION: THEORY AND PRACTICE IN CHRISTIAN EDUCATION

IN THE *PRAXIS*-ORIENTED CLIMATE that prevails in practical theology today, it may seem inappropriate to begin this opening section and chapter with an effort to reclaim the significance of theory. This concern is not to be reactionary, but to recognize that neither this chapter, nor this book, nor indeed any of the books stressing *praxis* could have been written without at least a rudimentary, antecedent view of theory. In some sense theory inevitably and more or less tacitly precedes *praxis* and remains in continuing dialectic with it. For the sake of coming clean with certain key presuppositions in this volume and with the suspicion that this prevalence of theory is true across the board in practical theology, I begin this chapter with a discussion of theory before we indwell the phenomenon at hand—the dimensions and dynamics of the practice of Christian education.

Indeed, throughout this book theory will function as a major concern on two levels. The manifest agenda will be to discuss the nature of Christian education, for which an explicit theoretical perspective will eventually be developed. But the tacit agenda to be made explicit at the conclusion of this book is to use this study of Christian education as a basis for articulating a comprehensive theory of practical theology embracing the whole field of human action in the light of God's power to transform that field through the presence and power of the Holy Spirit.

3

Some view of theory is therefore necessary for the project of this book. But more than that, theory, in many quasi or proximate forms as well as in fairly explicit and refined forms, is an inevitable part of our knowledge of anything.[1] For instance, in a celebrated conversation between Einstein and Heisenberg, Heisenberg said, "A good theory must be based on directly observable magnitudes." To this Einstein countered, "It is quite wrong to try founding a theory on observable magnitudes alone. In reality the very opposite happens. It is the theory that decides what we can observe."[2] Einstein's point, persuasive to Heisenberg, was not only the necessity for good theory but, indeed, its inevitable priority.[3] Thus, in the following chapters I will emphasize theory, because theory, however conscious or unconscious, inevitably exercises a controlling influence on all our observations.

Moreover, whether intentionally constructed or not, theory is the inevitable bridge between what we observe and what we practice. Thus, the old dictum "Nothing is more practical than a good theory" can be affirmed in reverse: "Since theory decides what we can observe, nothing is more misleading and impractical than an unexamined one." In other words, because theory has an inevitable and centrally formative influence on the intentional practice of practical theology generally and on Christian education in particular, it merits some careful attention here from the beginning. We must now examine the nature of theory more closely in itself and in its relationship to practice.

---

1. "Theory," as it is used here in its broadest, least formulated, and unexamined sense, resembles various preunderstandings as they appear in the writings of J. Habermas ("interests") or in H. G. Gadamer ("prejudices"). Although I do not ground this study on any specific contemporary theory of hermeneutics, it is clearly engaged in interpretive discourse.

2. Heisenberg, *Physics and Beyond*, 63 (slightly emended). What this encounter describes is a highly condensed leap from an earlier positivistic science based on logical empiricism to more contemporary postcritical understandings by Michael Polanyi, C. F. von Weizsacker, and Niels Bohr. Heisenberg was never a strict positivist since his formulation of the "uncertainty principle" qualified perceptions of the empirical data. His work acknowledged in part the general theory of complementarity that his teacher, Niels Bohr, formulated. Theory was for him in a continual reciprocity with perceived observables.

3. A brief note from the history of sciences makes this claim clear, though the interplay between theory and observation will continue to change both. Observations of the planet Jupiter from Earth have in recent centuries done a complete reverse. For an astronomer who accepted the Ptolemaic theory of planetary motions, the apparent changes in the position of Jupiter were clear evidence of its cyclical movement around the earth. For us today, the same observations tell us that the planet remains in orbit around the sun. The theoretical point of view decides what you can observe.

## (II) THE PRIORITY OF THEORY

We should remember from the beginning that the word "theory" comes from *thea*, an action of viewing, beholding or contemplating. Our word "theater" comes from the same root, which leads some to say pejoratively that theory connotes detached speculative spectatorship. However, in the case of *good* theater, what one views, beholds, or contemplates are often disclosures of immense existential and social magnitude. Classically, for example, in ancient Greek theater the dramas of Aeschylus, Sophocles, and Euripides had a powerful impact because they enabled viewers to see with deep personal recognition what could not otherwise be grasped due to socially constructed constraints upon Athenian self-understanding. Good theory, then, like good theater, breaks through the surface of collective public opinion. Thus, Aristotle constructed his famous "catharsis principle" based on his realization that seeing deeply and accurately beneath the surface of socially constructed and uncommon personal restraints functioned as a powerful influence in the preservation of the personal health and public welfare of society. On the basis of a similar principle nearly everyone knows of the one play by Sophocles, *Oedipus Rex*, if only because they know that the "Oedipus complex" has something to do with hidden sexual motivations. The expunging power of an accurate disclosure of widespread and buried human conditions is a mark of good theater and a dramatic illustration of what good theory can do.

Theory, however, can do more than simply unearth hidden, potentially antisocial impulses. It may also disclose hidden orders of intelligibility, meaning, and the presence of the sublime. According to H. G. Gadamer, the original context for *theoria* in the lives of the Athenian people was as participants who joined in pilgrimages, journeying to celebrations held in honor of the gods. *Theoria* referred to the observation and celebration of what the gods were doing. In order to overcome our forgetfulness of this deeper meaning of theory, we must see that at its roots, *theoria*, impinging significantly upon the present time and circumstances, refers to what we may call a vision of a higher but hidden order.

Note, however, that "theory" does not come from *theos*, as if theory enabled one to play God. The priority of theory does not warrant that we construct Procrustean beds for the sake of manipulating observable realities in terms of predetermined and inadequately examined presuppositions. In recent years, the emphasis on *praxis* with its stress on the interaction between reflection and action functions like a declaration of freedom away from oppressive theories that hardened into ideology and that disregarded observable conditions for the sake of a theoretical *tour de force*. Confronted with these false forms of theory, advocates of *praxis* separated *theoria* from *praxis*, as oppressor over the oppressed, master over slave—as in Hegel's famous political paradigm—which inspired Karl Marx's view of *praxis*. In doing so they misunderstand the power and significance of both *praxis* and *theoria* as they were interpreted in early Greek thought and in Aristotle's philosophy. For Aristotle, *praxis* was internally consistent with *theoria*. Moreover, by means of *theoria* one effectively indwelt *Sophia* or Wisdom.

To reemphasize, to assert the priority of theory does not mean we reinstate a hierarchy of the oppressive political sort, nor reclaim the Unmoved Mover. Nor do we encourage the theoretician to play God in an effort to coerce social conformity. Rather, we assert first of all that *praxis*, as Aristotle understood it in his own way, requires a larger, carefully articulated frame of reference according to which the metaphysical or theological significance of *praxis* can be examined. Second, we argue that true theory requires the establishment of a reciprocal relation (as opposed to a unilateral top-down hierarchical relationship) between *theoria* (as an intentional frame of knowledge) and *praxis* (as reflective practice.) The hierarchical or deductive use of theory makes the theoretician God-like. That is a mistake. But the corrective is not simply to go to *praxis*. Rather, we seek to preserve something of the original Aristotelian understanding of a reciprocal interplay between *theoria* and *praxis*. Out of this interplay can come *phronesis*—i.e., sound judgment as to the nature and activity of Christian education.[4]

We should also note here that "theory" does not come from *thelo*, "to long for" or "to wish for." Theory is not wishful thinking, speculative imagination working overtime to create impossible worlds. In fact, in Aristotle's highest state of theory, there was an eternal "beholding" of the universal that was by definition "a *wishless* absorption into the perception of the highest truth."[5] Thus, on the one hand, in our concern to construct an adequate theory, we cannot condone empty speculation. On the other hand, we do not want to kill the imagination. What is at issue here is the imaginative dream that may serve to heighten inspiration and/or deepen insight. As Allan Bloom once wrote in reference to Plato, "Utopianism is the fire with which we must play because it is the only way we can find out what we are."[6] The deadpan realist, who does not want to go beyond just what is happening, dismisses the dream too quickly, kills the flair, and locks us into the

---

4. Aristotle's language is a useful place to begin but, as we will show, these notions must be disembedded from both Aristotle's and Marx's understanding in order to be given the distinctly christological significance that preserves the integrity of Christian education theory and practice.

5. Windelband, *History of Philosophy*, 154.

6. Bloom, *Closing*, 67.

given. The wide-eyed enthusiast swallows it whole. Theory is not wishful thinking, but neither does theory denigrate dreams and visions—the stuff out of which some of the best theories (even in the hard sciences) are eventually fashioned.

Theory in Christian education, then, seeks a deliberate point of view that can be brought into a propositional form. However, it ultimately rests on, and is finally accountable to, the self-revelation of God as the whole, highest, universal, and living Truth with which we have to do. This Truth grounds, even as it infinitely exceeds, the most exhaustive systematic articulation of the potential relationship pertaining among the principles and propositions of the theory per se. Thus, careful development of how we may behold and participate in theological truth will lay the foundation for the vision of Christian education practice to be articulated in Section IV of this book.

Although all the following chapters unfold aspects of the meaning of theory in Christian education, we must ask here, at least in a preliminary way, how we understand good theory? Good theory is a comprehensive point of view that can be provisionally articulated as a set of mutually consistent, corrective, and enhancing principles. These principles derive in part from the matrix of experience viewed by the theory, but also from the highest truth to which they are finally accountable. They are intended to return to the matrix of experience as dependable guides to reflection, practice, and further inquiry.[7] Thus, there is a reciprocal relationship between theory and practice, but theory exercises marginal control over practice as its larger context of meaning.[8] This asymmetrical reciprocal relationship can be diagrammed succinctly as follows:

7. Although fundamentally different at points, this description of theory owes an obvious debt of gratitude to the work of D. Campbell Wyckoff. See Wyckoff, *Theory and Design*. This interplay between experience and reflection might be the introduction to a hermeneutical discussion and the contribution of Gadamer, Ricoeur, and others to the interplay described here. However, this discussion is directed toward an effort to preserve the more scientific approach (as distinct from technology—a distinction not made by Gadamer) in the genre of Michael Polanyi and Thomas F. Torrance.

8. This phrase "marginal control" is borrowed from the thought of Michael Polanyi, especially his classic, *Personal Knowledge*. It refers to his claim that all knowledge has both a tacit and an explicit dimension. "We know more than we can tell," his famous dictum regarding the tacit dimension, makes the claim that out of our tacit link to the universe through the body and the cognitive unconscious come all our scientific discoveries about that universe and our place in it. Although there is reciprocity between tacit and explicit expressions of knowledge, the tacit dimension exercises marginal control over the explicit in that it supplies the source, structure, and contours of new insight for every act of discovery.

Although it might seem that we should reverse our emphasis on theory vis-a-vis

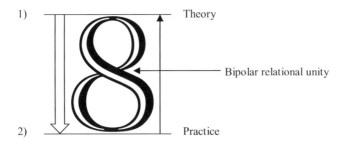

*Theological Model of Theory-Practice Relationality*

One's practice may radically challenge or change the form or the content of this meaning, but it cannot change the status of theory per se vis-à-vis practice. Good theory in Christian education, then, like good theater or, more archaically, like envisioning and participating in a festival for the gods, is an ongoing disclosure and articulation of a hidden, created order

practice in light of Polanyi and argue that practice has marginal control because it is less conceptually explicit, that would be a misunderstanding. Practice rarely focuses on insight-getting except within the preset limits of the practice itself because it is confined to an enculturated and socialized field of human action (see the following discussion of Parsons's theory). Theory, on the other hand, leads to insight and deeper inquiry into and beyond the field of action, challenging the contextual axioms that practice takes for granted. This is not to say that practice does not contribute fundamentally and significantly to theory, but the generation of insight in the context of practice must become theoretical before it can change the field of action presupposed by any practice.

In other words, theory may be thought of as an intellectual tool, i.e., an interpretative framework that one indwells in order to perform practical tasks. One might even say that practice is theory being indwelt. That is, in practice we are only subsidiarily aware of the presuppositions of theory because we are interiorizing them by indwelling them, thereby allowing us to focus on what practice is accomplishing. Thus theory, as an interpretative framework, acts as a tool tacitly shaping actual practice so that such practice will be exploratory in character. In this manner, theory allows practice to disclose and to be receptive to novel practical procedures while, at the same time, fostering new theoretical understanding (*Personal Knowledge*, 59–63). For future reference, the model at work here is discussed at length in the book *Knight's Move*, chapter 3.

In this model, the Möbius band, a unique topological phenomenon having only one edge and one side, suggests the dynamic interplay between the two polarities and at the same time suggests that in some deeper sense they are one and the same thing. The double arrow suggests marginal control in an otherwise reciprocal relationship between polarities (1) and (2). As we will see later in this chapter, proximate applications of this model have important ultimate significance in pointing toward the relationality described by the Chalcedonian interpretation of Christ's nature. In this respect, *theoria* and *praxis* are interrelated within a larger, indeed ultimate frame of reference, as Aristotle claimed. However, the nature of that ultimate reference frame is very different when it is conceived and constituted not metaphysically but christologically.

of things in relation to, and in light of, the truth of God's self-revelation. It draws relationality and illumination into proximate propositional forms of expression so as to attain an ever-deepening disclosure of what the self-revealed God is doing in, through, and beyond the present form of the created order to transform things in the field of practice and to transform practice into conformity to what God is doing.[9]

We seek here, therefore, a different and distinctly theological view of theory that leads to a different and distinctive view of practice. That is, practice is not primarily an expression of human action but a human response to divine action. This responsiveness is, of course, how we are to understand the title of the book of Acts. *Praxeis Apostoloi* (The Acts of the Apostles) is not basically a story of human acts and certainly not of human practices such as popularized versions of Alistair McIntyre's *After Virtue* would have it.[10] Rather, Acts takes account of human action in radical conformity to the actions of God's Spirit. The basically political concerns behind Aristotle's, Hegel's, and Marx's use of *praxis* are not abandoned. But for Luke, all political action is transformed in conformity to the politics of God.

## (III) CHRISTIAN EDUCATION: INDWELLING ITS HIDDEN ORDER

We will begin the process of indwelling and disclosing the hidden order of the field of Christian education by examining what is latent in the title, "Christian education."[11] Indeed, what is latent is a contradiction. The hidden

9. Editor's Note: The upcoming paragraph is, I believe, from an earlier version of the manuscript apparently excised from the later version. However, I have inserted it back here because I think it clarifies what Loder is after with his *theological* theory of the relation of theory to practice. I believe his theological theory of theory-practice is unique in practical theology today, and an important effort to recover the dynamics of the Holy Spirit in relation to the human spirit in all dimensions of human action. See Nelson, "James Loder," in *Psychology*, 241–43.

10. See, for example, Craig Dykstra's use of McIntyre's *After Virtue* in Dykstra, *Growing*, 67–70.

11. As Michael Polanyi (*Personal Knowledge*), Jean Piaget, with Rolando Garcia (*Genetic Epistemology*), and T. F. Torrance (*Theological Science*) point out, the beginning point for studying any phenomenon is to indwell its inner structure, to discover what internal relationships constitute its nature, and thereby to allow the phenomenon itself it disclose how it is to be known. Once one begins to discover what internal relations constitute its nature, the phenomenon then can be related to significant external relationships: historical, systematic, and pragmatic. This second move we will make in following chapters. The third and final step is to make, if possible, a move that transcends the sets of internal and external relationships, which will take us into a theoretical reconstruction of Christian education in light of its place in practical theology.

order appears to be disorder or at least disjunction. "Christian" does not easily fit with "education." In fact, they are in one sense in direct contradiction to each other. This contradiction is no historical accident. It is the crux of the matter.

## (A) Socialization: The Dominant Educational Force

Education concerns itself essentially with making the dynamics of socialization conscious and intentional. Socialization, as generally understood in educational terms, is the pervasive interactional process between persons and their human environment that brings them into an existing interpersonal or sociocultural context, establishing equilibrium or balanced functioning within and for that context. In essence socialization is the process by which a given social reality shapes and inducts new members.

Primary or unintentional socialization begins very early, even before birth, in the conditioning of the child. I recall when my daughter Tami was born, the seasoned nurse in attendance said she had never seen a more active child in the moment of birth. In fact, Tami continued to wave her arms, kick her feet, and scream her lungs out to the point where it was getting to be disconcerting even for the nurse. Tami didn't quiet down until she was placed in her mother's arms and heard her mother's voice say softly, "Hi, there." Suddenly, Tami became very quiet and for just a moment she focused on her mother's face. What was happening? Well, Tami, you see, had heard that voice before, while still inside her mother's body. The sound was familiar. Long before birth she was being conditioned to the sound that would facilitate subsequent socialization. Her mother's voice helped her overcome a very radically upsetting personal situation (i.e., the trauma of birth) and adjust to her new environment in terms familiar to the former one.

The same essential dynamic operating in primary socialization operates in secondary or intentional socialization. In the face of disturbances of all magnitudes, socialization establishes conventional grounds for gaining and maintaining equilibrium. This same basic process by which Tami was able to adapt to the new world of face-to-face relationships (primary socialization) is the process by which a student acquires a college degree (secondary socialization). As a student, when you first come into an institution of higher learning, you may face considerable disruption. But you have

Editor's Note: The reference to Piaget and Garcia and the book *Genetic Epistemology* at the start of this footnote may be a conflation. Piaget published *Genetic Epistemology* in 1970. He coauthored *Psychogenesis and the History of Science* with Rolando Garcia and published it in 1989.

mastered the conventions of schooling. You know from high school how to study, gather information, take tests, write papers, and meet professional and institutional expectations. This new learning environment requires you to perform all of those same tasks. Your reward if you succeed will be the degree or certification you attain by the process of socialization—by listening to the voices you have listened to in the past, and by utilizing what you already know and understand to meet the demands and expectations of the new, potentially threatening environment.

Thus, socialization begins very early before birth and continues as the child moves from family to school where similar processes are repeated. As the child moves from the school to the larger society, it is repeated again and again. There is always a move from one form of equilibrium into disruption to a renewed state of equilibrium or adaptation. Basically, then, socialization is a *tension-reduction, pattern-maintenance process* designed to serve the purposes of adaptation and incorporation into larger and more complex social milieu. Note that it operates regardless of the magnitude of the personal or social milieu in question as it implicitly and unconsciously perpetuates the predetermined goals and aims of that milieu.[12] In the largest context

---

12. This claim may seem overstated in terms of the power of the corporate milieu, especially in a supposedly open system. However, one powerful illustration suggests otherwise. Critics have noted, regarding the training of Harvard Law students, that while "an overwhelming majority of students in any entering class at Harvard Law School identifies itself as liberal to leftist in its political orientation, the majority of any graduating class chooses corporate law practice over public interest work." So writes the unnamed *Harvard Magazine* reviewer of Robert Granfield's book, *Making Elite Lawyers*. Quoting Grandfield: "George Bernard Shaw once said that all professions are conspiracies against public . . . professionals have the ability . . . to construe truth to serve their own self-interests." See *Harvard Magazine*, "Endpapers," 112. ("Endpapers" is the title of the book review section in *Harvard Magazine*.) The reviewer went on to summarize Granfield's argument, noting first of all that truth derived as expertise, whether in the medical, legal, therapeutic, or any other field, constructs social life by the symbolic boundaries it creates. Professionals gain and maintain cultural authority through these abstractions such that they are able to make sense and even control meaning amid the uncertainty of modern life. Lawyers thereby reduce the problems their clients face to a kind of game to be manipulated. Moreover, by upholding so-called legal justice in this way, lawyers actually distort the meaning of justice for their clients, especially those who are already marginalized in society. *Legal* justice (not *true* justice) becomes the goal. This reduction of justice to legalities disempowers those same clients and keeps those in power over them unscathed and morally absolved. Students who learn the law learn to place great value on the skill of advocacy without attending sufficiently to the content of what is advocated. The result of learning gamesmanship within the context of abstractions is that law students end up becoming incompetent and indifferent advocates for the less powerful in society. Thus, law students who dedicate themselves to public interest must have "deep personal commitment" to sustain that dedication. How deep and by what power do individuals actually succeed in challenging socialization within the legal establishment becomes an important question. And this issue for

of the natural order—i.e., in the universe—the drive toward equilibration is ultimately aimed at the lowest level of tension-entropy and the death of the universe. This is socialization, one of the two great forces in Christian education operating predominantly on the educational side of the Christian education antithesis-in-synthesis.

## (B) Transformation: The Dominant Christian Force

On the other side, we have Christianity, especially as understood in continuity with the principles of the Reformed theological tradition. Christianity perpetuates on the highest scale possible the second great force in Christian education—transformation. As a force of universal magnitude, transformation may be defined as *the patterned process whereby within any given frame of knowledge or experience, a hidden order of meaning emerges with the power to redefine and/or reconstruct the original frame of reference.*[13] Thus, transformation begets an order of meaning that decisively alters the horizon with respect to which it first occurs, even when that horizon is decline and ultimate death. In the natural order of things, the largest frame of knowledge we have is the universe. Even here, where it is usually assumed that entropy—the ultimate drift of the universe toward a final irreversible equilibrium—is inevitable physicists tell us that transformation, not equilibrium, may still be the final word.[14] Indeed, in the promise of the gospel, even death—human death and the death of the universe—gets transformed!

Harvard Law students is typical of the problem for individuals entering any profession in our culture. Thus, given the immense power of socialization at all levels of human action, is there any real alternative for those who would seek higher forms of justice? Christian education, especially at the level of theological education, ought to be most attentive to the dynamics Granfield points out and be ready to provide answers to these kinds of the questions as a means for providing alternative answers that promote just practice.

13. Editor's Note: As far as I know, this definition of *transformation* is Loder's own, which he used throughout his corpus. For a comprehensive discussion of the experiential origins and theological implications of this notion as a basis for Loder's analogy of the spirit, see Loder, *Transforming Moment*.

14. Illya Prigogine, a Belgian physicist, won the Nobel Prize in 1977 for demonstrating that in an open system new order emerges out of apparent disorder and randomness. Consequently, he and his followers have shown that entropy is not merely a downward slide toward disorganization but potentially the progenitor of new order. What can be suggested on the strength of Prigogine's findings on a number of varied physical systems is that from the largest conceivable frame of reference (namely, the universe) on down to every subframe of reference, to and including the development and formation of the human mind (Prigogine's included), this emergence of order out of disorder pertains. See Prigogine and Stengers, *Order*.

To allay any suspicion that I am propounding a metaphysical dualism between socialization and transformation, let it be understood that in theories of socialization, the drift towards entropy includes but predominates over transformation at all levels. Transformation, on the other hand, appears to be predominant in all stage transition dynamics of human development—i.e., in the psychosocial dynamics of adaptation as one moves from primary to secondary socialization as well as in the formation and transformation of cultures. However, whenever socialization is taken to be dominant, then all transformations get their historical significance and systematic meaning from the equilibration context in which they occur. When transformation is dominant, then it is clear that all socialization is unto transformation, preparatory to the emergence of a higher but hidden order in keeping with God's action in the world. In neither case is one force separable from the other. And in every case they are inextricably intertwined.

One might say, then, that transformation and socialization are interdependent in a way that is similar to the interrelatedness between the life and death instincts in Freudian thought or between assimilation and accommodation in Piagetian thought. The fundamental difference is that in both of these thinkers, the inevitability of the triumph of equilibration seems assured. The position I am taking here is closer to the thought of philosopher and scientist Michael Polanyi. Polanyi understood the irreducible openness of the universe and knew that every apparent equilibration of forces is best understood as an explicit context concealing a tacit dimension from which new forms of ordered openness may emerge. Thus, for him discovery was the core of the knowing act.[15]

It might be asserted at a deeper level that this is also Piaget's position, since he argued that the transformations in human development are stronger than the stages, which means that even for him equilibration repeatedly

---

The cosmological context of this discussion is important because it enables us to see that what we are dealing with in Christian education is not—to put it in the extreme—merely something done in a corner to prevent a socially marginalized institution from descending further into extinction. The magnitude of the forces involved is immense, and they extend farther beyond our individual efforts than even socialization theory imagines. Moreover, under proper circumstances and with an adequate theoretical perspective, we can determine from what nexus of influences and forces we will cooperate. But we are in no sense, even from the standpoint of the hard sciences, inevitably caught in a drift toward meaningless equilibration and disintegration at any level of the created order. Consequently, any implicit cooperation with entropic equilibrium, such as long-term socialization advocates, is neither proximately necessary nor cosmologically inevitable.

15. Editor's Note: Polanyi's thinking on postmodern scientific epistemology permeates Loder's thought, even when he is not mentioned explicitly. See Wright, "Personal Knowledge," 34–51, for my attempt to describe Loder's use of Polanyi.

gives way to the emergence of new orders of meaning. His theories, however, are rarely conceived this way since they have been forced into the service of socialization and made to serve conventional educational concerns. But Piaget's thought—which has been socialized by the American psychological establishment—is fundamentally different from his original work. Chapter 5, in large part devoted to Piaget's thought, will not only show that this is the case but also demonstrate how his original thought is, in several respects, including his cosmological perspective, paradigmatic for this present volume.

Does the emphasis being made here upon transformation mean that Christianity merely sacralizes transformation as an existing force, blessing this given condition in the universe? No. All such natural forces are in themselves without meaning and purpose.[16] Thus, all natural forces, including transformation itself, must be transformed. That is to say, Christianity's answer to the cosmological question of meaning and purpose lies in the contingent relationship between God the Creator and all of creation. This contingency is revealed in the relationship between God and humanity in Jesus Christ, in both his nature and redemptive action. To set transformation in the context of creation's contingent relationship to God is to see that all created forces, including socialization and naturalistic transformation, are in need of redemptive transformation through the mediation of Christ.

Thus, to return to our original point, only through the eyes of faith in Jesus Christ can we recognize the ontological priority of transformation over any other force in the universe. By faith we know that the pattern of this force, operative throughout creation, is analogous to the pattern by which all creation is renewed, and will be redeemed, by the *Spiritus Creator*. Although the main thrust of the foregoing paragraphs suggests the theological perspective from which this book is written, it should immediately disabuse us of the naïve assertion that since socialization takes place anyway, we should make it the central dynamic of Christian education. There are a great many forces that are inevitably operative in the course of the formation of personality and society. Each must be examined critically and appropriately as the lenses of faith may direct.

---

16. The term *force* in this usage refers generally to a dynamic tendency or a powerful patterned process that appears to unfold spontaneously compelled by an intrinsic logic of its own. My use of the term would include both physical and social forces. I am not referring specifically to the four fundamental forces that undergird and govern all physical phenomenon: gravitation, electromagnetism, and the weak and strong nuclear forces. Recently physicists have demonstrated that the latter three forces are manifestations of a single, fundamental force. Force in the soft sense is necessarily linked to these larger cosmological concepts, but that linkage can be bracketed for the present discussion.

Thus, we have said that transformation, as a pervasive natural force, must itself be transformed. The exact significance of this double transformation, however, must await the discussion in chapter 5 on the analogy of the Spirit. In the meantime, in the context of Christian self-understanding, let us understand that in the interplay between socialization and transformation, the former is to be in service to the later.

## (IV) THE CHALLENGING TENSIONS WITHIN CHRISTIAN EDUCATION

Since education is predominantly governed by the dynamics of socialization, and the Christian life is predominantly governed by the dynamics of transformation, we must examine Christian education as constituted by a tension that stretches across a deep but dynamic dichotomy. Built into the name of this discipline is, first, a far-reaching *educational* challenge to Christianity, and second, an even more compelling *Christian* challenge to education. If the radical claims of Christianity prevail in a way that eliminates this educational challenge, education seems unnecessary since all things are raised up into the truth of God by the power of the one true Teacher, the Holy Spirit. On the other hand, if the radical claims of education prevail, removing the challenge of Christianity, Christian education rests on an illusion of the future—illusory because all socialization, aiming as it does toward equilibrium, is subject to the law of entropy. And all equilibrium, as even human development teaches us, is in a steady drift toward disintegration and death.[17] Thus, the tension across this dichotomy within

---

17. It may be disputed that the effort to preserve an equilibrated condition is not necessarily a drift toward death and annihilation. However, on a personal level it is obvious that no equilibrium is a steady state, just as no stage in human development is a stable condition. It must either tend toward disintegration or it must be in the process of becoming part of a higher or more complex order of integration. Left to itself, any effort to preserve a given state of balance will gradually disintegrate, moving persons toward lower levels of equilibration that finally end in death, which is the inevitable fate of every human organism. Every developing personality begins to die at the moment of birth, and survival is maintained only so long as new patterns, formations, or levels of functioning are brought forth in the personality by the process of transformation. In effect there is no neutral ground, one must create or die. However, in the end the goal of perfect equilibrium, death itself, brings all transformational innovations to nothing.

In the larger corporate sense the same point may be argued. Although Ivan Illich's work is too schematic and idealistic on solutions, his analysis of this inevitable disintegrative tendency in all of the created order is very telling. In *Tools for Conviviality*, he outlines four basic phases in the disintegration process (passing two "watersheds") that afflict modern systems, professional and industrial, as they promote an illusion of progress. First the basic problem of education of the youth, cure of the sick, transportation,

this discipline is such that if either pole prevails unchallenged, the discipline itself collapses. To give a more concrete understanding and deeper feeling for this tension, I will develop the challenges that each polarity poses to the other. First, we'll look at the socialization-education challenge to Christianity. Then we'll discern the transformation-Christian challenge to education. In so doing we will play out the extremes in order to focus more clearly the crux of relationships between them.

## (A) The Educational Challenge to Christianity

The educational challenge was put most sharply to me when I was on the staff of the Menninger Foundation. There I attended a clergyperson's seminar that was led by the famous anthropologist Margaret Mead. She was well known for putting questions in a most provocative manner and this seminar was no exception. She said something to this effect: "In our modern pluralistic, industrialized, highly differentiated and mobile society, the functions and structures of the social order are becoming increasingly clear. Certain functions are absolutely necessary. For instance, doctors take an oath to heal the sick, so we know what they can and must do. Lawyers interpret the law of the land and protect the standards of legitimacy in the social system. But," said Margaret Mead, "what do you do?" She then added something like what I once heard the sociologist Talcott Parsons say: "Don't respond with anything that faintly resembles prophet, priest, and king imagery. The real prophets are those whose ideas change the world and shape the future— Freud, Jung, Marx, Darwin, and Einstein. The real kings are those who have political clout—legislators, governors, and presidents. The priests are those who understand the social system and can interpret it for the welfare of all

---

and the like are clearly stated, and adequate solutions are proposed and demonstrated. Then (the first "watershed") new knowledge, miracle cures in medicine, or rapid transit systems and air travel in transportation, for example, are applied to generate a new experience and effectiveness. But, then an inversion takes place (his second "watershed") as an emerging professional elite uses progress demonstrated in a previous achievement as a rationale for the exploitation of society as a whole. The net result is that an industry of professionals emerges to create more new problems that the original solution was designed to solve. A succinct example, not Illich's, is in the mental health industry where the helpful development of nosological categories has, by the influence of the professional elite, reached the level of popular literature, and now begins to tell people how to define their lives in pathological terms. In other words, they are taught how to get sick by the terms originally designed to aid the cure (e.g., Rapoport, *Boy Who Couldn't Stop Washing*). This same argument has been set forth with considerable wit and irony in an article by Tenner, "Revenge Effect," 27–31. Editor's Note: Loder engages Illich's insights again in chapter 7, using his work to again delineate important aspects of Loder's theological understanding of the "triumph of negation" in culture.

involved—i.e., like Margaret Mead and Talcott Parsons. So why do we need you clergy? What can you do?"

Now Mead's question is not hypothetical. When graduates in Christian education seek a job, the basic question inevitably becomes: "What can you do that we want done?" To put it in educational terms: "Can we count on you to bring people into the Christian community?" In Christian education, if you're going to "produce," you must know how to engage in intentional socialization. Thus, your answer must be some version of: "Yes, I know how to help you socialize people into the community of faith."

But as soon as you agree to socialization as the dominant force, you have sold out to Parsons and Mead. Do you run the socialization machine, or does it run you? From the standpoint of socialization, of course, it runs you. If it runs you, then when it comes to socialization, Parsons and Mead *are* the true priests. It is really the social scientist, the psychologist, the developmentalist, who understand the mysteries of human formation, and surely it is they who know best how Christians are made and developed?

Here I must try to portray the power and magnitude of socialization by examining what lies behind these claims. In this regard, I want to look particularly at the theorizing of Talcott Parsons. To set his position forth, I have constructed a neo-Parsonian diagram.[18] Some of you, already familiar with Parsons, are aware of certain critiques of his system.[19] For instance,

---

18. I am not concerned here with merely a lesson in the basic units of social theory and action. It is a sketch and topic outline of this volume, but as we will see transformation views these topics according to a very different dynamic than the socialization forces depicted. Also note in passing that Parsons's theory is the major generative source behind Geertz, Berger, Luckmann, Bellah, and Luhmann, according to Milbank, *Theology*, 106–10.

19. For an illuminating discussion and critique of Parsons's theory, see Gibson Winter's *Elements*. Winter contends that Parsons is too Freudian, reductionistic, nonrational, and insufficiently attentive to cognitive valuing processes. Quite so. But the force of socialization functions, as a force, in just this way. So when Winter objects that Parsons's model is insufficient to account for human behavior on any of the levels discussed, I agree with him, even to the point of incorporating some of his corrective themes, in chapter 7. However, all educational practices that drive towards predictable outcomes in terms of the present or expectable environment—and most all do—exercise a predominance of socialization over any of the other deep processes at work in the formation of human personality, society, and culture. Thus, for Christian education— which is supposed to be a *deep* process—to play into socialization as its dominant ally in the development of a Christian style of life is a deep self-contradiction. See also the basic theses of Milbank, *Theology*, which supports this same position with a somewhat different argument. See also other major critiques of Parsons's position in Mills, "Grand Theory"; Lockwood, "Some Remarks"; Dahrendorf, "Out of Utopia"; and Homans, "Structural, Functional," all found in Peterson, *System*. Editor's Note: For a reference to the "two Parsons" see footnote 22 below.

C. Wright Mills stated flatly, "Parsons has not been able to get down to the work of social science because he is possessed by the idea that the one social order he has constructed is some kind of universal model."[20] So be it. In using Parsons here, I am not saying that his is the final word on all versions of socialization. Rather, his approach, narrowly focused as it may be, defines effectively and thoroughly this major force in Christian education theory as I understand it. I am calling this *tension-reduction, pattern-maintenance* force "socialization." Others will perhaps define the term differently or want another name for the force, but that is a secondary discussion.

Here, I have modified, streamlined, and at points renamed parts of the model, but it is, I believe, faithful to Parsons's basic intention to describe the structure and dynamic in all fields of human action.[21] Parsons divides the whole field of human action into four basic systems—biological, psychological, social, and cultural.[22] The four systems are interrelated as follows:

20. Mills, *Sociological Imagination*, 48.

21. The structure of this set of boxes may appear to represent a closed system such as persons in family systems therapy use to characterize dysfunctional families—that is, families in which patterns of interaction (e.g., codependency) produce persons trapped in roles that make them unable to leave the family and unable to be themselves within the family. Such family systems are closed by a set of interlocking double-binds and though such a family may continue to exist, it produces emotionally impaired persons such as the Adult Children of Alcoholic personality type. Parsons' system is not of this sort. In fact, his once widely read *Family: Socialization and Interaction Process* makes it clear that families are open-ended systems standing in the transition between personality formation (Box A) and the social order (Box I). Families are supposed to generate new members for the larger society and culture. Parsons understood children to be part of the public function of the incest taboo—to send the new generation outward and populate the land but always according to the dynamics of social ways according to the dynamics of socialization learned at home. My point here is that Parsons's understanding of an open system governed by the structure and dynamics of socialization is in a more fundamental sense opposed to, and dominant over, the renewing power of the dynamics of transformation. Whether Parsons realized it or not, the whole field of human action described this way must, in the end, remain captive to short-term satisfaction and long-term disintegration.

22. Some commentators on Parsons's theory find a disparity between two sets of writings, the political and the sociological. The sociological Parsons from whom we are drawing the above diagram appears to be conservative and deterministic, but the political Parsons takes on specifically historically defined issues and problems in ways that appear to transcend the system. For a further discussion of the "Two Parsons" see Buxton, *Talcott Parsons*, 3–13.

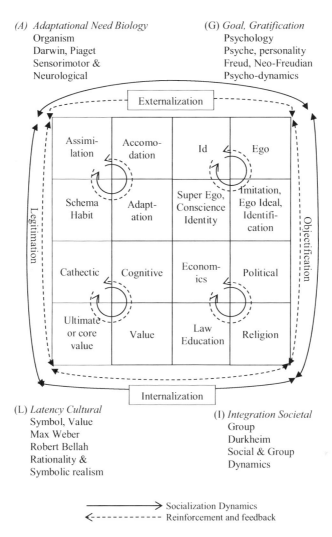

(A) *Adaptational Need Biology*
Organism
Darwin, Piaget
Sensorimotor &
Neurological

(G) *Goal, Gratification*
Psychology
Psyche, personality
Freud, Neo-Freudian
Psycho-dynamics

(L) *Latency Cultural*
Symbol, Value
Max Weber
Robert Bellah
Rationality &
Symbolic realism

(I) *Integration Societal*
Group
Durkheim
Social & Group
Dynamics

The basic unit of the biological system is the *organism*. The basic unit in the psychological system is the *psyche*. In the sociological box, it is the *group*. In the cultural box it is *symbol* and *value*. Note that Parsons's system is an *isomorphic* system of action. Thus, each subsystem functions as a miniature of the larger system. In other words, each subsystem structurally and functionally replicates and completes the larger system by exercising the same dynamics.

In this neo-Parsonian diagram, the four phases of interactive subsystems follow a dynamic pattern of action that proceeds ultimately in a clockwise direction.

1. One may begin with "adaptational" needs and patterns in Parsons's A box. This *biological* subsystem can be designated in textbook Piagetian terms (although Parsons does not use this terminology) as assimilation, accommodation, adaptation, and *schema* or habit.[23]

2. In response to such needs and the tension they generate, "goals" that will gratify the need and reduce the tension are sought. Goal setting and getting as action and as agency are represented in Parsons's G Box. In the *psychological* box, the four phases can be designated in Freudian or neo-Freudian terminology as id, ego, imitation/ego-ideal/identification, and superego/science/identity.

3. When the goal is attained, some equilibrium is established between the organism or person and its natural and/or interpersonal environment. Agencies and actions concerned with "integration" in the public domain are represented in Parsons's I Box. In this *social system* subcategory the phases can be designated economic, political, religious, and legal/educational.

4. Actions that are effective in attaining such integration thereby become valuable for the whole context of human action. Consequently, they are crystallized into symbolic forms creating enduring cultures as "latent" patterns (Parsons's L box) for determining the legitimating future action in meeting needs (Parsons's A box) the next time they arise. In this *cultural* subcategory the four phases may be designated cathectic, cognitive, value, and ultimate value.[24]

In addition to the Parsonian scheme, I have added terms to the diagram used by Berger and Luckmann in their collaboration *The Social Construction of Reality* and incorporated by Thomas Groome in *Christian Religious Education*. The terms are *externalization, objectification, internalization,* and *legitimation*. We can understand these terms in relation to these neo-Parsonian categories in the manner already suggested.

23. In chapter 3 of this book, the "textbook Piaget" will be laid aside for the deeper dynamic views of his life and thought. As assimilated by the American psychological establishment, the textbook Piaget illustrates this patterned socialization process quite well. This socialized distortion of Piaget also illustrates the damage that conformity forces can work on an open-ended, genuinely transformational approach to human development.

24. Obviously each of these subcategories could be elaborated to book-length discussion, but it is their place in the overall scheme that we want to designate here. Each box will be elaborated in the chapters that follow, but if readers would like an illustration of one part of the system, refer back to footnote 12, which describes the power of the legal system to set up and perpetuate a form of "legal" justice that merely legitimates the existing system rather than moving toward any larger sense of true justice.

1. Needs are *externalized* into goals designed to meet those needs.

2. Attained and frustrated goals are *objectified* into integrated adaptational systems of social interaction designed to overcome frustration and systematically insure future attainment.

3. Integrations (inclusive of their affective component) are then *internalized* as effective habits that extend into personal, social, and cultural values.

4. These value orientations eventually seek to *legitimize* the organism's subsequent adaptational needs and direct human action to repeat the cycle.

Parsons is said to have called the birth of each new generation of children a recurrent barbarian invasion requiring socialization. This neo-Parsonian scheme shows in brief compass how all human action, however barbaric or nonconformist, may ultimately be brought under the power of the social system. Subparts of the theory may vary, but the essential claim is that socialization moves over time, and in spite of repeated feedback and reciprocity (the counterclockwise motion), in a tension-reduction, pattern-maintenance direction (the clockwise motion) that finally exerts power over all human action in every realm of that action.

The customary analysis of socialization into primary and secondary socialization will be further discussed momentarily. Also, I will address the more differentiated aspects of the process in due time. However, what needs to be stressed here is the subtle, pervasive power that the force of socialization exercises over human action at all levels. At this point, a few illustrations must suffice.

As we have said, primary socialization takes place first and in relation to our primary groups, the family of origin. Secondary socialization is intentionally built on primary socialization and extends to society at large. Most primary socialization takes place without our recognizing it, so its power is largely latent, but nonetheless pervasive. Social psychologist Harold Garfinkel tapped into this phenomenon in his *Studies in Ethnomethodology*. I am told that professor Garfinkel would send his students home on vacations with instructions as they got off the train or plane or bus to act as perfect strangers to their parents, or whomever was meeting them, for as long as they could handle it. The pain that the students felt in reacting as a stranger to those who were eager to greet them is existential evidence of the power of primary socialization.

The power of socialization can also be shown by how it excludes you rather than by how it consumes you. The power can be overwhelming even to those who know most about it. A noted sociologist I know found that his experience going to India to visit and participate in a theosophical society meeting was so overpowering that he finally had to leave because of the density of the strangeness he encountered there. Similarly, Carl Jung, who was supposed to be the master of archetypes that cut across all cultures, was reportedly so deeply disturbed by the social realities he encountered in Africa that he returned prematurely to Zurich.

In Parsons's system, we, as religious persons, are taken in, given a function, and consumed by the system. As leaders or members of an organized ecclesiastical body, we belong in the little subbox in the bottom right hand corner of the diagram. We are neither prophets nor priests nor kings. We are merely factors in the system. Are we not destined to let the social system determine how and to what ends we may function? Will we not become fundamentally a by-product of this larger social reality? If we want to really make a difference, as Margaret Mead, Talcott Parsons, and other social scientists have argued, isn't it the case that we should become social scientists? *Doesn't Christianity really work best when it sacralizes what keeps the social system in good repair anyway?*

For example, in light of socialization, a Christian funeral and burial service is best understood as a means of social control. The shock, frustration, guilt and aggression set is motion by a death can be assuaged through such services. In these circumstances identities can be reconfirmed, common life blessed, and ultimate meaning articulated. Thus, the church is effective because it allows grieving, underlying regrets, and resocialization to be dealt with in a controlled manner. Socialized memorial services prevent disruptive motives from being released into the social system at large to cause disturbances in other sectors of the society. Thus, what works for social cohesion also perpetuates the value of the Christian religion—a nice arrangement. Other examples could be multiplied. For instance, disabling anxiety built up through a sense of guilt may be released through a sacrament of penance invoking confession and giving assurance of pardon. These examples and others all go to show that Parsons and Mead are right. Isn't ministry as educational either irrelevant to or merely a perpetrator of a useful myth? Don't the social scientists understand how to make it all work much better than we witnesses of Christ do? Because socialization is its central dynamic, the heart and soul of education, it poses the sustained educational challenge to Christianity's very identity.

## (B) The Christian Challenge to Education

On the other hand, the Christian challenge to education is even more pointed. As we have said, the dynamics of the Christian faith are predominantly transformational. As such, they consistently and repeatedly draw upon a reality that transcends the social system and thereby that seeks to redefine the system (or any part of it) in terms of that transcendent reality. Transformation, then, describes a dynamic that is basically different from socialization, even though it is often presumed and included in the efforts of socialization. More specifically, when the nature of Jesus Christ serves as the transcendent reality toward which emergent coherent orders of meaning point, transformation becomes life in the Spirit of Christ. As such the predominance of transformation over socialization focuses in dynamic terms the Christian challenge to education. Let us illustrate with a dramatic case in point.

Out of his passionate faith and concern to rescue the church from its cultural captivity, Søren Kierkegaard, the nineteenth-century philosopher and theologian, wrote in his posthumously published book *Attack upon "Christendom"*: "All Christian education is based upon a sheer lie."[25] In nineteenth-century Denmark civil religion had run its full course, so that to be born into a Christian family in Copenhagen was, at that time, to be automatically a Christian. Danish civil religion was an extreme case of the dictum that you can grow up Christian and never know the difference.[26] But from Kierkegaard's radical standpoint, revelation meant and means that there is no possibility for teaching Christianity. Socialization dynamics, regardless of how well rationalized they are, are fundamentally irrelevant to the Spirit of God. Only God's Spirit is the Teacher. "The Spirit will lead you into truth." So, from this standpoint, why are we doing anything about Christian education at all?

"Ah," you say, "but we can teach the Bible. That is the truth that will solve the problem." No, not according to Kierkegaard, as one of his famous

25. Kierkegaard, *Attack,* 199, 223. Editor's note: I found variations of this sentence in three places in a section of *Attack* titled "The Instant." Loder appears to be quoting in part from the table of contents of this section (199), which is repeated as the subheading (122). It reads: "That the Christian education of children in the Christian home, so much extolled, especially in Protestantism, is based upon a lie, a sheer lie." Several paragraphs later, Kierkegaard repeats the charge in this way: "The truth, however, is that this (the pride of Protestantism), this Christian education of children in the Christian home is, Christianly speaking, based on a lie, a sheer lie."

26. This statement is an allusion to Horace Bushnell's supposed thesis in *Christian Nurture* "that the child is to grow up Christian, and never know himself as being otherwise." See chapter 2 for a discussion of the actual meaning of the dictum in the larger context of Bushnell's thought, which differs from its meaning as an isolated statement out of context.

parables makes clear: Once upon a time, a man escaped from an insane asylum. As he climbed over the wall and walked to the nearby town, he knew something was still wrong with him, but he didn't want to be put back in the asylum. So he tried to think what he might say to the townspeople that would convince them that he was sane. As he walked along the road, he picked up a little ball and began to toss it up and catch it, toss it up and catch it. As he tossed the ball he thought to himself, "the ball is round, the ball is round." Then it occurred to him, "The world is round!" So he ran into the town and looked everyone straight in the eye and told them with great enthusiasm, "The world is round! The world is round!" And of course, they put him back in the asylum.[27]

The man did not lie. He spoke essentially true words. But his relationship to the truth made that truth into a bizarre statement. His words were inappropriately appropriated. The true words were spoken in a spirit that belied them. Thus, even the devil can quote Scripture. Indeed, the devil can *teach* Scripture. Therefore, it is not sufficient to socialize persons into the use and practice of established Christian truths. Christianity will not yield to habit, however well ingrained it may be. The dynamic of habituation and socialization are not sufficient—and even sometimes look bizarre—in their efforts to be bearers of Christian truth. The decisive question is, how is the truth related to you and to us, to the people of God? Or as Kierkegaard once put it, "What is the *how* of Christianity?"[28]

To begin with, Christianity is participatory truth, not a speculative or abstract truth. Thus according to one commentator, Lot's wife turned to salt because God does not tolerate spectators. The spirit of detached speculation contradicts divine action. As a theologian you may recognize my general point as a restatement of the struggle in the fourth-century church called the Donatist controversy. In this debate Augustine, the bishop of Hippo, argued at one point that the effectiveness of the sacrament was not dependent

27. Kierkegaard, *Unscientific Postscript*, 194–95. Editor's Note: Loder here paraphrases Kierkegaard's tale.

28. Kierkegaard, *Journals*, 123 (See also *Papirer*, 10:2, 43, in Diem, *Kierkegaard's*, 145). Although I have used Kierkegaard as an example of the challenge to socialization and education, it should not be assumed that this opposition between socialization and transformation can be reduced to corporate vs. individual behavior. Kierkegaard's emphasis on the individual was for the sake of the corporate life of Christianity and for the sake of the witness of the church to the entire political order. Bruce Kirmmse makes this point with impressive documentation in his book, *Kierkegaard*. Editor's Note: The reference to Kierkegaard is not an exact quote, but a kind of summary of Kierkegaard's discussion in section #1405. Loder's footnote originally referred to the Danish translation.

upon the moral character of the priest. But then it was also Augustine who finally said that the effectiveness of the Donatist sacrament was annulled because it was being done without *caritas*. Of course, earlier than that Paul had warned the Corinthians against taking the sacrament unworthily and getting sick (1 Corinthians 11:27–30.). By what spirit, according to what dynamics, do we know the truth individually and collectively?

Kierkegaard's point is that there must be a coherent relationship between the content of the faith and the dynamics by which it is conveyed. If that coherence is not there, the faith is not delivered. So if the truth is to be efficacious, how we stand in relationship to it is decisive. But human beings cannot determine that coherence, since such coherence can only be created and communicated by the Holy Spirit. Christian truth is not teachable. Only the Holy Spirit can render the Bible as the Word of God. Only the Spirit enables us to know how to view divine action. Only the Spirit makes the sacraments efficacious. And if our lack of love grieves the Spirit, then we take the sacrament to our detriment.

*But what is Spirit/spirit?*[29] Whatever we may say about spirit, we must say it is transformational in character. In its unity of power and meaning, it manifests power to transform personal meaning, social orders, cultural values, and even to transform the body—to heal and restore it. In the radical formulation of this perspective, socialization and education are not only fundamentally impotent and incompetent, but if a person ever assumes that he or she can communicate the truth of the gospel by means of socialization, that one is implicitly guilty of Pelagianism. By way of the paradigm case of Søren Kierkegaard, this is the Christian theological challenge to education.

## (V) THE POLAR FORCES IN TENSION

But now we must back off and look again at the protagonist in this dialogue. After all, Margaret Mead was a good Episcopalian, an admirer of the Roman Catholic theologian Teilhard de Chardin, and sometimes a defender of the faith.[30] Parsons, teaching at Harvard at the same time Tillich was lecturing there, affirmed the position Tillich held in relation to ultimate meaning—and perhaps more. Kierkegaard, to educate future generations, wrote

29. Editor's Note: Loder capitalized "Spirit" here and did not include "/spirit" in the original manuscript. But the context is somewhat ambiguous in the sense that his subsequent description of "Spirit" as transformational describes both the Holy Spirit and the human spirit in an analogical sense. So I added *"/spirit"* to this short sentence to capture the analogical relationship of Spirit/spirit.

30. See Mead's debates with James Baldwin in their book *Rap on Race*.

in just fourteen years all those books that it has taken scholars decades just to translate. Currently all twenty-four volumes of his writings are being retranslated in what must be seen as a major effort to educate. Thus, in the *de facto* situation of Christianity and education, the challenges do not represent absolutely opposite positions. Nevertheless, in these polarities one can see the extremes between which Christian education must move and by which the crux of the discipline is described.

Furthermore, the mutual challenge of the forces is not merely an analytical and/or historical dichotomy; it ramifies into practice. If the tension is effectively collapsed in either direction Christian education collapses into a closed and finally vicious circle. On the one hand, Christian education practitioners often come under the overbearing influence of socialization. As a consequence, they begin to produce programs and a wide variety of attractions that serve only the faddish, attendance-getting needs of the institution. Educators soon lose the reason they felt called into the profession in the first place. On the other hand, there are those spiritual educators who "go transcendent." They usually do so in one of two ways: (1) *scripturalism*, concentrating on the Scripture itself by itself—i.e., just do what is says and it will do the rest; and (2) *spiritualism*, becoming transcendent to the point of irrelevance—i.e., creating coded language for in-group experiences that outsiders do not have and do not understand.

Ironically, both expressions of biblical fundamentalism and ingrown spirituality unwittingly capitulate to the socialization dynamics that Margaret Mead and Talcott Parsons understood so very well. Consequently, those approaches lose, by their very one-sided zeal, the transcendence they had hoped to gain. The dynamics of authoritarian conformism and cultic indoctrination are well known to all social theorists who study the church.

Christian education theory must repeatedly work to expose the underlying dynamics of the theological-educational relationship, even as it preserves the essential tension at the heart of the discipline. This tension is essential not only for sound theory, but also for how one practices education. Thus, the essential integrity of the field and the vitality of practice depend upon keeping the integrity of this bipolar tension. One cannot collapse them together into an undifferentiated unity. One cannot rend them apart and still have a Christian education worthy of the name.

Mere concern to hold on to the bipolarity, however, does not resolve the issue. Rather, it only drives us to face a basic theological question: How far does the truth of Christianity admit to being taught? To contemplate and answer this question is to reveal one's fundamental view of the relationality between transformation and socialization. Which dynamic force is the predominant one in the polarity? How will this tensive relationship be constituted and executed in practice? How do we understand the relation of the Holy Spirit to the human spirit at work in this creative tension?

My answer will be elaborated in particular ways in all the following chapters. Note here in general, however, that the fundamental reality and master image guiding all these chapters is the relationship between God and humanity in Jesus Christ. There is, in other words, a profound paradoxical interplay between transformation and socialization in Christian education embedded in and analogous to the relation between God and humanity in the God-Human, Jesus Christ. The basis of the analogy is complementarity[31] in which two contrary and mutually exclusive categories of understanding are both required to account for the whole, because the exclusive opposition *between* them is essential to a comprehensive or complete understanding *of* them. Further, the whole may be viewed from the standpoint of either category, but not without implying its opposite. Finally, as God is the definitive category in the God-human relationship, humanity as in the particular human Jesus is reciprocally significant yet subordinate in the mutual indwelling of the two polarities.

The significance of transformation, especially transformation transformed by *Spiritus Creator*, lies in its power to disclose what may be a radically new coherent order of intelligibility which is itself disclosive of God's very nature, the uncreated Source and Ground of creation. In this respect, transformation stands toward the Godward pole in this analogy. Socialization moves in the opposite direction, driving toward establishing a steady state, ensuring extension of the status quo and eventual death and annihilation. Thus, socialization tends toward the human side in this analogy.[32] In other words, the theological baseline for this study is that the

31. This concept of complementarity is taken from the philosophy of Niels Bohr. See Loder and Neidhardt, *Knight's Move*, chapters 4 and 5, 61–122, for a comprehensive discussion of complementarity for theology and science dialogue.

32. Four key issues are important to note here even though they will receive fuller treatment in subsequent chapters. *First*, I do not suppose that this bipolar relational unity constitutes a complete Christology or even the essence of Christology. But I do claim that no Christology could be adequately formulated that did not make use of the form of logic modeled here. *Second*, I do not suppose that God's self-revelation in Christ is in itself a sufficient form of relationality by which to guide the subsequent discussion. But I do suppose that this relationality is the necessary basis upon which we can comprehend the ultimate and sufficient form of relationality inherent in the Holy Trinity. *Third*, the appearance of this relational logic in other contexts (e.g., complementarity in physics, self-relationality in human consciousness) does not detract from the uniqueness of the revelation of God in Christ, but rather indicates the pervasive way in which the created order reflects his nature. Just as it is only through "the *Eidos* of the Son" (Athanasius) that the Godhead can be known, so also it is only through that same *Eidos* that the natural order can be comprehended as "creation," contingent upon the

inherent nature of Jesus Christ is definitive for Christian education and for our practice of it.[33] His nature analogically delineates the necessarily tensive relationship between the two forces that constitute the dynamic structure of the discipline. This relationship is also reflected in the dialectic of Christian action inherent in life in the Spirit.

In that light we can comprehend Paul's admonition, *"Work out your own salvation with fear and trembling, for God is at work in you, both to will and to work for God's good pleasure"* (Phil 2:12b–13 RSV). What this verse suggests is that Christian education, understood in the context of this chris-tomorphic bipolarity, is an awesome task.[34] It may be indicative that the Greek words for "fear" and "trembling" are the roots for the English "pho-bia" and "trauma." The Christian education enterprise is called to participate in the very nature of God's revelation in Jesus Christ, and that is surely a task of cosmic magnitude. Thus, Christian education and Christian educators must remain in the dialectic described aptly years ago by Karl Barth.

> As ministers we ought to speak of God. We are human, however, and so cannot speak of God. We ought, therefore, to recognize *both* our obligation and our inability [this with fear and trem-bling]—*and by that very recognition give God the glory.*[35]

sustaining grace of God. *Finally*, the analogical move from two natures to two dynamic processes may seem to be as unwarranted as it is ungrammatical to turn nouns into verbs. However, as we will see in the following chapter on Piaget (beyond the textbook Piaget), this is precisely how he moved from thinking about organism and environment (two nouns) into thinking relationally about "functional invariants," i.e., *assimilating* (verb with organism dominant), *accommodating* (verb with environment dominant) as constituting *adapting* (verb representing dynamic equilibrium) in a relationality he claimed constituted the basis of all *intelligent* knowing. Thus two processes moving in opposite directions constitute the unity of intelligence. In theological context, this shift is more complex, but it is essentially the same basic move toward stressing the dynamics of relationality inherent in more fixed substantive entities. For a discussion of this move in theological terms, particularly as it constitutes the core of Kierkegaard's project, see Loder and Neidhardt, *Knight's Move*, chapter 12.

33. Here readers may again refer back to the model described in footnote 8. The significance of this normative view of relationality for Christian education and for practical theology will continue to be unfolded in the following chapters. Suffice it to say here that christomorphic relationality is the interpretative framework within which other analogous relationalities find their larger context of meaning. For a full develop-ment of this argument, see Loder and Neidhardt *Knight's Move*, section 1, *In Quest of Spirit*, 19–122.

34. Editor's Note: "Christomorphic bipolarity" is an allusion to the Chalcedonian doctrine of the two natures of Christ translated for its communicative value in a scien-tific culture.

35. Barth, *Word of God*, 186 (italics original); the bracketed phrase is added. For a further discussion of the relationship between Barth's dialectic and Niels Bohr's concept

This is the crux of the dialectic at the center of Christian education, and it can no more be broken than Jesus Christ's divinity can be divided from his humanity, or his humanity from his divinity.

## (VI) CONCLUSION

Thus, the crux of Christian education is ultimately grounded in the bipolar relational unity of Christ's Person. Fully God and fully human, his Person defines and indeed constitutes both the disturbing discontinuity and the glorious unity that resides at the center of this field. An elementary principle for Christian education, then, is that its two great constitutive forces are held together and apart as the God-Human Jesus Christ holds the nature of humanity and divinity together and apart.

---

of complementarity, see Loder and Neidhardt, "Barth, Bohr" in Richardson, *Religion and Science*, 271–98.

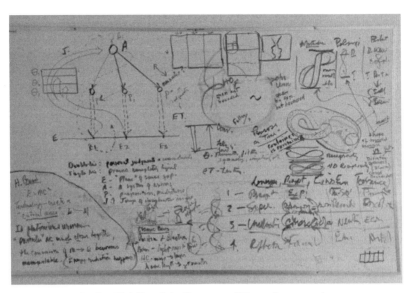

*Loder-Neidhardt's diagram of Complementarity
between Christ & Culture (Theology and Science)
circa 1990*

# Socialization Dominance

*The Malleability of Culture*

# 2

# Socialization and Transformation

## A Brief History

## (I) INTRODUCTION

IN HIS CLASSIC BOOK *Dogmatics in Outline*, Karl Barth voiced his "amazement" at the "mighty relationship" between God and human beings revealed in Jesus Christ.

> Starting with Jesus Christ and with Him alone, we must see and understand what in the Christian sense is involved in the mighty relationship, to which we can only point again and again in sheer amazement, about which we cannot help being in danger of great error, when we say *God and man.*[1]

We want to follow Barth's lead and allow the outworking of that "mighty relationship" to guide our discussion of the dynamic character of Christian education through this book. The following subsections contain two brief historical typologies to illustrate the long-standing relational interplay between socialization and transformation in biblical and cross-cultural perspective. Following this initial discussion we will envision this interplay in civil religion and in various vignettes in Christian education. We will conclude the chapter with an analysis of a paradigm case from the important Christian education theorist C. Ellis Nelson.

---

1. Barth, *Dogmatics in Outline*, 66.

33

From the standpoint of faith, these historical sketches are meant to offer glimpses of the universal unfolding in time of the ultimately irreducible relationality of God and humanity in Jesus Christ. Thus, the history of Christian education theory and practice may be broadly characterized as "pointing again and again in sheer amazement" to the unique relationality that lies at the very core of his Person. But at the same time we risk the very "danger of great error" to which Barth's quote draws attention. This history is an exploration of the vast scope of the dynamics of Christ's nature which, on the one hand, have been characterized as socialization with its inclination toward equilibrium and the death of creation, and on the other hand as transformation with its drive toward the disclosure of the divine presence in and through creation, revealing proleptically the ultimate destiny of the history in which it partakes.

The translation of the substantive nature of Jesus Christ into this bipolar relational dynamic has been spelled out elsewhere.[2] But the task of this book centers on showing that such a translation has interpretative power for reenvisioning the history of this field and for moving it into the future under the guidance of a dynamic interpretation of the *hypostatic union*, as the unified bipolarity of the person of Christ has been classically designated. I do not presume that this effort represents the only possible interpretation of Christ's nature. Nor do I assume that this is an exhaustive account of the spiritual nature of Jesus Christ. I do claim, however, that such a viewpoint has explanatory value which lends added dimension, integrity, and flexibility to the overall vision of this field, especially as it may be reinterpreted, past, present and future, in light of the presence and power of the Holy Spirit.

## (II) HISTORICAL PATTERNS, PARADIGMS, AND CASES

As we discuss the following paradigms, beginning with a biblical and historical typology and moving into the contemporary Christian education scene by means of cases and further types, we note that there is a significant increase in the use and explanatory significance of transformation as the dominant dynamic by which this field is coming to understand itself and its purposes. This common usage does not mean to say that there is agreement as to the meaning of the term. But it is significant that this theme is now stressed at the center of a field that has long been dominated by conceptions of socialization. To show that transformation ought not and cannot be reduced to a new name for the old socialization is, of course, part of the agenda of this book.

2. Loder and Neidhardt, *Knight's Move*, especially chapters 12 and 13 (265–308).

We turn now to the first paradigm that expresses perhaps the starkest contrast between these two dynamic patterns, socialization and transformation. Still, readers should keep in mind that these two patterned forces are inseparable in thought and action. There is no socialization that does not call upon transformation, and there is no transformation that does not presuppose some socialization. The following tale of two cities sets up a typology in which the relative dominance of one force over the other is dramatized, but this emphasis should not obscure the ultimate inseparability of these intertwined forces.

## (A) Babylon and Jerusalem: The Tower and the Church

"The Babel story is a masterpiece of narrative art," says Bernhard Anderson.[3] In terms of literary criticism, there can be little doubt that the story of the tower of Babel (Gen 11:1–9) forms a consistent multidimensional whole. Yet it is also thematically tied into other narratives, most notably to the story of the fall of humankind that precedes it and to the Abraham narrative that follows it in anticipation of the birth of God's people at Jerusalem. Both the Babylonian story and the Abraham narrative concern the rebuilding of human culture after the great flood, and therefore have to do with the redemption of history after consuming devastation. In this respect, the Babel story also parallels the fall from paradise in Eden and the dissemination of the people across the earth, to which the Abraham story also responds.

This parallelism between Babylon and Abraham (Jerusalem) suggests the major distinction that we must appreciate if we are to fully understand the force of the typology. In the first instance (Babylon) we are concerned with the work of the human spirit to reconstruct history in its own terms. In the second instance (Abraham/Jerusalem) we see the radical transformation of the human spirit by the intervening power of God's Spirit, redeeming history in God's own terms. The first scenario suggests humanity written as large as possible into the heavens ("*let us build a tower to heaven*") with the ironic result that, as von Rad comments, "Yahweh must draw near, not because he is nearsighted, but because he dwells at such tremendous height and their work is so tiny."[4] The satirical force of the biblical description

---

3. Anderson, *From Creation*, 168.

4. Von Rad, *Genesis*, 149. Von Rad attributes the quote to Otto Procksch from his 1924 commentary. This interpretation contrasts with a linguist's view that the tower somehow threatened God. See Pinker, *Language Instinct*, 16. The contrast illuminates the reductionism implicit in coming to an understanding of God through faith in culture as against coming to an understanding of culture through faith in God.

obliterates any claim that the human spirit can be equated with the Spirit of God. Yet as we will see in Jerusalem, the pentecostal narrative in Acts 2 clearly confirms the integrity of the human spirit when it is transformed into agreement with God's Spirit.

### (1) Babylon: The Biblical Paradigm of Socialization

Let us turn to an elaboration of these two paradigm cities. The term "Babel" signified the center of the earth, and the name "Babylon" means *Bab-ili*— that is, the "gate of the god" (Marduk), the place where heaven and earth meet and touch each other. "Babylon" is thus the source and center of all countries, "the navel-string of the countries." Indeed, one of the fifty names for Marduk is "the Lord of the lofty navel-string." The "gate of the god" (Marduk), which became the name for the city as a whole, originally designated the sacred precincts of the temple tower of Marduk, situated in the center of the city. Almost certainly the "tower with its top in the heavens" of the Genesis account is this temple tower. This edifice was built according to the structure of a ziggurat (literally, "mountain peak"), famous throughout the ancient world and known as "the house of the foundation of heaven and earth." The name of the city of Babylon, "navel of the earth," locates the navel-string that connects the lofty heights of heaven to the earth, which lies like a prostate body, belly upward. Furthermore, the tower was arranged in a tripartite fashion so as to correspond to the supposed tripartite structure of the universe: (1) The waters of the netherworld (the anteroom contained a large water basin called *Apsu*), (2) earth, and (3) heaven. The ziggurat of Babel functioned as the center of the New Year festival rites that reiterated the primeval victory of Marduk over Tiamat, in the course of which the *Enuma Elish* epic was recited.

The account of creation in Genesis may be seen as an attack on the whole ziggurat mythology. The cosmic significance of the ziggurat is fully recognized, but at the same time it is exposed as an inordinately ambitious human effort at self-realization on a superhuman level. Thus Babylon becomes the center of the confusion of languages, humankind is scattered abroad, and the name Babylon becomes an enduring signifier of God's judgment upon human attempts to be like God.

As we suggested earlier, we miss the point of this judgment, however, if we do not see it as leading up to the appearance of Abraham who, from chapter 12 onward, becomes the principal figure in the historical drama. Abraham is God's effective reply to the tower of Babel. God calls Abraham to leave Ur of the Chaldees, cradle of the Sumero-Babylonian religion. Then

God promises to make Abraham into a great nation. And God's judgment now becomes the beginning of a new history which God will bring into being in ways that are far removed from the mythic system that attempted to locate God at the center of the earth in a tower that connects heaven and earth like an infant to its mother's body.

Recall here Parsons's pattern of human action summarized in chapter 1. Note that Parsons's model describes in scientific terms the fundamentally organic foundations that reside in this narrative account of the origins of the culture of Babylon. Psychological and social factors eventually give symbolic and cosmological expression to the organic concept of birth, and the result is an ultimately closed system sacralized by the priests of Marduk, who regularly celebrate the divine origins of the whole system. The dynamics at work in Babylon are not altogether different from contemporary systems of socialization that attempt an all-inclusive integration of organic, psychological, social, and cultural organization, as we will see in the subsequent discussion.

Before turning to the antithesis of Babel at Pentecost, an account of the Jerusalem temple as a halfway house in the creation of God's people must be given. The temptation of Israel to build a temple in order to emulate other nations and kingdoms seems to be universally human. The temple through many indications was built to replicate in many of its aspects the tripartite structure of the ziggurat, and the lowest part had the same name as the corresponding part of the Babylonian ziggurat: "bosom of the earth." Other evidence could be cited to suggest the physical similarity between the temple and the ziggurat. But the striking thing is that the cosmic significance of this symbolism seems to have held no intrinsic significance for the Israelites.

Indeed, the detailed record of the building of the temple was marked by matter-of-factness. Not a word was said that suggests any exercise in magic or mythology, practices that usually preceded the building of pagan temples. If Israel borrowed from the pagan ziggurats some design and various appurtenances, they gave the entire endeavor their own meaning and significance that decisively broke away from pagan symbolism. The sacred quality of the temple came from God alone who said, "My name shall be there!" This reference was to the ark of the covenant, which housed the tablets of the law and was kept in the holy of holies. But Yahweh was never considered the God of the lofty navel-string. Yahweh is the God of history. Indeed, the long poles by which the ark was carried were left in the rings of the ark to remind Israel that the ark really belonged to the God who is "on the move." God alone creates, redeems, and restores history.

Therefore, the temple in Jerusalem was at best a halfway house, as the prophets clearly saw. Nathan's resistance to David's building the temple should be put alongside Samuel's resistance to the introduction of a kingship for Israel (1 Samuel 8). There is, for example, vehement protest against the patterns of kingships shared by other religions of the ancient Near East in Ezekiel 28, where the prophet denounces the king of Tyre. Here, the prophet denounces kingship mythology in a way parallel to the denunciation of the earlier Babylonian mythology. Pagan kings were either considered to be god incarnate (Pharaoh) or a servant of the gods (as in Mesopotamia), who ruled over the land as the chief instrument for the integration of society, nature, culture, and the gods.[5]

By comparison to these pagan forms, the relation between the Hebrew monarch and his people was as secular as was possible in a society in which religion was a living force. Israel maintained an undiminished distinction between creation and the Creator upon whom it is contingent. In doing so, she foreshadowed a more radical desacralization of the natural order that ultimately opened the way for modern science, as we will argue in the following discussion. God's eternal purpose was to create a people from the seed of Abraham, namely Jesus, who would not need a temple made with hands. Nevertheless, the human need to bring the whole field of human action, including religious life, under the control of socialization and patterns of culture is a powerful force to which even God gave some provisional space and time. However, eventually the tendency of socialization to dominate the transforming work of God was once and for all overthrown in the creation of the Christian church at Pentecost.

## (2) Jerusalem: The Biblical Paradigm of Transformation

We turn now to this prototype of the new Israel, who, as the people of God, was constituted by the living presence of Christ, as the antitype of Babylon. We carefully note that in *all* the Gospels, John the Baptist declares Jesus to be the One who will baptize the people in the Holy Spirit. And so it was. At nine o'clock in the morning he was crucified, blood burst from the wounds in his body, and the veil of the temple was torn from the top to the bottom. And, at nine o'clock in the morning the Holy Spirit, the new life of Christ, was poured out on the frightened group of disciples who obediently but

---

5. Editor's Note: I did some of the initial research on Babylonian mythology for Dr. Loder as his assistant in 1994, most of which shows up in the manuscript (i.e., von Rad, C. Westermann, B. Anderson, and others). But some of the particulars of his discussion appear to be from sources other than the ones I provided him.

uncertainly awaited his return in an upper room in Jerusalem. The roar of the Spirit, harbinger of the new Jerusalem, was so loud and the tongues of fire above their heads so striking, that a great crowd made up of multiple nations gathered to see what had seemingly made them drunk with ecstasy. The power of the Spirit testified through Peter's sermon to the essential nature of Jesus Christ and the claim he made upon the lives of all who were present. Three thousand persons were converted to Christ because all heard the message in their own tongues.

I want to offer six observations on this decisive event that serve to focus our discussion of this antitype to the Babylonian mythic system. *First*, Pentecost is clearly revealed as the work of God in history since it is portrayed as a hierophany that fulfills the prophecy of Joel—the climax of centuries of waiting for the Messiah. *Second*, of course, this event not only fulfills prophecy but, as with all major turning points in the history of Israel, history is redirected by a hierophany that is not itself historically definable. On the day of Pentecost, Jerusalem resumes its eschatological role as the mountain of the Lord. But now the city was no longer only the place of gathering but also the central point of departure for the apostolic mission to the world. Thus, Pentecost reveals and initiates the beginning of the "new nation" that God is creating, promised long ago to Abraham and fulfilled through Abraham's Seed, Messiah Jesus. This event depicts God's answer to Babylon and the beginning *in* history of the divine transformation *of* history.

*Third*, in contrast to the assertions of the Babylonians that their ancient, mythically enshrined god Marduk is the source of the earth and of the nation, Pentecost reveals that in the unity of God and humanity in the Person of Jesus Christ the origin and destiny of the universe is disclosed. Through him and for him all things have been created. Yet he does not dwell in temples made with hands. Moreover, he cannot be conceived in some isomorphic relationship between humanity, earth, and heaven, but in his transcendence he gives relative autonomy to creation, even as creation remains always under his redemptive care. This contingent relationship between God and creation shatters the closed mythic systems of Babylon, and it releases the power of the human spirit to discover through the arts and sciences the richness of creation in all its aspects, yet within the context of its ultimate purpose to glorify God.

*Fourth*, Pentecost reveals a transformation of the Mosaic law so carefully concealed in the ark of the covenant in the holy of holies of the temple. It is not accidental that Pentecost occurred on the same day that the Jews ordinarily celebrated the giving of the law to Moses. So, when the veil of the temple is rent from top to bottom, the "law of the Spirit" replaces the law of Moses as its fulfillment and transformation.

*Fifth*, the significance of tongues is decisive for our understanding of the Spirit in relation to culture since it is by the Spirit, at a level deeper than culture, that thousands of people of diverse cultures and languages were all enabled and empowered to find communion. They were bound together in a way that poses the exact opposite result in the tower of Babel story where tongues were confused and nations were scattered all over the earth.

*Finally*, all five of the above points make the decisive claim that what is invisible ultimately rules over what is visible, what is intangible and un-controllable as the wind ultimately rules over the tangible and controllable aspects of human life. However, this overruling does not occur apart from— nor is it finally antithetical to—its design for the fulfillment and flourish-ing of visible and tangible aspects of human affairs. It is an overruling that dwells in and fulfills the very terms of that over which it rules. The nature of this rule is evident in the fact that, although the Spirit transcended all cul-tural distinctions and differences, each person was made to hear *in his or her own language* the gospel message. Cultural distinctions were not obliterated, but they were made to serve the spiritual nature of Christ. In other words, at Pentecost the Spirit reconstituted the church in a fashion that replicated the asymmetrical bipolar model we have used to describe the nature of Christ. That is, the Spirit replicated functionally what it revealed theologically. Karl Barth describes this work of the Spirit through history in this elegant way.

> The work of the Holy Spirit, however, is to bring and to hold together that which is different and therefore, as it would seem, necessarily and irresistibly disruptive in the relationship of Jesus Christ to His community, namely, the divine working, being, and action on the one side and the human on the other, the cre-ative freedom and act on one side and the human on the other, the eternal reality and possibility on one side and the temporal on the other. His work is to bring and to hold them together, not to identify, intermingle nor confound them, not to change the one into the other nor to merge the one into the other, but to coordinate them, to make them parallel, to bring them into harmony and therefore to bind them into a true unity.[6]

The tower in Babylon and the outpouring of the Spirit at Pentecost in Jerusalem epitomize then, the antithesis between the two great forces of so-cialization and transformation that we are and will continue to discuss. They dramatize the extreme case when one or the other force becomes dominant.

6. Barth, *CD* IV/3.2, 761.

In what follows we will attend to the interplay in more subtle forms, but this archetypal comparison and contrast should help disclose and illuminate this distinction in whatever historical phenomenon we investigate.

## (B) Ontocratic and Theocratic Typology in History

In 1964 a challenging and controversial volume, *Christianity in World History*, appeared on the theological scene. In this book, which Hendrick Kraemer, the well-regarded Dutch theologian called "an event," Arend van Leeuwen set forth a typology based in principle on the distinction described in the previous section.[7] He designed his discussion to guide the mission of Christianity into the modern world. He articulated two contrasting worldviews in this book, the *ontocratic* and the *theocratic*. By the *ontocratic* pattern van Leeuwen meant an understanding of reality in terms of cosmic totality, a total order of harmony between the eternal and the temporal, in which the earth, humanity, and divinity were understood to be analogical replications of each other. All the hierarchical structures within this pattern were sacralized by divine ordinance and preserved by a priestly caste. Of course, he was thinking of early civilizations of the Near East as well as of the great cultures and religions of the Far East. He argued that the latter had produced a way of life that had for centuries, in the face of radical political changes, remained seemingly unchangeable. The type is recognizable, even if it does not do full justice to Eastern civilization and religion. As Karl Marx once wrote, "The structure [underlying] the economic elements of society [i.e., Asiatic societies] remains untouched by the storm clouds of the political sky."[8] Something here seemed rooted in the very being of the earth, humanity and God, and so remained highly resistant to fundamental change, even in the face of sweeping political upheaval. What Marx had noted in the context of Parsons's action system was the immense staying power of culture at the point of ultimate value.

Against the *ontocratic* pattern van Leeuwen set the *theocratic* pattern, which he argued characterized the people of Israel and later the Christian church. Israel and the church became bearers of an understanding of reality that was destined from the outset to break out of the *ontocratic* straightjacket

---

7. Kraemer, "Foreword," ix. Editor's Note: Kraemer wrote: "From time to time the appearance of a book is an 'event.' Dr. van Leeuwen's book definitely falls into this category. Whether looked at from the angle of cultural history, cultural philosophy, theology, or Christian missions, it fully deserves the description of an 'event.'"

8. Van Leeuwen, *Christianity*, 175. Editor's Note: Van Leeuwen quotes from Marx, *Articles on India*, 76.

to become repeatedly the source of revolutionary action. God, in this view, is Creator, and the created order is set in a contingent relationship to God. As mentioned before, by this understanding of contingency the realm of nature and the orders of society and culture were desacralized in relation to God the Creator, who worked in and through history. Desacralization prepared the way for the rise of modern science and technology. Indeed, several historians of science and theology have argued that the Judeo-Christian doctrine of *creatio ex nihilo* broke open the Hellenic metaphysical unity of God and nature and thereby all the natural orders of creation were given relative autonomy. With laws of its own, the created order became subject to experimental science and to technological manipulation. In van Leeuwen's *theocratic* worldview, all relatively autonomous systems of the natural order remain open-ended and contingent upon God's sustaining, intervening, and redeeming grace, and they derive their ultimate meaning and purpose from that God.

At the time of van Leeuwen's book came out, it appeared that the rise of science and technology might, perhaps, become a viable expression of the *theocratic* worldview.[9] The *ontocratic* worldview, ancient and long-standing as it might have been, seemed then, and continues to be seen now, to be headed toward breakdown as the Western world order advanced. But notice that this advance is not based primarily on scientific discoveries but is linked to the spirit of the Western mentality rooted in its Judeo-Christian history. After all, several significant discoveries (e.g., gunpowder, the compass, and the printing press) were made in China long before the West came upon them. But these inventions could not flourish due to the *ontocratic* worldview that failed to legitimate rapid technological advancement. Now, with the advance of Western science and technology under the spirit of creativity, which was fueled by Western religious resources, it seemed that *theocracy* was and is on the rise worldwide. But, of course, van Leeuwen's typology brought the enduring issue of distinguishing between spreading the gospel and the advance of Western civilization into sharp focus.

What was not sufficiently understood in the debate that swirled around van Leeuwen's literary "event" was that the *ontocratic* pattern, as it appeared in the ancient as well as the contemporary Eastern world, was only one very obvious manifestation of the power of socialization through enculturation

---

9. There is in van Leeuwen's book no distinction between science and technology. Such a distinction is imperative for a theological perspective on contemporary science. See the lengthy treatment in Loder and Neidhardt, *Knight's Move*, 1–15. In brief, note that discoveries in technology are patented but discoveries in science (e.g., relativity theory) are open to all. In essence, there is a distinction between open-ended and closed-circuited knowledge at stake here.

to create and perpetuate a seemingly intractable religious and cultural order. On the Western side, advances in the sciences and their technologies at any or all levels are no guarantee against the pattern-maintenance, tension-reduction proclivities of socialization. Technological expressions of science do not secure the open-ended spirit of Western civilization. Rather, modern science and its technologies, like any other cultural artifact, will itself become subject to those same dynamics that Parsons' system describes. Indeed, what is Parsons's action system but a highly differentiated and sophisticated *ontocratic* pattern done up in the language and concepts of the social sciences? All aspects of the pattern are isomorphically analogous and are "sacralized" by "the priests" of the system who teach that this field of action is all there is, and our "salvation"—if there is any—will begin and end right there.

Because Parsons's system is itself a cultural artifact, it illustrates what it also describes. Thus it is a clear account of the power of socialization, which may operate with far greater subtlety than even its keenest practitioners may realize.[10] However, the main point here is that the seductive power of socialization makes it evident that the typology van Leeuwen described is not fundamentally an ancient-modern or an East-West dichotomy. Rather, the evidence for his typology is perhaps better interpreted dynamically as a socialization-transformation struggle played out in multiple cultures through different epochs in both East and West.[11]

10. As I have already noted above, some scholars have argued that there are two "Parsons." The one is the system maker who constructs isomorphic patterns that operate according to the dynamics of socialization, and the other is far more political and even activist. The latter comes to the fore when Parsons analyzes particular issues. See Buxton, *Talcott Parsons,* 1–13.

11. This discussion borders on a philosophy of history, but since it is not our purpose to develop such a position, we must attempt to place this discussion briefly in that context. For instance, the dialectic between socialization and transformation might mistakenly be seen as a manifestation of the Hegelian view of the progress of the consciousness of freedom. Georg Wilhelm Friedrich Hegel's writings constitute a full-blown universal philosophy of history with premises and implications that are unacceptable to the position taken in this volume. Nevertheless, within Hegel's grand scheme, transformation, as we have defined it, might be seen as the drive toward an expanded consciousness of freedom; and socialization, as discussed above, the counter force which presses toward constraint and socially acceptable forms of the constriction of the consciousness of freedom. In each instance of conflict between these two forces, the resolution will sooner or later work toward the superordination of transformation over socialization in Hegel's view.

In a recent widely discussed volume, *End of History,* Francis Fukuyama argues that precisely this drive toward a full consciousness of freedom for *all* persons has been achieved with the collapse of Communism and the unchallenged ascendancy of democracy. Intriguing as his theses was, it did not stand the test of hard scrutiny and was

However, in sympathy with van Leeuwen's concern to preserve the integrity of a worldview that affirms the contingent relationship between God and God's creation, between the Spirit of God and the creations of the human spirit, between the nature of Christ and the nature of any civilization, the ensuing discussion of this volume must drive home some hard distinctions. One of van Leeuwen's refrains, taken originally from Genesis but extended throughout the entirety of Scripture, was "God divides in order to create." Similarly we must make some critical distinctions so we can participate more consciously and intentionally in the creative acts of God, not confusing them with human forms of legitimation in any social or cultural milieu.

For instance, our discussion must distinguish between the human spirit participating in the transforming power of God's Spirit as against the potentially transformational power of the human spirit trapped in "sacralized" patterns of socialization. We must further distinguish between socialization that is actually in the service of a deeper transformation by the power of the divine Spirit as against socialization that is crying "liberation" in the name of God, but is all the time entrenching its "liberation" in some new, more sophisticated form of the *ontocratic* pattern. The spiritual presence of Christ is hidden within and beyond the patterns that socialization produces,

---

rejected by many notable scholars such as Daniel Bell, who made a similar observation some thirty years before in his volume *End of Ideology*. See also Fukuyama, "End of History?," 3–18, and "Responses to Fukuyama" by Bloom, Hassner, Himmelfarb, Kristol, Moynihand, and Sestanovich in the same issue, 19–35.

For our purposes, the terms *transformation* and *socialization* are much closer to the precise issues raised by Christian education than any of the Hegelian terminology, even when it is done up in contemporary political jargon. Moreover, in our position, even though a dialectic is involved that can be studied historically and cosmologically, the dialectic we are working with requires the mediation of Christ, not the kind of spiritual *Aufgehoben* Hegel affirmed. In effect, the distinctiveness of Christ in Christianity and in world history, to which this volume holds, sets it apart from Hegel and from all other great philosophies of history such as those offered by Oswald Spengler and Arnold Toynbee, as well as lesser positions such as those of Auguste Comte, Herbert Spencer, and Karl Marx.

A related position closer to the position of this volume is that of Wolfhart Pannenberg. For him the resurrection of Jesus Christ is the proleptic revelation in history of the end of history. Transposing our terminology into Pannenberg's context, transformation is in the service not simply of the historical triumph of human freedom (Hegel), but it is in the service of that unique freedom for individuals, societies, and cultures that comes from conformity to the nature of the resurrected Christ. Although the following discussion departs from Pannenberg at many points, his philosophy of history is closer to our point of view than Hegel's or those of any of the other philosophies of history mentioned above. Editor's Note: Loder does not cite a source for Pannenberg here. He probably has in mind Pannenberg's *Revelation as History*.

and Christian education should make the distinctions that will release the power of his Spirit for the transformation of all human orders of existence.

## (C) Civil Religion in the United States

A third type of illustration of the transformation-socialization dynamic appears in the phenomenon of civil religion. The essential point here is that the broad sweep of socialization in American society has undergone repeated transformations embracing ever-widening dimensions of human existence at the hands of explicit religious claims. Moving beyond the essay discussed below, we would stress that under leadership of such people as Martin Luther King Jr. the theological potential for transformation, always latent in a socialized milieu, was actualized, raising permanently the horizon of socialization toward higher standards in society as a whole. This latency of transformation is not to argue for permanent and inevitable progress. Rather, the higher standards expressed in the previous sentence refers to an expansion of the range of human consciousness into the major dimensions of human existence.[12]

In this respect, even the secular course of events may approach the revelation in history of the ultimate meaning of history given proleptically in the Event of Jesus Christ. Analogous to the fashion in which the violence and suffering of the American Civil War permanently altered socialization patterns in this society to include the potential death and loss of the nation, I am arguing that the periods of Great Awakening have moved American social consciousness to a permanent need for grounding society in religious values. Even though these religious values lose all critical power through being socialized, they nevertheless remain the permanent endowment of the history of their society and the latent *pentecostal* potential for a transformational awakening to the divine presence acting redemptively in history.

The pervasive power of socialization as we have been describing it is familiar to all students of civil religion in America, and has been described by

---

12. See Loder, *Transforming Moment*, and chapter 5 in this text. These dimensions are discussed at length in the following chapters. For now let me assert that the major dimensions of human being, always present tacitly but only explicitly known as such by faith, are Self, World, Void, and Holy. The complete comprehension and integration of these dimensions is given in the nature of Jesus Christ. In him all things cohere, yet, in spite of the universal scope of his being, he is particular in his love for each person. This love takes death and ultimate nothingness into itself, transforming it into a darkness that heightens the sense of his holiness by contrast. The argument in this text is that we are, both individually and corporately, drawn historically by his Spirit into a heightened consciousness of his four-dimensional nature.

several key historical observers of the American scene. However, it has been dramatized most effectively for contemporary social and religious thinkers by Robert Bellah, onetime student and later colleague of Talcott Parsons, in one of his early, most widely read essays, "Civil Religion in America."[13] Comparing the religious claims implicit in the inaugural addresses of Washington and Jefferson, with Abraham Lincoln and John F. Kennedy, Bellah showed that the root metaphor behind Washington's address was explicitly stated later in Jefferson's Second Inaugural. In that address, Jefferson declared, "I shall need, too, the favor of that Being in whose hands we are, who led our fathers, as Israel of old [read here Abraham as well as Moses], from their native land and planted them in a country flowing with all the necessities and comfort of life."[14] Europe is "Egypt" and America is the "Promised Land." God led a "Chosen People" to establish a new sort of social order that shall be a light to all the nations. The manifest destiny of the nation to move westward with their religious education as well as with their drive for wealth, property, and power was compelled forward by this vision of America as the new Israel. But in these addresses there was no mention of Christ, nor any significant use of christomorphic imagery.

When we come to Lincoln's speeches, the situation is different. Here the ultimate meaning of the nation was at stake and Lincoln related slavery, war, and the issues surrounding states' rights to an ultimate context of meaning. Bellah argued that with the Civil War, new themes of death, sacrifice, and rebirth entered civil religion as a single theme that was symbolized in the life and death of Lincoln himself.

> The Gettysburg symbolism (". . . those who here gave their lives that the nation might live") is Christian without having anything to do with the Christian church . . . With the Christian archetype in the background, Lincoln, "our martyred president," was linked to the war dead, those who "gave the last full measure of devotion." The theme of sacrifice was indelibly written into the civil religion [of America].[15]

The power of socialization becomes most evident on Memorial Day, which grew out of the Civil War and gave ritual expression to the themes of

13. Bellah, "Civil Religion," 3–23. When Bellah left Harvard and went to the University of California at Berkeley, it was a public sign of his separating from Parsons's thought. Thus his more recent works (e.g., *Habits of the Heart*) show far less the impact from his years at Harvard in association with Parsons. However, some scholars still recognize Parsons's influence even in Bellah's later works.

14. Bellah, "Civil Religion," 7–8. Editor's Note: Loder inserted the parenthetical remark, "Read here Abraham as well as Moses," into Bellah's quote.

15. Ibid., 10–11.

sacrifice, new birth, and redemptive suffering in light of the American vision. Thus, Memorial Day functions to integrate each local community into the national cult. Those who have talked about our "American Shinto" are talking about civil religion. But even more profoundly they are talking about the relentlessly subtle and pervasive power of socialization that sweeps up and consumes everything in its path, including theological language and symbols. This consuming force does not mean that socialization eliminates the significance of deity, but it relegates deity to the realm of ultimate appeal by the nation. Bellah points out that the religious dimension of *public* life, precisely because it is public, remains aloof from the concerns of *private* life and so from any specific religious organization or set of beliefs that don't easily conform to the socialized order. The net result is that religion and all that it implies takes on the form, shape and direction dictated by the unfolding of the socialization dynamics at work at the time.

Perhaps not surprisingly, it is only in the face of a rupture of the social fabric and through suffering that transformational dynamics surface to call the axioms of the existing order into question. Again, Lincoln is the prime example of this phenomenon. But it is notable that Martin Luther King Jr. appealed precisely to that higher and ultimate order that Kennedy articulated when he said, "the rights of man came not from the generosity of the state but from the hand of God."[16] The critical incidence of transformation comes at the point where what is publicly recognized as the ultimate court of appeal is brought directly into conflict with the particulars (persons, organizations, institutions, ideologies, and the like) of a well-socialized sphere of human action, including the private sphere. Transformation does not call into question the nature of these ultimate claims. It calls those ultimate claims into engagement with specific aspects of the interlocking arenas of a society turned in upon itself by socialization dynamics. This engagement does not ever work smoothly because transformation and socialization are fundamentally contrary to each other until the socialized sphere of action yields to the transforming vision, or until the power of socialization succeeds in suppressing the emergence of a new axiomatic order. The dramatic and powerful interplay of these immense forces of influence, operative in all arenas of human action, and dramatized for the church in Jesus's cleansing of the temple, is the concern we are out to investigate in the following chapters.

16. This phrase comes from Kennedy's only inaugural address, January 20, 1961, quoted in Bellah, "Civil Religion," 3.

## (D) The Sunday School in American History

The history of the church-related school in the United States may seem to be an unlikely candidate through which to engage such worldwide issues raised by van Leeuwen, Parsons, and Bellah. But this history actually provides an excellent paradigm case for examining such matters. Here in more manageable form are all the issues of interdisciplinary conflict, cross-cultural exchange, and social, institutional, and cultural meanings in dialogue with theological and biblical claims about what God is doing in the world. In such schools, the worldwide issues take on very direct, hands-on significance. Moreover, from such schools have arisen extremely influential and formative movements and leaders in the development of the American way of life.

In their book *The Big Little School* Robert Lynn and Elliott Wright documented the history of the Protestant Sunday school and made the point (which their title summarizes) that this "little school" has had a "big" impact on the values that shaped personal, familial, educational, and political life in our country. Major issues of classism, racism, and sexism were all defined (for better or for worse) for the *vox populi* of the nineteenth and twentieth centuries by the Sunday school—perhaps as much as by any other single influence.[17] In making their case, the authors document, without naming it as such, several ways in which the ever-present interplay between socialization and transformation worked to shape the life of the church in America and to shape America according to the images of the church. Two contrasting vignettes will enable this discussion to illustrate some of the subtlety and irony that is present in a dynamic analysis of the history of the church-related school.

In 1830, just at the end of the Third Great Awakening, the American Sunday School Union took on a formidable task. They resolved that within two years and "in reliance upon divine aid" to establish "a Sunday School in every destitute place where it is practicable, through the Valley of the Mississippi." This plan, which was warmly approved by the Presbyterian General Assembly, aimed to cover two-thirds of the then-known landmass of the nation, from Harrisburg, Pennsylvania, to the Rocky Mountains, and from Canada to the Gulf of Mexico.[18] A young St. Louis fur trader wrote his mother in Connecticut shortly after that 1830 decision:

17. Sawicki, *Gospel in History*, 274–75. Sawicki cites statistics that indicate that by 1905 approximately one in six persons in the United States were members of a Sunday school.

18. Lynn and Wright, *Big Little School*, 40–67.

We are fast growing to a giants statue [*sic*]. The days of our childhood will soon be past. If nothing but the love of country actuate us something must be done to dispel ignorance & drive away vice. So thought the members of the [Presbyterian] General Assembly when they lately met in Philadelphia. They were however inspired by higher motives. The glory of God & the love of souls influences them. When they passed a resolution to establish Sunday Schools in every settlement in this valley, within the short space of two years, a resolution fraught with greater consequences to the Nation than any ever before adopted.

But why am I speaking of these things. *An excitement has gone forth. An excitement that the power of man can neither gainsay or put down. It exists not in the East alone. It has passed the boundry [sic] which separates the East from the Western States. It has reached this place.*[19]

This "valley campaign," as it was called, surely gave every evidence of being initially empowered by the Spirit of God. But the initiative was, at the same time, carried forward by strong political forces and figures, chief among them the New Jersey politician Theodore Frelinghuysen. As a Whig, he opposed Andrew Jackson's prevailing politics and political style. Accordingly, the movement tended to be led by Whigs or conservatives. The valley campaign had a great impact on the Mississippi Valley through the hardy and heroic journeys of missionaries into the hinterlands of the "new Israel" that America was called to be and to become. However, it gradually became evident that socialization forces had narrowed the vision and brought that original inspiration for spreading the gospel under their control. This control was particularly evident by 1840 when it was openly disclosed that the mission did not extend to immigrants, blacks, or the oppressive urban climate, and it was vigorously opposed to "the Romanists." Evidently, "every destitute place" included only those places that the Whig and conservative influences deemed appropriate. The rest were, according to Frelinghuysen, "refuse" and "dregs."

This brief account of an historic sequence illustrates the way in which the transformative power of God's Spirit can work to break through the *status quo*, to create new life in the face of formidable obstacles and circumstances, only to become finally subject to the consuming powers of socialization, where personal interests and political and social predispositions prevail. However, significant changes in the structure of human life in America had been indelibly established. The Sunday schools paved the way for the public schools by carrying the Protestant ethic into the frontier. The

19. Ibid, 51 (italics original).

horizons in all fields of human action had been raised as consciousness of the transformative potential of the Spirit became manifest in the lives and works of those missionaries.

The contrasting vignette comes into focus when the supporters of the Sunday school organized again to revive its effectiveness. According to Lynn and Wright, this initiative gained momentum from the so-called Illinois Band under the leadership of B. F. Jacobs, who was the organizational genius behind the International Sunday School Convention (ISCC). Jacobs and his organization kept the movement alive during the 1880s and 1890s. But here socialization, operating under the apparent claims of grace, brought forth a repressive educational monstrosity known as the Uniform Lesson series. Under this plan, all persons of all ages across the nation would study the same lesson every Sunday, with no apparent continuity from one Sunday to the next. Learning faith would be socialized to enhance effectiveness and control. Of course, this effort was doomed to failure precisely because the dynamics of transformation implicit in the Scriptures will finally *not* be suppressed. This suppressive approach eventually led to the decline of the ISSC as the twentieth century began. This decline and eventual demise of the ISSC meant a wider scope for the actual practice of transformation was needed. Ironically, a more transformational approach came at first through the hands of secular progressive and liberal figures such as George H. Mead and John Dewey, who appreciated better than supporters of the ISSC the dynamic nature of human beings. *"The children of darkness are wiser in their own time than the children of light"* [cf. Luke 16:8b]. Ultimately, the trans-formational dynamics are stronger than socialization and will seek a more dynamic way. The story goes on, of course, as the dialectic between these two forces continually unfolds into ever-deeper ironies of history.

The general argument here is that the dynamic interplay between so-cialization and transformation crystallized into key turning points in each historical episode. But whatever the outward claim, transformation turns the tide. Taken together, all of these historical vignettes suggest that regard-less of the scale of our study, across the world, across the nation, across the church school, or across the street, these two forces come into evidence as the definitive dynamics with which we have to do. Ignoring these funda-mental forces that shape our common life, whatever their manifest form, is to continue to perpetuate a naïve distortion of the nature of Christ. To attend to them is to recognize that the pentecostal power of the Spirit, even under secular guise, moves history into an ever richer and deeper consciousness of the major dimensions of human existence and thence to the nature of Christ in whom we see our nature fulfilled, comprehended, and transformed.

## (III) THEORIES OF CHRISTIAN EDUCATION IN AMERICA: A TAXONOMY

We turn now to the contemporary professional discussion of Christian education, gaining insight from a volume titled *Educating in Faith: Maps and Vision*, by Mary Boys. In this study, reminiscent of H. Richard Niebuhr's classic *Christ and Culture*, Boys constructed a typology for the field of Christian education in the United States from the time of the First Great Awakening to the present. Indeed, her four types, which she calls "classic expressions," are quite similar to Niebuhr's types, but with some significant differences. After reviewing her categorization in relation to Niebuhr's classic typology, and noting the prevalence of the transformational theme even in arenas that relate Christ to culture in other ways, we will bring our discussion to focus on the theoretical thinking of one of the great masters in this field, C. Ellis Nelson. This procedure will allow us to place transformation in the contemporary professional discussion and to make the case for its fuller development in relation to specific issues raised by a major theorist.

Professor Boys's first category is *evangelism*, paradigmatically represented in Jonathan Edwards and Charles Finney[20] and coming forward to contemporary Protestant fundamentalism and the electronic church on the right, the Sojourner Fellowship on the left, and the well-known Christian education theorist Larry Richards and the National Association of Evangelicals in the middle. Here in various forms is Niebuhr's "Christ *against* Culture" pattern moving toward a transformational position through variations from right to left on the meaning and scope of conversion.

Boys's second category is *religious education*, represented paradigmatically by Horace Bushnell (1802–1876),[21] George Albert Coe, and Harrison Elliott. This expression is brought up to date in views as seemingly diverse as Unitarian Universalism on the left and Roman Catholic educator Gabriel Moran on the right, with Paulo Freire and the Alister Hardy Research Center in the middle. The "Christ *of* Culture" pattern articulated by Niebuhr is here amply represented in its diversity, yet with its common theme that socialized religion, not the distinctiveness of Christ, is the operative theological concern. Socialization and enculturation are clearly predominant, but

---

20. Boys, *Educating*, 13–38. Finney's inclusion here is somewhat anomalous since, following his own conversion and great success as a preacher, he socialized evangelism, making it an intentional effort to bring about conversion through natural means.

21. Ibid, 39–65. Bushnell's inclusion here should not obscure his very carefully considered evaluation of revivalism, both pro and con. Moreover, his profound personal transformation, said to be "the central point" in his life, places him closer to the preceding category than the others included in this "classic expression."

transformation is presupposed in all these representative views. There is, in fact, serious attention given to transformation in the educational process itself in Freire and Gabriel Moran, and the Alister Hardy Research Center was founded on lives transformed by visits from a transcendent Other.[22] Even the Unitarian Universalist position not only includes understandings of the Judeo-Christian tradition, but through education in its themes of evaluation, scientific method, dramatic process, and radical pluralism, it seeks social change. Transformation is here, but it is fragmented, watered down, and constricted to the life of the human spirit, which in turn remains within the confines of a human action system under the definitive power of socialization.

Boys's third category, *Christian education*, is paradigmatically represented by the great neo-orthodox theologians, Karl Barth, Reinhold Niebuhr, and Paul Tillich.[23] Here Boys might have pushed back history a bit further to Kierkegaard, from whom all three of these theologians learned the dialectic of Christology. She brings this classic expression forward in ways that are no less diverse than the others, putting Randolph Crump Miller, James Smart, D. Campbell Wyckoff, and C. Ellis Nelson all in this group. The major thematic distinction overlooked by Boys's development of this classic expression is between *natural* and *revealed* theology. The major theologians who establish the keynote for this expression would find Miller's allegiance to A. N. Whitehead and empirical theology, Nelson's confidence in the human sciences, and Wyckoff's emphasis on socialization, unacceptable. On the other hand, James Smart's faithfulness to Barth's theme that the Word of God is self-authenticating actually proved to be educationally ineffective when it was appropriated in the *Christian Faith and Life* series. Theologically this category includes both Niebuhrian categories, "Christ and Culture *in Paradox*" and "Christ the *Transformer* of Culture," and consequently raises the important question at the core of our discussion: Can Christianity that does not go to the one extreme of socialization or to the other of an outright educational drive to convert, actually be taught? If so, how can it be done with integrity on both the Christian and the educational side of the issue?

22. Editor's Note: Alister C. Hardy (1896–1985) was a marine zoologist at Oxford and Fellow of the Royal Society who, upon his retirement founded the Religious Experience Research Unit in Manchester College, Oxford. Dr. Loder had a keen interest in Hardy's research into religious experience, since he believed deeply that such experiences needed scientific investigation. See Loder, *Transforming Moment*, 14, 16–17. Loder's writing of *Transforming Moment* was made possible in part by a research grant from the Center for Theological Inquiry and by a sabbatical at Oxford University as an advisor to the Alister Hardy Research Center. See Wright, "James Loder," 28.

23. Boys, *Educating*, 66–79.

The fourth category in Boys's map of the territory comes from her own tradition, *Catholic education–catechetics.*[24] Acknowledging the indebtedness of this category to H. R. Niebuhr's "Christ *above* Culture" pattern and to the towering figure of Thomas Aquinas, Boys develops post–Vatican II implications for Christian education in the Catholic tradition. Describing a spectrum that extends from Catholic schools as countercultural on the left to peace and justice centers on the right, she describes the overall tendency of Catholic education as moving towards transformation. She herself finally aligns her position with the conversionist tradition represented by Bernard Lonergan and Walter Conn. She even goes so far as to suggest that the viewpoint to which she has come almost returns to Jonathan Edwards's theme that wholeness of person, especially including the affections, is tantamount to holiness. Mention of Edwards invokes the Reformed theological tradition and again raises the question of natural theology, a major concern to which we will return in the discussion of C. E. Nelson at the end of this chapter.

Reflecting back upon Boys's helpful work, we note that her map of the field is fairly closely related to denominational boundaries and to the classical Niebuhrian types. However, there is an emerging consensus in the field that transformation is the central theme that requires emphasis, articulation, and explanation in the context of this otherwise highly socialized discipline of Christian education.[25] At the same time, there is essentially no corresponding emphasis upon the presence and power of the Holy Spirit or upon the human spirit by which transformation must be understood if it is to mean anything more than a crypto-Hegelian move in a positive direction.

In effect, then, the direction toward which this field is moving is very promising. But the theme of transformation does not necessarily portend anything more than a resocialization of the human spirit under the rubric of "transformation." If there is to be a genuine appropriation of this emerging potential for a vital renewal of spiritually empowered conviction, from individual to worldwide significance, then there must be a forthright engagement with the socialization-transformation relationality and with the doctrine and the reality of the Holy Spirit, which in turn must be understood

---

24. Ibid, 111–52.

25. In support of this conclusion, note that Sawicki wrote her substantial history of the church-related school and its ministry through the lens of "the transformation of human existence," Sawicki, *Gospel in History*, 28. Editor's Note: Sawicki's full sentence reads this way: "The question of the what and how of the transformation of human existence gives us the lens through which we are going to scrutinize the history of the church, and particularly the history of the ministry of the word." Also note the prominence of the theme of transformation in Moore, *Religious Education as Social Transformation*; and in Browning, *Fundamental*.

and engaged through a deep comprehension of the human spirit in all its major dimensions.[26]

## (IV) THE HOLY SPIRIT IN THE CONTEMPORARY DISCUSSION OF CHRISTIAN EDUCATION THEORY

This concern for the Holy Spirit is, of course, not a new idea, but it is a sadly neglected one whose time is long overdue.[27] In 1965, Edward Farley, in a two-part article in the journal *Religious Education*, challenged the field of Christian education by provocatively asking: "Does Christian education need the Holy Spirit?" Farley focused attention on a "basic linguistic confusion in language about Christian education."[28] He noted the tendency of Christian education to identify "instruction" with "nurture," i.e., to use the terms interchangeably. His proposed remedy was to limit the scope of Christian education to classroom "instruction." Along with this proposal, he expressed concern over "the way the Holy Spirit was appealed to and used in much of the literature of Christian education."

> A rather typical passage will describe Christian education as helping or enabling or aiding man [*sic*] to respond to revelation with the qualification, "under the guidance of the Holy Spirit." The formula seems to be Christian education plus Holy Spirit equals salvation and or sanctification. When this is the case the Holy Spirit becomes a kind of *explanation* for the X-factor in salvation not covered by human effort. The picture we are left with is one of God using the enterprise of Christian education to sanctify us.[29]

---

26. Editor's Note: For Loder's schematization of the history of socialization-dominant or transformation-dominant theorists of Christian/religious education in the United States, see the table at the end of this chapter. This table seems to have been part of the manuscript Loder wanted published, and I have included it for that reason. Readers may want to look at this table now as a summary of what they just read.

27. Notably the distinguished British theologian Colin Gunton, in his 1992 Warfield Lectures at Princeton Theological Seminary, made clear the pressing need for an adequate pneumatology, especially in light of our postmodern world that remains saturated in the modernist thinking of the Enlightenment. Editor's Note: These lectures became Gunton's book *Brief Theology*.

28. Farley, "Strange History," 339–46.

29. Farley, "Does Christian Education Need the Holy Spirit? Part II," 430 (italics original).

While granting that "education cannot be carried on in the church in an identical way with education beyond the church,"[30] Farley argued, "the Holy Spirit is simply superfluous in the program of Christian education."[31]

In response to Farley, four replies were published the following year in the journal *Religious Education*. These rejoinders, written by persons who were themselves critiqued in Farley's indictment, were not only swift but contemptuous.[32] Consequently, the most constructive response to the real issues raised by Farley came from someone *not* referred to in the article—C. Ellis Nelson. In his 1967 seminal work *Where Faith Begins*, Nelson clarified the relationship between "nurture" and "instruction" in Christian education. Referring directly to Farley's articles, he wrote—

> Although many problems will emerge in this curriculum plan, it does have the possibility of freeing the church school for instruction. Edward Farley has recently pointed out that American religious education for over a half a century has confused nurture and instruction, assuming that the church school can nurture faith and planning its curriculum for that purpose. But, he says, we would be better served if we used the small amount of time available in the church school for honest instruction and let the nurture take place elsewhere. His basic thesis is sound. This approach would give us a strategy whereby a church school would be more sharply defined as instruction in the Christian faith, and the fostering and living of faith would be more consciously seen as a function of the whole congregation and of the home.[33]

In the process of clarifying the relationship between "nurture" and "instruction" in Christian education, Nelson defined effectively and precisely the socialization dynamic of Christian education. But, unfortunately, he failed to define with the same precision the "X-factor"—the dynamics of transformation—Farley's second concern. As a consequence, with this book, Nelson continued to invert the transformation-socialization relation heavily on the side of socialization. Christian education came to mean the socialization of persons into a particular community of faith with its particular understanding of theology. Because of its importance historically and

---

30. Ibid, 432.

31. Ibid, 431.

32. Editor's Note: These "contemptuous" responses recorded in volume 66 of *Religious Education* appeared as Hunter, "Box Theory," 5–8; Cully, "Christian Education," 8–10; Wyckoff, "Instruction," 10–2; and Smart, "Holy Spirit," 223–29.

33. Nelson, *Where Faith Begins*, 208.

to the present state of the field, we will now discuss this significant work in greater detail, as a case illustration of how the domination of socialization in Christian education theory works and of the problems the approach elicits. However, this text must first be understood in the larger context of Nelson's writings as a whole.

## (V) C. ELLIS NELSON'S *WHERE FAITH BEGINS*: A SOCIALIZATION-DOMINANT THEORY

### (A) C. Ellis Nelson the Man

In the discussion of Nelson's thought and writings we must first acknowledge that the profound scope of his personal faith and the range of the literature he has produced exceeds anything that may be said here about this one particular book. A survey of his career reveals an astonishing variety of experiences, and he has held responsibilities in Christian education that cover the entire spectrum of this discipline. He taught and wrote about Christian education from the level of children's work in church school to graduate studies in theological seminary. As president of two theological seminaries, Louisville (1974–1981) and Austin (1984–1985), he built a distinguished record at the upper echelons of this field. Having stressed from the beginning of his career that Christian education should concentrate on adults and that the church should address the social and cultural milieu critically, he wrote for audiences as diverse as the legislative council for the State of Texas on public school education and for the National Council of Churches, as well as for nearly every aspect of the current Christian education establishment.[34]

Many of the themes that characterized his career come to focus in his book *Where Faith Begins*. Although, by his own admission, this book stresses continuity in Christian education at the expense of the discontinuity of convictional experiences,[35] it does an excellent job of raising the key issues which come into focus when someone who holds to a Reformed theological perspective takes the socialization approach to Christian education. However, not all of the themes stressed in his earlier years appear here. Early in his career Nelson developed a very effective understandings of sin and its

---

34. Editor's Note: C. E. Nelson died in 2011. His papers are located in the archive of Stitt Library, Austin Presbyterian Theological Seminary, Austin, Texas.

35. See Nelson, "Accountable," 172.

implications for education. In these writings he was strongly influenced by neo-orthodoxy and existentialist understandings of anxiety as a concomitant factor in the sinful condition of humanity. However, these expressions of the discontinuity with culture and history, which are implied in the Reformed doctrines of sin and redemption, do not enter in any significant way into his discussion in *Where Faith Begins*. This book was written at a time when the validity of any theological language was seriously challenged by a social and cultural milieu epitomized in the Death of God Movement, and at the same time the human sciences were advancing rapidly. Hence his emphasis on socialization is in part a response to a particular cultural and historical era in which he lived and wrote.

However, unlike most books written in that period, Nelson's is still in print and widely read by theorists who know that theological reflection continues to make the social sciences a foundation for articulating and communicating the faith. Here one may note George Lindbeck's book *The Nature of Doctrine*, and other attempts to interpret theology as a cultural phenomenon. The point to be stressed is that we are here working in Parsons's cultural box, which poses the question, to what extent do symbols and symbol systems shape the lives of persons or communities, and to what extent is this shaping significant for Christian education? I want to examine Nelson's work carefully here for three reasons: (1) its classic status in the field, (2) its power to set forth the critical issues for theoretical thinking about Christian education, and (3) its comprehensive approach. Unlike other more episodic and nonsystematic writers in this field, Nelson presents a comprehensive treatment.

Let it be clear that we are here examining a *text*, not a *man*. Nelson's work has extended beyond this particular book and he has attempted to take a fuller account of transformation in other works—e.g., *Congregations: Their Power to Form and Transform* and *How Faith Matures*. However, what we have in *Where Faith Begins* is a classic text in socialization theory in Christian education. It is also one of the most comprehensive theories this field has ever produced, so it has much to offer as a key to future theory construction. Let's examine the text in some detail.

## (B) *Where Faith Begins*: An Analysis

Nelson states the main thesis of his book as in the following way.

> My thesis is that faith is communicated by a community of believers and that the meaning of faith is developed by its members

> out of their history by their interaction with each other and in
> relation to the events which take place in their lives.[36]

The first thing to be noticed about the thesis is that there is no distinctive theological term anywhere in it, except "faith," which is the phenomenon to be accounted for. This omission is the essence of the matter. In this text, Nelson wants to account, as fully as possible, for theological meaning and experience generally, and faith in particular, in nontheological, social scientific terms when possible. How does he propose to do this?

He begins by telling us that he has a fundamentally objectivist (an historical-critical) approach to Scripture.[37] On the basis of his historical-critical reading of the Scriptures, he claims that the socialization process is a natural human phenomenon that operated in biblical times even as it does today. For example, in Judaism the law was to be written on the doorpost, and on stones along the highway. The advantage we have today over educators from biblical times is that we understand the socialization process better (*ala* Parsons, Margaret Mead, Peter Berger and Thomas Luckmann, and so on). Consequently, we can manipulate socialization dynamics more intentionally to serve our purposes of Christian nurture.

We have in the socialization process and in our ability to emulate the canons and achievements of the natural sciences, according to Nelson, an analytical and interpretative basis for controlling human behavior. We may lead (enculturate) persons into radically different styles of life, or shape their style of life from birth. Here by "style of life" Nelson means one's whole way of being in the world. With it he contemporizes the notion that Christians are followers of the Way (Acts 9:2). Thus, he claims to get from the Bible both his basic aim—i.e., the creation of a style of life, as well as the process designed to produce it—i.e., socialization.

In shaping a style of life, Nelson says that the basic formative unit is the small group in which there is face-to-face interaction. The prototype of the face-to-face group is the family where *primary* socialization takes place. Primary socialization, you will recall, is centered in childhood where children develop their first self-concept, sense of group life, value system, and worldview. Following primary socialization comes secondary socialization. Secondary socialization is any intentional process that inducts already socialized persons into new sectors of the larger society, like school or church.

---

36. Nelson, *Where Faith Begins*, 10.

37. Nelson does *not* appear to have a postcritical or contemporary hermeneutical approach to Scripture (Ricoeur), allowing reappropriation of the text at the level of a second naiveté.

A family or face-to-face group has in it the same basic patterns (remember the isomorphisms in Parsons's boxes) that the larger social system does. So to be socialized into a family is to undergo the kinds of dynamics on a small scale that you go through on a larger scale as you move out from the family into larger contexts of social interaction. In stressing the cohesive power of the small group, Nelson is on good ground. Social scientists agree, and so do military strategists. One reason Nazi fighting units were so resistant to Allied propaganda in World War II was the tight face-to-face structure that was used in the construction of the Nazi battalions.

Closer to home, television must be understood not as entertainment or information, but as business. It is a selling medium. Forty percent of the American population is consistently influenced by it. Another 20 percent is influenced some of the time. The remaining 40 percent of the population is immune to its commercial effects. As a consequence, marketers gear television to reach the first 40 percent. When new values (products) are introduced, they are positively associated with values held by small groups in the first 40 percent. Thus, advertisers play to what is already valued by families in the 40 percent of the American population who can actually be influenced by commercials. That is, they play to values already grounded in the primary groups of that 40 percent. For example in the 1960s, the dominant male image in American culture did not permit men to wear hair spray. To introduce "the value" of hair spray to men, television commercials showed macho men wearing it—i.e., astronauts talking about what spray they used.

The core, then, of Nelson's view of the church as an educational force in the society and world, is the small group with face-to-face interaction. Nelson can move from discussions of small group interaction into all that the church intends to be because for him the church is the empirical congregation. If a congregation maintains good small group interaction, it can develop for its constituents the contemporary meaning of faith, because given proper socialization techniques and procedures, the "Christian faith can be communicated."

Thus, having asked and answered the questions, what is the reality we want to communicate? and, what is the natural agency for communicating that reality? Nelson declares that he wants to communicate faith—the God of the Bible—and that the agency for doing this is the prudent use of socialization dynamics. He proposes to combine context and process in enculturation. This is the essence of his argument. Let us look beneath to its underlying assumptions.

## (C) Enculturation in Nelson's Theory

If enculturation into the Christian tradition is to occur, one must first understand from a social scientific point of view what is meant by "culture."[38] For Nelson, culture is symbolically constructed configurations of learned behavior embodying the core values of a given group, in this case, the Christian church. This means for Nelson that explicit instruction must take place in the church for adults. These adults are in turn called to nurture their children in the Christian tradition at home and in church gatherings. Notice here that Nelson has a sophisticated notion of tradition. It is not a digging up of the past. It is not a matter of simply memorizing catechisms. His is a lively, living understanding of culture. He is socially and scientifically sophisticated enough in the social sciences to know that it is not enough to just lay things on people. He understands tradition in terms of *traditio*—that is, the act of passing on or handing down a symbol system and a set of values from the past to the future. Still, even though he is thinking of tradition as a living process, the tradition envisioned is primarily the life of the society and culture.

How exactly does culture work to shape personality and lifestyle? Nelson isolates four variables that we may look at more closely. The first three variables are perception, self, and conscience. Taken together, these variables yield up the fourth variable—identity. Note that for Nelson culture shapes perception. A classic though debatable thesis in anthropology and linguistics is the Sapir-Whorf hypothesis. It states that in the enculturation process language controls perception. For example, the Eskimos have many different words for "snow." Thus, the Eskimos are enculturated into actually perceiving snow in a much more subtle and highly differentiated fashion. The French have many more words for "love" than the English—so that explains that! The idea here is linguistic version of Einstein's statement with which we began in chapter 1: "Theory controls what you can see."[39]

38. *Enculturation* means the socialization process viewed from the standpoint of the primacy of culture and of a particular culture being taught.

39. A classic phenomenological illustration in anthropology of theory controlling observation comes from Colin Turnbull, who studied the pygmies inhabiting the jungles of Malaysia. Turnbull took one of the pygmies, Kenge by name, who had lived all his life in the dense jungles, and led him out to the edge of the jungle. As they approached the edge, they looked over the hill down to the plain where there were some water buffalo. Kenge looked down and saw the water buffalo. Since they were quite a ways away, he called them insects, because they were small. Turnbull tried to explain that they were big animals. "No they are insects," said Kenge.

The reason Kenge believed the buffalo were insects is that living in the jungle all his life had shaped his perceptions. The idea of depth perception, the capacity to measure the size of things in terms of their distance is shaped by the culture that interprets this

Since "the self" emerges from how one is perceived by others, cultural influences shape it. That is, selfhood emerges as one perceives one's "self" being seen in a certain way by others. This condition of "being seen" by others who are important to one's life (i.e., the small face-to-face primary group) is then put into interaction with one's perceived needs for trust, worth and achievement. Out of this interaction emerges the sense of self, which in turn feeds back into the culture as one finds his or her own way of meeting the expectations of the important persons in one's life. This issues in self-perception and self-understanding—and a self-concept.

With the development of one's sense of self, a person is able to enter into group interactions—i.e., to see how to "fit in" on the basis of how one is perceived and how one perceives oneself. Thus, appropriate social role behavior becomes increasingly manageable, and so in successful adaptation, the larger corporate life affirms and consolidates the developing sense of self and one's self-image (ego ideal). This accrued sense of self is not simply a by-product of group interaction. It is a consequence of the primary culture that first taught the person how to look at the world, what to perceive, and how to value it. This culture—i.e., these configurations of learned behavior embodying symbols and symbol systems—allows persons to use language and symbol to claim and reinstate their identity.

In terms of enculturation dynamics, one may claim one's identity via a value-laden symbol system: "I am a Kennedy" or "I am an American." And from Nelson's position, the dynamics of enculturation are what motivated Luther, in confrontation with temptation and the devil, to cry out, "I am baptized." Or it is enculturation that enabled Jesus to use Scripture in the wilderness to affirm his identity. Less dramatically, we ourselves regularly practice the reinstatement of our identity via acts of worship. Whether alone or together, we call upon the dominant symbol system of the tradition to tell us once again who we are. "We are Christians!" We are enjoined weekly to

---

jungle as the outer boundary of the world. So Kenge figured, the water buffalo had to be ants. Turnbull said, "Okay, we will go and see." And so they got into the jeep and drove down to see how big the water buffalo actually were. Now, imagine Kenge's angst. He is riding in this jeep and the "insects" are getting bigger and bigger and bigger. He is terrified, traumatized, and crouches into his seat. He accuses Turnbull of witchcraft. You may think this example is extreme, but everybody is raised in an unexamined cultural forest of some kind. The culture or symbol system that you are raised in—the African jungle or the Wall Street jungle—largely determines your perceptions; what and how you see. Or, to change the analogy, fish will be the last to discover water. Nelson is arguing that the culture we learn will tell us how to see things and determine its meaning for us. Editor's Note: Loder does not give the reference here for Trumbull's account. But he refers to the story in *Transforming Moment*, 73–74, in which he cites it as taken from Zimbardo, *Psychology and Life*, 235. The original story is found in Turnbull, *Forest People*, chapter 14 (249–60, especially 251–53).

reenvision our real needs, our sense of self, our role in corporate life—all in relation to the ultimate meaning of our lives given in the symbol systems of worship and the Word.

In summary, Nelson's governing theme is that the tradition—i.e., the Christian culture—has the power to shape perception, self, values, and identity. These elements combine to give persons a Christian style of life—the unity of how they see themselves in society and in culture. That is lifestyle.

The wider impact and importance of this process is that the congregation witnesses to the community at large. By its very life, it makes a statement of what it stands for theologically. Everything it does—the buildings, the budget, everything—interprets the faith of the Christian community to the larger culture Thus, Christian education is not confined to the church school. It permeates the whole work of the church and hopefully society. The educational work of the church is to perpetuate a self-conscious interpretation of the Christian life, not only for individuals, but also for the church and for the world to which the church bears witness.

What we must do, then, in Christian education is develop critical intelligence, adult leadership, a curriculum, and forms of learning that interpret the events in people's lives. We must also stress primary socialization, family life through the key medium of primary groups, and so pass on the tradition in an intimate way. In general, Nelson calls for a new deliberateness or confidence in Christian nurture, because he believes that by the explicit use of socialization and enculturation, we can effectively communicate the Christian faith. But, we may now ask, what are the ambiguities in Nelson's thesis?

## (D) Problems Internal to Nelson's Argument

Problems with Nelson's argument begin to emerge at the end of chapter 1. Nelson states, "Faith is what we want to communicate." "Faith" here "derives its meaning from the object of that faith relationship—God."[40] But wait; in his main thesis he said that faith derives its meaning from "the members of the community and out of their history." Does the meaning of faith come from God or from the community? Clearly, Nelson wants to have it both ways without developing any consciousness or concepts of the dialectic involved. When it comes down to it, he wants to communicate "the God of the Bible." How he wants to communicate God is through the methods of social science with special emphasis on small group interaction, as primary society. Now we have a perfect case illustration in Christian education

40. Nelson, *Where Faith Begins*, 32.

theory of Søren Kierkegaard's escapee from the asylum. Nelson has the right content (God) but the wrong spirit (socialization). The result is theological and spiritual confusion.

Notice a second major ambiguity, the uneasy and confusing combination of tradition and experience. Nelson writes,

> What is unique in Christian worship is an experience with the God of the Bible. It is experience of the most intense kind and is personal to the extent that one feels that the whole world is less real than the presence of God; but the difference is that one experiences the God who is described in the Bible. That is why it is so important to read the Psalms—to catch the flavor of their devotion, to relive the affirmations they made about God—or to sing the songs of the Christian church throughout the centuries and thereby renew our relation with the past. Likewise, we read and expound the Scriptures because we have in the past revelation of God an image of God that can be activated in our mind by the Holy Spirit. So, to discuss worship only in terms of experience is not enough. Christian worship is an activity in which a person participates in order to relive the traditions of the faith and to explore the images of God displayed in the Bible.[41]

Picking up the theme of worship, Nelson describes an event—an experience—wherein "the whole world is less real than the presence of God." Worship is a "unique" experience, "an experience of the most intense kind," fully "personal." Note here that Nelson is speaking of supernatural reality communicating itself in a fashion that is in itself no way bound to the socialization process. "The whole world is less real than the presence of God." The whole world!

But is supernatural reality of which Nelson speaks the same reality social scientists want to focus on and reduce everything to? Social sciences name such transcendent experiences hallucinatory. From a social scientific standpoint, if you have an experience of the presence of God, and you believe it is more real than all the rest of the world, you are hallucinating! But Nelson, you see, wants to call the hallucination *revelation*, God's communication of Godself. How is it that at this critical point Nelson arbitrarily departs from the social sciences, when he has said that he wants to employ the social sciences precisely to give meaning to the experience *via* these communal dynamics?

If you are going to go with the social sciences, go all the way, or at least come clean about the difference. This serious flaw in Nelson's argument

41. Ibid, 103.

prompts these questions: If the whole world is less real than the presence of God, then why don't we just declare that presence? Why don't we point to God's own way of communicating Godself, namely, by the Spirit? One may argue that Nelson does mention the Holy Spirit. Yes, but what does the Holy Spirit do in Nelson's thinking? The implication is that the Spirit does nothing more than inject life into what enculturation has already done. The Holy Spirit is conformed to socialization and sacralizes enculturation, merely confirming Farley's X-factor charge.

Cynically one might respond that Nelson talks this way because, from a social scientific standpoint, he by his own premises is only socialized into thinking of hallucination as revelation. That is, by his own premises, he cannot understand revelation except by socialization. But if one is consistent with the claims of the social sciences, one must recognize hallucination for what it is. If you depart arbitrarily at critical points such as this, then you lose the premise for the whole argument. If Nelson is only socialized into thinking of hallucination as revelation, then, you see, Parsons and Mead really understand Nelson better than Nelson understands himself.

If we are going to extricate ourselves from this dilemma, then we have to declare another order of reality—nothing less than God's presence, which is God's freedom to act. Why not talk about God and the action of God's Spirit? Why not talk about the intervening action of God? But if we do that, how will we educate? The ambiguity has come back to focus on the *crux* of Christian education.

Remember that we are not concerned here with abstractions. The real human problem is that *not* solving the issue of divine action is sooner or later depressing and discouraging to the practice of Christian education. Christian educators are often seen by others and by themselves as a demoralized group of people with low self-esteem and a bad reputation for being gimmicky, willing to buy almost any new thing to make a program come to life. One good reason for this low status may indeed be that Christian educators have become the victims of their own programs. They have to keep inventing incentives to keep people coming, to keep things moving. Thus, Christian education easily degenerates into an anxious pragmatism. Such pragmatism eventually demoralizes faith, because faith has sold its birthright for a mess of socializing programs.

So, my basic objection to Nelson's approach is that it seeks to socialize the transforming work of God's Spirit. It needs to be the other way around. The power of God's Spirit dwarfs the power of society and socialization and needs to be taken seriously in theory and practice. If we are going to maintain integrity with the theological language we use, we had jolly well better be working with the transformation of socialization by the Spirit, not the reverse. Let me formalize my response to Nelson in positive and negative terms.

## (E) Positive Aspects of Nelson's Theory

*First,* on the positive side, Nelson takes theory seriously. He has to be commended for moving Christian education out of the Sunday school rooms and making it relevant to the full-scale operations of the church, both contemporary and historical. Nelson has to be credited for raising Christian education to the place where it becomes responsible for developing a pervasive critical intelligence that repeatedly weighs experience against tradition. The scope of his conception of Christian education is good. *Second,* he moves clearly from foundation disciplines through the theoretical formulations to guidelines for practice. By so doing, Nelson on the one hand highlights the major tension in the field between the programmatic and the pragmatic, and on the other hand highlights a larger theoretical context within which these programs can be understood.

*Third,* Nelson examines the understandings of the social sciences seriously and looks at the dynamics of human interaction analytically with an eye to bringing them into line with theology. His is a very competent interdisciplinary study, self-consciously sustained, responsible for the most part in its attempt to say what the social scientists have said. In terms of concern for the interdisciplinary relationship between the social sciences and theology, he at least preserves both sides of the tension between Christian and education—socialization and transformation.

*Fourth,* by making lifestyle or style of life the objective of Christian education, Nelson has again, I think, made an appropriate emphasis. He is not simply concerned to pass on cultural information, or to get biblical knowledge across at a higher level. Nor is his concern simply formational in the sense of teaching character and values. He is concerned about creating a whole style of life. Also helpful and commendable is his understanding of lifestyle. Lifestyle, as Nelson understands it, is not the sort of thing that one simply picks up here and lays down there—lifestyle on the cheap. Rather, he emphasizes the style of life that emerges over the course of a lifetime of responding to the faith tradition. Surely he is right to place this kind of serious emphasis on the significance of lifestyle in this strong sense of the word. Nelson want lifestyle to cost us something.

*Fifth,* Nelson's focus on event and the narrative quality of events in our lives is an important consideration. Narrative is one important means from which we do indeed derive meaning for our lives. Events have a narrative quality—a beginning, middle and ending—which in turn drives persons and communities toward higher meanings and toward ultimate meaning. Narrative functions as a decisive unit of Christian education and reveals Nelson's early anticipation of the rise of narrative theology.

*Sixth* on the positive side, I also want to commend Nelson for the practicality and wisdom of starting with adult discipleship. The logic of trying to bring adults to the place where they can understand and celebrate the Christian faith is very important for eventually enabling children and youth to appropriate a meaningful and credible faith. Children inevitably learn what adults prioritize and celebrate. What adults invest emotion in children come to care about and learn for themselves. If we have our family prayers, but we've got to hurry and finish because we have to watch the football game, then we have not taught prayer but the importance of the football game! Children learn what parents celebrate, what they invest emotion in, and what they're willing to suffer for. In this sense, beginning with adults is practical and accurate in terms of how lives are shaped in faithful ways. Let us now turn to the negative side of my critical assessment.

## (F) Negative Aspects of Nelson's Theory

*First*, on the negative side, when Nelson says "church" he means the *empirical* church, which implies a focus on a religious institution that social scientists investigate in depth. Nelson does not just focus on the empirical church as a sociological phenomenon. He also attends to the inner workings of that sociological entity, the face-to-face groups that constitute the empirical church. The empirical church is both a macro and micro system for Nelson. However, unwittingly it seems to me, he draws an artificial boundary around the empirical church as if it were not fully subject to the same socialization forces that control the rest of society. Actually, the same plurality of lifestyles, in a strong or weak sense, that run through society as a whole also run through the church and into its small groups. If we look at the empirical church, we also see the world. There is no protective envelope around the church.

Thus, if Nelson is going to take social science seriously, he must see the church as located by the priesthood of sociologists in the lower right hand subbox of Parsons's diagram. He must see it as operative in the *tension-reduction, pattern-maintenance* social system I described in chapter 1. There, I referred to funerals as an example of what the church does. The church helps maintain the social system by managing the tension produced by potentially disruptive problems intrinsic to the larger society. The problem here is that Nelson, for all of his efforts to take the social sciences seriously, does not actually take them seriously enough. Consequently, socialization dynamics subvert his best efforts to use them. All the time he thinks he is using socialization, the larger socialized system is using him—or us if we take his position!

For instance, Nelson seems uncritical or unaware that the employment of these methods serves to conform his theory and practice to the values of our achievement- and production-oriented society. The achievement-oriented society wants to know how to manipulate the social and human machinery to produce predictably desirable outcomes. Nelson is uncritical of this kind of objectivism foisted on him by the method he has chosen to use. He seems unaware that the production of Christians through the socialization process is far more fundamentally a reproduction and exten-sion of our production-oriented society than it is an expression of genuine Christian community of the Spirit. Thus, the socialization forces with which Nelson wants to work are actually working on him before he starts to use them. His position represents, it seems to me, a naïve view of the empirical church. And since the church cannot be the buffer society wants to make it, he becomes a victim of the dynamics he actually wants to utilize. So, we have to take the social sciences more seriously than Nelson takes them, so that they function with integrity in terms of their true contribution to theory construction in relation to his Reformed theological perspective.

*Second*, corresponding to the first concern, Nelson's use of theology as a tradition imported by the socialization process puts theology under the power of socialization in a way that violates his own theological self-understanding. Nelson is a Presbyterian who stands firmly within the Re-formed tradition. Nelson would therefore appropriately align himself with the Niebuhrian category of "Christ *the Transformer of* Culture."[42] But his theory of Christian nurture actually better signifies another of Niebuhr's categories, "Christ *of* Culture."[43] Thus, the way Nelson places his theological convictions in the service of socialization to construct his theory violates his own theological tradition. Nowhere in the book is this issue of theologi-cal integrity confronted. What he supposes to be a biblical and theological incorporation of socialization turns out to be just the opposite. Ironically, Christian education's concern to foster theological self-criticism intrinsic to the church's gospel is impossible from the standpoint Nelson's position, for his position is subject to the control of the socialization dynamics that

---

42. See Niebuhr, *Christ and Culture*, chapter 6 (190–229).

43. Ibid, chapter 3 (83–115).

inevitably suppress self-criticism in the name of pattern-maintenance, tension-reduction stabilization.

We must also, then, take theology much more seriously than Nelson takes it. Where is his theological understanding of the empirical church in light of the communion-creating power of the Spirit? Where is his theological understanding of experience of divine action? Where is his theological understanding of the Spirit's transformation of language and perception? What is Nelson's pneumatology—his theological understanding of the process of education governed by the pedagogy of the Holy Spirit?

*Third*, because of the crucial issues that we have been discussing, the so-called crux of Christian education remains unresolved in his thinking. In a sense Nelson's theory wobbles back and forth between the polarities of socialization and transformation, eventually throwing us into pragmatic ways of thinking shaped by the interests of socialization. This ambiguity results in a kind of demoralizing and degenerating kind of Christian education practice wherein his theory "sacralizes" what churches would be doing anyway. Negative practical outcomes result from this socialized construct, and these outcomes and the theory that sponsors them must be confronted by a theological understanding that exposes this ambiguous and incoherent position in light of an alternative practice resonant to the presence and work of the Holy Spirit. Only in the Spirit can we recognize the domesticating power of socialization on the church and thereby open ourselves to the transforming power of Christ shaping our theory and our practice. Before we develop such a focus on the Spirit, first let us examine a possible rejoinder to my argument.

## (VI) GOD AND THE SOCIALIZATION PROCESS

### (A) Incompatibilities between God's Action and Socialization

You may ask, why doesn't God just use the socialization process? And I would respond, God does use socialization. But in the final analysis socialization and God's action are as incompatible as the profane is to the holy. However, God can make use of even that which is incompatible with the divine nature, but not without that incompatible nature undergoing transformation. Thus, theologically, one is forced to assert that God's actions use socialization precisely to transform it. Transformation is necessary precisely because of certain basic incompatibilities between socialization and God's action. Let me list four.

(a) Socialization obscures rather than exposes divine action. The action of God upon us in the midst of socialization's obscurantism discloses God's presence as the source of our life.

(b) Socialization prizes the self-perpetuation of the group above all else, survival and satisfaction even above truth. The transforming work of Christ's Spirit prizes truth above survival.

(c) In socialization, God consciousness cannot exceed corporate consciousness. Corporate consciousness stands above God consciousness. That is why when you have an experience of God's presence, the social scientist will say that you are hallucinating. He or she understands everything transcendent as a distortion of the highest socialization reality—corporate consciousness. Theologically, God consciousness must exceed corporate consciousness.

(d) The driving end of socialization is tension reduction, pattern maintenance—stability. But what is perfect stability? Death! The tension-reduction, pattern-maintenance drive toward homeostasis is essentially, fundamentally, and finally in service of disintegration and entropy—death-dealing, not life-giving. The transforming work of Christ's Spirit is inherently life-giving. Oftentimes, it operates most decisively in contexts of disequilibrium, or it uses equilibrium as a context for breaking in with new, unexpected, often gracious but disturbing awareness.

In sum, to take the action of God's Spirit and the action of God in the community, and to bring them under the canons of social science is in these very fundamental ways a violation of what we would want to say theologically about God's action. God stands over and against the socialization process. When God uses socialization, it is to transform it, which means that socialization is in the service of transformation. But if we take Nelson's premise, experiences and events that bring us into relationship to God socialize transformation at best. The theological premise about the priority of transformation over socialization makes all the difference.

## (B) A Poignant Illustration of Cultural Depravity

Finally, let me push the issue further and ask, does a given culture really shape a lifestyle? Nelson's answer is that it does, and it is accomplished by enculturation. But can a Christian style of life really issue from enculturation? A poignant experiment designed by Stanley Milgram suggests that it cannot. Milgram, while a professor at Yale University, conceived of a now infamous experiment in which he asked for volunteers from the larger New Haven area to participate in a learning experiment at Yale.[44] Volunteers were to be paid $4.50 to contribute to "science" and to "learning at Yale." All these details are important! As soon as I say, "$4.50," "science," and "learning at Yale," I am talking about things highly valued in American culture. Yale is power. Money has power. Science is power. You are going to contribute to scientific research. Stanley Milgram is a professor at Yale. This is something!

In the experiment Milgram paired off volunteers as teacher and learner. The sneaky thing about the experiment was that the learner was not really a volunteer. The learner, who was strapped down into a chair wired to electrical currents, was actually in cahoots with Stanley Milgram. The teacher was instructed to give the learner a set of paired words to learn. When I say "blue," you say "sky." When I say "tree," you say "leaf." Every time the learner made an error, the teacher administered fifteen more volts of electricity through the chair. What was the implicit rationale for inflicting pain on another human being? "We are doing this experiment to study the relationship between pain and learning. You are contributing to science and Yale and you are being paid."

A panel of psychiatrists was asked to estimate ahead of time just how far any "teacher" would go in giving volts to people for missing questions. The scale on the voltmeter went up to four hundred and fifty volts. The psychiatrists confidently predicted that no more than 4 percent of the teachers would go beyond three hundred volts. Only one-tenth of 1 percent of all the volunteers would ever go to four hundred and fifty volts, they said, potentially "killing" the learner.

So here we are. The teacher gives the key word, but the learner (who, you remember, is in cahoots with the experimenter) cannot remember. The teacher gives him fifteen volts. The learner tries again. Wrong! Thirty volts! By the time the meter gets up to a hundred and fifty volts or so, the learner strapped down into the chair cries out, "I don't want to go on! Get me out of here!" The teacher, looking at the experimenter, says, "Do I have to go on?" Milgram responds, "You agreed to go on. I'll take the responsibility." ZAPPP!!!! Of course, the learner is acting, the apparatus only goes to a fifteen volts maximum. But the teacher doesn't know this! The panel of

44  Editor's Note: Loder does not give the reference for this experiment. He probably means Milgram, "Behavioral Study," 371–378; or Milgram, "Some Conditions," 57–76; or both. He may also have had in mind Milgram, *Obedience to Authority*. Milgram's film *Obedience* captures the research he conducted at Yale University in May 1962, and this film is available through Stanley Milgram Films on Social Psychology. I imagine Loder may have viewed this film version since his in-class descriptions of the experiment were so vivid. They felt like eyewitness accounts.

psychiatrists estimated that only 4 percent would go to three hundred volts and that less than 1 percent would go all the way to four-hundred and fifty volts. Do you know how many people went to three hundred volts with the learner crying, "I've got a heart condition! Get me out of here!"? Seventy-eight percent! Moreover, 65 percent went all the way to four hundred and fifty volts—all because the learner could not remember the connection between "blue" and "sky." All because Stanley Milgram stood there in his scientific garb and said, "I will take responsibility. In the name of science, Yale, and $4.50, electrocute him." That's the power of socialization in a scientific culture!

Milgram gave the teachers leverage to say, "To hell with your experiment. I'm not going to kill some guy because you want to do an experiment." But, you see, in none of the experiments did the majority of participants opt out. Twenty-two percent or thirty-five participants exercised their individual initiative and opted out of the experiment: "Keep your $4.50, Yale, and science. Goodbye." But this was the distinct minority. Apparently, relatively few of us have the power to choose against an experiment like this.

In the original write-up of his experiment, Milgram said the problem was that people did not have "a language of nonconformity" to resist the pressure.[45] But this explanation is an enculturated way of putting the issue. Culture (language) no doubt shapes behavior. But culture is also the root of the problem. One of our Princeton Seminary graduates, who knew the Christian language well, went all the way to four hundred and fifty volts. Even Christian enculturation—the language in which we say *"for freedom Christ has set us free"*—may only be teaching us conformity and obedience to the authorities of culture. What is missing is not a language of nonconformity. What is missing is the compassionate *power* of nonconformity. Power without compassion is tyrannical and fanatical. Passion without power is sentimental. Only the Spirit of Christ, who combines power and compassion, who can breathe divine life into the dry bones of the Christian

---

45. Editor's Note: I could not find this reference to "a language of nonconformity" in the original write-up mentioned here. It may be that Loder had access to a mimeographed copy of Milgram's report to the National Science Foundation's gathering on January 25, 1961, titled "Dynamics." In another discussion in which Loder mentions Milgram, he notes that intimacy, not language, provides the empowerment needed to resist the dehumanizing influence of socialization. In the social sciences, Loder drew on research by Charles Hampden-Turner in *Radical Man*. See Loder, *Logic of the Spirit*, 273. Loder deepens Hampden-Turner's model theologically to imagine an intensification pattern he calls "the practice of love in *koinonia*" (ibid., 274–78). Without Christ's Spirit, the move toward intimacy based on ego risks despair. Loder writes: "What makes [the theological model] work is the matrix of grace in which the identities involved are dialectical and the distance is already bridged by the Spiritual Presence of Christ" (ibid.).

language system, transforming all enculturation and the people of God in terms of Christ's nature. What we need, after all, is the presence and power of the Spirit who will lead us into all Truth beyond our culturally conditioned truths and give us deep compassion for the other whom Christ loves.

## (VII) CONCLUSION

Let me conclude by referring back to the typological contrast with which we began this chapter. Pentecost makes our point very dramatically. Fifty days after Passover, the disciples experienced the descent of the Spirit on the day the Jews ordinarily celebrated the giving of the law of Moses. The Spirit enabled a radical transformation of law and tradition whereby in Christ we live according to the "law of the Spirit." The Spirit of Christ is not culture-bound, but transcends and transforms culture. Here the cross-cultural significance of tongues is revealed. Pentecost reverses Babel and unifies humanity, not primarily in cultural terms but in the Spirit's communion-creating power. Beyond cultural barriers, those present at Pentecost heard and understood deeper than their enculturation allowed them to hear and understand. Thus, the law of the Spirit was at work to transform the Mosaic law and all cultural laws that legitimate spiritually restricted forms of human action, enabling those present to embrace the underlying unity of humanity offered to the world in Jesus Christ through the power and presence of his Spirit. The Spirit is the power of Christian education.

### Transformation/Socialization Dialectic in the History of Christian Education in the United States: Key Theorists, Events, and Works[46]

| Transformation Dominant | Transformation/Socialization in Balance | Socialization Dominant |
|---|---|---|
| 1. *Jonathan Edwards* (1703–1753): "Surprising" conversions reveal the priority of transformation under the sovereignty of God. *First Great Awakening* (1730–1760). | | |
| | | 2. *Charles Finney* (1792–1875): Used "technique" (i.e., "conversion bench," music) to socialize the conversion process. *Second Great Awakening* (1800–1830). |
| | 3. *Horace Bushnell* (1802–1876): His *Christian Nurture* (1847) affirms socialization of the child within the context of transformative nurture in the godly home: "The child is to grow up Christian and never know himself otherwise." | |
| | | 4. *George Coe* (1862–1951): Appropriated Bushnell's aphorism, but argued that scientific expertise, not conversion, should determine and guide religious development. *Religious Education Association* (1903). |

46. Editor's Note: I have added the subtitle "Key Theorists, Events, and Works" to Loder's title, reordered some of his descriptions to make them more uniform, and updated the years of death for those who died after Dr. Loder died: Randolph Crump Miller, Edward Farley, C. Ellis Nelson, and D. Campbell Wyckoff.

| Transformation Dominant | Transformation/Socialization in Balance | Socialization Dominant |
|---|---|---|
| 5. *Karl Barth* (1886–1968): H. Shelton Smith's essay "Let the Religious Education Reckon with the Barthians" (1934) argued for religious educators to engage "crisis" theology and its implications for transformative education in the church. | | |
| | | 6. *Harrison Elliot* (1882–1951): Argued in his book *Can Religious Education Be Christian?* (1940) for educators to continue in the liberal tradition of the Religious Education Association. |
| 7. *H. Shelton Smith* (1893–1987): Professor of American Religious Thought, Duke University (1931–1960). His book *Faith and Nurture* (1941) offered a strong theological critique of liberalism in religious education. | | |
| | 8. *Lewis Sherrill* (1892–1957): A colleague of Reinhold Niebuhr and Tillich at Union Theological Seminary (New York), he wedded an immanent understanding of the spiritual with psychological processes that engender maturity. | |

| Transformation Dominant | Transformation/Socialization in Balance | Socialization Dominant |
|---|---|---|
| | 9. *Randolph Crump Miller* (1910–2002): His *The Clue to Christian Education in the Church* (1941) emphasized "Theology in the background, faith and grace in the foreground." Education uses language of relationships, keeping God at the center, in kind of natural theology reminiscent of William Temple. | |
| 10. *James Smart* (1906–1982): Old Testament Professor; stressed Bible and self-authenticating power of the Word in his book, *Teaching Ministry of the Church* (1954). Wrote the "Christian Faith and Life" curriculum. | | |
| | | 11. *Edward Farley* (1929–2014): Taught at Vanderbilt University. His 1965 essay "Does Christian Education Need the Holy Spirit?" created a stir for arguing the Holy Spirit functions merely as a kind of X-factor in Christian education. Church schools should emphasize instruction and leave nurture to the home. |

| Transformation Dominant | Transformation/Socialization in Balance | Socialization Dominant |
| --- | --- | --- |
| | | 12. *C. Ellis Nelson* (1916–2011): His book *Where Faith Begins* (1967) can be read as a measured response to Farley, arguing that the God works through the socialization process to bring about faith in communities. |
| | 13. *D. Campbell Wyckoff* (1918–2005): Taught at Princeton Theological Seminary (1954–1983). His *Theory and Design of Christian Education* (1961) is considered a classic in curriculum theory emphasizing transformational outcomes. | |

# 3

# Lifestyle

*Taking Social Reality Seriously*

## (I) INTRODUCTION: LIFESTYLE AS THE PROPER FOCUS OF CHRISTIAN EDUCATION

IN THE PREVIOUS CHAPTER, I commended C. Ellis Nelson for stressing lifestyle as a basic unit of Christian education. This focus is, in my judgment, better than stressing curriculum, personality, character, or even the congregation. Lifestyle is the most comprehensive concept that preserves both the dynamics and the structure of human formation over a lifetime. It is both corporate and cultural as well as individual and organic. Lifestyle relates to the *whole field of human action*.

Nelson wanted to advocate lifestyle in terms of socialization within the church. As we have argued, the problem is, he uses socialization without taking it seriously enough. In this chapter, we want to talk about socialization and take it as seriously as possible. To do this is in some ways to further Nelson's agenda—i.e., to bring socialization into the educational ministry of the church. However, we will find that this agenda is much larger and more complex than he envisioned. That is to say, the empirical church, the church with which Nelson and practicing Christian educators must concern themselves, exists in a much larger social and cultural milieu. This larger milieu creates and generates the lifestyles that permeate and shape the church. What we really have, therefore, is not the church creating lifestyles but the lifestyles generated in the larger sociocultural milieu creating the forms and patterns of life in the empirical church. The lifestyles generated by society at large tell the church how to appropriate its own traditions, not the other way around. In other words, whether we like it or not, lifestyle, as generated by the larger society (not by the church) already serves as the basic educational unit in a socialization model. It behooves us, therefore, to examine in some depth certain powerful lifestyles that enter in and pervade church life. Our concern here is to focus more precisely on the depth and quality of human existence that must be addressed, both Christianly and educationally, if we are going to do anything more than sacralize the status quo drift of society and culture at large. Thus, an examination of dominant lifestyles in our society will give us some idea of the magnitude of the task before us.

## (II) LIFESTYLE DEFINED

To begin with we must ask, what is meant by style? Alfred North White-head said, "style is the fashioning of power."[1] If you think of "power" in this phrase as being the energy of a lifetime, then lifestyle refers to how one fashions the energy of a lifetime. Thus, what we are *not* talking about here is something that changes from one physical setting or context to another. Such a weak usage of the term is popular, but evanescent and chimerical. For example, you have a lifestyle as a student while you are in school. But in the summertime the lifestyle of the beachcomber prevails. On Sundays, the lifestyle of a Christian might emerge, or of a sports fan, each one impacting how you dress, speak, or show emotion. These are descriptions of lifestyle in the *weak* or popular sense.

The lifestyle I am talking about is lifestyle in the *strong* sense, and as such it does not change with setting and context. Lifestyle pervades the different physical contexts, different social milieus, and selects, shapes, and reconstructs those various contexts and milieus according to the structure and dynamics of that style. Thus, I am talking about something here that has *pervasive* cross-cultural significance. Lifestyle is not an ephemeral thing, but a powerful, formative force shaping the whole of one's life.

Let me give you a somewhat more technical definition of lifestyle that sums up this discussion in the language and structures that we have been using. A lifestyle is a relatively stable, patterned process whose core characteristics govern life in all four major areas of socialized human action. Thus,

---

1. Whitehead, *Aims of Education*, 23–24. Editor's Note: See Loder's essay "Fashioning of Power," 187–208, for his theological interpretation of Whitehead's notion of lifestyle as the "fashioning of power."

one's basic needs (organic), understanding of human personality (psychic), ways of entering into small groups and large groups (social), and ways of dealing with value and symbol (cultural), are all governed by the core characteristics of a given style. These core characteristics are formed early in one's life through the influence of primary groups and transposed back into the culture at large from which they derive.[2]

## (III) LIFESTYLES OF WESTERN CULTURE

Now let me try to give you some illustrations of lifestyle. What I want to do is to explicate four lifestyles dominant in our society and culture that pervade the church and its ministry. I don't assume that these four styles are exhaustive. But I do argue they are central and predominate, so that they govern a great deal of our common life. Each of these styles is sufficiently prevalent to have generated a great deal of empirical research, so there are good social science reasons for selecting them. Moreover, these particular styles are a prevalent part of Western society's self-understanding.

As these lifestyles impinge upon central theological and ecclesiastical concerns, we become aware of how these concerns become self-alienating within and for the Christian life because of the power of socialization. That is to say, although these styles of life are socially and culturally encouraged by the power structure of American and Western society, uncritically appropriated—i.e., untransformed—they actually *alienate* us as individuals and as a church from the biblical and theological foundations of our faith and distort our Christian witness in the world.

The four lifestyles I want to use to illustrate this alienation—achievement, authoritarian, protean, and oppressive—can be roughly correlated with the four boxes in Parsons's diagram outlined in chapter 1.[3] Thus, the *achievement*-oriented style, which gets obsessed with motivation and setting and achieving goals, corresponds to Parsons's G box (psychic). The *authoritarian* lifestyle, which gets hung up primarily in terms of conformity to the external standards of the group, connects to Parsons's I box (social). The *protean* style of life generated by the diffusion and pluralism of symbols and values in our highly mobile society corresponds to Parsons's L box (cultural). And the *oppressive* style of life, where initiative toward setting

2. There are other ways of talking about core characteristics: (1) Ego posture: "I'm okay, you're okay" or "I'm not okay, you're not okay;" (2) Mazeway: Each person develops a way through the maze of organism, personal, social, and cultural organization (Wallace, *Culture*).

3. See Loder's neo-Parsonian discussion and diagram in chapter 1, 19.

realistic goals is frustrated and the mere satisfaction of basic needs becomes predominant, connects to Parsons's A box (organic).

## (A) The Achievement-Orientated (-Obsessed) Lifestyle

I will begin with a discussion of achievement-oriented behavior and lifestyle, because it is the easiest for Presbyterians to recognize in themselves and their congregations. Achievement-oriented behavior was first identified as a style with core characteristics by David McClelland at Harvard, who worked on this concern for many years.[4] At first he thought the achieving lifestyle was a good thing. In fact, he began to develop achievement-oriented behavior as a solution to a number of human problems, including alcoholism. You can read about this research, the way it was originally generated and some of its subsequent implications, in Roger Brown's *Social Psychology*.[5] But later on McClelland began to realize that this behavior becomes a problem in our society and may even be a cause in precipitating such problems as alcoholism. He then began working on ways to control what has become an obsession in American and Western society.

What lies at the core of the achievement-oriented personality? Let's begin biologically, psychoneurologically, and physiologically with the organism. There are two countertendencies in every human being. One is *ends-means instinct*. When you are first born you are endowed with the instinct to grasp, to go get things. You have powerful prehensile capacities that govern your adaptation. You know how to grasp things, go for things, and you know how to suck. It's all built in. The instinct requires development, but it is still the organic foundation of our setting and getting goals. Right there, potentially, is the beginning of the achievement-oriented personality. If you really are an achievement-oriented mother, you will actually notice how your child—let's say you are breastfeeding—how your child "roots" for the breast. (This image is a rather indelicate allusion to pigs, but developmental psychologists use it). If you are an achievement-oriented mother, you will help your child get the nipple as quickly as possible, because that reinforces the intentionality of your child. (No doubt the forerunner of the

---

4. Editor's Note: Loder studied under McClelland at Harvard and he served on Loder's dissertation committee along with Hans Hoffman and H. Richard Niebuhr. See Loder, *Religious*, 10.

5. Brown, "Achievement Motive," 423–76. This chapter in Brown is a write-up of McClelland's work. See the references at the end of this chapter for McClelland's publications on the subject, 475. Editor's Note: See also Loder, "Fashioning of Power," especially 187–95 for an earlier discussion of these matters by Loder and his reference to McClelland, endnotes 2 and 3.

fast food industry in an achievement-oriented society). The child learns to refine random behavior, becoming more exact and efficient. You may laugh. But achievement-oriented people are really interested in this sort of early training, because they consider it the essential key for getting into Harvard. Setting and getting goals is rooted in the organic nature of the personality, and even in the earliest months of life can become a deep preoccupation for achievers.

The other basic tendency is something called *ascriptive worth potential*. This tendency embodies the need to be held, to just be valued for being there, which the experience of being held signifies. Some ethnologists think that the reason why all little creatures are cute reflects this profound need to be held. Cute things call out from us the affirmation of ascriptive worth. But being held is not just an arbitrary pleasure but be a matter of life and death. There was a king once who wanted to find out what the original language of the human race was. So he took newborn children before they had any contact with language anywhere and isolated them. He fed them and took care of their physical needs regularly, but no one was allowed to hold them or speak in their presence because he wanted to see what language would spontaneously emerge. What happened? All the children died because they were not touched or held.[6]

In Harry Harlow's famous research with monkeys at the University of Wisconsin–Madison,[7] Macaque monkeys were separated from their mothers at birth and placed in cages with either artificial wire "mothers" or cloth "mothers." The baby monkeys, it turned out, preferred the cloth "mother"— which they could nestle with—over the wire "mother," even when only the wire "mother" gave them milk. You, too, need to be held. You have to have *ascriptive* worth, worth not given because of something you do. Worth must be given to you just for being there. Ascriptive worth is the context in which rewards for achievements are properly placed.

Initially children hold these two tendencies in balance. But something happens to this balance in our achievement-oriented society. We gradually and persistently inform the child in subtle ways that she is really worth a lot more for what she can do than she for just being there. In effect the

6. Editor's Note: Loder does not give the reference to this anecdote.

7. Editor's Note: Loder gives no references to Harlow's research. But he may be referring here to *Learning to Love*, especially 17–31, where Harlow describes the phenomenon Loder notes in the following paragraph. Harry F. Harlow (1905–1981) was a prominent psychologist best known for his maternal-separation, dependency needs, and social isolation experiments on Rhesus monkeys that manifested the importance of caregiving and companionship in social and cognitive development. He did most of his initial research at University of Wisconsin–Madison.

dominance of setting and getting goals gets firmly established in psychic life (Parsons's Goal Box). This dominance was borne in on me with some shock many years ago. Our daughter Tami was very little then. I was down in the kitchen one morning, half asleep, muddling around assembling breakfast, when she came into the kitchen on her way to school. She said, "Good morning, Daddy." Tami is irrepressively effervescent, so hers was a very expressive greeting. However, I responded with a muffled and indifferent, "Morning." Then she said, "I tied my own shoes this morning." I wheeled around and excitedly responded, "You did!?" Tragically, you see, I didn't care that she was just there. I cared that she tied her shoes. Without even realizing it, I started rewarding her more for what she could do than for just being. My reaction revealed my pervasive and unconscious imbibing of an obsession with achievement that just took over. Since then, the best thing I was able to do with my two daughters, Kim and Tami, was to tell them what I am learning. So now they say, "Do you want to know what grade I got in such-and-such a class?"

"Yes, what did you get?"

"We're not going to tell you! It's not good for you."

Over a period of time children develop what is technically called a *reaction formation*. That is, they learn to do the opposite of what they really want to do with all the energy that they would have done the first thing. A child would like to have affirmation just for being there. But as a result of the reinforcement and socialization that begins to reward the child more for what she can do rather than for being there, she learns to put all the energy that she would like to have put into holding and being held into going and getting. Thus, we gradually teach the child that she has to earn her hugs and kisses. In a reaction formation, you use all the energy you would like to use one way, but in the opposite way. I take this reactive response as the basic ego posture—the core of the achievement-oriented personality—the one dominant form of defense for achievers in a competitive society. Subsequently, identity and conscience are formed around this heightened need to achieve by the society that creates and sustains this obsession.

If we move this analysis to the social context, we realize that Princeton is a great place to study this phenomenon. Right along with this early ego posture, we push early independence training. We want our child to grow up and be on her own. "Handle it yourself. Don't ask me. You can do it!" We act with our children as if *doing* was the *only* point. Early independence training gets our child ready to exercise resourcefulness, to meet the competition that will come from the world as soon as she leaves the family. Thus, we want to get her, if possible, into the best available nursery school, as early as possible, in order to develop her achievement-oriented and competitive mindset from the outset, to give her an advantage. Of course, we have her best interests at heart. We want her to succeed in an achievement-oriented society! It is not that we are bad parents. Princeton parents take wonderful care to make sure their children get the fullest possible advantages in order to survive and thrive in an achievement-oriented society.

So, as our child moves from the family into the larger sociocultural milieu of school, she will find the same kind of achievement obsession there she found at home. Teachers will tend to reinforce what she can do over and above who she is, because it is well known that teachers who privilege ascriptive worth—being sensitive, friendly, and congenial—over achieved worth are less effective in raising students' SAT scores. So according to one study by social psychologist Urie Bronfenbrenner, the best teachers in terms of SAT scores (the supposed measure of how you are going to do in our society) are those who practice what he called "cold democracy"—i.e., the impersonal practice of fairness.[8] Each child does his/her own work. What is best for each is best for all. So let's all try to be the best, because that is best for all. No special pleading. No special considerations. Achievement is a powerful social force. If you can compete successfully, the concern for achieving is almost impossible to resist.

Aware of the negative effects of competition and achievement-orientation one private school in Princeton decided not to give grades to the students. Instead, teachers committed themselves to writing long personal comments to help the parents understand what was going on with their child. Do you know the reaction they got? The parents went to the school and said to the teachers, "We don't understand what these comments mean. Would you please give our child a grade so we will know how well s/he is doing?" So, the teachers agreed. Why not? It's a lot easier to give grades! With minimal comments and grades, the parents were happy, because now their children could be moved rapidly and efficiently onto the ladder of success in the ritualization of progress.

The goal of this progressive education is to go from the best private prep schools to the best Ivy League schools to the best graduate schools to the best management team possible, in order to arrive at the top of the organization by the time you are thirty-five. Achievers make sure nothing like marriage or children interrupts them. If you are married, make sure it is a contractual arrangement in which each partner promises not to impede the achievement potential of the other in any way. "Get to the top by the time

---

8. Editor's Note: Loder does not cite a source here for Bronfenbrenner's notion of "cold democracy."

you are thirty-five" is the mantra of success for achievers, cheered on by an achievement-obsessed society chanting, "Go for it! Go for it now."

Ivan Illich criticizes this achievement obsession in his book *De-Schooling Society*. Ours is a "schooled" society, he insists, in the sense that all the way from the bottom to the top, there are grade-levels that require increasing mastery. Your task is to always be promoted from one grade to another—up, up, up the ladder—through repeated "ritualizations of progress."[9] Illich asks whether this obsession with progress is a good idea, or whether it is destructive to our humanity or to the well being of our society. Other voices have chimed in as well. For example, more than one author has written a book on the Peter Principle, which discloses an irony endemic to the inevitability of progress when persons excelling in one arena get automatically promoted to a higher level where their innate incompetence shows. So, you may be a great salesman, but have no skills to manage others. But, because you are such a good salesman, and because we are caught in the ritualization of progress, you get promoted to manager. You are a lousy manager, but you have earned it! And both you and others pay the price.

Ironies like this are pervasive, not just in schools but throughout the larger social context that achievers have created. The social perpetuation of the achievement-oriented personality is so important to us that we have created cultural or symbolic sanctions (Parsons's Latency Box) to perpetuate this dehumanizing obsession as the normative state of affairs. The achievement-orientation habit gets set down in fixed, even "sacred" cultural forms. In other words, the achiever can by means of something akin to Weber's famous "Protestant ethic" look at the whole cosmic order to see God sanctioning the achievement-oriented mentality.

I am sure most of you know the rubric "Protestant Ethic." But let me just spell it out briefly to refresh our memories. The rubric comes from Max Weber's famous and much debated text, *The Protestant Ethic and the Spirit of Capitalism*, and it is based on a popular perversion of Calvin's doctrines of justification and sanctification. That is, the "Protestant ethic" is a perversion of Calvin's original intention, which was to say that rewards *may* be a sign of grace. Calvin never taught that rewards were a means of proving or earning grace. Roger Brown notes that the Reformation engendered a kind of characterological reformation in which Protestantism (as studied by Weber) was contrasted with the Roman Catholicism of that time. Protestants worked hard, denied themselves, made gains, and plowed the gains or a portion of the gains back into the advancement of the business, in order to insure future gain for which they themselves might never benefit. But the rewards

9. Illich, "Ritualization," 464–72.

that accompanied this kind of diligent intensity gradually became signs of God's favor.[10] Eventually the sovereignty of God and doctrine of election, the major theological premises behind Calvin's formulation of this position, become less and less significant. The priority of the works ascended, and we begin to see works as a way of getting and proving grace.

So it is at the present time. For the achiever, God is at work sacralizing what the achiever would do anyway. An achiever can go to virtually any church and find that achieving is what is often and essentially preached and taught. Achievement enters into counseling and administration, and, indeed, into every aspect of ministry. Winning and getting on top is somehow legitimated by the grace of God. Of course, we all want achievers in our churches, don't we? Achievers, after all, make the best elders. In one of the studies that McClelland conducted to distinguish achievers, his subjects threw wads of paper into a wastebasket. Now the really dependent types got right up close and dropped them in. The really creative, innovative types took hook shots from midcourt. But not so, the achiever! The achievers stood back just far enough to make the throw interesting, and just close enough to never miss! Now that is what you want in an elder. Achievers also make excellent students in adult classes. The achievement-oriented personality will come to your adult church school class and learn everything you say. She will ask the best possible questions. She will read the best books. She will read the bibliography you only suggested and feed it back to you in detail.

So, now let's return to Nelson and the socialization argument. If you try, as Nelson advocates, to pass on the tradition to a group of people, a congregation that is predominantly made up of achievers, what are you going to get? What you will get is mastery of the tradition according to the spirit of the achievement-oriented society. Now you have another version of Kierkegaard's madman running through the town saying, "The world is round." Thus, Nelson, as representative of the entire socialization emphasis in Christian education, does not take socialization near seriously enough. For when we push the socialization paradigm as hard as it will go, we see that these larger patterns swallow up the Christian tradition and create parishioners in the image of a Christianized achievement-oriented society. What's wrong with that? We know what could be said theologically about this. But we do not have to go to theology to see the devastating problems associated with this obsessive lifestyle.

---

10. Editor's Note: Loder did not cite the source of Brown's judgment here, but it was probably Brown, "Achievement Motive," 451–54.

The ironies and contradictions embedded in the achievement-oriented lifestyle are indeed deep and devastating. In fact, research on the phenomenon shows that obsession to achieve is a socially accelerated form of self-destruction. For instance, there is the study by Maccoby titled *The Gamesman.* Maccoby is a social psychologist who interviewed top executives in our society and labeled most of them—not all of them—"gamesmen." Why "gamesmen"? He used this term to communicate that these executives do not so much win to survive as they survive in order to win. They believe the excitement and meaning of life depends upon winning. What's wrong with that?

What is wrong with gamesmanship is that it reveals that a kind of perpetual adolescence has taken hold of us. "Winning" is the way an adolescent thinks. And what happens as you continue to perpetuate this winning mentality, this kind of obsessiveness? You begin to empty yourself inside. What Maccoby found was that many of these wealthy and powerful achieving adults are inwardly empty. Without a game to play to win, they feel lost. They have no inner resources. They have no way to draw upon an inner life, and therefore, no way to really care for somebody unless they can be shown how care itself is an achievement. In the context of this pervasive mentality, ascriptive worth is almost completely lost.

Brofenbrenner in his study of achievement-oriented behavior found that the achievers were "more planful and purposeful, but also more tense, domineering and cruel."[11] Furthermore, the physiological consequences of the A-type personality are familiar and devastating. You may want to look at a book titled *Type A Behavior and Your Heart* by Friedman and Rosenman. No doubt you have heard about A-types. These authors describe them in considerable detail. A-type behavior can be hard on your heart and you are much more likely to have chronic heart difficulty, heart attacks, if you are

11. Bronfenbrenner, "Effects," 347–56. Editor's Note: Loder put this description of achievers in quotation marks. But I think this phrase is a summary statement not a quote. In another essay, Loder offered this same description at the end of an expanded comment but without quotation marks.

> One can only estimate the effect of this surge toward "excellence" upon recent youth movements in the United States. But in an article written in 1961, Bronfenbrenner, reflecting upon these trends toward re-enforcement of the achievement-orientation, came to some very disturbing conclusions. Citing studies by Baldwin, Kalhorn, Breese, and Haggard, he concluded that these patterns of child rearing, peer group development, and the public school emphasis upon excellence tended to produce a person who is purposeful, but who is also more aggressive, tense, domineering, and cruel.

See Loder, "Fashioning," 189–90,

this type of person. This tendency is particularly true if your achievement-oriented motivation derives from a basic distrust of human nature and of your closest associates in particular. Furthermore, it breeds loneliness. Loneliness is also, by the way, hard on your heart. You may want to look at another book, titled *The Broken Heart: The Medical Consequences of Loneliness* by James Lynch, in which he shows the devastating effects of this kind of loneliness on the heart.

The destructive nature of the achievement-obsessed lifestyle is graphically revealed in the remarks achievers make. One obsessed achiever I know, who is a well-known person whose books you have probably read, said he never used to be able to get to sleep at night until he began to think about his next promotion. Another overachiever, displaying the self-emptying qualities of this lifestyle commented, "I just hope I die before I ruin my reputation." A woman achiever remarked, "I don't want any more love than I deserve." Do you realize what futility it is to have to deserve the love you get? You have to *keep* deserving it. And *keep* deserving it. And *keep* deserving it. That is not love; that is self-destruction.

In one large church I know there was a chemical engineer who escaped from the terror of Cambodia's "killing fields." Eventually he made his new home in the United States and found employment in a large chemical company. After being on the job for a while, the refugee confided to his minister, "The terrors of escaping from Cambodia were nothing like the pressures of working in this chemical company." Employees were forced to participate in a ranking system. If you were number 5 on a scale of five research chemists and there were losses or you did not produce, they lopped you off. You had to stay on top to keep your job. "This kind of pressure," he said, "was incredible, worse than escaping from Cambodia."

*Please note that I am not trying to take achievement out of life!* That is not the point of my critique. You have to achieve, that is, by instinct you have to put ends and means together. Achievement itself isn't the issue. As already noted, it is instinctually built in from the beginning. What I want to do is take the *obsession* out of achieving, the *addiction* out of it, so we don't make achieving try to do what only receiving ascriptive worth can do—anchor our lives in the presence and power of God's *agape* love.

In order for church educators to liberate achievers out of this pattern of self-destruction, they have to get at the core of the achievement-obsessed lifestyle. If they cannot help achievers deal with this core, educators will end up basically socializing self-destruction in the name of grace. The hidden curriculum in all of this, as Illich says, is the "ritualization of progress." Unfortunately, the constructive side of Illich's critique does not help us, because it doesn't affect the core of the achievement-oriented personality.

Any efforts directed toward the Christian education of achievers, without getting at this core, become futile because this socially and culturally accelerated lifestyle will devour whatever ecclesiastical or theological instruction you give people. Again, we reiterate that educators like Nelson do not take the power of socialization seriously enough. They simply do not see that educationally we must have access to a merciful power far greater than our sociocultural obsession with achievement if we are to engage in a transformational *Christian* education that really matters.[12]

## (B) The Authoritarian Lifestyle

Let me now move on to the second lifestyle, which is equally prevalent and equally, if not more thoroughly, researched by social scientists—namely, *authoritarianism*. A German psychologist named E. R. Jaensch conceived the original study on the authoritarian personality in 1934. Jaensch, working for the Nazis, endeavored to describe two personality types, the S-type and the J-type. He had the same idea of lifestyle and type that I am talking about—i.e., a core ego-structure that governs behaviors across the widest range of experience. In his study, the S-type was the sensitive type, the type that was aware of ambiguity and ambivalence; the type that was aware of inner feelings and their connections to the outer world. S-type persons maintained an interest in poetry and literature and art. These persons were oftentimes willing to be passive or compliant for the sake of a higher value.

Then there was the J-type—*J* for Jaensch I suppose. These were the ones who were strong, stable, knew right down the line the difference between good and evil, right and wrong and how to hold that line. Of course, what Jaensch was actually doing, it turns out, was working on the kind of research that would help determine what makes a good fascist. So Jaensch, in distinguishing between the S-type and the J-type in 1934, was doing research in defense of the J-type to facilitate discrimination against the S-type, a Jewish stereotype. Today, looking at this kind of research, we affirm and endorse the reverse transvaluation. With an historic transvaluation of

12. Editor's Note. It might be helpful to emphasize here that Loder's critique of the achievement-oriented personality may have been directed ultimately toward himself. This suggestion anticipates his discussion in chapter 8 in which he describes his own transformation from being an achieving Loder bound to a family mystique to being his own person in Christ, such that he now "owned" the image that formerly owned and determined him. He could now place the Loder image in the service of Christ and be liberated from any obsession to achieve that dehumanized himself or others around him, and thereby misrepresented Christ.

values, we see the J-type as the real problem and the S-type as having much more to offer.[13]

Ironically, however, even though we have changed the way we evaluate S and J types, because we denigrate Nazism, there is still a rising positive value on the authoritarian-type personality under other rubrics. Particularly, authoritarianism is represented in various spheres of American life: particularly in religion, in education, and in the military. In fact, some say there is a clear drift in our society toward totalitarianism, perhaps following Plato's prediction that democracy eventually dissolves into a kind of anomie that makes it ripe for totalitarian takeover. Some years ago, Robert Heilbroner created a sensation with his book, *Inquiry into the Human Prospect*, when he predicted that ultimately our democracy would yield to a police state. In other words, according to these political philosophers, democracies all tend, more or less, towards authoritarian-type structures that they deem necessary to secure their own survival.[14]

Whether these predictions are accurate or not, even within the present structure, our culture has established several institutions that attract authoritarians. If you lean toward the authoritarian type, you may quite comfortably find your home in the military, in many churches, and in many businesses. And many public school administrators may bring or develop authoritarian leanings in their jobs because their legitimate concern to create true learning environments is stifled or destroyed by the chaos and violence threatening their schools. For us, however, the question remains: what is the core of this lifestyle, and what are its power and its patterns of self-destruction?

The research on this phenomenon by Theodore W. Adorno and others was published in 1950 in a book titled *Authoritarian Personality*.[15] These researchers argued that the origins of the authoritarian orientation and spirit could be traced back to early toilet training and the child's first encounter with the social constraints to basic instincts. Shamed into social conformity of this type, children become susceptible to a distorted resolution of the Oedipal crisis between ages three and five. Recall that the Oedipal or Electra struggle is motivated at an unconscious level by primitive urges toward sex and violence (rape and murder). In its "normal" resolution, the little girl identifies with her mother while the little boy identifies with his father. This need to identify is first of all because the child is small and the parents are

13. Brown, "Authoritarian," 477–78.

14. Editor's Note: We can only wonder how Loder would write this whole section in light of the rise of authoritarian eruptions that plagues our world today.

15. A summary of Adorno et al., *Authoritarian Personality* can be found in Brown, "Authoritarian Personality," 478–79.

big. The child wants to be where the power is. Also, as a child, the need to get your own way, to have your needs gratified somehow, is important. Furthermore, same-sex identification allows the child to anticipate his/her entrée into the larger society. The little boy anticipates how to be a man by identifying with the father-type. The girl anticipates how to be a woman by identifying with the mother-type.

Now this identification process is actually a very complex systemic phenomenon, but I am just giving you the basic path. Thus, the fundamental solution on how to enter the world as an adult and get the love of the other parent indirectly is right there in front of the child through this identification process. If you can identify with the parent of the same sex in this way, you solve a plethora of problems all at once. If one is in an opposite-sex single parent home, the child may find identification figures in relatives or friends. So about age three to five, the child resolves the question of sex role identity in the family constellation by identifying with the parent of the same sex in order to know how to be an adult and to get, indirectly, the love of the other parent.

But if the power struggle has been too great, and the family dynamics are governed by fear from unpredictable threats of violence, then the identification dynamics ominously change. In the authoritarian situation, the child learns to identify with the parent who has the most power. This distorted identification happens no longer for the sake of basic need satisfaction and the construction of a viable role in society, but out of fear of punishment. Normally identification takes place as the basis of enhancing the future. But in the authoritarian personality it takes place to avoid the chronic punishments of the past. Thus because the parental training patterns have instilled so much uncertainty and so much fear in the child, the child has no way of dealing with the big people who have all the power except to give up and identify with them. So the basic rubric is, always identify with the aggressor. If you can't beat them, join them.

Let me give you an illustration of this kind of identification with power. After I had lectured on authoritarianism once, a student from the class came to my office to talk. "I know I'm one of those people," said. "Let me tell you a story about how I was raised," and he told me this story.

> I was sitting at the breakfast table one morning. It was a perfectly happy, joyful, and pleasant day. The sun was shining, the birds were singing, the breakfast was good, and everything was fine. All at once, out of nowhere, my father looked over at me and said, in a menacing voice, "You do that again and you're going to get it!" Cautiously, I took a couple more bites of cereal, not

knowing what my crime had been. Suddenly my father thundered, "You did it again!" He picked me up and literally threw me through the air into my room and slammed the door. "Don't come out until I tell you!" was all he said. A little bit later, from inside the room, I heard the TV going. I opened the door just a little bit and saw my father out there watching the football game. He noticed the door was ajar and called out, "Hey, kid, come on out and watch the game!" Suddenly everything was great again.

How did this boy learn to survive this context? He never knew what was coming, when, or from where. The only way to survive this environment was to identify with his father. Whatever he said, you do it. Don't try to make sense of it. The further consequence was that when the authoritarian gets frustrated, the authoritarian in turn finds someone weaker—the dog, a Jew, or a minority person—to kick around. So authoritarian followers often become authoritarian leaders or bosses.

Therefore, the fear of punishment and the consequent guilt feelings generated by capricious parenting exists as the seedbed for the traumatized child to tragically identify with the aggressor adult. Such parenting is primarily motivated out of that adult's felt needs, rather than the child's real needs, and reproduces the development of the authoritarian personality in the child. The child raised in this situation eventually learns to pay exclusive attention to what the parent wants, insists upon, and demands. He represses anything of his own space, world, self-understanding, or sensitivity, and is ever after deeply preoccupied with the issue of social control (Parsons's Integration Box).

This particular student who came to talk eventually left the seminary and went into the military. You might be happy to know, as a postscript, that eventually he grew to the place where he was taller and stronger than the father. One day his father was sitting in the living room and told his son to do something unreasonable. He refused. So his father said, "You do it or I'm going to beat the hell out of you!" And the son said, "No, I'm not going to do that." And the father said, "You damn sure will do that!" Then the boy stood up, now about two inches taller than his father and repeated, "No, I'm not going to do it." That was the end of that. The father backed off. Incidentally, this anecdote reveals that power language may be the only language some authoritarians understand.

Several characteristics of authoritarianism growing out of this core ego posture and its patterns of defense can be delineated.

(a) *Strong over Weak*. The authoritarian is preoccupied with the difference between who is strong and who is weak. The authoritarian begins to look at everything through this lens alone. Of course, the authoritarian wants to be either the strong one or identified with the strong one or group. From this place of strength, one takes out all frustrations on the weak one or the weak group.

(b) *In-Group over Out-Group.* The authoritarian seeks to construct clear-cut distinctions between those who belong to the in-group and those who remain outside. They construct a hard line between the two, with no ambiguity in their judgments. "Are you one of us? Or are you one of them?" The authoritarian sets very absolute distinctions between in and out.

(c) *No Inner Life.* The authoritarian rejects or represses (or both) anything that has to do with inner feelings, inner resources, or the inner life generally. The technical term for this repression is "anti-intraception." The authoritarian does not know and does not want to know how he or she feels, does not want to be in touch with his or her unconscious or internal motivations. Therefore, s/he can't be in touch with the inner feelings of others.

(d) *Stereotyping and Superstition.* The authoritarian is given to rigid stereotyping and superstition, both of which hinge upon the rigid repression. Stereotyping helps the authoritarian repress feelings, ambiguities felt on the inside. Superstition follows the Jungian mantra "What you do not recognize and face in yourself happens outside of you as fate." So if you are a very superstitious authoritarian, what does that imply? You will say things like, "As I was going home, there was a branch that fell on my path. It must mean something! Everything means something." Of course, it may mean nothing more than that there was a high wind. But the authoritarian is easily afraid because he/she is repressing so much stuff that there is a chronic fear of loss of control. Superstition is a way of exercising control over the exigencies of experience, trying to establish meaning out of accidents because accidents imply that "I am not in control."

(e) *Preoccupation with Perversity.* The authoritarian is also deeply preoccupied with all the deep, dark dirty things that are going on in the world. There are deep, dark dirty things going on in the world, by the way, but the authoritarian finds them even when they are not there. He attacks them "out there," because of what is going on "inside." For example, one day I visited in New York City with an authoritarian friend of mine. As we were walking down Forty-Second Street on the way to the bus terminal, someone walked past whose gender was not immediately apparent to us. My authoritarian friend watched this person for a few moments and then let loose with an "Aagh!"—a deep guttural growl. For the authoritarian you must always repress any kind of ambiguity concerning sexual identity. To suggest that male has a female side and vice-versa is automatically perverse.

(f) *Aggression toward Punishment.* The last characteristic is authoritarian aggression. Authoritarian aggression is out to punish any and all who do not agree with what the in-group is saying and supporting, out to punish those who in any way seem to be participating in evil. The point is never to see and understand and then move toward some sort of forgiveness and reconciliation. The point is to punish, to shape them up.

One of the ways one's dominant lifestyle defenses get exposed comes by attending to what emerges when one undergoes deep stress. You can put a fairly affable, genial, get-along-easy-with-everyone kind of person under stress, and s/he will become very authoritarian. We can try to educate authoritarian personalities to be less so, but these efforts won't really make any difference because, under the inevitability of stress, they become authoritarian again. You have to get to the core of the condition. To be honest, just as there is a bit of the achiever in all of us, there is also a bit of the authoritarian in all of us. If you don't believe that you can become authoritarian, you don't have children! Wait until you have children! Children bring out the authoritarian in us all. As the bumper sticker put it, "Because I'm the Mommy!" Sometimes the only way to manage stress is to become a little authoritarian. But being a little authoritarian at times is quite different from being enslaved to an authoritarian personality and the dehumanization of life and relationships that inevitably follows from this lifestyle.

Before moving on to social context, let us note in passing that one can be an authoritarian liberal just as much as an authoritarian conservative. "I can't stand the Fundies!" is about as authoritarian as any "Fundy" will ever get about his liberal opponent. So the lifestyle is a dynamic and structural pattern in which the content of what is expressed may shift dramatically even as the authoritarian spirit remains the same.

Let us now address authoritarianism in the social context. What does the authoritarian want in a school? In the actual classroom experience, he wants well-ordered lessons and exact assignments. He is not interested in personal initiative, either in himself or in his students. Often in fact, the authoritarian does not know what to do unless told. He is very preoccupied with getting it right. He does not care about knowing his own mind, relying on his own judgment, or exercising his own critical faculties. He just wants to get the right answers. In one authoritarian classroom I know about, the children were assigned a "creative" paper. They were told to write a paper creating their own ideas, expressing their own creative impulses. But when the papers came back graded, the only things marked on any of them were mistakes in spelling and grammar. Ironies continue. "All right children! Attention! We are going to have a little time of creative drawing and a little creative self-expression. Does everyone have his or her things out? Does everyone have everything on the desk? Are you ready now? You're not! Shame on you! Ready now! Create!" Thus, in the name of encouraging the human spirit, we have actually engaged in its contradiction—conformity to an external authoritarian milieu.[16]

As I have said, some social institutions seem to be made for enabling this kind of socialized authoritarian personality—in the military, in some churches and seminaries, perhaps in accounting firms, or routine assembly-line plants, or in school administration. There are also definitive cultural patterns, systems of symbols and values that can be used to justify and enable the authoritarian spirit to thrive. For example, real authority becomes authoritarian by the dynamics of this style. The Bible is a primary example. When that which has genuine authority becomes authoritarian, it generates the core characteristics described above—strong/weak, in-group/out-group, or the like. When the Bible becomes authoritarian, it may take on the false authority often attending those who defend "the inerrant Word of God," as the old Princeton theology put it. So just do what the Bible says. As another bumper sticker had it, "The Bible says it! I believe it! That settles it!" The deep irony is that the real power of the Word of God is here replaced by fear-driven need for control. Fear of weakness masquerades as strength of conviction.

I remember giving a series of lectures in California some time ago. After the lecture on authoritarianism, a person came up to me and said, "I know I am authoritarian, but what do I do? I actually read the Bible and do what it says." The most fruitful part of our conversation took place when we started to talk about life in the Spirit in relation to the Bible. We noted that the Bible does not say of itself that it can be read and followed by strenuous human effort. The Bible says the Spirit works in us through Scripture.

16. An illustrative example of conservative authoritarian rhetoric concerning education can be found in Falwell, "Freedom's Heritage," 63–65. The article is remarkable for its verbal affirmation of the human spirit and its systematic advocacy of an authoritarian approach that would control, if not crush, the spirit. A critique of authoritarian discourse and education may be found Jorstad, "Politics," 66–76. Jorstad is also critical of the fundamentalist appropriation of authoritarianism, especially where it accelerates free enterprise and the capitalist economy. Concern for the oppressed, in such a milieu, is utterly forgotten. They are after all the "weak" ones, the nonproducers.

We can do nothing without the Spirit. This conversation became fruitful because we talked about what the Bible itself says about its nonauthoritarian authority. Authoritarianism must be brought to the Scripture, not vice versa. The key to the difference between authoritarianism and authority lies in the degree to which self-knowledge and self-understanding are suppressed or are enhanced.

But there are ironies intrinsic to the authoritarian lifestyle itself. Nevitt Sanford indicated in his book *Self and Society* that he had found many male authoritarians longing to express inner feelings—feelings that socially speaking we would classify as feminine ideas and imagery. He found a longing in these men for the sensitive and the intuitive dimensions they had repressed. But at the same time, he found them afraid to talk about these inward feelings we call introspection. Sanford found that he could make headway against this particular mentality when he showed persistent care for them as individuals. He did everything he could to eliminate the fear that they would appear weak or that they would be overwhelmed by anything. He cared for them. But at the same time, in this context of care, he asked them questions that radically contradicted their assumptions. He presented ambiguities and ambivalences in the midst of the context of caring, and he found that by so doing, he could begin to make some progress against this deeply entrenched mentality.[17]

In relation to Sanford's findings let me add a comment: We should realize, recognize, and appreciate that talking to authoritarians often leads them to feel vindicated in their own fears and insecurities. That is, authoritarians will talk to you in such a way as, if possible, to threaten you. Unconsciously, they want to make you angry so that the fear that justifies their position can be further justified by your anger. Have you ever tried to talk to an authoritarian? Don't you feel frustrated? The authoritarian makes you feel like he or she feels on the inside—insecure, not in control, and angry at the world. The more you react in accordance with the way he or she feels on the inside, the more proof the authoritarian has of the necessity for maintaining the authoritarian pattern. So the authoritarian generates the environment that entrenches the mindset. This need to control the environment is one of the reasons authoritarians find it so hard to break out of the authoritarian lifestyle. And that is why Sanford's efforts to create and maintain an environment of nonthreatening care are so crucial for dealing with authoritarian personalities.

17. Sanford, *Self and Society*, 162–64, 194–200.

## (C) The Protean Personality and Lifestyle

A third basic lifestyle, which is perhaps the most tempting option for young people in American society today, has been described by Robert Jay Lifton, a teaching psychoanalyst at Yale University, as "The Protean Personality."[18] You will recall that it was the Greek god Proteus who continually changed his shape and nature from wild boar to lion to fire to blood in order to avoid his proper function, which was to prophesy. Lifton argues that three massive sociocultural threats merge to explain why this lifestyle has become so socially acceptable and so widespread in the last half of the twentieth century. The three threats are "nuclearism," psychohistorical dislocation, and the flooding of imagery into society. Let us discuss each threat in brief.

*Nuclearlism.* Nuclearism is the mentality created in the aftermath of Hiroshima, as the horror of our being able to destroy civilization became so imminent and so seemingly inevitable that it elided any frame of meaning. This mentality believes, in line with Bertrand Russell's concern, that we will destroy civilization because we can, since we have never been able to refrain—and will never be able to refrain—from acting on what we capable of doing. Before the Cold War ended, this growing threat engendered a pervasive fear that most of the present generation would not live out their lives. When high school students were surveyed, a surprising majority believed they would die in a nuclear war. Anxieties arose when we learned that the government had appointed committees to figure out ways to deliver the mail and collect taxes after the holocaust hit the United States. Today, the horror of world-destructive war continues to dilute our capacity to construct meaning. This despair contributes to the second threat contributing to proteanism, psychohistorical dislocation.

*Psychohistorical Dislocation.* Nuclearism together with the rapid changes in industrialization (e.g., increased differentiation of the work force and the creation of multinational corporations) uproots meaning. Rapid technological changes reorder our frames of reference almost week by week. The dazzling pace of technology moves so fast that we hardly have time to *ask* what it all means, much less find meaning. All this experiential change ushers in a radical undervaluing of the former ways humans devised for giving life significance—i.e., tradition, church, family life, neighborhood, town, schoolhouse, family business, enduring marriage and so forth. All we are left with in this dislocated world is our *self.* So the key concept in proteanism is *"the self in process."* We must continue to create and improve our

---

18. Lifton, "Protean Man," 298–304. See also Lifton's book-length treatment, *Protean Self.*

self to meet each new advancing situation, since no foundation for meaning is equal to all situations that arise.

*The Flood of Imagery.* The third major social threat contributing to the rise of the protean personality in our society is the bombardment of the culture with ever-newly-minted streams of imagery. With children typically spending more time in front of the computer or the television than they spend in school, the sheer exposure is overpowering. Of fifth to ninth grade school age children, 51 percent watch three hours of television per day. An estimated six hundred thousand children routinely view adult-geared programming between twelve midnight and two a.m. every night. By the time children reach eighteen years of age most have watched seven hundred thousand commercials! These viewing habits play into the emerging industry of 'virtual reality"—the ultimate trip that promises even more virtual experience. Eventually, because we no longer believe in the real world's capacity to give us stability and meaning, these "virtual realities" become more "real" than reality itself.[19]

Don Barnhouse (a child prodigy who entered the ministry after studying physics and the effects of nuclearization at Harvard) illustrated the power of "virtual reality" through media in a lecture he gave at Princeton Seminary on the schematic world of television.[20] He recalled for us his experience of doing commentaries on a Philadelphia news program, how people would come to the television station to see the celebrity anchor man in person. But instead of watching him, they watched the monitor of his image during the show's taping. Next, he told of one of his parishioners asking a group to pray for a character in a television soap opera. Finally, he noted that kids from the church he attended habitually cut school so as not to miss episodes of the soap opera *General Hospital.* Thus, not only in sheer time and exposure, and even more importantly in its impact on social learning, the media threatens to powerfully subvert our embodied existence.

Another aspect of the media that is important for protean behavior is the familiar argument that television tends to eliminate childhood. Scholars

19. Editor's Note: Obviously these statistics are outdated as are the changes in technology that make watching television rather anachronistic. But since the media saturation is so much more overwhelming today than Loder describes, his essential point remains even more valid and even more urgent.

20. Editor's Note: I could find not such a lecture on television in Princeton's library or media service. And Loder does not mention the actual title or date of this lecture. The seminary's online database gives two references to Donald Barnhouse: (1) a sermon titled "Why Do We Worship God in Jesus Christ?" (1965) and (2) a lecture titled "Omni Words (1994). In an older resource, the "Listening Library Catalogue," only the earlier sermon is noted. I am unclear as to whether Loder based his comments on either of these two sources, or heard Barnhouse in a different context.

note that childhood was created by the printing press, since to be an adult evolved to be one who could read. Europeans discovered that learning to read was best facilitated in childhood by special instruction, which made reading serve as enculturation's bridge from infancy to adulthood. Today the television and the computer—new technological inventions that threaten to replace all books—serve to reduce the gap between childhood and adulthood—or, we might say, to eliminate childhood by eliminating adulthood. Fundamentally this elimination of childhood occurs because the media, in order to hold its audience, must tap every existing social taboo. Thus, long before children know how to think about thinking, they get exposed to a steady diet of violence, brutality, murder, and misogyny. They view multiple forms of confusing sexual expression (i.e., incest, promiscuity, adultery, homosexuality, and sadism), and the dehumanization that flows from portrayals of indifference to the suffering of others, uninhibited greed, linguistic violence, drug abuse, and so forth. Moreover, television's content incessantly directs viewers toward purely commercial values, which thrive on the principle, if you like it, you'll buy it. Is the McDonald's commercial of the happy family visit real? Who cares? The point is, you like it, so you'll buy it. In the process our sense of conscience is radically eroded. In its place we inquire after only as to whether or not we like something; whether or not it feels good, makes us perform better, or what have you.

Developmentally, the core of the protean personality arises from parenting patterns that combine high expectations with low personal involvement. On the one hand, the pattern devolves to a situation of sheer neglect as it was in this particular military family I know. The father, a military doctor, was largely absent on assignment. The mother, independent and absent emotionally, took little interest in her children's lives. When their little boy blew two fingers off his sister's right hand with their father's gun, the only punishment he got was a reprimand: "Don't do it again." On the other hand, the pattern may manifest itself in the context of attentive and sensitive parents who understand everything but stand for nothing. Either way the result is the same. There are no boundaries. There is no firm basis for social conduct and behavior to guide the child's experience. In effect, the child is raised without an ethical or moral context—essentially told that she must find her own way and mold herself. The parental illusion is that they are raising the child effectively for living in a pluralistic society, equipping them to live in a context full of ethical ambiguity and relativity. In reality, under these circumstances the child's personality may be formed more by the media than by any other force. "Virtual reality" becomes definitive, and external reality merely the stuff to be molded by the steady flow of images.

I recall seeing Bill Moyers's report on the historical evolution of the camera.[21] There was a time, he noted, when we believed, "The camera cannot lie." Today, however, we know better. We know that many mysteries cannot be resolved by recourse to some imagined infallible photographic evidence. In fact, we are increasingly aware that photographic images are not so much representatives of reality as they are strategies of persuasion. The old adage "What gets your imagination gets you" can now be seen as a self-fulfilling prophecy in a society in which, in its adulation of the power to create "virtual realities" oriented to the commercial interests of the human creator, we show ever-increasing indifference to the objective reality that surrounds us—including the people who surround us!

For the protean personality, the developmental consequence is that a person can be one image today and another tomorrow without any sense of conscience to mediate a deeper sense of oneself. One may graduate from high school, drop out of college, hit the San Francisco scene for a while, grow tired of that, decide to study orthodoxy in Jerusalem, return to the United States, go into business, enter a management training program for three or four years, then switch over into a counseling program for high schoolers, and so on, and so on. Thus, we may describe four major characteristics that mark the lifestyle of the protean personality.

(1) *Self-Evasion and Cynicism.* The constant shift in personal and professional identity generates a deep ideological hunger and cynicism in the personality. Here, creativity runs amok, engaging in a futile search for an evasive transcendence that can tie a knot in the thread of a life. Such endless self-creation functions as self-evasion.

(2) *Inability for Relationships.* There is a longing for nurturance in the protean personality coupled with a paradoxical rejection of commitment. Instability in identity results in an inability for nurturing relations. Covenants become ever-renewable contracts.

(3) *Vague, Disempowering Guilt.* Third, protean personalities are marked by a vague yet pervasive sense of guilt that is ever transposed into moral confusion and indifference to society. Proteanism disempowers democratic involvement and disinclines covenantal commitment.

(4) *Dynamism without Substance.* An endless cycle of "dying and rising" becomes the key process that structures the personality. In this

---

21. Editor's Note: Dr. Loder gave no information about this program, and I could not find it. Researchers at several libraries also failed to turn it up.

dynamic fluidity there is no developed sense of purpose or meaning in life from sources that transcend the self.[22]

We can recognize that proteanism has become an identifiable personality in our postmodern context. Lifton quotes from a young teacher who expresses the protean personality quite succinctly.

> I have an extraordinary number of masks I can put on or take off. The question is: is there, or should there be, one face which should be authentic? I'm not sure that there is one for me. I can think of other parallels to this, especially in literature. There are representations of every kind of crime, every kind of sin. For me, there is not a single act I cannot imagine myself committing.

The teacher went on to compare himself to an actor on the stage who performed with a certain kind of "polymorphous versatility," referring, slightly mockingly no doubt, to Freud's term "polymorphous perverse" to describe diffusely inclusive infantile sexuality. The teacher then asked,

> Which is the real person, so far as an actor is concerned? Is he more real when he is at home? I tend to think that for people who have these many, many masks, there is no home. Is it a futile gesture for the actor to try to find his real face?[23]

The psychological key here is the absence of any superego. Hence the cultural icon for the protean personality is no doubt Jean Paul Sartre, whose protean traits seem so much an embodiment of twentieth-century humankind in the nuclear age. In an essay published in *The Acquisition and Development of Values*, Lifton quotes the American critic Theodore Solotaroff, who speaks of Sartre's fundamental assumption that "there is no such thing as even a relatively fixed sense of self, ego, or identity—rather there is only the subjective mind in motion in relationship to that which it confronts." Lifton noted that Solotaroff characterized Sartre as "constantly on the go, hurrying from point to point, subject to subject, fiercely intentional, his thought occupies, fills, and distends its material as he endeavors with other lives, disciplines, books and situations."[24] Then Lifton quotes Solotaroff quoting Sartre from his (Sartre's) autobiography.

> Had my father lived, he would have lain on me at full length and crushed me . . . I move from shore to shore, alone and hating those invisible begetters who bestraddle their sons all their lives.

22. Lifton, "Adaptation," 38–41.
23. Ibid, 39–40.
24. Ibid, 40–41.

I left behind me a young man who did not have time to be my father and who could now be my son. Was it a good thing or bad? I don't know. But I readily subscribe to the verdict of an eminent psychoanalyst: I have no Superego.[25]

In this case—as in all other lifestyles we are discussing—Christian language and values may be appealed to and appropriated in an effort to legitimate a lifestyle that is not really Christian at all. We must recognize, then, how the protean spirit distorts Christian meaning and life even as it may use Christian language or symbols. One may, for example, speak especially of living "in the Spirit" or of "dying and rising with Christ" or of "freedom from the law" in terms of having no superego. Such a distortion of Christian freedom shows little concern for how the Spirit enables obedience and covenantal faithfulness to a reality that transcends the self not by obliterating the superego but by transforming it in the service of Christ.

The key irony here is that studies of protean personalities show that they tend to return at about age twenty-eight or twenty-nine to values held when they were about seventeen. Thus, proteanism is itself only an illusory form of self-processing. Consider the case of David, who was raised in a fairly large family of five children. The control patterns in his home were inconsistent and inaccurate. More particularly he never felt he was "seen." There were high parental expectations for him, but low personal investment with him.

David started out in college studying engineering like his father. But in his senior year he began to battle depression and came to talk. A young woman had got to him, touched the place where he longed to see the "face"—i.e., a prototype of a loving presence that does not go away and that gives order to life, first experienced in infancy.[26] She was a drama major, so he began to invest his attention into drama and poetry, with the result that the other side of his personality flourished. In this creative milieu David became cynical about all boundaries, values, and goods. The drama and theater was as true to him as the society that was supposedly real. He began to enter into the classic protean pattern, moving to Boston and then to New York City, and always related to this girl whose lifestyle was even

25. Ibid, The quote is from Sartre's autobiography, *Words*, 19.

26. Editor's Note: Loder develops this theme of the "face" in the next chapter. He refers there to research into infantile development when the child fixates on the face/presence of the mother in order to organize his/her personality around an interpersonal presence. This infantile experience of the "face" becomes a prototype for Christ as the Face of God ordering conversion experiences. Only the divine Face/Presence can serve as the true ordering reality of human beings and communities and bring redemption. All other "faces" or "presences" ultimately go away.

more protean than his. Finally, he followed her out to San Francisco. They lived together, but the pattern was beginning to drive him back into depression. He lost motivation. Unable to move, he would lie in a half-wake state, unable to work, incessantly making excuses. And so he came to talk again.

In our conversations, David became very aware that his girlfriend couldn't be the face for him. She was better at living the lifestyle than he was, and it made him depressed because he really wanted some responsibility and continuity in the relationship. He longed for a covenantal relationship and he longed for creative freedom. This double-bind was killing him. He finally came to a point of decision. He would cut off the relationship and seek the intimacy of the spiritual life for which he longed in Christ. This anecdote illuminates our discussion in two ways. First, David followed the pattern that at ages twenty-seven to twenty-nine (he was twenty-nine) the protean personality returns to values held around the age of seventeen. Second, the human spirit's quest for intimacy and love is deeper than the ego defenses that create the protean personality. True spiritual intimacy accomplishes that deeper reach when the self is grounded in the Holy Spirit of God and not the defensive ego.[27]

## (D) The Oppressed Mentality/Lifestyle

The fourth major lifestyle pattern implied by the sheer fact of the other three is the *oppressed* mentality. Oppressive lifestyles are generated out of the chronic realization that one will never be an achiever, one will always be in the out-group, dispossessed and powerless, with no way out, totally hopeless of change. The central dynamic here is passed on from generation to generation as parents communicate to infants (often by neglect or parental dependency and aggression) the sorrow, helplessness, and futility of life, as well as their frustrated longings for a higher way of life that eludes even their best, honest efforts. The result is a chronic erosion of self-esteem, and the psychological denial of aggression.

Abram Kardner and Lionel Oversy described the core psychological structure of this mentality some years ago in an article on "the Negro personality."[28] Below is an adaptation of that model (originally designed to apply to oppression in the black culture) to describe the dynamics of oppression in any oppressed minority. The authors set it up as follows:

---

27. See cases of protean orientation in chapter 6.
28. See Kardner and Oversy, "Negro," 259–66.

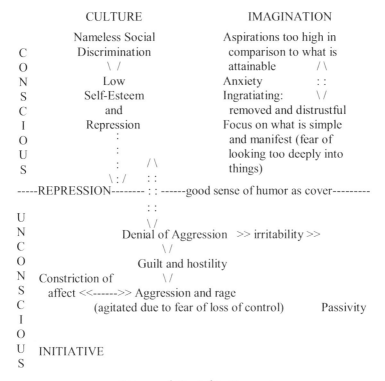

**Oppressed Mentality Dynamics**

In social contexts such as school, the oppressed person has no confidence. He or she resigns him- or herself to the bottom of the class, often drops out, lacks motivation, and fantasizes about the destruction of the enforced regime of public education and the nameless oppressor—"the system." The personality oppressed by the social system cannot learn, but must by law stay in the social context, where nonlearning and losing out become chronically and systemically reinforced day by day.

In cultural contexts, the dynamics of oppression, often reinforced by religion, support Marx's claim that religion functions as an opiate of the people. Indeed, oftentimes a great many oppressed persons receive commendation by their oppressors for their "Christian humility," not realizing that there is no humility without a strong sense of personal identity. Of course the longing for a better life makes oppressed persons fair game for opportunistic and exploitative evangelists and the emotionalism of certain sects in which the practice of religion consists largely of catharsis and re-socialization in the oppressive context. A classic study by Liston Pope, *Millhands and Preachers*, written many years ago in Gastonia, North Carolina, showed how important it was for the oppressed millhands to go to church on Sunday because the pent up hostilities associated with life in the mill needed to be drained off in a cathartic worship service. Otherwise the number of accidents and absences in the mill would increase.

In relation to this style of life, I want to stress the insightful educational implications of Paulo Freire's two works, *Pedagogy of the Oppressed* and *Education for Conscientization*. He, more than any other educator, was able to identify and liberate the dynamics of oppression to instigate change. As he himself said, he did not go far enough since he did not have sufficient understanding of the direction the revolution he started should take. He did not know how to avoid the consequences of revolution that Paul Lehmann described: "Revolutions devour their children."[29] Nevertheless, he managed to use education very effectively for the undoing of the binds implicit in the structure of oppression.

Freire addressed what he called "the culture of silence" in oppressive contexts with a literacy program. Here recall Betty Friedan's heralding of the feminist movement by describing women's oppression as a "problem with no name." The continuation of oppression depends on and thrives in contexts in which three "silent" conditions exist: (a) those in which oppressed persons are not conscious of their condition as an oppressive social construction of reality; (b) those in which oppressed persons are unable to name their oppressor as oppressor; and (c) those in which oppressed persons lack a sense of self-determination to take the cultural action necessary to liberate themselves and their oppressors. Freire coined the term *conscientization* to communicate what a liberative educative process must achieve in light of any and all oppressive "cultures of silence."

In order to overcome the "culture of silence" and liberate oppressed persons Freire went with his team into the migrant worker camps of Brazil and Chile where they lived for about six months with the people. There they discovered key generative terms like "slum" (*favela*) that named the workers' context. In class sessions with the workers, Freire broke the word *favela* into syllables and taught the workers to rearrange the syllables to make and pronounce new words. For example,

> *favela* à *vela* à candle à *vivo* à I live

When oppressed persons or communities discovered they could read and write, they realized also that they could *name*, and hence "conscientize,"

---

29. Editor's Note: Loder does not give the reference here, but he is probably referring to Lehmann's opening chapter of *Transfiguration*, 3, 7. Lehmann draws on Hannah Arendt in this discussion and takes up her thesis in *On Revolution* that "all revolutions devour their own children."

their situation. Being able to name their situation did two things for the workers. *First*, it gave them a sense of power over the oppressor by working a kind of personal redevelopment within them. That is, developmentally, a child's sense of autonomy and initiative comes with, and depends in part on, the use of language. To be able to read and write, to speak for oneself and therefore to create culture, gives rise to a new sense of selfhood. The experience of literacy for the migrant workers was so deeply moving at this level that they would enthusiastically ask Freire, "What shall we do?" Reminiscent and in terms of the Milgram experiment cited at the conclusion of the last chapter, Freire gave to these people "a language of nonconformity" that worked only because it linked speech directly to the empowerment of the human spirit. What dawned on them in this context was what Freire called their sense of "ontological vocation"—their call to name and create their own world. This vocation depends upon a person's ability to problematize—to name the problem in their existence and determine in corporate agreement, what shall we do?

However, naming the problem is only the first step in the liberation of the human spirit. *Second*, naming the oppressive context calls out for a larger, transcendent context in which humanization becomes a true possibility. This larger, transcendent context is needed, for as Daniel Schipani pointed out in his book, *Conscientization and Creativity: Paulo Freire and Christian Education*, the underlying aggression when released may be too strong, and the reaction more violent, than the original oppressive situation engendered. So what is needed is a larger context in which to understand the liberated human spirit. From a theological standpoint, this larger context is the context of worship in which the human spirit is taken up, transformed, and confirmed in the Spirit of God. We will have much more to say about the context of worship as the only suitable context for the liberation of the human spirit out from all the dehumanizing lifestyles we have discussed in this chapter.

## (IV) CONCLUSION[30]

I have sought in this chapter to further C. E. Nelson's concern to identify the power of socialization for its impact on the educational ministry of the church. However, in doing so I have reversed and negated Nelson's judgment that socialization is the key that unlocks our prospects for understanding

30. Editor's Note: This chapter contained no conclusion. In order to follow Loder's general pattern of recapitulating his argument at the end of each chapter, I wrote this conclusion in a way I imagined he might write it.

and developing a Christian style of life. I have argued that socialization is not the positive transformative power Nelson claims it to be. Rather, socialization is the controlling force in a fallen world that generates destructive lifestyles that permeate and determine the church's empirical existence in ways that quench the Spirit and falsify Christ's witness. The Apostle Paul admonished the Roman church: "*Do not be conformed to the world but be transformed by the renewal of your mind.*" I argued in this chapter that the dehumanizing power of conformity lies exactly here in the socialization dynamics Nelson wants to sanctify. But these dynamics cannot be sanctified in the way Nelson suggests, because they serve the *pattern-maintenance, tension-reduction* concerns that permeate unredeemed cultures in the interests of survival, preservation, and satisfaction. They domesticate the transformational potential that the Spirit seeks to awaken and enable in the socialized context to bring about new life. "*Do not be conformed to the world but be transformed*" (Rom 12:2).

I identified four dehumanizing lifestyles that socialization dynamics tend to generate and reproduce in our cultural context. Each of these lifestyles fundamentally distorts the true spirit of Christian faithfulness and thereby destroys both the communal integrity of congregational life and the community's witness to Christ in the world. The false lifestyles discussed in this chapter were (1) lifestyles dominated by an *achievement* obsession that erodes our ability to really care for the other, destroying motivation; (2) lifestyles dominated by an *authoritarian* paranoia that hollows out the inner life and destroys the social order by recasting it in terms of "us" versus "them"; (3) lifestyles characterized by a *protean* obsession with continual self-creation that diminishes commitments, engenders cynicism, and dissolves cultural cohesion; and (4) lifestyles developed amid *oppressive* contexts in which both those oppressed and those who oppress are enslaved in a fated world of winners and losers.

Churches captured by these kinds of socialized lifestyles may on the surface be liturgically sound, orthodox in thinking, active in outreach, and growing in numbers. But they will remain spiritually corrupt and bear the seeds of their own destruction unless and until they are transformed by a truly sanctifying power of greater magnitude than socialization—the Holy Spirit. The Spirit must be allowed to work in all dimensions of human existence, including the formation of the personality itself, if sanctification is to truly take hold in human experience. Our next chapter contends that for the most part theorists of human development and Christian education continue to generate their insights within the framework of unredeemed socialization dynamics—a framework that makes little room for the work of the Spirit.

# 4

# Human Development and Personality Formation

*The Socialization Approach*

## (I) INTRODUCTION: DEVELOPMENTAL INTERACTIONISM

YOU WILL RECALL FROM our study of Nelson's theory the emphasis he made on cultural, societal, and personality socialization. We have discussed and critiqued the first two of these dimensions. In this chapter, before moving in the next to the task of constructing a transformational theory of Christian education, we must examine the foundations of personality formation as it appears in Christian education theories dominated by socialization.

The specific definition of human development with which we will be working is as follows: *Normal human development is an emergent reality, a resultant of the interaction between a personality and its environment, whereby the potential structures of the personality are given particular and varied shape over the course of a lifetime.*[1] This definition reflects an *interactionist* or a *constructionist* understanding of human development, since it is being

---

1. Much of what I will be discussing in this chapter was originally published in another form. See Loder, "Developmental Foundations," 54–67. Editor's Note: Loder's understanding of development was shaped in part in relation to Bernard Lonergan, "Elements," 431–87, see especially ibid., 451–55. This generic definition reflects Lonergan's influence but is not, as far as I can tell, a direct quote from Lonergan.

thought of as the emergent result of organism-environment interaction. In interactional theories, development takes place between two polarities, between the organism and the environment. For example, language is a potential of the personality that is given particular and varied shape as the child interacts with her cultural environment. A child babbles spontaneously, but if language is to emerge this babbling requires a linguistic environment. In a nonlinguistic environment, children babble for a little while, but eventually it (the babbling) drops off. Children raised in such an environment—as in the case of children who are kept in an attic or raised by wolves—do not learn to speak human language.

There are four phases of language development: First, *holophrastic* speech occurs, in which a child will use just one word to convey a whole environment of meaning. The child will say, "Ball." What she may means is, "I go get the ball"; "Let's play ball"; "See the ball"; "Aren't I smart, playing with the ball"; and so forth. Second, *patterned* speech emerges at twelve to eighteen months of age, in which the "combinations of words may often seem random and the meanings bizarre, but this is not the case. Even the first word combinations are organized according to definite principles."[2] In context, "Bill ball," may mean, "Bill, throw the ball"; or "I see Bill and the ball." Third comes *grammatical* speech. By the age of four grammatical structures begin to emerge, and the child often becomes more grammatical than the environment. For example, a girl might say "sheeps" instead of "sheep." In any case, the flow of speech in one's native tongue, from Swahili to German to English, will begin sometime after the age of four.

Finally, *intelligent* speech develops when intelligence brings language under control by about age seven. Still, the interplay between language and intelligence will continue for the full course of one's lifetime. In our culture, children learn to speak English, not Chinese, because the particular language and the particular structure of the language learned reflect the dominant linguistic community in which the child is raised. Language as an example of development is an emergent reality that comes out of the interaction of the language potential of the personality with a particular linguistic environment.

By locating development in the interaction between the personality and its environment, and by asserting that it is an emergent *gestalt* that synthesizes environmental influences and personality potentials, certain views of development are inevitably discounted. For instance, *preformationism* is discounted. Anton van Leewenhoek held this naïve, seventeenth-century notion. Studying sperm under his microscope, he thought he saw miniature

2. McNeill, *Acquisition*, 19.

animals. He hypothesized that these miniatures simply expanded into maturity. By this view, development takes place in a balloon fashion in which the preformed life in miniature simply expands. Before you laugh too long at the idea, understand that as soon as you address and/or treat a female child like a "little lady" or a male child a "big man" you are exhibiting a preformationist mentality. When you say, "Act like a lady!" or "Be a man!" you exhibit preformationist morality. Thus, although denigrated in theory, preformationism is still alive and well in dehumanizing practice.

A second view to discount here is *predeterminism*. This view assumes that preset biological mechanisms exercise exclusive determination over development. Predeterminist G. Stanley Hall, founder of child psychology in the United States in the late nineteenth century, propounded a developmental Darwinism summed up in the phrase "ontogeny recapitulates phylogeny." This view fails to take sufficient account of the uniqueness of human development, assuming, as it does, that children's minds develop into adulthood in the same way mature frogs develop from tadpoles. Predeterminists imagine the inevitable unfolding of a developmental process governed mostly by the organ itself. In this view, the innate biological forces that impact human development are overestimated while the human capacity to create oneself uniquely in relation to one's environment is underestimated.[3]

A third view that is also discredited by the basic premises of interactionalism is *environmentalism*. This view of the early behaviorists, notably John Watson, assumed that by controlled training any newborn child could be molded into any type of adult. Contemporary behaviorists such as B. F. Skinner take more account of genetic factors and neurological findings than Watson did, but they make similar claims regarding the power of the environment to determine the shape of adult personality. Environmentalism makes the same mistake as predeterminism, but from the outside in rather than from the inside out. It fails to take account of human uniqueness, assuming that persons can be shaped in all registers of behavior by the same techniques that shape the responses of laboratory rats and pigeons. In this kind of discussion, two questions are traditionally raised: How much is nature? And how much is nurture? Interactional developmentalists, however, do not concern themselves so much with this quantity question. Rather, assuming that there is interaction of some degree, they want to know not, how much? but, *how* does development takes place?

---

3. Lower organisms are largely genetically programmed for their environment before birth. But humans are born unfinished—i.e., a large portion of the cerebral cortex has to create and be created in relation to its environment. This "deficiency" is why it is so unfortunate to socialize the potential of persons without giving full play to the dynamic power of that potential, which transformation implies.

## (II) STAGES OF DEVELOPMENT

The interactionist view of development has been most influential at the foundational level in Christian education theories. As already described above with regard to language, interaction in development takes place in stages. Generally, Christian educators focus primarily on stages of development when they use the developmental material foundationally. The reason for educational interest in stages is to determine readiness for learning. As Christian educators, we are interested in the stage of the learner, because we want to teach in accord with the learner's readiness to learn. More broadly speaking, we want to cooperate with growth—i.e., with the developmental process inherent in the child. We do not want to be either neglectful or intrusive in our educational interventions.

Let me at this point give you my definition of a stage. A stage is *a relatively stable equilibrium between personality and environment, which is incorporated into subsequent development of the person.* By way of our previous example, "patterned speech" is incorporated into but transformed by "grammatical speech." When the child is born, thrust into a new environment, her life is characterized by a great deal of random activity. She's grasping, sucking, kicking, screaming, and so on. But then at about eighteen months, if she develops positively, she gains a very significant level of equilibrium characterized by a sense of basic trust (but never apart from a degree of mistrust) in relation to her environment. If she develops negatively, she gains a qualitatively different equilibrium characterized by a dominant mistrust (but never apart from a degree of trust). This equilibrium, whether positive or negative, signals the completion of the first stage of ego development

## (A) Ego and Repression

In addition to stages, another central concept in theories of human development surrounds the term *ego* in the psychoanalytic tradition. All of the major theories refer primarily to ego development. Ego by definition is *the intrapsychic agency that balances psychic reality over against environmental reality by means of the Reality Principle.* The Reality Principle ensures that the ego learns to order the personality's development according to realistic assessments about what it means to survive and to thrive with maximum satisfaction over the course of a lifetime. Ego orders all that is going on *outside* the self—social restraints, cultural demands, environmental conditions, and so forth, with all that is going on *inside* of the self—the demands from the unconscious, the body, appetites, desires, dreams, the sense of conscience, and so forth, according to the Reality Principle. In this crucible ego asks a dizzying array of questions: Can it really happen? Who are the real people? How can I really tell? What am I relating to? Am I putting too much of me into them—i.e., projecting? "Or are they projecting, dumping too much of themselves onto me and calling it me?" Ego can be diagrammed as follows:

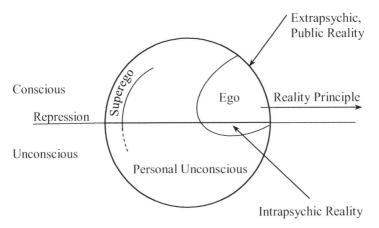

**The Structure of the Ego**

The ego accomplishes its task by the primary maneuver of repression. *Repression* means *unconscious* forgetting, as opposed to *suppression*, which means *conscious* or intentional forgetting. In terms of repression, we recognize the enormous amount of stimuli that confronts us unconsciously each moment, most of which we have no control over and for which we cannot take account. Thus, a considerable amount of repression is absolutely necessary. Without the capacity to repress, you could not sit there and read this book. You repress most of the stimuli that are bombarding you all the time. If you did not repress stimuli, you would be reduced to a mass of confusing responses. Thus, primary repression is actually healthy, provided it is flexible and reversible and not secondary, rigid, irreversible, and restricting. Secondary repression occurs when you begin to constrict your world because you feel so threatened. The ego excludes those things from consciousness that are going to get in the way, or disturb, or demand immediate gratification and so defeat the healthier focus on long-term gratification. Ego with its sense of time, space, and distance, its sense of what is happening out there, negotiates with the environment for the benefit of your survival and your satisfaction.

When we speak of development then, we mean the development of the ego's increased competence to establish equilibrium between personality and environment, to manage ever-greater complexity with ever-greater efficiency. For an understanding of this development, let us turn to Erik Erikson, a neo-Freudian who worked in the psychoanalytic tradition.

## (B) Ego Development: Erik Erikson

Erik Erikson (1902–1984) was one of the very first in the psychoanalytic tradition to take psychoanalysis of children seriously. Originally he was an artist, wandering around and through Europe. After receiving an invitation to go to Vienna, he became involved with Sigmund Freud's psychoanalytic circle there, and was eventually psychoanalyzed by Freud's daughter, Anna. All of this background is important for understanding that Erikson was not a medical doctor and received only honorary doctorates. He worked with and trusted his intuitions such that the genius of his literature depended upon his ability to make intuitive leaps into what constitutes a definitive stage of human development. His theorizing was not imaginary, but it was imaginative. That is, his argumentation worked effectively to disclose rather than to obscure what is present in human development. He made his arguments. He took up cases. But this research generally served and supported his intuitive powers.

Erikson believed that in each stage of its development, the ego comes up with a qualitative new sense of itself. The term *sense* is used with discretion here because in Erikson's thinking the subject himself cannot objectify the patterns of ego formation Erikson described. Rather the subject, sensing the patterns, tests his intuitions out in behaviors responding to the social and cultural context to discover whether or not they prove valid. Each ego state is a kind of multidimensional equilibrium, which for all of its interrelatedness to physical, psychic, social, and cultural factors has a relatively stable autonomy of its own.

The dynamics of development follow from stage to stage, as one ego state finds itself too heavily and persistently conflicted from such factors as physical growth, emerging competencies, and environmental demands. For example, take the case of language again. Children know that the language in their environment carries meanings beyond their group. This conflict gives rise to new competencies. When confronted in this way, the ego either expands in complexity toward a new sense of stable autonomy, or it may be overcome by negative environmental factors if its creative, conflict-resolving potential is not permitted to function with sufficient support. Thus, development in Erikson's scheme follows a conflict-resolution process over the course of a lifetime.

Erikson described eight stages through which the ego moves as it increases in its capacity to manage the complexity of the self-environment interaction with greater and greater simplicity and vision. Each stage embodies a new instance of equilibrium.[4] The eight stages of this dynamic development are as follow:

| Psychosocial Crises | Radius of Significant Relations | Related Elements of the Social Order | Rudiments of Ego Strength |
|---|---|---|---|
| Basic Trust vs. Basic Mistrust | Maternal person | Religion and the cosmic order | Hope |
| Autonomy vs. Shame, Doubt | Paternal person | Law and social order | Will |
| Initiative vs. Guilt | Basic family | Theater and ideal prototypes | Purpose |
| Industry vs. Inferiority | Neighborhood school | Technological elements | Competence |
| Identity vs. Role Confusion | Peer groups, model of leadership | Ideological perspectives | Fidelity |
| Intimacy vs. Isolation | Partners in friendship, sex, competition, cooperation | Patterns of cooperation and competition | Love |
| Generative vs. Stagnation | Divided labor and shared household | Currents of education and Tradition | Care |
| Ego Integrity vs. Despair | "Humankind" "My Kind" | Collective Wisdom | Wisdom |

### *Erickson's Eight Stages of Psycho-Social Development*

Erikson called the first stage Trust vs. Mistrust. What does that mean? In simple terms, Erikson means that by the time a child is eighteen months

---

4. It is probably not sufficiently stressed just how Hegelian Erikson's scheme is. Erikson always asserts that a positive ego state, or a successful resolution, represents a synthesis of affirmative and negative aspects in the struggle for adaptation rather than a liability.

of age, his whole psyche, including his body and sense of his environment, has made up its mind—its ego—as to whether it can predominantly trust the environment or not. The random behavior of the newborn, which include sucking, grasping, reaching, reacting, crying, smiling, sleeping, and so forth, all come gradually to focus on this one major issue—do I trust or mistrust myself in this threatening environment?

The mother's task here is to construct with her body, by stroking and nurturing the child, an environment that stimulates the comfort, support, and assurance that the child became accustomed to for nine months in utero. The child makes this transition from womb to trust, not simply by replicating the earlier situation, but also by learning what can be reached and not reached, what soothes or hurts to bite, and how it feels to fall and be left alone or to be cuddled. He learns trust not simply by trusting everything, but also by learning to mistrust certain things, situations, persons, and impulses while continuing to reach out in exploration of his world and himself. Thus, the child's trust incorporates limits and grows all the more trusting because he learns both what must be trusted and what must be mistrusted.

All subsequent developments in the ego are based on this primary issue. Thus, if ego is to be healthy, there must be equilibrium established that gives the predominance to trust over mistrust. Still mistrust must also be included for the sake of boundaries and survival. In terms of our earlier discussion, ego development is a combination of socialization and transformation in which socialization is dominant, so that all the transformations that occur here are in the service of conformation to existing sociocultural norms. For example, in the next stage, the child learns to say "I" as her sense of autonomy emerges, but always over against the threats of the social environment, which are expressed in terms of shame. By the end of the second year a second equilibrium has been established, which has built upon the first. In resolution of the Autonomy vs. Shame stage predominance must be given to autonomy, but still shame is included as a social limit. One does not want to grow up shameless.

Another key technical term in Erikson's approach that you should know is *epigenetic*. Epigenetic means that a certain scheduling is involved in human development such that the child must deal with certain appropriate crises "on time." This notion has its basis in the step-by-step physiological development of fetal organs. Each organ has its appointed time for emergence. If it does not arise at that time, it will never be able to express itself fully because the appointed time for some other part will have arrived. This newer organ will tend to dominate the less active organ. Moreover, failure of one organ to develop fully tends to impair the whole developmental schedule and the hierarchy of organs. By analogy and extension of this physiological model, Erikson proposed that ego development over the course of a lifetime follows an epigenetic schedule through the eight major stages noted above. Each phase, characterized by a critical opposition in one's sense of self, emerges according to this schedule. The phase then passes with the resolution of the opposition in a dominance of one side over the other.

The model taken rigidly would seem to say that each resolution is destiny for that person. But Erikson did not hold strictly to this view. Such a view would seriously undermine psychotherapy and analysis. On the contrary, the whole conceptual scheme is to be heuristically used as a model of ego structures for reflection upon therapy, development, and education. The epigenetic notion connects the stages, making them interdependent and putting them on a time schedule that becomes generatively heuristic for the therapeutic task.

Erikson's acceptance in religious circles has been built in part on his developmental view of *virtue*, another important concept. In *Insight and Responsibility*, he set up a schedule for the developmental emergence of virtues—pervading strengths—that follow the epigenetic sequence. He described how the ego comes to manifest its structures of biosocial adjustment at any particular stage in relation to macrostructures of the social order and even the cosmos. Such manifestations are reciprocal interactions between the ego and its environment, which have been stabilized as strengths (virtues) upon which the ego can rely. Virtues build into the personality qualities of actual life that combine over the course of development to integrate the whole person in relation to the world.[5] What Erikson gave to us is a cumulative sequence by which the normal ego develops its capacity to manage greater and greater complexity in relationship with the most important people in one's environment, with greater efficiency.

As we have said, all major theories of human development focus on ego development. For instance, there are those who focus on the ego's development of intelligence (Jean Piaget), moral development (Lawrence Kohlberg, Carol Gilligan), or its comprehensive capacity to relate to universals, sometimes called "faith" development (James Fowler). We move now to discuss these three aspects of ego development before making a theological response to this same body of work.

5. See the diagram of Erikson's theory above.

## (C) The Developmental of Intelligence: Jean Piaget

Within the interactionist approach to development, Jean Piaget is considered to be a structuralist. That is, he focused his attention on the emergent structures within the ego, especially intelligence. He is less concerned with *what* you know than with *how* you think. By analogy, one might be more interested in grammar and how it works than in semantics or anything that was actually said. Furthermore, as an heir of the French intellectual tradition (René Descartes, Jean-Jacques Rousseau, Claude Levi-Strauss), he is more interested in the development of intellectual aspects of the ego than in interpersonal relationships or the unconscious life.[6]

First, a brief biographical note on Piaget himself is helpful. He did most of his work in Geneva, Switzerland, but he also taught philosophy at the Sorbonne and worked with Simon (of the Simon-Binet intelligence test) in Paris before he began the work in Geneva for which he is famous. When he was a boy, Piaget wandered around the lakes of Neuchâtel making remarkable observations. He had an enduring interest in biology. For example, he noticed how the mollusks splashed back and forth beneath the water of the lake, as part of their adaptational endeavors, and he eventually wrote a paper on the topic. He was instinctively a very shrewd observer of all he saw. When he was just ten, he wrote and published his first professional paper on an albino sparrow that he observed in the park. By the time he was twenty he had published some twenty-five professional papers. On the basis of his published work, a museum in Geneva even offered him the curatorship until they found out that he was only fifteen years old!

Piaget was a *bona fide* genius, and his insights derived most frequently from his astute powers of observation. That is why, when he finally came to do the research that has made him famous, he accomplished it by observing only two or three of his own children, a scandal according to the canons of psychological research in America. Nevertheless, these observations on his own children and the research that issued from the observations have

---

6. Editor's Note: Loder had a long-standing interest in Piaget. Not only did he read Piaget's corpus, but he also received an American Association of Theological Schools research fellowship to do postdoctoral work at Piaget's Jean J. Rousseau's Institut des Sciences de l' Education in Geneva in 1968–69. He probably should be considered one of the foremost interpreters of Piaget in the United States, explicating Piaget's potential for integration with epistemology and theology. After Loder's death, one of his students recovered an eighty-page chapter on Piaget and a table of contents that seemed to be part of a mammoth work on practical theology that he apparently planned to write. These materials are in the Loder archive at Speer Library, Princeton Theological Seminary.

influenced American psychology more than the work of any other theorist with the exceptions of Freud and Skinner.

Piaget's early observations of children focused mainly on the development of the structures of intelligence. These structures in turn influenced his understanding of development in other registers of behavior such as language, imagination, and moral judgment. The basic unit of development for Piaget is the organism interacting with the environment. The dynamics of development are assimilation, accommodation, adaptation, and *schema* or habit. He called these interactions "*invariant functions*." When Piaget looked at mollusks, birds, people, indeed every kind of biological phenomenon, he saw that every organic form of life functions fundamentally in this invariant interactionist way.

*Assimilation* has to do with the way the organism takes something from the environment into itself. *Accommodation* has to do with the way the organism alters or modifies itself to attain what is in the environment. The interplay between the inner frame and the outer frame—i.e., the inner life of the organism and its outer environmental life—eventuates in *adaptation* or stages of relatively stable equilibrium. The dynamics of adaptation, then, are what give rise to *intelligence* in humans, because, for Piaget, intelligence is simply a highly differentiated, highly efficient way of adapting to one's environment. Thus at the level of mind, the structure of intelligence will be the outcome of the interplay between assimilation and accommodation in the child.

The nature of this interplay is important. For example, the dominance of assimilation over accommodation is *play*. In play, you take something like a piece of chalk and make it into all sorts of things, from a gun to a cigarette to a small microphone. When you do this, you are taking something that was made for a specific environmental use and assimilating it to your own internal frame of reference. You are imagining it for your own purposes. Thus, assimilation over accommodation is the formal definition of play. On the other hand, the dominance of environment over organism, or accommodation over assimilation is *imitation*. That is, when one is simply imitating another, one allows something or someone in the environment to temporarily become one's internal frame of reference. Thus, we must play and imitate or indwell something in order to come to know it, to become intelligent about it. Over time, basic structures develop in the intelligent ego to give us rapid access to known objects, words, and ideas. These are the structures of intelligence that provide the grounding for highly efficient methods or procedures of adaptation to highly complex situations. Thus, the interaction between play and imitation yields intelligence.

For Piaget there are four stages through which intelligence develops in order to maximize this innate potential. The first is *sensorimotor* intelligence. The second is *intuitive* or *preoperational* intelligence. The third is *concrete* operations. The fourth is *formal* operations. By "operations," Piaget is thinking of mathematical or logical procedures: adding or subtracting, classifying or deducing.

*Sensorimotor* interaction is the first stage of intelligence. An example of sensorimotor behavior is the child grasping. Grasping is, after all, the intelligent thing to do when you need to get hold of something. Or, the child is sucking. That too is an intelligent move. Infants know they need to grasp and suck in order to survive. In order to suck or to grasp, you have to assimilate and accommodate. You assimilate by taking the food in, but you have to accommodate your mouth to the food. The interplay keeps you nourished. At a somewhat more advanced level the child puts things together and pulls them apart, puts them together again and pulls them apart again. Did you ever watch a child doing this? It's beyond interesting. What are they doing? They are adding, subtracting, multiplying and dividing. In physical ways, the child is laying the foundation for the highest forms of intellectual sophistication. We should note that although we move beyond this stage developmentally, we may return to it to get new ideas. This works because our bodies are our basic link to the universe. Michael Faraday and James Clerk Maxwell both relied on *embodied* mathematics to lay the foundation for the theory of relativity. So sensorimotor intelligence predominates in terms of the child's relationship to the environment until the age of about eighteen months, when the symbolic function emerges.

The move from sensorimotor to *intuitive* or *preoperational* intelligence occurs with the emergence of the capacity of the child to construct the environment mentally in symbols. By the time the child is eighteen months, there is some patterned speech, but that is not the key. The key is the ability to reconstruct in one's imagination a situation in the past and play it out in the present or future. Piaget illustrates this capacity from an event in the life of his daughter Jacqueline. Jacqueline and the family were visiting with friends one Sunday afternoon, when the little girl in the other family threw a tantrum that Jacqueline simply watched. The next day smiling all the time, Jacqueline threw the identical tantrum at home. Piaget said, "Aha! The move from stage one to stage two, from sensorimotor behavior to the capacity for preoperational thinking." In other words, his daughter had developed the ability to grasp a situation, put it into her head symbolically, and then reconstruct it imaginatively in a new situation.

You need to be able to exercise this quality of intelligence in order to advance to the next stage in intelligence. So preoperational intelligence, or intuitive thinking, depends upon the constructive capacity of the imagination. Note that thinking here is not imaginary but imaginative. That is, intuitive thinking allows you to reenter the real environment through the powers of symbol and imagination. This period from two to seven is probably the least studied of Piaget's stages. But a great deal is going on in the life of the child at this stage, including the emergence of grammatical competencies. Piaget was primarily interested in how one develops logical thinking, and during this time, the child develops the capacity to generalize, classify, and subclassify.

Toward the end of this period, around the age of five or six, the child learns spontaneously to think *transductively*. In transductive thinking you have an understanding of classification, but you don't know how to relate the classes logically. Therefore, a child just moving out of the preoperational period will typically say, "Italians eat spaghetti, we're eating spaghetti, so we must be Italian." You can tell the child is beginning to classify and is aware of categories and generalizations. But she is not able to put the categories and generalizations in relationship to each other to advance thought and understanding.

After the age of six, transductive thinking becomes deductive and inductive thinking. The child begins to relate classes and classifications of things systematically and to appropriate the relationship between deductive and inductive thinking. A little later, about age seven, the development of *logical* thinking begins to take over language and intelligence. Children begin their study of formal mathematics, and they learn in more formal and objective ways just how to do the addition and subtraction they did intuitively and preoperationally before. Sometimes they can learn it earlier than age seven, but this is the generalized norm that Piaget found in the hundreds of children he eventually studied throughout the Genevan school system. What characterizes this period, from about age six or seven to eleven, is that the child is increasingly able to do the kind of logical thinking that one would find in a textbook in mathematics, or any kind of text that requires systematic reasoning.

But the child's thinking during this period remains bound to *concrete* reality. The child thinks logically, but only about concrete things. The child can think about the problem in the text only in the way the text or the concrete situation sets it up. What the child is *not* aware of until age eleven is that he or she is thinking. At the age of eleven, the young person can begin to think about thinking. This stage is the final major advance in intelligence in Piaget's model. When you can think about thinking, you learn to set up the world in terms of propositions you create. You can imagine and structure realistic problems. You can explore hypotheses out of your intellectual imagination and examine them mentally for their capacity to solve a given problem. You can anticipate conclusions, eliminate certain hypotheses, and bring the most likely ones to an empirical test. In effect, when you have reached the level of formal operations, you can do conventional "scientific thinking."

There is an interesting period at the beginning of adolescence when it first dawns on the child, "I can think!" She experiences what Piaget called "the omnipotence of intelligence," believing she can solve any and every problem there is. That's a good, healthy kind of narcissism. Only gradually do adolescents learn that problem solving is a little harder than they first thought. But the structural impetus to this sense of intellectual omnipotence is the new capacity to think about thinking. This development is extremely important. According to Piaget, the attainment of this formal operational thinking capacity is the goal of the development of intelligence.

Two more points about the overall movement toward intellectual development in Piaget's thought need to be made. First, movement through these stages, as emphasized by all the structuralists, is fundamentally a move from egocentric mentality to the widest exocentric mentality possible. Children are egocentric, not in the sense of morality (selfishness), but because there is in them a mental structure of egocentricity. Young children simply cannot think any way but in reference to themselves.

Tami and I used to go out for a walk when she was three. As we went out the front door down the walkway I would say, "Where do we live, Tami?"

She responded by pointing behind her and saying, "Right back there." Okay. We continued walking down the street, but then turned the corner.

I would say again, "Tami, where do we live?"

"Right back there." Again she pointed behind her.

I said, "No, over there. We turned the corner."

She would say, "No! Right back there!"

Why did she make this "mistake"? For three-year-old Tami, everything was understood in reference to her. It's not because she was selfish. But the structure of her intelligence was not able to get outside of itself and allow her to think from a larger perspective.

A second observation that needs to be made in reference to Piaget's theorizing is that the sequence of intellectual development is not inevitable, as it was in Erikson. You do not necessarily progress beyond concrete operations. Still the progress you make will be sequential. In other words, the sequence is *invariant*, but it is not *inevitable*. In point of fact, no matter whose view of development one studies within the structuralist frame of reference, or what particular register of the ego's behavior you investigate— moral judgment, language, imagination, intelligence, or relationality—one moves sequentially from egocentricity toward a more exocentric and universal understanding.

## (D) Moral Development: Lawrence Kohlberg and Carol Gilligan

Lawrence Kohlberg used Piaget's same structuralist assumptions but applied them to the development of moral judgment—a study that Piaget had already begun in Geneva. If you look at the following chart, you can see how Kohlberg set up the stages in the development of moral judgment.

**Preconventional**

    1. Heteronomous Morality

    2. Instrumental Exchange

**Conventional**

    3. Mutual Interpersonal Relations

    4. Social System and Conscience

**Postconventional Principled**

    5. Social Contract, Individual Rights

    6. Universal Ethical Principles[7]

Obviously in accord with Piaget's view of intelligence, Kohlberg theorized that the direction out of the earlier stages is from egocentrism to exocentrism and universality. Moreover, the sequence is invariant. One cannot move from stage 2 to stage 4 without going through stage 3. Indeed one cannot even understand the position of those who are two stages above one's own. Thus, a person at Stage 6, refusing on ethical grounds to fight in an unjust war, might be seen by a stage 4 person as being in Stage 2, selfish and only willing to do something in a context of equal exchange. Also, one tends to be particularly critical of persons who are just one stage below, as if that stage were particularly threatening or especially despised because it is the one most recently transcended.

    Of particular interest to us is the work Kohlberg did during the 1960s at Harvard University with Harvard students related to motivation. He found several students who responded to his testing approach at a stage 6 level, but who in effect said, "So what?" In other words, they had no answer to the question, why be moral?" Kohlberg tried to construct a stage 7 to

---

7. Editor's Note: This chart is Loder's distillation of Kohlberg's theory.

establish the subject's philosophical or theological basis for whatever stage was indicated for the first scale. This effort eventually proved unsatisfactory and was not finally incorporated before the time of Kohlberg's death. His effort points, however, to a perennial problem largely overlooked by developmentalists: what is the meaning and purpose of the development that one is undergoing?

Before we move on, we must look at Kohlberg's most effective and widely read critic, Carol Gilligan. First methodologically, she is rightly critical of Kohlberg's testing procedures, which were based upon a subject's response to *hypothetical* moral dilemmas (e.g., should a man steal a drug to save his wife's life if he can get it no other way?). In distinction, Gilligan interviewed actual women who faced the question of whether or not to have abortions—i.e., real ethical dilemmas they were suffering. Also, Gilligan was rightly critical of a male bias in the scheme that claimed universality. Because most women in Kohlberg's testing came out at stage 3, she claimed that the whole scheme had a built-in male bias favoring the development of autonomy and universality at the expense of relationality. For Gilligan, Kohlberg's work not only reflected male bias but also, more seriously, an unfair ethical posture.

Gilligan, therefore, developed her own scale, still working as a structuralist. The content of the women's comments (what they decided to do in response to a real crisis) was not as important as how they thought about doing what they did. Her study first appeared in the *Harvard Educational Review* in 1977. Since then she has written *In a Different Voice*, which considerably expanded upon her initial study and departed from the use of any hierarchy. She did subsequent work researching the adolescent development of boys as well as girls. Gilligan's original sequencing of the stages of moral development is as follows:

I. Orientation to Individual Survival

First Transition: From Selfishness to Responsibility

II. Goodness as Self-Sacrifice

Second Transition: From Goodness to Truth

III. The Morality of Nonviolence, An Ethic of Care[8]

If you look at the chart, you can again see that the movement is out of egocentrism into exocentricity. But now movement transpires through a deepening and widening sense of the significance of relationality. This focus seems much closer to the sort of ethic we would want to affirm theologically.

8. Gilligan, "In a Different Voice," 481–517.

But still the larger theological or philosophical question, why be moral? remains unanswered in Gilligan's work as well.

## (III) FAITH DEVELOPMENT: JAMES FOWLER

The theologian who has worked most fully and is most widely read within the structuralist approach is James Fowler.[9] In Fowler's work, we have the integration of Erikson, Piaget, Kohlberg, and other theories of development into a structuralist view of the whole person. According to Fowler, everyone has "faith," which he defines as our comprehensive way of seeing and knowing the world. Since everybody has a way of seeing and knowing the world, everybody has faith.[10]

The basic structure of faith in Fowler, derived from H. Richard Niebuhr, is triadic, interrelating the self, others, and shared centers of value and power. Faith is also dynamic, a verb not a noun. That is, you are always using your way of knowing and seeing things to navigate through life. Thus, it is by "*faith-ing*" that you compose the world and put yourself into it. But of course your perception and knowledge of the world is continuously developing. So faith develops. Faith development is, thus, development in one's way of seeing and knowing oneself in relation to the world and the constructs of ultimate reality the world possesses. Again movement is out of egocentricity and toward universality, the universality of seeing and knowing.

Fowler designed an interview format that allowed people to tell their life stories in response to specific questions. Once they had been transcribed, he scored each interview on each of seven variables. In this way he sought to discern the stage structure of the person's faith. Faith always has a triadic

---

9. Editor's Note: Loder's academic dialogue with James Fowler was ongoing, substantial, and intense. When Fowler's book *Stages of Faith* and Loder's book *Transforming Moment* came out in 1981, the Religious Education Association sponsored a debate between them at Michigan State University early the next year. The two authors summarized their critiques of each other's work from the debate in the journal *Religious Education*. See Loder and Fowler, "Conversations," 133–48. Loder also used Fowler's research method in his doctoral seminar on human development for many years. He also wrote a substantive critique of Fowler's paradigm in *Logic of the Spirit*, 255–64. Richard Osmer, who studied under Fowler, also became a colleague of Loder's at Princeton for ten years. See Osmer's pre-Princeton article in *Religious Education*, "James W. Fowler," 51–68 for his early assessment of Fowler's work in relation to Loder's Reformed tradition.

10. More specifically, Fowler says that everyone who is not contemplating suicide has faith. Actually, his principle even applies in this extreme situation, because suicidal persons have faith that suicide will set things right.

structure, but as faith develops, the triad can be analyzed through seven lenses (variables). Let's briefly describe these variables.

(1) *Form of Logic.* This variable has to do with the stage of intelligence. Do I use formal operations to put my world together? Or, do I use concrete operations? Am I still thinking in the early forms of logic, even though I am a mature person age-wise?

(2) *Form of World Coherence.* A second variable concerns how I put my world together. Is the way I tell you about my world mainly narrative? When you ask me a question, do I tell you a story? Narrative may be a relatively immature way of putting a world together, as opposed to giving you a more conceptual or universalistic position. But not necessarily so.

(3) *Role-Taking.* The third variable has to do with how I see myself in relationship to the other persons who compose my world. Is it mainly my perception of them that dominates? Again the more complex and universal the mutuality of perspective and role-taking, the more advanced one's faith. I have a more mature faith if it manages more role complexity with greater coherence.

(4) *Locus of Authority.* This variable has to do with the authorization of action. Do I still do just what my mother says? Or is the locus of authority somehow more in me? Or is it in me and coming out of me in terms of my relationships—i.e., in terms of what significant others view as authoritative? Do I build up beliefs and ideologies that move toward a more universal perspective?

(5) *Bounds of Social Awareness.* The fifth variable has to do with the largeness of my world. If you talk to me about my world, do I bring in national and international affairs? Or is my world just my wife and me and our own two kids? The larger one's awareness, the less egocentric one's faith.

(6) *Form of Moral Judgment.* Fowler depends entirely on Kohlberg here. In this variable, the more universal one's rationale for judgment, the better and more mature is one's faith.

(7) *Role of Symbolization.* The seventh variable asks, does the person use language and symbols naively or with discernment? "That's the cross, and it has power in itself. That's why I wear it." Or do I demythologize the cross, always asking the question, what does the cross mean? But even that is relatively immature, because when you attempt to say what the cross means, it is necessarily impoverished. You can't really say

what it means. In the mature stages, you have to *reinvent* and *reincor-porate* symbols in a much more diverse sort of way, eventually getting to the place where you understand what is behind the symbols well enough to begin to invent new symbols. Now you are in stage 6 on the symbol scale.

Those are Fowler's variables.[11] Their relationships can be diagrammed as follows.

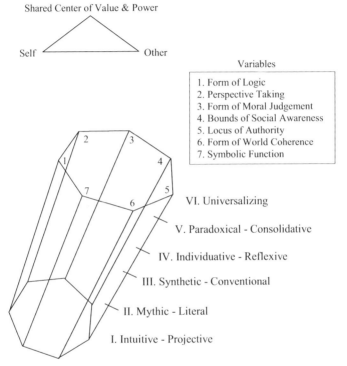

Variables

1. Form of Logic
2. Perspective Taking
3. Form of Moral Judgement
4. Bounds of Social Awareness
5. Locus of Authority
6. Form of World Coherence
7. Symbolic Function

VI. Universalizing

V. Paradoxical - Consolidative

IV. Individuative - Reflexive

III. Synthetic - Conventional

II. Mythic - Literal

I. Intuitive - Projective

### Fowler's Structural Model

Fowler argues that all the variables appear to develop at the same rate of change, hence the stage. The six stages that he isolates follow essentially the structuralist pattern, moving out of egocentrism to a more universal per-spective. Fowler places most Americans in stages 3 or 4 of faith development. Those in stage 4 (*Individuative-Reflective*) tend to think in dichotomizing sorts of ways. I'm not putting stage 4 people down; I'm just putting them in the system, which means that they want to get their system together. They

11. Editor's Note: Fowler charts these variables in *Stages*, 244–45. For Loder's schematization of these variables, see *Logic of the Spirit*, 256.

want to know where they stand. They want to know if they are Barthian. If a Barthian, they want to know how a good Barthian thinks. As dichotomizers, they tend to caricature people who are not in their system. Back of this, they are more dependent upon groups, face-to-face type relationships, and more interested in telling their own story about their life than in hearing yours. According to Fowler, one really cannot move beyond stage 4 until one has reached the age of thirty or suffered irreversible losses, since stage 5 means that one is taking account of the essentially disruptive quality of life itself.

In stage 6 (*Universalizing Faith*), persons get to the place where they see the whole world in terms of the nature of being. Fowler apparently found only one person whom he thought interviewed in terms of stage 6. Some people thought it was Thomas Merton, but we don't know. Let me turn now to a sustained critique of Fowler's faith development paradigm.

## (A) Critique of Fowler

From my point of view, Fowler's greatest contribution has been the interview method he developed as a way of gathering data on the formation and development of the phenomenon he calls "faith." There is increasingly less doubt in my mind that he has constructed a reliable method for gathering information from people through which to assess stages of faith. Some of my students and I consistently get results that, within certain limits, corroborate his findings.[12] However, in my judgment the more fundamental question his research raises is: What developmental phenomenon is he studying? More pointedly, how is his work to be understood as faith development in any definitive biblical or theological sense?

### (1) Fowler's Socialized Understanding of Faith vs. Biblical Faith

In my judgment, we have in Fowler's work one of the most pointed examples of the triumph of socialization over transformation. His work is no doubt a sensitive, insightful study of the ego's competence in structuring meaning in a way that enables adaptation to the largest sociocultural environments we inhabit. But as such, Fowler project seems only potentially, not necessarily, related to faith in a biblical or theological sense. In fact, my own predisposition would be to say that the main title and subtitle of Fowler's book should be reversed to read, *The Psychology of Human Development and the Quest*

12. Editor's Note: As a PhD student I remember well using Fowler's research methodology and interview process in Loder's seminar on human development. The discussions of our lengthy, transcribed verbatims were deep, illuminating, and provocative.

*for Meaning: Stages of an Aspect of Faith.* Fowler wants to concentrate on the human aspect of faith. But the decisive question for Christian education is, how do Fowler's constructs relate to biblical understandings of faith that are inherently transformational specifically because of *divine* agency? To focus the sorts of issues that emerge from such a question, let us engage Gerhard Ebeling's study of faith in the Synoptic Gospels to draw out some of the discrepancies between Fowler's view of faith and the synoptic accounts.[13]

Ebeling says, first of all, that faith gives *certainty to existence.* "It is taking sure steps although there is no road visible, hoping although there is nothing to hope for, refusing to despair, although things are desperate, having ground under us although we step into a bottomless abyss."[14] The source and substance of such faith clearly resides beyond the ego's capacity to construct meaning. The second aspect of the synoptic understanding of faith is that it is directed toward the future. Indeed, faith *really brings about the future.* That is to say, faith has to do with an event. Faith directed toward so-called facts is really only faith insofar as a future opens up in light of, but from beyond, these facts. As an event, faith is an act of creation, including but always transcending and transforming any given state of equilibrated development.

Third, faith in the Synoptics is understood as power. It is really *participation in the omnipotence of God,* but via human weakness. Mountains and mustard seeds are no more strikingly contrasted than when Jesus claims that faith the size of the latter will move anything the size of the former. Faith as power comes forth precisely in the face of human powerlessness. Hence it is seen not as an exercise of human potential but of existential participation in God's power, which participation discloses human power as weakness. Fourth, faith comes forth in the *encounter with other people.* Preeminently, of course, faith occurs in the encounter with the living Christ. But the authority of Christ also works through encounters with other persons who are graciously empowered to invoke faith. Faith has its origin in a divinely endowed, humanly embodied, living authority that evokes the personal response of faith in others. The rise of faith depends upon encounters with witnesses of faith. In no way does faith develop as an organ of the human personality, arising automatically from within the structural potential of every person-environment interaction.

Fifth, faith is *specific* rather than general and abstract. Faith masters and overcomes particular, specific situations on the basis of the transcendent ground of its existence. Faith is something exceptional. It does not appear as the inevitable subjective design of given situations, but repeatedly proves

---

13. Ebeling, *Word and Faith*, 201–46, especially 240–46.
14. Ibid., 240.

or authenticates itself in existential situations. Faith is not a phenomenon automatically present to supply the general structure of awareness, but is everywhere and anywhere accessible and effective in shaping the future of concrete particulars.

Sixth, faith *saves*. Both *pistis* (faith) and *soteria* (salvation) are characteristically associated in the synoptic accounts, but the manner of their interaction is exceptionally fluid. Whatever the manner and form of their interaction, the point is that with the arrival of faith on the scene, between God's action and human affairs, the decisive encounter has occurred. Massive facts will now have to yield. The cause of the future has been espoused and the old—all that comes from the past to discourage the present—has been declared to be past. Where there is faith, existence becomes whole and is healed, not as an expression of human fulfillment but by and for the purposes of God.

My aim here is not to be biblicistic but to come to terms with that which is so central to what the Christian tradition has meant by the word *faith*. On this score Fowler has missed the mark. I would also note here that Fowler's view of faith has not answered the question, why have faith? any more than his sources in Kohlberg, Piaget, and the like. However, it is precisely through New Testament faith that the believer knows the *why*. To take away that answer in the name of socialization and developmental psychology is a grievous error—all the worse so for its popularity as a resource for Christian educators.

## (2) Methodological Concerns

A second group of questions might be labeled methodological. Here I refer to areas in which Fowler's position does not seem to be sufficiently self-conscious or self-critical. First among these is the intrinsic difficulty of making the developmental sequence normative. This difficulty focuses on the problematic standpoint of the observer. Let's ask, for example, where would anyone have to be, in the system's own way of accounting for things, to be preeminently interested in stages and the staging of the whole of human development? It seems unlikely that one could be beyond Fowler's stage 4, because to a person in stage 5, *paradoxical* faith, the stages would be ambiguous. And to someone in stage 6, *universality*, they would appear to be of minor interest and certainly not normative. Indeed, insofar as they were thought to be normative, they would actually represent an error with respect to the stage 6 way of constructing meaning and being, since the normative goal of Fowler's sequence is precisely this universalizing stage.

What kind of a model sets up within itself a normative goal that if it is attained would expose the model's focus on stages to be inadequate and even fundamentally in error? The problem by which Fowler's system seems to contain the seeds of its own falsification apparently stems partly from his failure to clarify the faith standpoint from which faith itself is being observed, and partly from making the *universalizing* stage the normative goal for faith development.

The extrinsic difficulty in making the developmental sequence normative is that development in faith seems to reflect, rather than correct, the ritualization of progress in an achievement-obsessed society. Fowler himself recognizes and decries this societal dilemma, yet the sociology of these stages seems to make them a party to that very dilemma. Biblical faith is supposed to foster healing, sustain health, and promote wholeness of life through participation in the Spirit of Christ (salvation). But faith development, in light of our analysis, seems implicitly, if not explicitly, to be contaminated by the sickness of a society that systematically makes any human advancement an automatic good, that is obsessed with self-fulfillment, and that has more to do with seeking some sort of cosmic Peter Principle than the reign of God.

A second methodological concern relates to the nature of structure in Fowler's position. In general, the notion of structure varies from Kohlberg to Piaget to Erikson and from all of these to Noam Chomsky, Claude Levi-Strauss, Jacques Lacan, and Roland Barthes. One might even argue that Friedrich Nietzsche is the founder of the structuralist enterprise. Given such variety, what is the basis for Fowler's view of structure as against the alternatives? To specify this question, why has he made his selection of the seven variables we describe above determinative for the constitution of a faith stage? Could not other variables as fundamental and as systematically central to his enterprise be chosen?

For example, take *perception*. Might one not examine the developmental history of perception as it emerges from centration and egocentrism and reaches toward its highest transformation in the vision of God? Or take *volition*. Why not study volition as it emerges from primitive self-assertion reaching its highest transformation in willing the will of God? Finally take *sense of humor*. Could humor not be understood as unfolding from a basis in gross bodily action, as in slapstick, through Kierkegaardian notions of irony and religious humor, to the holy humor of Christ where it has the power to disclose the presence of the kingdom of God (i.e., *"Take the beam out of your own eye . . ."*)? On this issue and elsewhere I find Fowler's the notion of structure is not firm enough to establish a clear basis for discrimination. So many vital areas are left vague and unaccounted for by this faith system such that in using it one is faced with the necessity of having faith in the development of the theory rather than having a discriminating theory of faith development.

A third area of methodological concern is what this investigation excludes in order to gain information about one's supposed faith. Take the case of Mary, which Fowler uses as a basis for demonstrating his approach. While Fowler indicates the story is not typical, the case he describes at length shows quite vividly, by the time Mary is classified in stage 3, how much of the person of Mary is lost in the application of the theory.[15] If we are studying true faith, ought we not to be studying what makes one more, not less, oneself—more human? Ought we avoid the dehumanizing reduction of a person to a category? Some sense of having lost Mary as a person seems to have prompted Fowler's inclusion of Erikson's scheme as a postclassification attempt to account for the dynamics of her case, which no doubt the readers cannot help but see and feel in reading her story. But when Fowler uses Erikson, the sensitive, insightful, dynamic analysis that Erikson's position is capable of generating does not emerge. Erikson is used for his system of stages, and Mary is once again located on a map. Surely Fowler provides useful information, but his discussion does not seem to penetrate beneath the surface of Mary's life of faith. A richer and more variegated method of interpretation would be required for such an inquiry.

### (3) Overlooking Negation Incorporated into Human Development

The last critical issue to bring up here is that Fowler's interviewing method, generally so very helpful, carefully ignores the profound depth of the negative side of human development. Every developmentalist knows that you begin to die the minute you are born. To overlook the negative depth to human development is another grievous error, particularly when you are interested in constructing a theological understanding of human development in any Christian sense. The existential abyss underlying human existence and development has to be taken into account if we are going to think theologically about that existence and development against the backdrop of the human condition. Thus, normal faith development, as described by Fowler, is theologically abnormal because it eliminates the negative dimension that must be there if we are going to understand human existence theologically.[16]

---

15. Mary's case is given and interpreted in Fowler, *Stages*, 217–68.

16. Editor's Note: A similar critique of Fowler's *Stages* is found in Loder, *Logic of the Spirit*, 255–59,

## (IV) CONCLUSION

As we have tried to show, the figures we have reviewed in this chapter—Freud, Erikson, Piaget, Kohlberg, Gilligan, and Fowler—all concern themselves with variations on ego development. But ego development in all its dimensions is itself governed by the power of socialization, which is preeminently concerned with survival and satisfaction according to the Reality Principle. Consequently, the ego as a human construct may be understood as the tragic source and victim of socialization incorporated, since all the ego's amazing and potentially transformational developmental potential finally remains captive to the *pattern-maintenance, tension-reduction* forces of death.

Therefore, the transformation of human lifestyles in any theological sense must therefore deal with and effectively cooperate with the redemptive transformation of the ego by the power of the Spirit. To understand and to talk about this kind of transformation we must necessarily develop an understanding of human development that is both fully interdisciplinary and fully theological, one that effectively integrates divine and human agency in their proper relationality in a way that ramifies through all dimensions of human existence.[17] This concern forms the content of section III of this book.

---

17. Editor's Note: James M. Nelson, who teaches in the Department of Psychology at Valparaiso University, gave an insightful comment on the uniqueness of Loder's theological understanding of human development in his massive overview of the current discussion on psychology, religion, and spirituality. Prior to reviewing Loder's theological interpretation of human development in *Logic of the Spirit*, Nelson wrote: "The work of James Loder (1931–2001) is important because he offers one of the few models of development that has both theological and psychological sophistication. He believed that theological as well as psychological perspectives were necessary to understand human development." In relation to Fowler's work, Nelson wrote, "Loder's theory is based on the idea that human development is shaped by spiritual transformation, while more psychological theories like Fowler's argue that spiritual transformation is embedded in human development, a view that tends to privilege psychological concerns over theological or spiritual ones." See Nelson, *Psychology*, 241–43.

# Theological Considerations

*The Holy Spirit and Human Transformation*

# 5

# Transformation in Theology
## Analogy of the Spirit

## (I) INTRODUCTION

WE BEGIN HERE BY agreeing again with C. Ellis Nelson that "style of life" is the basic unit with which we have to deal in the discipline of Christian education. Nelson discussed lifestyle in terms of the importance of communicating a biblical and theological culture (i.e., tradition and Scripture) through the dynamics of socialization. But we saw that the incommensurability between the theological and biblical context, on the one hand, and the process of socialization, on the other, created an impossible situation, not unlike the man in Søren Kierkegaard's writings who escaped from the asylum and went shouting into town, "The world is round!"

We next tried to show that this impossibility was not merely an ideological incommensurability, but a matter of power and influence. The dynamics of socialization in the society at large have far greater power to persuade than any recital of the symbolic content of theology or any critical form of reasoning. Hence, wider cultural and social lifestyles subvert what can be said theologically, as seen in our discussion of behavior oriented by the obsession with achievement, authoritarianism, proteanism, and oppression. We have argued, finally, that personality formation, as psychodynamically understood, is also a by-product of the socialization dynamic. Naturalistic formation does not, therefore, provide any real leverage upon the predominant power of socialization. In fact, the major views of personality formation, intelligence, moral judgment, and faith development are of a single force with the socialization dynamics discussed earlier. Hence, the critiques of Erikson, Piaget, Kohlberg, Gilligan, and Fowler support the conclusion that the ego is nothing other than socialization incorporated.

We need, therefore, to start from a different place. We need a standpoint that is inherently theological (i.e., accounts for divine action) and also that has the capacity to reverse the predominance of socialization over transformation in all forms of human action. Theologically speaking, transformation, not socialization, must be the predominant concern of Christian education because this dynamic process is commensurate with the content we seek to convey. To that end, my starting point will be an analogy of the Spirit that conceives of divine and human action working together in proper relationality according to the nature of Jesus Christ.

## (II) THE DYNAMICS OF KNOWING IN THE SPIRIT: THE DIVINE PEDAGOGY

It seems to me that the most obvious educational starting point in theology is the biblical premise that the Holy Spirit is the Teacher. In the power of the Holy Spirit, the Scriptures become the Word of God in human experience. The power of the Holy Spirit brings Jesus Christ out of the remoteness of history into the present, creating faith through the power of grace. This action of the Spirit is our epistemology for Christian education. For all that pertains to teaching and learning in the Christian context, our fundamental epistemology and guiding assumption has to be this conviction: the Holy Spirit leads us into all Truth. The question, then, is how are we to understand this assumption and its relation to Christian experience?

## (A) The Analogy of the Spirit

I think that one way to understand the Spirit is by using an approach that appears in Scripture at several points. Scripture suggests that an analogical relationship pertains between the human spirit and the Holy Spirit. George Hendry argued for this analogy in one way by correlating the Genesis J documents regarding "spirit" with the P documents regarding the *imago Dei*.[1] He concluded that the human spirit is the image of the divine Spirit. I once

---

1. Hendry, "Human Spirit," 96–117.

heard Princeton Seminary's Old Testament scholar Henry Gehman confirm this insight as well, but this is only one scriptural indication of the analogy.[2]

The apostle Paul makes the analogical relationship suggested in the Genesis account explicit in 1 Cor 2:10b–11. *"For the Spirit searches everything, even the depths of God. For who knows a man's thoughts except the spirit of the man which is in him? So also no one comprehends what is truly God's except the Spirit of God."* Here, the Spirit of God who searches the deep things of God is likened to the spirit of the person who searches the deep things of the person. Moreover, in Rom 8:16 Paul writes: *"It is the Spirit himself bearing witness with our spirit that we are children of God."* Here the conjoined activity of human spirit and Holy Spirit suggests a commonality along the lines of one's being the image of the other, suggesting that an analogy pertains between the actions of the human spirit and the actions of the Holy Spirit. A further indication of this analogy is the paradox of divine/human intentionality as in Phil 2:12b–3: *"Work out your salvation with fear and trembling, for God is at work in you to will and to do for God's good pleasure."*

If we are going to think of human spirit and Holy Spirit in terms of an analogy, then we have to think about what analogy requires. Analogy requires recognizing both similarity and difference in a relation. Analogy is concerned with both how two things in relation are alike and how they are not alike. Thus, in setting up an analogy we clearly want to avoid what some theologians tend to do, namely, reduce human spirit and Holy Spirit to the same thing. We want to keep the difference because that seems to preserve the way in which Scripture talks about "spirit." Moreover, the preponderance of opinion among Reformed and Lutheran theologians favors keeping the distinction. Pannenberg and certain process thinkers may want to make the Holy Spirit and the human spirit one. But Luther, Calvin, Barth and Tillich are among those who want to keep them distinct. I am arguing that it is more faithful to Scripture, and to our experiential understanding of life in the Spirit, to preserve the distinction, but also to keep them in an analogical relationship. This means that human spirit and Holy Spirit are distinct but not ultimately separated, any more than an image can be separated from its original.

So, assuming both that the human spirit and the Holy Spirit cannot be reduced to one reality and that Holy Spirit and human spirit cannot be radically separated as if they were two totally unrelated realities, let us first

2. Editor's Note: Loder does not indicate where he heard this teaching of Gehman's. Henry Gehman was the William Henry Greene Professor of Old Testament Literature at Princeton Theological Seminary from 1942 to 1958. Loder may have taken one of Gehman's classes and heard him lecture, or read one of Gehman's books as a student.

inquire about the connection between them. How are they similar? To begin to answer this question, I want to talk a little bit about the nature of the human spirit under the theme of creativity.

## (B) The Human Spirit

One way to begin a discussion of human spirit is to go to George Thomas's study, *Freedom and the Spirit*. Thomas was for several years the head of the Religion Department that he founded at Princeton University, and a frequent colleague of the faculty at Princeton Seminary. In *Freedom and the Spirit* he explores the origins of the understanding of human spirit in Western thought. He finds that at certain points human spirit is equated with reason. At other points, it is equated with love (particularly *eros*), personality, universality, freedom, and creativity.

I would argue in a theological context that the underlying logic or grammar of the human spirit in all these cases is best understood by centering on *creativity*. That is, I want to argue that creativity is generative and formative of all of the other modes or expressions of human spirit—inclusive of, but not limited to, the ones that George Thomas listed. To pursue this theoretical discussion here, however, would take us too far afield. Instead, I want to try to give you a minor experience of the human spirit's creative power. I do this in the hope that you begin to recognize, first of all, that the underlying structure of creativity serves as a logic or grammar for all other forms of spirit. Second, I hope that you can recognize that you and I are already spirit in the most fundamental sense—more than we are reason, consciousness, or even experience. To make these two points, I am going to take a little specimen of human spirit in creative action and have you try to experience it.

### (1) Catching the Human Spirit in the Act of Knowing

I want you to try to solve the nine-dot puzzle. The problem is to draw four straight lines continuously through the nine dots without taking your pencil off the paper.

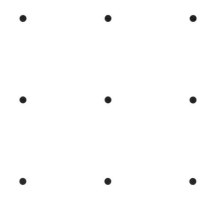

***The Nine Dot Problem***

If you already know this problem, then you can try the six-stick puzzle. In this puzzle, there are six sticks three inches long. You are to arrange those six sticks in such a way as to create four equilateral triangles, three inches on a side.

Now as you try to think about this exercise, you may go through some kind of scenario like the following. Starting out you might think to yourself, "I'm reading this book to learn about Christian education, not puzzles. I don't like doing stupid puzzles. But okay, if he wants me to, I'll play his little game." So you take the four lines and you start to figure—"One, two, three. I've got one line and two dots. That's not going to work. I'll start again. I'll be cagier this time. I'll go this way and that way and this way. Now I've got one line and three dots." You're beginning to see that none of your strategies is going to work. In fact, you're getting frustrated. You say to yourself, "Why should I bother making this effort? This is nonsense! I want to learn profound verities about God and humanity and the salvation of the world. Why should I bother with nine dots and four lines?" Let's say you get really upset and growl to yourself, "I'm not going to read this book anymore! I'm getting out of here!" You get up from your chair, throw down the book, and mumble to yourself, "What a stupid waste of time!" What you don't yet realize is that while you no longer have the puzzle, the nine-dot problem has you! It has taken up residence under your skin. You may have put it out of consciousness, but out of consciousness is *not* out of mind. Something is working on you unconsciously. You just think you need a change of pace. So you say to yourself, "I'm going to take a drive."

You start out down the highway. You come to a traffic light. Sitting there in front of a traffic light waiting for it to change, you experience that marvelous little moment of semiconsciousness while staring off into blank space. Then, just before the horn behind you starts honking, there comes a moment of insight. Oh!—a release of something! The solution dawns on you, and you say, "Oh! Oh!" The horn behind you is honking, but you don't even care. "Oh, I got it!" You pull over to the side of the road, open the glove compartment, take out a little pad of paper, and you write: "Like this—four lines, nine dots. I got it!"

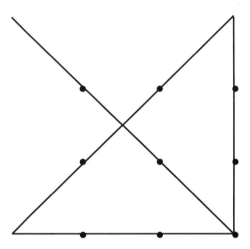

**The Nine Dot Problem Solved**

You turn the car around, drive back home, pick up the book to look for the printed solution. You find you did get it right. With great satisfaction you declare, "I got it! I got it!"

Now if you have been working on the six-stick problem, then you can try all kinds of things. Until finally, it dawns on you in a similar way that you cannot solve the problem in the frame of reference in which it is posed. You have to move into three dimensions.

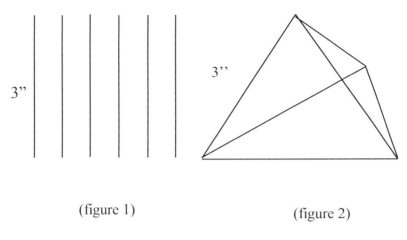

(figure 1)                    (figure 2)

**The Six-Stock Problem**

Now you've got four equilateral triangles, three inches on a side. By the way, if you actually solved this problem, some years ago you could have gotten into MIT. This puzzle used to be on one of their entrance exams!

## (2) An Analysis of the Human Spirit's Action in Knowing

Now what's going on? The first thing that is going on is your acceptance of the *context* within which the conflict is given. You accepted the puzzle as a problem. Some bright students have said to me in the past that the puzzle is really not a problem. All you have to do is draw three straight lines through the dots and somewhere out there in infinity, because space is curved, parallel lines meet and come back. The only problem is what to do with the extra line. And I say, "That's your problem. The problem as I gave it in context includes you and your drawing four lines without lifting your pencil from the paper. You have not accepted the context in which the problem was given." The point about this is that the human spirit always moves within a context, even as it always involves a felt sense of disequilibrium, things not working within that context. So you have context and conflict as keys of the movement of the spirit in you.

As human spirit, you embrace the *conflict* (puzzle) and hold on to it. It hooks you, because once you have a conflict that bugs you, it gets your attention and it binds psychic energy. You and I are made with a profound ambivalence towards conflict. We can't live with it and we can't live without it. If everything is running smoothly, you want a little difficulty or problem to challenge you. Once you have the problem, then you have to solve it. So if the conflict is there, you wrestle with it, and it binds energy. What your psyche is trying to do after a conflict binds the energy is to work out a resolution to the conflict and release the energy.

So what goes on then? After the conflict is accepted, indwelt and worked on in context, yet without resolution, then there is a period in which the problem goes underground. Thus, you work on the problem unconsciously, as when you are sitting in front of that traffic light with the puzzle out of consciousness. Conflict engaged at his level ushers in an *interlude*. In the interlude, your psyche scans for solutions, puts the parts of the puzzle together in different ways. It looks for prototypes, ways in which similar problems have been solved before. You don't know that all of this is going on under the surface, because your psyche is at work unconsciously trying to resolve the dilemma. So there is an interlude, scanning for prototypes and solutions.

Then finally what happens is *insight*. In this particular case, what your psyche does is ingenious. *It reverses the figure and ground* of the conflict. So instead of trying to assimilate the four lines to the nine dots, you assimilate the nine dots to the four lines. The insight bisociates two frames of reference—i.e., it puts them together in a meaningful way, in a way you had never perceived of them coming together before.[3] The insight comes with the force of assurance that the solution is solid, that you know you've got it, even before you have tested it out. The insight is felt with intuitive force. "I know I've got it! That's it!"

Once the insight is accurate and sufficient, then the energy bound up with the conflict is released. This is the "Aha!" experience. With the *release of energy*, the phenomenal world is restored, but at a higher level. You see everything clearer than before. This clarity in turn initiates a concern to *validate* your solution. Is it the case that the insight, felt with intuitive force, really does check out in terms of the shape of the problem? This is the coherence test. Having satisfied yourself that it does, you still want to give it a public test. You go back to check out your solution with the one in the book. Validation, then, is a question of both coherence between insight and problem, and a test of correspondence to see whether your insight satisfies (corresponds to) the public arena.

The result of this spiritual process is that you performed a creative act. There is a transformation of the horizon within which you perceived the original puzzle. That particular puzzle can never be a problem for you in

---

3. Editor's Note: The concept of bisociation will be discussed below.

the same way again, because you are in the world with respect to it in a fundamentally new way.

## (C) The Definition of *Transformation* and the Logic of Transformation

So let's recall our definition of *transformation*. In contrast to socialization, we define *transformation* as follows: *Within a given frame of knowledge, transformation is a patterned process whereby hidden, internally coherent orders of meaning are awakened and empowered to reconstruct that original frame of knowledge and experience.*

The sequence that we have just described as a creative event is a patterned process, which I have called the *logic of transformation*. The classic example of this logic is Archimedes being commissioned by King Hiero II of Syracuse to find out whether or not his recently minted crown was really solid gold. The king wanted to know whether the goldsmith who made the crown had mixed a little alloy in there, scraping some gold out for himself. Now the king likes the crown so he doesn't want it melted down. So he says to Archimedes, "I want you to find out if my crown is solid gold without destroying the crown."

Now Archimedes, in effect, has a nine-dot problem that really matters. He cannot melt down the crown, and yet he has to meet the conditions set by the king's command. He is under this commission. He struggles with the problem, but cannot solve it. Instead of going on a drive, he goes to soothe himself in the public baths of Syracuse. As the irregular shape of his body sinks into the water, he sees the water rise against the smudges on the wall of the bathhouse. (There were smudges on the walls of the public bathhouses in Syracuse!) Right at that point, something marvelous happens in Archimedes's spirit. There is a *bisociation* that takes place between the irregular shape of his body and the irregular shape of the crown. Noting the displacement of water, he knows he can measure the volume of the crown. Since he can figure out what one would call the specific gravity of gold, which is the weight per unit volume, he can then tell in fact whether or not the crown is really solid gold. The insight hits him like a bolt of lightning. He jumps out of the bath and runs naked through the streets of Syracuse shouting, "Eureka!" (No doubt one of the first great streakers of all time!) Fortunately, he could account for himself with an empirical test afterwards, which is to stress the need for public validation to complete the creative sequence.

## (1) Key Factors in the Process

Now there are two things I want to point out specifically in this process. The first is the term *bisociation*. Philosopher Arthur Koestler invented the word, but it has found its way into a variety of psychological textbooks.[4] It means that two frames of reference not ordinarily associated with each other come together surprisingly to create a meaning neither one of them could possibly carry by itself. I usually tell a bad joke at this point, because humor is one of the best ways to illustrate bisociation. Humor in fact depends upon bisociation, the bringing together of two otherwise unrelated frames of reference in a surprising way to give a meaning you hadn't thought of. Koestler's illustrative joke is, "A sadist is someone who is kind to a masochist." If you didn't erupt in uproarious laughter, you are not alone. Actually, no one ever laughed at this joke when I told it in any of my classes. But they always laughed or smiled when I told them they laughed when they didn't. It's the same thing, because there is a bisociation of the assertion that you laughed with your not having laughed. The bisociation of laughing with not laughing works just as well as bisociating kindness with sadomasochistic behavior.

Thus, a key notion in creativity is bisociation, which describes two frames of reference habitually dissociated from each other coming together to create an insight, to produce an order of meaning that is otherwise unexpected. The reason I focus on bisociation is that it is the simplest unit of insight. The nature of insight can get very, very complicated. But the simplest unit for getting an insight is two frames of reference—just two of them—habitually dissociated coming together to create a meaningful unity.

The second thing in the process that I want to stress is that the *energy* tied up with the conflict is *released* when an insight comes. In the case of the joke, whether you responded with amusement or outright laughter, a release of tension accompanied the insight. The failure to release energy is usually an indication that you don't have the right insight or that you have an escapist kind of resolution that allows you to elude the problem rather than solve it. What happens when the energy is released is quite important. With the release of energy through insight, you are put back into your context with eyes open to yourself in that context in a new way.

Do you know what it is to have a conflict, something going on inside you that won't let you see people, relate to them? Or you are with someone, you are talking with them, and they are wanting to say to you, "What are

---

4. Koestler, *Insight*, 36–53; and Koestler, *Act of Creation*. Editor's Note: Loder thinks of bisociation as a kind of shorthand for the crux of the imaginative act, the "smallest unit necessary to an imaginative resolution and reconstruction of the problematic situation." See Loder, *Transforming Moment*, 38.

you really thinking about? What's really going on?" Conflict can remove you from your environment. So when the conflict is released, even if it is just a little one, the released energy works to put you back into the environment, so that the objects and things of the environment become richer. They have more texture. You can see things with keenness and sharpness that you couldn't see before.

### (2) The Sequence as a Whole: Continuity and Discontinuity

Now let met make three additional comments on the sequence as a whole. *First* of all, understand that the sequence is a kind of linear *gestalt*.[5] Creative process has a kind of narrative quality. Once you accept the conflict, your spirit cannot rest until you have worked the resolution all the way through. The spirit in you wants to unfold the sequence from beginning to end. Your spirit has what Frank Kermode calls an inbuilt "sense of an ending."[6] He illustrates this sense using common experiences. If in the context of clocks, somebody says, "Tick," what do you say? "Tock." In the context of dogs, if I say, "Bow," what do you say? "Wow." What Kermode is talking about is the force of grammar that makes you want to resolve something that has you in conflict. Suppose someone speaks to you: "I'd like so say something . . . Hmmm. You know. I heard. But what can I say? Remember . . .? No. I could, you know. You know what I mean. I'll work it out. We should . . . I will. What else can I say?" You become frustrated at first, because meaning is grammatically structured. So even if the parts aren't there, or make no sense, you will try to put it together, because you have within you a sense of an ending. If I start a sentence and don't finish it, you feel like you have got to finish it for me. I don't even have to try to get you to do that. I want to argue that the structure of transformation is like that. Once you get into it, you have a sense of the continuity of the thing and you want it to work out. You can't rest until you complete the sequence and make meaning.

*Second*, remember that this is a discussion of the human spirit. This pattern combines continuity and discontinuity, and this apparent contradiction is absolutely crucial for any understanding of the spirit, whether in reference to the Holy Spirit or to the human spirit. In reference to the discontinuity of the Holy Spirit, both the Hebrew *ruach* and the Greek *pneuma* can mean "wind," as in Jesus's comment: "*The Spirit blows where it will.*" In relation to the human spirit, one of the main characteristics of spirit is the

---

5. For an explanation of why creative process or transformation is a linear gestalt, see chapter 6.

6. Kermode's book is titled *The Sense of an Ending*.

discontinuity of spontaneity. However, the discontinuity of the Holy Spirit and the human spirit is never sheer discontinuity, never sheer or random wind or sheer or random spontaneity. In both the Holy Spirit and the human spirit is also a kind of predictability, a kind of recognition. I might say, paradoxically, that I recognize the newness as something I have known before. Or I already know what this surprising phenomenon means.

Thus, one of the fundamental, phenomenological characteristics of spirit, Spirit, or both is this combination of continuity and discontinuity. The transformational process integrates both. There is a rush of discontinuity in the moment of insight. But the pulling through of things, as a result of its working like a linear *gestalt*, gives you this sense of continuity. The result, as I say, is a transformation of the horizon within which the conflict originally existed.

*Third*, as a result if these two considerations—the linear gestalt and the combination of continuity and discontinuity—it is possible to enter this transformational logic at any point. In the illustrations given above, the process was entered at the point of conflict. But you can also enter at the point of insight. Sometimes you know the answer to something before you know what the question is! You know you know something *very* important, but you don't know what the question is that you have the answer for. That's not sloppy thinking. That was Einstein's experience when he read Newton's *Principia Mathematica*. He had an intuition that something was wrong with the theory. He also had the intuition that he could figure out what was wrong with it even before he knew what was wrong. This same phenomenon happens in religious experiences. You have an experience that you know is very important, but you don't yet know why it is important. It just stays with you. Studies of religious experience show that they are important, not only in the moment of having them, but over long periods of time.[7]

So it is possible to enter in the middle of the transformational sequence. Because of the *gestalt* quality, when you enter in the middle, you want to work back to the conflict, as well as forward to the place where there is the release of tension that gives you a new sense of meaning. In other words, no matter where you enter, you will want to work through the sequence to complete the whole. This flexibility is very important educationally, because in education we tend to start at the end, with the conclusion (i.e., interpretation) and fail to engage the entire sequence. The problem is that oftentimes we don't care if our students work back and forth through the process or not. We don't care if the conclusion has anything to do with the creative act.

---

7. Editor's Note: One of the purposes of Loder's *The Transforming Moment* was to make religious experiences an important theme for scientific investigation.

Too often all I want to do as the teacher is to make sure you get the right conclusions. If, on the other hand, you are sensitive to the students' need to move through the whole process, then you give them the opportunity to discover for themselves the significance of the conclusions. You cooperate with the human spirit's response to any startling conclusion. And that's when teaching takes place.

To take a negative case in point, in one adolescent Sunday school class, the teacher asked, "Why do we worship Jesus?" The students raised their hands, giving all wrong answers. Then the son of a seminary professor leaned back in his chair in the back of the room and said in a bored, desultory voice: "Because he was God." "That's right!" the teacher responded. And he proceeded on with the lesson. Note what happened. The young man's conclusion gave testimony to the most marvelous creative act imaginable—the incarnation of God—and it was treated like a proposition about what they were going to have yet again for lunch. Now when this young person first heard this truth—that Jesus was God!—I am sure it wasn't treated like that. When you first hear something like this, you want to know how in the world anyone can make such an incredible statement. If you entered the sequence at any point, something in you wants to get the whole. It is possible to defeat the spirit. It is possible to quench the spirit. But something in us wants the whole, if at all possible.

## (D) The Logic at Work

Earlier in this chapter I said that I thought that the creative process could account for our understanding of freedom, reason, universality, personality, love, and so on. Instead of spelling this out for each case, let me simply give you some examples of how the pattern of the spirit works. For instance, in the case of personality, the logic of transformation describes the stage transition process by means of which every register of human behavior is generated. So the pattern is fundamental to the formation of the personality, to the dynamics of development. Indeed, Piaget himself knew about the dynamic core of human development when he said that the transformations fostering development are stronger than the stages.

In the case of freedom, the concern is with that which gives you the self-transcendence to choose for or against the objective versus the subjective side of your environment. The only way you can do this is by getting an insight that frees you to see the alternative within the environment that you can then choose for or against. You see, you don't get freedom just by acting without restraints. You get freedom by being put back into the binding context in some new way. As a consequence of the release of energy, we say, "Oh I see; now I can choose." That's the quality of freedom given by creative insight. Basically what I am arguing in these very cryptic demonstrations is that creativity operates as the fundamental notion among these several other expressions of spirit. The structure of creativity, the grammar or logic of transformation is the structural commonality that characterizes the human spirit in a wide variety of contexts.

Another example is how the logic underlies the therapeutic process. At the Houston Medical Center a few years ago, a Houston psychiatrist reviewed my book *The Transforming Moment* in my presence.[8] "At first," he said, "I didn't really understand what Dr. Loder was getting at. Then I began to think about it. The first thing that occurred to me was the way my patients started to get better after I showed up late or forget an appointment." What had the doctor noticed? He noticed that by being late or forgetting an appointment, he broke out of the nine dots of this professional role. He became a human being to his patients. His clients began to sense the therapist's humanity. The clients were thereby freed to reconstruct the relationship with the therapist on that basis, not on the basis of role structures.

The psychiatrist continued, "Let me give you another illustration. I went to an athletic event at the Houston Astrodome." I don't know if you know the Astrodome, but he described it as this huge arena where it is very difficult to go out the same door you came in because all the doors look exactly the same all the way around. So he said to himself: "I'll park the car under an Exxon sign and go to the athletic event. Then when I come out, I'll find the Exxon sign and thus my car." So he went into the athletic event, came out, and started to walk around the Houston Astrodome. But he couldn't find the Exxon sign. So he said, "What do you do when your Exxon sign goes out?" That is a theological question. You become spirit. You start reconstructing the world. The psychiatrist began to think about the cobblestones in the street, the other buildings that were related to where he had parked. About an hour later he found his car. Perhaps an external proof of the theory was that his wife believed him after he got home!

The psychologist elaborated further. "Looking at my therapy, I had another case that made the same point within the human context." He described his work with a nine-year-old boy who had a psychological tic. The boy's story was that his mother had fallen in love with a young man from their little town in Texas when she was very young. She loved this guy so much, but he left town and married another woman. With her lover gone, she married someone else. They had a son, this nine-year-old boy. When

8. Editor's Note: Dr. Loder does not identify this psychologist.

her childhood lover came back to town divorced, the boy's mother divorced the boy's father to marry her sweetheart. It was subsequent to these events that the tic developed in her son. Physically, the tic jerked the boy's head horizontally from side to side. In the course of therapy, the psychiatrist explained to the boy that he was using the tic to communicate his confusing situation. He was using the tic to say, "Which is my father? This one or that one?" At the same time he was shaking his head: "No, I don't like being confused."

Then the psychiatrist prescribed a strategy for the boy. "It is very important that you preserve your tic until everybody understands exactly what you mean. Don't give up the tic." At that point, of course, the boy gave it up because part of the function of the tic was to exercise defiance. If the tic became permissible—or more to the point, prescribed—then the defiance drained out of it. And so his tic disappeared. However, the family was so used to the tic that they didn't actually know how to relate to the boy any more when he came home without it. Their Exxon sign had gone out. They had to begin to reorganize themselves without it. Once again I am highlighting the pervasive quality of the human spirit in human experience.

## (III) THE HUMAN SPIRIT TRANSFORMED: FOUR DIMENSIONS OF KNOWING IN THE HOLY SPIRIT

All of the above is my working conception of the human spirit. But having said this much, I must add now that my discussion is *not* yet theologically or biblically significant. Thus far we have understood the pattern of transformation on the basis of which I anticipate the Holy Spirit and the human spirit may be judged to be similar. To show how transformation operates as patterned process for discussion of the Holy Spirit, we must transpose the pattern into a theological frame of knowledge. In the foregoing, I have described the way the two dimensions—the self and the world—create and compose each other in a relationship that constitutes what we call *personal* reality. We have to move this two-dimensional understanding of spirit into four dimensions if we are going to understand its theological significance, because all theological thinking is inherently four-dimensional. This move across the analogy from the human spirit to the Holy Spirit, from two to four dimensions, is a radical shift in consciousness.

Let me give you an illustration of the qualitative difference I have in mind from when the Rapaport Sorting Test was subjected to a standardization process. The Rapaport Sorting Test is a psychological test to determine whether or not schizophrenia is present in the subject you are examining.[9] The testing instrument consists of a lot of little farm animals, people, houses and fences. As psychologist you sit the subject down and dump the objects out on the table. You say, "Make some sense out of this." If they cannot make sense out of this farm world, then maybe they cannot make sense out of their Lived World, and this failure may be an indication of schizophrenia.

When the guild first tried to standardize the test, members took it to the fellow who was head of research at Johns Hopkins. They sat him down and dumped the stuff out before him on the table. He looked at it for a little while. Then he put the farmer up above the window, the lady down on the floor, the mouse under a chair, the cow on the chair, and the fencing all over the room. At first, it looked like research at Johns Hopkins was in serious trouble! That is, until he explained to them the frame of reference within which he was working. As a result, they had to revise the test. They had to get it off the two-dimensional table and move it into a much larger frame of reference. I want to make this same kind of shift now. I want to get our discussion out of the two-dimensional, tabletop perspective into a much bigger frame of reference because it is that larger frame of reference that is inherently biblical and theological.

The first two dimensions have to do with the human spirit, because the human spirit describes how we create and compose the world in a human sense. What we want to do is shift to a frame of reference that includes these first two dimensions but then goes beyond them to include the whole scope of human existence. This task calls us to learn to think in terms of four dimensions—the Self, the World, the Void, and the Holy—i.e., four dimensions of the one reality we inhabit. The gospel reveals that human existence in a redeemed creation consists of these four dimensions.

## (A) The Self

First of all, there is the Self. Now the Self, as the first dimension, exists phenomenologically as the "I," the chooser, the source of one's choices and beliefs, who says, "I did this," or, "I did that." The fundamental question here is not one's identity crisis. Self is a structural reality, something that is always there but is not always in evidence. For example, I used to drive my daughter Tami to school in the mornings. We would have little chats about various things. Sometimes we broached profound questions like, how do I look? But at other times other matters took precedence.

---

9. Editor's Note: Loder does not give the source of this anecdote.

"You know, Daddy," Tami said on different occasions, "you're you and I'm me. You will never know what it is like for me to be me. And I won't ever know what it is like for you to be you."

And I would agree. "Yes, you're you, and I'm me, and that's fine."

"But, no, isn't that sad?" she would say.

"No, it's not sad. It's a nice arrangement. You can be you, I'll be me, and let's got to school!"

"No, no!" She would get very frustrated.

She used to talk about this concern so often that I got concerned. Being an academic type, I have to read about something before I understand it. So, eventually, I read an essay by Thomas Nagel titled, "What Is It Like to Be a Bat?"[10] Have you ever been in a room with a bat? We live in a big house, and sometimes in the summertime the bats come over from the graduate school to join us in the evenings in our bedroom. It is a startling experience to be suddenly awakened by the "whoosh" of bat wings overhead. Nagel has picked a most likely subject for trying to understand the internal nature of an alien presence. He tried to understand what it's like to be a bat. He supposed he was flying around blind, able to respond only to sonar vibrations, or sleeping hanging upside down on all kinds of things. He tried to get inside the bat's frame of reference. Finally, he had to conclude that no matter how he tried to understand what it would be like for *him* to be a bat, he could never structurally understand what it is for a *bat* to be a bat. Think of that. That is what Tami was trying to tell me. No matter what you understand about me, you will never understand what it is for me to be me.

If you don't like my homely, phenomenological illustration, then I have some more sophisticated ones. Take Wilder Penfield's studies, particularly in *The Mystery of the Mind*. He was the first neurologist to do open-skull surgery on conscious epileptic patients. While his patients were still fully awake but under local anesthetic, he opened up their skulls. He took his electric probe and went over the cerebral cortex touching different places. When he would touch one, the person would say, "I hear music." Touch another and they would say, "I remember that scene or episode." This research was the source of *I'm OK—You're OK* and transactional analysis. On the strength of such studies, Thomas Harris claimed that we all have tapes in the brain that tell us whether we're okay or not. You can find them with a sensitive electric probe. As Penfield searched around over the cerebral cortex and touched different places, he got different reactions. But most intriguing was Penfield's further finding that when the person would move an arm, a leg, or hear music, the person would say, "You did that, I didn't." He tried

10. Nagel, "Bat?," 391–414.

everywhere he could to locate the "I" that says, "You did that, I didn't." But he could never locate it. Now Penfield was old enough, wise enough, and well established in the profession not to have to apologize to anybody. He, therefore, concluded—if you just look at the data you have to agree—that there are two essences.[11]

Of course, the "two essences" thesis violates all the canons of neurological research. But if you look at the evidence, you have to say that there are two essences, one that is subject to the sensitive probing of the electrode and another one that comes forth saying, "I." This "I," in Penfield's mind, blazes new trails through the neuronal connections. It reprograms programmed behavior.

Several well-established scientists like Karl Popper (*The Self and the Brain*) and Nobel laureates Sir John Eccles and Roger Sperry (right and left hemispheres of the brain research) all hold to the "two essence" theory. They maintain that the only way to be true to the evidence is to argue that there is an "I" that operates as the composer of one's world. Now you can be a little more technical and say that the person said "I," not "*Ich*," nor "*Je*," or something in some other language, so that it is culturally bound. That's true. Nevertheless in any language, the "I" does the unique thing that Penfield describes. So you have to say that the "I" both *is* a body (is embodied) and *has* a body (is able to change the nature of the body in which it is embodied). This "I" is the Self, the first irreducible dimension of what it means to be human.

## (B) The Lived World

The second dimension concerns what the Self does. What the Self *does* is repeatedly compose the Lived World. You live in a world—not a world that is out there, but a world that you compose from what is out there. I'm not saying there is nothing out there. I am saying what is out there is something you constantly construe in order to make the world livable. As an illustration of this, hold this book at arm's length, close your right eye, and focus

11. Penfield, *Mystery*, 114. Editor's Note: Penfield wrote: "I conclude that it is easier to rationalize man's being on the basis of two elements than on the basis of one." Penfield ended this book with his "Christian testimony" and his call to science: "I was brought up in the Christian family and I have always believed, since I first considered the matter, that there was work for me to do in the world, and that there was a grand design in which all conscious individuals play a role. Whether there is such a thing as communication between man and God and whether energy can come to the mind of a man from an outside source after his death is for each individual to decide for himself. Science has no such answers" (115).

on the upper square with your left eye as you bring the book slowly towards you. At a point along the way the $x$ to the left of the square disappears. Continue moving the book towards you and it appears again. Why is that?

The answer is that there is a blind spot where the optic nerve connects to the eyeball. Everybody has a blind spot in both fields of vision. So you go around with two holes in your field of vision? No, you don't. You cannot live in a world that is punctured with holes. You must compose a livable world, so you compose the holes out. To prove this to yourself, close your right eye again, but this time focus on the lower square as you bring the book towards you. Now your mind fills the gap completing the broken line. A better, stronger illustration was the psychological experiment in which people were given glasses that reverse the image on the retina of the eye. These glasses reversed the reversed image so you saw everything upside down, and left and right were reversed. That's very confusing! But if you left the glasses on and moved around, at the end of seven or eight days the world appeared right side up again. People even skied with these glasses on!

You are constantly in the process of composing and recomposing the world. The reality that you and I think is so tough and firm and real is simply the interrelationship between the "I" (the Self) and the Lived World the "I" composes. We can get very, very rigid about this. If you have children, parents, they can make you very rigid. "No! That is not true. No! No! There are no green fairies dancing in the flowerpot. Let's just grow up. Let's be realistic." Or, "No, you can't have more money. It's not realistic for me to pay for everything." In all kinds of ways you construct a whole world on the basis of these first two dimensions.

These first two dimensions constitute the reality that socialization dynamics govern. They are also the dimensions within which transformation of the human spirit occurs, but only implicitly and tacitly. The social and cultural milieus you inhabit are the extension and elaboration of these two dimensions of human existence. But two dimensions are not enough, even though the ego calls these two dimensions the *real* world. Now, before I go on, I want to emphasize that this so-called *real* world we create is very fragile. It is so fragile that we have to sleep six or eight hours every night in order to get up enough energy to put it back together again every morning. Seventy-two hours without sleep and you can't tell the difference between inside and outside anymore. You begin to dream while you are awake—it's called hallucinating. Depending upon your relative psychological balance, therapists either let you sleep it off or they put you some place where you can work it through. You are only seventy-two hours away from hallucinating! Seventy-two hours and the whole thing collapses—this almighty normative reality by means of which we put down everybody who has ever had an experience that doesn't fit it—like those who have religious experiences!

So the "*real* world" is very fragile. But this fragility also means that it is flexible. We can do wonderful things with this flexible world. The best illustration I have of this flexibility is the plastic surgeon Maxwell Maltz, who wrote a little paperback entitled *Psychocybernetics*. Maltz discovered that when he changed people's faces, they changed their personalities. Then he discovered he didn't actually have to change their faces. All he had to do was change how they *thought* about their faces to change their personality. Why does this changing of thought work? It works because the fragility of our reality gives it flexibility. We can do wonderful things. We can also do horrible, abusive things. But we can do wonderful things. We can mold it, make it great—it's great stuff!

## (C) The Void

But our socialized constructions of "reality" conceal two other dimensions of human existence that are absolutely crucial to our understanding of spirit within a theological frame of reference. The first dimension it conceals is what I will call the *Void*, the presence of existential absence, which is the third dimension of human experience. Let the Void be the name for the ultimate aim of all proximate forms of nothingness. Void is the implicit aim of conflict, absence, loneliness, or death. These are some of the faces of the Void or ways in which an ultimate nothingness can intrude into the self-world relationship and violate the reality that we construct between self and world.

We don't like to think about the Void, but it is constantly intruding, constantly poking its way into the ego-constructed reality that we so carefully try to preserve. Thus, we automatically tend to compose it out, like we compose out the blind spots mentioned above. The best phenomenological description of this intrusion of Void comes from Jean-Paul Sartre. Picture Sartre in the café on afternoon waiting for his friend Pierre to show up at 2:30. It's 2:29. Sartre figures Pierre will be on time. He usually would be here. It gets to be 2:30. He looks around, but Pierre is not there. It's 2:32, then 2:35. He looks around again. Pierre is still not there. "I wonder what happened to him? He's usually so punctual." A quarter of three: "What happened to him? Perhaps he or I got the time wrong." Ten of three . . . Five of three . . . "I'd better call his office and find out what happened." Three o'clock. "He's not coming. What went wrong? I have to find out and see what is going on." What is happening to Sartre? He is sensing the presence of an absence. And when you sense the presence of an absence, you go to work to compose it out because it is a blind spot, an empty place, a face of the Void. You have got to compose it out so that the world can become livable again.

I go home sometime after lectures and go into the big old house that we live in and say, "Arlene, Arlene!" No answer. Immediately I tend to ask myself, "Where is she? Oh, yes, she was supposed to be at such and such a place." My questioning reveals that I don't want to notice the absence. Absence is something I don't want anything to do with. In fact, it doesn't occur to me to look at the significance of the absence. I compose it out as fast as I can.

I know you know what this experience feels like. I know you know if you know what *loneliness* is. Loneliness is the chronic sense of the presence of an absence. Harry Stack Sullivan, the noted psychiatrist, said that he could get people to relive almost any trauma except the trauma of loneliness. From this standpoint of the Void, loneliness was and is too close to the experience of one's own death. You have to keep that awareness screened out. Those of you who have lost a loved one have experienced the strongest metaphor, the most powerful face, of the Void.

Have you ever gone to a room where someone you have known and loved lived and died? My only sister died when she was thirty-nine years old. We went out to California to take care of things. We walked into her room and there were all kinds of things half done—a half-finished manuscript, a rented TV set, a half-finished work of art, clothes hanging in the closet that she would never wear again, and ten thousand shoes. All the time we stood there a pervasive sense of the presence of an absence reigned. Death is the strongest metaphor we have for nothing. I want you to feel this absence as much as you can. It is very important to try to feel it. So let me die for you as I do annually for my students.

For the sake of the scenario, let's say it is November a few years ago when our children were still at home. I am working late in the study and it's about two o'clock and I think, "Well, I better take a walk to sort of clear my head, or I won't be able to sleep." So I put on my boots. It's been raining, so I put on my raincoat that has some leftover camping gear in the pockets. I decide to take the walk down by Carnegie Lake. Carnegie Lake is very quiet at two o'clock in the morning. There are practically no lights down there. It's very dark. Maybe there is noise off at the university somewhere, a dorm party or some folks making their way to the local convenience store, but that's about all. You hear almost nothing. So I'm walking down there along the shores of Carnegie Lake, when suddenly I stumble on a root and fall. As I fall I bump my head. It knocks me out and I plunge into the water. There's just a momentary splash. Then the water just smooths out. Because of all the gear I have in my coat, because of my boots and so on, I sink down to the bottom. There's lots of stuff on the bottom of Carnegie Lake. My coat catches on something down there. I get tangled up in the junk, my lungs fill with water and I die. And the water on the surface just smooths out over me . . .

About three o'clock in the morning Arlene wakes up and she reaches over to my side of the bed. I am not there. "Jim?" There's no sound. I left the light on downstairs. She turns it off. "I wonder where he went. I better go back to bed. I've got to get Kim and Tami to school in the morning." She goes back to bed. Ding-a-ling. It's seven thirty. "Get up, Kim! Come on, Tami! You have to hurry up and get to school. Hurry up, let's get breakfast." "Where's Daddy?" "I don't know. He must have gone out early. But you're going to miss the bus. Hurry up and go! Go! Bye-bye."

At ten o'clock someone from the seminary calls and says, "Is Dr. Loder all right? He missed his class this morning. Is everything okay?" And so a little search commences. The police get involved. They hang around for a little bit, but can't find anything. They never think to look in Carnegie Lake because he never walks down there. They wait a week. They wait two weeks. They are pretty sure he is not going to show up. Well, we have to do something about his classes, right? Students get a chance to register for other classes. Some work out a way to get credit for the course. There is a faculty meeting. Colleagues call for a little memorial minute to be placed on the faculty records. There's a little memorial service. A couple of tears flow here and there. My wife is informed that she can live six months in the big house but that's all. Then she has to move out to make room for another faculty family. So she gradually packs up the boxes wondering less and less, "What in the world happened? Where is he?" All the boxes are packed up, the furniture loaded onto the moving van.

Arlene takes the girls out west to Spokane, Washington, where her family lives. She mourns for a little while, but then she gets a job and returns to teaching. Life begins to return to normal. Kim and Tami grow up and finish high school. They go off to college. They get into their studies and they go on dates. Inevitably the guys they date ask them, "Hey, whatever happened to your old man?" And each one simply replies, "I don't know, but come on, let's have a good time. Don't let that spoil the evening." Everything, like the dark surface of Carnegie Lake, is smoothing out. The books and articles gather dust; people read them less and less. They mention him less and less. There's something in the records, but who was that guy? A hundred year from now? Two hundred years from now? Nothing! Not a ripple . . .

Now this may not be exactly how it happens, but it *will* happen. It will happen to you and it will happen to me. One for one every time. Death is the perfect statistic. A hundred years from now, two hundred years from now, five hundred years from now, *nothing, absolutely nothing*—I tell you an uncompromising truth—it is all going to come to nothing. Well, what are we doing—me writing a book, you sitting there reading it as if it really mattered? A hundred years from now, two hundred years from now, nobody gives a damn! They won't know you or me. They won't care!

Now you see what Void does. The nothingness makes everything we are doing, everything we think matters, *absurd*. The Bible insists that you look at the *whole* history of the universe and at the *whole* of human experience. If you look at what we are doing now from the perspective of the Void, then what we are doing now is patently, absolutely absurd. End of chapter . . . end of book . . . end of sanity![12]

## (D) The Holy

But there is a fourth dimension. The fourth dimension is the *Holy*. The best definition I have of this comes from Rudolf Otto's classic work, *The Idea of the Holy*, in which he defines the Holy as "*the mysterium tremendum et fascinans.*" The Holy is just as radically other, just as distinctly disruptive as the Void. Like in the presence of the Void, every time the Holy appears the first two dimensions are shattered. Every time God shows up, those to whom God appears are down on their faces saying some version of, "My God! It's God!"

The reality-shattering experience of the presence of the Holy creates a real pedagogical problem for God. How do you teach anybody anything if every time you show up they are down on their faces, scared to death? So it is no surprise that when God appears almost the first thing that God says is, "Don't be afraid!" Why does the appearance of God always have to say, "Don't be afraid"? The gospel reveals that when the Holy shows up, it shatters two-dimensional reality and reveals something radically new. You cannot put it together yourself. "Don't be afraid." Mysterious! Tremendous! The holy enters into the first two dimensions with a power and vitality that creates things that are awesomely new.

Consider some of the faces of the Holy. When I first started to lecture on this topic some years ago a student came up after class and said, "Would you lay your hands on me and pray for me, so that I might receive the Holy

---

12. Editor's Note: I heard this dramatization of Dr. Loder's death several times while I was his TA for ED 105, and I recall the vividness of the sense of finality he gave to it. At the conclusion of the story he would move his arms slowly like an umpire signaling "Safe!" to dramatize the water smoothing out over his destiny in death as his voice softened into a haunting hush and then complete silence.

Spirit?" I said, "Sure, I'll lay my hands on you and pray for you." Right in the middle of the prayer, however, the student interrupted me. "Wait! No! I'm not ready for this yet." What spooked him? What was he waiting for? Did he anticipate the Spirit might interrupt his hoped-for success as a sophisticated and effective minister? Here is no doubt a very contemporary example of the power of the Holy coming near. "Wait a minute! Don't mess up my reality with something so radically other that I can't control."

The Holy can also be much quieter and even more powerful. Once I counseled a married couple at a time in which the man had been unfaithful. We were trying to deal with his wife's grief and the trauma of the broken relationship. In the course of several weekly sessions the woman experienced a powerful conversion by the Spirit of God. When they came to the next session, the wife said to her husband, "George, I'm ready to start over. I am ready to completely begin again. It's a whole new world for me." Now George had the problem! But he couldn't understand what had happened. You see, his wife had forgiven him unconditionally. She was ready to forget even that he needed forgiveness. She didn't say, "I forgive you, but don't forget I have forgiven you. You owe me one." She didn't say, "I am going to forgive you for the sake of the kids, but when they're gone, then I'm gone!" She gave no conditions, no strings attached. Out of nowhere, "I forgive you. I'm ready to start all over again." Now George didn't know what to do with that. It was mysterious, tremendous, fascinating. She was a new person, and George was forced to deal with himself in a much more profound and frightening way than before. The Holy had come to this couple.

Another example comes from the life of Madame Julia de Beausobre.[13] She was a woman raised in the Russian mystical tradition who had been imprisoned into a training camp by Russian officers and subjected to systematic thought reform. This training officer knew exactly what to do. Talk about a sadist; here he was. He knew exactly how to break her down. When she would cringe and cry in the corner of the cell, he loved it. If she tried to fight him off that would also whet his appetite. No matter what she did, he knew how to break her down.

At first, she prayed, "Get me out of here. Why am I here? Get me out of here." Then she started to pray a somewhat different prayer, along the lines, "What are you doing?" She prayed with a different assumption now. I

---

13. Editor's Note: Loder does not reveal here the source of this episode from the life of Madame Julia de Beausobre, who suffered in the Bolshevik Revolution. But in *Transforming Moment*, 85–87, he discusses this same event at greater length and refers to two of de Beausobre's books, *Woman Who Would Not Die* and *Creative Suffering*. The episode is also recorded in Constance Babington Smith's 1983 biography of de Beausobre, *Iulia de Beausobre*, chapter 5 (31–38).

am not giving you prayer formulas. I'm just saying she came at prayer with a different assumption. When she began to pray this way, a new consciousness began to permeate the situation. She could see who she was and who the training officer was. She felt herself grounded on a rock. In fact, she felt herself to be part of the Rock. The more the guy worked on her, the stronger and deeper that connection felt. The Rock began to shine, and she began to convey a kind of serenity. She got so serene that he actually lost interest in tormenting her and finally left her alone.

The point here is that we don't understand the Holy because we avoid the Void. In fact it is the people who have been to the bottom of the Void who know best that there really is a fourth dimension. There really is another reality. You can say, "Well, that's nice, but that's ridiculous. That's absurd." And to you I say, "Right, all you have is a choice between two absurdities—either the absurdity of nothingness or the absurdity of faith." No choice to play it cool. No choice to be rational, to be reasonable, to be successful, to have a nice happy time, to make your life work out, to set up your retirement plan. These are choices for socialization. But socialization is nothing but the absurd choice for nothingness. You see, all you have is a choice between two absurdities. It is an old biblical story, right? You have to choose. The choice is between the absurdity of faith or the absurdity of nothingness.

## (IV) DESCRIPTIONS OF LIFE IN THE SPIRIT: FAITH AWAKENED IN FOUR DIMENSIONS

These, then, are the four dimensions within which the Holy Spirit of God lives and moves, bestowing grace and engendering faith. In light of these dimensions, for me *faith means abiding in the fourth dimension while the power of faith transforms the other three dimensions.* The effect of abiding in the fourth dimension is not to become so transcendently spiritual or spiritualistic that out of every pore there oozes some sort of heavenly glow. Abiding in the fourth dimension means that you are put back into the ordinary world, just like when the energy is released in creative experiences and you are put back into the ordinary world with a new awareness. The ordinary world then becomes the bearer of the extraordinary, and the transformed "I" knows it. Under conviction, the "I" takes on a dialectical quality present throughout Scripture. In the genre of the prophets, the dialectic was expressed as, "*I, yet not I, but Yahweh speaking to you.*" In the genre of the gospels Jesus expressed the dialectic as, "*I, yet not I, but the Father.*" In the genre of Paul it's "*I, yet not I, but Christ.*" Abiding in the fourth dimension you say, "I, yet not I," because the "I" is transformed to bear witness to the presence of Christ in the world.

The Lived World also gets transformed. The socialized world that you are working and building, and extending yourself into with so much effort has been exposed by the presence of Christ to be the larger world you know Christ is composing. The world becomes the habitation of the kingdom of God. Even the Void gets transformed. The Void no longer reigns as this deep silence behind silence, this utterly absurd nothingness. The Void becomes instead a shadow, a foreshadowing of the power of grace that truly reigns. Void becomes the optimal occasion within which you can recognize grace as thoroughly gracious. When the Holy appears in the context of the Void, you know you have nothing to fear. The Holy gets its sharpest, clearest definition in the context of the Void, such that the Void itself becomes a bearer of grace. Only in the context of Void do we know grace purely as grace, not as an extension of ourselves. When the Holy comes to us in the midst of the Void, we know that we can thank God in the midst of our suffering. You move into the life of the Holy, and that life goes from strength to strength. God's holy presence becomes the ultimate milieu within which all other dimensions are embraced and seen in their true context.

## (A) Transformation in Four Dimensions: The Emmaus Road Event

What I want to do now is connect the logic of transformation to the four dimensions of reality, so that you can see the completion of the analogy, as similarity in difference, and difference in similarity. In other words, to see transformation operating in four dimensions will be to see how we can understand the work of the Holy Spirit in analogical relationship to human spirit. In order to make this connection, I want to look at the so-called Emmaus Road narrative in Luke 24:13–35. In this story, we have in narrative form an accounting of how the Holy Spirit works in human experience in four dimensions. My basic assumption here is that what the risen Christ did tangibly with the disciples to bring about the redemptive transformation of their history then is consistent with what the Holy Spirit continues to do tangibly to bring about the redemptive transformation of our history today. Whether you see this text as an actual historical episode or as just the way the early church sought to portray the living Christ instructing her through the Spirit, I think the point is essentially the same. In this story, we have a paradigm for redemptive transformation in four dimensions, and therefore a narrative account of how the Holy Spirit works.

Let us read through this postresurrection passage verse by verse. Note that I have inserted some interpretative observations along the way (the bracketed, nonitalicized text).

> *That very day two of them were going to a village named Emmaus, about seven miles from Jerusalem, and talking with each other about all these things that had happened. While they were talking and discussing together, Jesus himself drew near and went with them. But their eyes were kept from recognizing him. And he said to them, "What is this conversation which you are holding with each other as you walk?"* [All the way through this narrative, don't miss the divine courtesy. Jesus takes their humanity seriously]. *And they stood still, looking sad. Then one of them, named Cleophus, answered him." Are you the only visitor to Jerusalem who does not know the things that have happened here in these days?"* [Why aren't you laughing? That's a joke. Jesus is the only one who *does* know what's been happening. Can't you see Luke writing this with a big smile on his face!] *And he said to them, "What things?"* [There is the divine courtesy again. Like a Rogerian counselor, Jesus encourages them to bring what they have to the conversation. Tell me what's in you. I want to know from you about you."] *And they said to him, "Concerning Jesus of Nazareth, who was a prophet mighty in deed and word before God and all the people, and how our chief priests and rulers delivered him up to be condemned to death, and crucified him. But we had hoped that he was the one to redeem Israel. Yet, and beside all this, it is now the third day since this happened. Moreover, some women were at the tomb early in the morning and did not find his body; and they came back saying that they had even seen a vision of angels, who said that he was alive. Some of those who were with us went to the tomb, and found it just as the women had said; but him they did not see."* [Notice the implicit intrusion of the fourth dimension as hope. They are not convinced, but they are not totally unconvinced] *And He said to them, "O foolish men, and slow of hearts to believe all that the prophets have spoken! Was it not necessary that the Christ should suffer these things and enter into his glory?" And beginning with Moses and all the prophets, he interpreted to them all the scriptures the things concerning himself.* [Now notice Jesus takes them back. They're scanning—looking for prototypes, a basis upon which to understand what has happened.].
>
> *So they drew near to the village to which they were going. He appeared to be going further, but they constrained him, saying, "Stay with us, for it is toward evening and the day is now far*

*spent."* [Notice, again the divine courtesy. In effect Jesus says to them, "You are getting warm. You are getting close to something that is hidden. Are you sure you want me to come in? Because if I come in it is going to change your life." You're never going to be the same. Are you sure you want the help I am going to give you? And they say, "Yes, we want it." Their hearts were strangely warm, like in the children's game when you say, "You're getting warm. You're getting warmer. You're hot!" because the person is getting near to the hidden thing.]. *So he went in to stay with them. When he was at table with them, he took the bread and blessed it, and broke it, and gave it to them. And their eyes were opened and they recognized him; and he vanished out of their sight.* [See below on the significance of this vanishing]. *They said to each other, "Did not our hearts burn within us while he was talking to us on the road, while he opened to us the scriptures! And they rose that same hour and returned to Jerusalem; and they found the eleven gathered together and those who were with them, who said, "The Lord has risen indeed, and has appeared to Simon!"* [And they said, "No, no, that's our line."]. *Then they told what had happened on the road, and how he was known to them in the breaking of the bread.* (Luke 24:13–35 RSV)

Luke presents us here with a narrated event of redemptive transformation in four dimensions. Four-dimensionality is the larger context in which I want to understand socialization. The socialized, Self-World reality for these two disciples is Israel. Israel is not just an empirical reality. Israel was the composed, constructed, and carefully rationalized world of the whole Hebraic tradition and culture. That world was being threatened by corruption from the priests within and by Rome's oppressive occupation from outside. Jesus was supposed to save Israel from this corruption and oppression. But now this erstwhile savior is dead and he didn't save Israel. The two-dimensional world of these disciples had fallen apart. Corruption from within and oppression from without promised to continue unabated. All hopes were dashed.

So the disciples are depressed. And they take a walk. Did you ever take a walk when you were depressed? They are in conflict about their socialized world. They don't so much have a conflict as the conflict has them in the context of Israel. Note that in their despair there is some lingering hope because the women had come to them with their amazing report. But socialized Israel did not put much stock in women's testimony. So the hopelessness of the conflict dominates their consciousness. Into this existential conflict, an unidentified stranger shows up to meet them in their despair.

Now the constructive aspect of the process of transformation begins. Jesus leads them in a deep searching out of prototypes in the history of Israel, in the history of their world, concerning Jesus himself. Luke portrays an interlude in which the disciples are being led by the visible but unidentified stranger to look back for something that will put their lives together again in a fresh way commensurate with the depth of the conflict. This movement deeper into the conflict is like the "Inner Teacher" that Calvin and Augustine talked about. The "Inner Teacher" works in you to pull things together in new ways that correlate with God's reign.

And so, the instruction of the Stranger starts to take effect. Through his study of the Hebrew Scriptures, the disciples sense something brewing in their spirits. The are "getting hot." Like players in the children's game, they are getting close to something hidden. What is hidden begins to emerge and assert itself into the conflict. They are beginning to get it. Everything is about to fall in place. When Jesus "*appeared to be going further*," in effect Jesus says to them, "Are you sure you want this?" And when they say, "*Stay with us*," in effect they say, "Yes, we want this." And so Jesus goes in, breaks the bread, and hands it to them. The broken bread is a charged symbol. It symbolizes *his* brokenness, which takes into itself *their* brokenness. He says, "Here, take this in. Swallow it if you can. Can you swallow this?" And you see they are convinced. Their brokenness is taken up in his brokenness.

They are convicted—convicted more deeply than they were convicted before. That is, they see that he has come not just to save Israel, but the deep resonance of brokenness means that he was sent to save the whole world. How convicted are they? They didn't even know who he was. The prophet sent to Israel? No. He is the Son of God sent to the whole world. Blinded by their enculturation, they didn't know what was going on. The pain of conviction was driven down deep within them. The conflict is worse than they thought it was. The conflict is driven deeper. But at the same time, the bread is held in resurrected hands. They see him presenting to them a four-dimensional reality in his own nature, saying, "Take this in if you can."

What's the epistemological effect of this encounter? Luke says, "*Their eyes are opened and they recognized him*"! But as soon as they recognized him, Luke notes, Jesus "*vanished from their sight*"! Now we must ask: "Why when their eyes were opened did they see less? Here we have a truly marvelous arrangement, nothing less than the twist that makes the transformational experience redemptive. They see less when their eyes are opened because when you truly recognize the presence of Jesus, you realize that you cannot compose him as an object in your world. You don't compose him into your world. He composes you into his world. He becomes the lens through which you now see everything and compose reality. He cannot be an object out there. You are the object in what he is doing. Here is the figure-ground shift that shakes the foundations of the world to reveal the kingdom. Of course he had to vanish. As soon as you see who he really is, he has to disappear in order that you can be composed into his world.

This narrative reveals the highest meaning of having a vision of Christ. A vision of Christ is not something out there, but something that comes into one's socialized world and then heightens your capacity to see what is really going on in terms of the four-dimensional reality that is in his person. To have faith in him means then that he becomes the one who represents the four-dimensional reality in whom and by whom we reside in the fourth dimension while these other three dimensions are transformed. He is the one who holds us together because he is the one who holds all things together.

Then what happens in the story? The disciples ran out into the darkness back to Jerusalem. Of course, we know it's not too smart to run around outside of Jerusalem in the dark! That is, it's not too smart unless you are no longer afraid of the dark, afraid of the Void! These disciples have awakened to the presence of the Creator of the whole world, so that light or dark are both the same to them. With the release of tension bound up in the existential conflict comes a new capacity to be thrust into the world without fears, boundaries, or restrictions. So they go running back to Jerusalem. They go in where the other disciples are together. And before they can say anything, the disciples sitting there say, "Hey, guess what! Jesus has risen from the dead and appeared to Peter!" They probably wanted to say, "No, no, that's *our* line. Jesus has risen and appeared to *us*." What does Luke portray here in this scene of mutual testifying to Jesus Christ's resurrection? He portrays in narrative form the *koinonia*, the church!

Note then, that the church is the social reality created by the presence of the living Lord, not the social reality created by socialization. The church is truly social, truly concrete, more embedded in creation, more embedded in the world than any socialization process could ever produce. Socialization may follow from the *koinonia*. But socialization is not the essential reality of *koinonia*. *Koinonia* is the church, the gathering of persons through the communion-creating power of Jesus Christ. That's what the Spirit of Christ is doing. The Spirit is working transformation, holding up the nature of Jesus Christ and four-dimensional reality, and driving conviction as deep as possible in order that the reality of Christ may become as meaningful as possible. If you refuse the Void, you refuse the integrity of grace. If you refuse suffering, then you refuse the mercy of God.

## (B) Luther's Experience and Doctrine of the Holy Spirit

To put the Emmaus narrative of redemptive transformation in more tradi-
tional theological terms, let us look briefly at Luther's doctrine of the Holy
Spirit. For Luther, the Holy Spirit has a grammar of its own, its own kind of
logic. Luther's understanding of the pattern emerged from his own struggles
with God.[14] He experienced a massive amount of personal anguish over
his own socialized world, struggles over law versus gospel, slavery versus
freedom, damnation versus salvation. There were countless interludes in
Luther's life, hours of conversation with Staupitz, his father confessor. But
of course, the socialized Staupitz did not want Luther to talk about these
anguished struggles with God. He wanted Luther to confess the normal sins
of pride or lust or cowardice or something. "Don't talk about God. Tell me
something I can forgive you for." But Luther insisted, scanning, always scanning. What does it all mean?

Famously, the resolution, the key insight, the figure-ground shift,
comes to Luther as he sits on the privy in the tower contemplating the just
God and the just God who condemns. There he reads in Rom 5:1: "*Therefore,
since we are justified by faith, we have peace with God through our Lord Jesus
Christ.*" The clouds departed and the dawn broke through. The just God
does not condemn; the just God *justifies.* Luther testified of this awakening:
"This came with great relief to me on the privy in the tower. It was given to
me by the Holy Spirit." Don't ever think the Spirit takes you out of the body
and quote Luther. Luther's spirituality is very much embodied, very earthy.
There is this great release, and, as Luther said of himself, "I was fired into the
world with a velocity not my own."

In the classic theological terms, the basic structure of the experience is
*mortification* followed by *vivification.* The Spirit works to mortify in order to
vivify. Between the mortification and the vivification there is this anguished
struggle, what Luther called, the *Anfechtungen* (i.e., struggles with God), the
temptation that occurs in wrestling with God at an existential level. But the
mortification of socialized existence is there so the vivification can come
in four dimensions, the sign of true conviction by the Word of God. So
the upshot of the vivification is that one is now a grateful recipient of the
Eucharist, and of the Word of God.

In the analogy of the Spirit, the grammar or the logic of transformation
is the constant and the authentic connection between divine and human
agency. The grammar is the same, providing continuity for the human spirit
and the Holy Spirit to work together. The analogy works on the similarity

---

14. See the discussion of Luther's doctrine of the Holy Spirit in Prenter, *Spiritus
Creator.*

side to foster continuity. But the human spirit, of course, is ontologically distinct from the Holy Spirit. The unredeemed human spirit composes the world in two-dimensions under the power of socialization. Its origins and destiny are the human psyche (ego). In contrast, the Holy Spirit works in four dimensions. Its origins and destiny are with God because the Holy Spirit *is* God. So the pattern of transformation is both familiar and radically new. The similarity of the pattern allows us to recognize the work of the Spirit in the milieu of spirit that lies at our core. If the Spirit's grammar was wholly and totally and only radically other, we couldn't even say it was radically other. But the human spirit requires an ontological ground beyond its own capacity to generate life and meaning. The human spirit must be transparently grounded in the power that created it in order to be fully human according to the *imago Christi*. The Spirit comes to us from beyond our social constructions of reality but intervenes within them to awaken the human spirit to the presence of Christ, enabling transformation in four dimensions. Thus, we are enabled to recognize this Spirit in similarity and in difference. When the human spirit, whose nature is transformational, testifies with the Holy Spirit, then human transformation is redemptively transformed. The human spirit turns beyond ego toward God, living now in four-dimensional depth and breadth in the power of the Spirit.

## (V) CONCLUSION

In conclusion, I have argued in this chapter that in Christian education the Spirit of Christ needs to be understood as the Teacher. Moreover, Christian education must be fundamentally transformational, four-dimensional, and christocentric, through the power of the Holy Spirit. In the following chapters, I will unpack these aspects of the work of the Spirit in personal, social, and cultural contexts, bringing my own perspective into relationship with the perspectives we have been working on in previous chapters. Our goal is to continue to move our concept of lifestyle from a two-dimensional to a four-dimensional horizon revealed in Christ.

# 6

## Person

### Human Development
### and Personality Transformation

## (I) INTRODUCTION

PRELIMINARY TO THE DISCUSSION of personality transformation in this chapter, I want to lay down as a foundation three propositions that are fundamental to the formation of the individual personality at the level of the human spirit. *First,* socialization focuses on the stages of human development because it is there that adaptation to the sociocultural milieu can be observed. In contrast, transformation focuses on the stage-transition dynamics not the stages. This transformational perspective argues that as we move from one stage to the next in the formation of the personality, we pass through the transformational sequence we have already identified—(1) conflict, (2) interlude, (3) insight, (4) release and restoration, and (5) proving out the insight again and again—in every register of behavior. To illustrate in brief, recall that in conflict with the complexity and richness of a language environment, the child struggles to bring forth the new structures of grammar that are then proved out with incessant talking! And so it is for the stages of ego formation and every register of human behavior that emerges from that ego.

*Second,* in light of the pervasiveness of the stage transition dynamics I argue that since each stage only appears temporarily and is to some extent statistically determined, the deeper continuity of the personality is maintained by the transformational dynamics. This deeper continuity is the human spirit creating and composing new worlds out of the deep resources within the personality in its interaction with the environment. In other words, the second proposition maintains that the transformational dynamics are more psychologically real and stronger—in terms of endurance over time *and* in terms of its capacity to overthrow the stages and create new ones—than the stages and their socialized equilibration.

*Third*, recall that in the transformation of the personality by the mediation of Christ, according to the analogy of the Spirit, the human spirit—which tends to be in the background behind socialization and ego development in the normal course of human development—now moves into the foreground. Transformation initiates a fundamental figure-ground shift—that which was in the background becomes the central figure. Without losing its integrity as the transformational process inherent in the personality, the spirit now exercises its creative power by drawing upon inner resources conformed to the nature of Christ and to the aims of the Spirit. In the transformation of the ego, the human spirit, already operative in the personality, is decentered from the ego (one of its most substantive creations!) and recentered on the person and nature of Christ. When the spirit is transformed, whatever one subsequently creates or generates of oneself now becomes an expression of Christ's nature and in conformity to Christ's Spirit.

As we now turn to the formation of a Christian style of life, recall the structure of a lifestyle. The core of any naturalistic lifestyle is the ego and its defensive postures. Thus, ego transformation is fundamental to the creation of a Christian style of life. Through Christ's transformation of the ego, the core of a Christian style of life is created. Moreover, a Christian lifestyle must be expressed contextually and deepen itself in all of its organic, social, and cultural contexts. That is, the integrity of a truly Christian style of life redeemed in the Spirit must engage the whole field of human action, even as the Holy Spirit engages and transforms every aspect of that field. Also note that even though I am beginning here with the transformation of the ego and so with the transformation of the individual person, a Christian style of life may also be initiated and empowered from any one of the other various fields of human action—organic, social, or cultural. Surely the transformation of the core calls for the transformation of the whole, while the transformation of the whole depends upon the transformation of the core. So, I am not advocating a conversionist, isolationist or individualistic approach to transformation and education. However, the transformation of the core—the ego's preferred line of defense—is decisive if we are to educate for a Christian style of life.

Now we must ask, how does such ego transformation occur and to what end does it move? Let us begin by inquiring into what constitutes the true aim of transformation. Then, in the course of examining this aim, we can discuss the question of how this aim is to be attained.

## (II) THE GOAL OF EGO TRANSFORMATION: LOVE

Stated concisely, for a Christian style of life to emerge, the goal of ego transformation must be understood as *the power to give love and to give it sacrificially with integrity*. Following the logic of transformation, we will begin with a diagnosis of the key conflict facing the socialized ego—integrity of love.

The first time I told my wife that I loved her, I set up a proper venue with great care. There was a marvelous dinner, flowing water, soft lights, and quiet privacy. Sensing the opportune moment, I leaned over and said softly with an appropriate amount of congruent affect, "Arlene, I love you." She immediately responded, "No, you don't." Her response was, to say the least, rather disconcerting. But of course, she was right, absolutely right. Arlene had raised the decisive question: What has to be there for one to be able to say, 'I love you' and really mean it?

The Bible claims that God is love and that we are created to love God and one another. In perfect accord with this Judeo-Christian claim, some of the best secular interpreters of human nature also claim the primacy of love in human existence as well. For example, Ashley Montagu, the popular anthropologist at Princeton University, held that the fundamental motivation of all animals, especially the human type, is to give and receive love. Moreover, according to one article, Montagu sent his evidence to Einstein. He then visited Einstein and was able to persuade him that this was the case, over against the more Freudian view that Einstein supposedly held prior to that encounter.[1] Probably the "love" Einstein was thinking about was closer to Spinoza's concept than to Ashley Montagu's. But in any case, if both the Bible and Einstein agree on this matter, shouldn't we pay attention?

We must now ask, however, if love is so fundamental to our nature, why is it so hard to say "I love you" and *really* mean it? Ironically, the answer I propose to give to this question arises from an account of one of the most magnificent achievements of the human spirit, the creation of the human ego. But, as we shall see, this creative act is also the defensive act

---

1. Editor's Note: Loder did not cite a source for this anecdote.

that imprisons the human spirit in the ego. The human spirit is, so to say, fundamentally imprisoned in one of its own creations. What follows is an account of why human spirit begins and ends in the human ego, and why the ego must be transformed if the human spirit is liberated to testify with the Holy Spirit that we are children of God, empowering us to live a Christian style of life.

## (A) Ego Formation Theologically Considered

The understanding of ego formation that helps us to see our situation most clearly comes from neo-Freudian developmentalists like Rene Spitz in his *The First Year of Life*, Erik Erikson in *Toys and Reasons*, and Ana-Maria Rizzuto in her *The Birth of the Living God*. According to these observers, the first year of life is the definitive time for the development of ego generally. What happens in this first year determines the nature of the ego's formation. Thus, the first year of life is foundational to lifestyle. Formation of ego is the core of the core. That is to say, ego formation itself is the primary problem, and later on in human development it gets further distorted through its socialization into achievement, authoritarian, protean, and oppressive styles of life as discussed in chapter 3.

Rene Spitz charted four basic steps in the formation of the ego.[2] The four steps are based on the four primary organizers of the personality during the early months of life, which he called the Mouth, the Face, Anxiety, and Negation.

### (1) The Mouth

The child is dependent and receptive during the first two and a half to three months of life outside the womb. So the first organizer of the personality is the mouth, the central organ through which the child survives and thrives. The mouth is the organizer through which the child indwells the world and takes in the world and knows the world. We need to emphasize here that the mouth is an *impersonal* organizer of the personality at this early stage.

---

2. Editor's Note: Loder summarized Spitz's work on ego formation in both *Transforming Moment* (162–64) and *Logic of the Spirit* (89–95).

## (2) The Face

At three months the definitive *interpersonal* event occurs—i.e., the "face" phenomenon. Spitz observed at this age that when a configuration of a face drawn on a stick is raised up and down before the infant, the infant smiles. A mirroring relationship with the mother follows, because in response to the child's smile, the parent smiles back. So significant is this "face" phenomenon to communicate interpersonal connections between mother and child that it functions like an imprinting on what it means to be human. Imprinting is a phenomenon that ethnologists like Konrad Lorenz applied to animals. For example, little ducks need to imprint on the momma duck. Indeed, there is a certain period of time after its birth when the duckling must be with the mother duck in order to find out what it is to be a duck. If during this critical period, the little duck is with Konrad Lorenz, a dog, or some other animal, its confusion fouls up the little duck's mating patterns. Imprinting defines what it means for a duck to be a member of a given species.

I am arguing here that the imprinting of the child on the human face during infancy is the human equivalent of this animal pattern. The imprinted face tells the child what it means to be human. What does the face tell the child? It says, to be human is to be confirmed as a self by a loving other, who holds and feeds you, who constitutes your universe and addresses you *interpersonally*—i.e., face-to-face. In countless ways the child is constituted by the supportive presence of the nurturing person. But this focus on the face as the decisive interpersonal organizer of the child's personality implies transcendence as well. Thus, for the child, the face signifies what I like to call *the cosmic ordering, self-confirming, presence of a loving other*. Through the encounter with the face, the child reconfigures her whole existence as essentially and concretely personal, substantially relational, and implicitly religious. At three months this interpersonal, relational, and cosmic ordering of life crystallizes for the developing person as the center of existence.

## (3) Anxiety

The baby continues to develop until he or she is able, at about six months, to recognize the mother's face and to see it over against other faces. Ominously, however, he or she now recognizes that the mother's face goes away and that other faces take its place. These other faces become for the child a threat. In other words, the baby begins to respond with *anxiety* to the interpersonal relation, because he/she wants the *one* face that will not go away. Suppose you are a father in a home in which the mother is your child's primary caretaker. You go off to work in the morning and come home at night, all eager to see little Johnny, future quarterback for Notre Dame. You set your briefcase down and stroll over to the crib, only to be greeted by an anxious look that breaks into frenzied "Waaaaaagh!" In effect, the child says to you, "Go away. You don't have the right face. You are not the face that constellates my world." In this way and many others the child begins to experience the imminent sense of the presence of an absence, resulting in continuous anxiety as an existential depth (recall the discussion of the Void).

Thus the security once supplied by the face gradually disappears. To make matters even worse, about this same time in the life of the child, she learns to anticipate the outer imposition of "No!" from these parents who also go away. As parents, we say "No!" in a thousand different ways. "No!" may be communicated in the way we hold our children when their pants are dirty, or in our frustrated response to their having dumped their cereal on the floor too many times with an outburst. "No!" is communicated through our body language, through voice inflection, and even through our eye contact. This combination of the *internal* loss of security once supplied by the face together with this *outer* no-saying by the big people produces an existential traumatic condition for the child's spirit wherein inside and outside structures collapse. That is, when what you fear inside also happens outside; there is no longer a place for *you*. You are crushed, traumatized and negated.

Imagine you are standing on a particular street corner when a car jumps the curb. You are knocked down and taken by ambulance to the hospital. While in the hospital you remark, "Well, I refuse to be afraid to go to that street corner again." So as your injuries heal, you go back to the scene of the accident. Suddenly, *Wham!* It happens again! You get out of the hospital this time and you think, "Boy, I'm not going to be chicken about this." So you go to the corner again. *Wham!* A car hits you a third time. Now three times is enough. No one is going to drag you to that corner again. Being there traumatizes you, because the thing you fear inside is matched by the events that happened outside.

The infant child faces a similar situation, because the fear of inner emptiness is matched by outward no-saying and loss. Thus, the child senses the "presence of absence" in a fundamentally existential fashion. In order to survive, the spirit of the child makes an ingenious, but tragic, response to the trauma. This tragic response becomes the fourth organizer of the personality.

## (4) Negation

At fourteen months children enter the fourth phase of ego formation, which is *negation*. In this stage, they do a primal version of what we described earlier as "reaction formation"—doing the opposite of what they really want to do with all the energy they want to do the first thing. Children learn to inflict "No!" on the environment before the environment inflicts "No!" on them. Thus, with all the energy they longed to put into face-to-face affirmation, they say "No!" instead. By the time a child reaches two years old, an existential sense of "No!" essentially organizes their personality! At the phenomenological level, we call this age the "terrible two's." Everything is negated. "Do you want a cookie?" "No!" "Okay, I'll eat the cookie." "Noooo! That's my cookie."

The activity wherein negation organizes the child's relation to the world is called *repression*. Fundamentally, repression provides the needed capacity to divide between inside and outside, between conscious and unconscious. We compose the world in a way to keep it "out there" while at the same time we attempt to preserve our internal sense of self in relation to it. No-saying is thus internalized and it becomes the psychic function of repression.[3] We can see that repression develops this way by looking at how repression becomes undone in therapy. Clients often revert to negation as a way of going deeper into the psyche than their ego defenses would ordinarily permit. That is, the unconscious can confess if it denies what it discloses. "No, that was *not* my mother I was in bed with in my dreams." Negation is both the developmental foundation of repression and the therapeutic way of undoing it. Thus, negation as repression is the foundation of the ego, and all subsequent ego competencies are built on this no-saying capacity.

What does this mean for human development? It means that the ego, this great creation of the autonomous child, is fundamentally defensive and operates in the service of concealing the anxious sense of absence, loss, and abandonment lurking under the surface of existence. Indeed, haunting all of the ego's activities—language, intelligence, emotion, and so forth—is this profound sense of the Void we cannot face. Further, this repressed sense of the Void means that the carefully contained creation of the two-dimensional world governed by socialization is itself fundamentally based upon existential negation that we continually must compose out of private and public life. Remember the blind spots composed out of our awareness as discussed in the previous chapter? Defensiveness becomes the work of the

---

3. Freud documented this claim in his famous paper, "Negation," 338–48; and Spitz, *No and Yes*; and Spitz, *First Year*.

ego, which it performs pervasively with systematic regularity with the support of socialization.[4]

Thus, on the one hand, the construction of the new order of ego in the face of imminent nothingness represents a magnificent defensive achievement of the human spirit. On the other hand, it means that to keep the ego's world intact, the significance of the face as the primary interpersonal organizer of the personality—the imprint of what it means to be human—has to be systemically buried under repression, under the negation that is the foundation of the traumatized ego. The result is a kind of cosmic loneliness, a deep longing in all of us for a "face" that will do what a "face" is supposed to do and not go away. Once formed, the ego continues to compose the world so as to continue to bury the "face" and to ward off the threat of nothingness and abandonment. Recall Sartre trying to recompose the world in the absence of Pierre. All of us try to recompose the world in the presence of absence, the face of death that haunts existence.

The secret, however, secretes. Sylvan Tomkins, a research psychologist for many years at Princeton University, saw this longing for the "face" as the foundation of the human quest for universality, the ego's search for comprehensive meaning to compensate for the loss that the "face" signifies. I want to stress the power of our longing for a "face" that will not go away. This longing is powerful enough to stop any hard-driven achiever.[5]

Have you ever watched achievers getting out of an airplane? They arrive at Kennedy or Newark. They fly in from someplace to do big business on Wall Street or some equivalent market. Sometimes I have watched these hard-driven people get off the plane in which a woman near them holds a small child, say a little girl. Now, before this little girl gets to be fourteen to eighteen months, she hasn't been socialized enough to know that you are not supposed to look at people in the eye. So the little girl's stare catches the achiever's eye. And the hard-driving achiever stops in his tracks, smiles, forgets who he is, and says, "Hi there. Aren't you adorable?" Ah, the secret secreted! There is a longing, a deep, abiding longing, even in the spirit of the achiever, for the "face" that will not go away—i.e., a longing for the "face" that will give the achiever a place in the cosmic order and communicate self-worth through a loving presence that is not earned. This longing secretes from under the achiever's ego defenses, and the child's eye-to-eye contact brings it out!

4. Editor's Note: Loder argued in *Logic of the Spirit* that human development emerging out of these early dynamic but repressive movements should be understood essentially as "the triumph of negation" in human experience and theologically as the recapitulation of the fall in human experience. See below.

5. Tompkins, *Affect*. See Loder, *Logic of the Spirit*, 95–96.

The "face" not only has the power to momentarily rehumanize the achiever. It can also undo, at least for a moment, anger that has built up over a lifetime. My best and favorite illustration of this power at work is the angry little lady I saw one evening in Davidson's Market in Princeton. She came into the store about five o'clock. She looked like she had been working all day scrubbing floors in some dingy, grubby hotel someplace. She was gnarled and petulant as she pulled her basket free and set off to conquer the store. Now Davidson's is always crowded, with lots of people jamming the aisles. This lady went ramming down the vegetable aisle, squeezed by the milk coolers, rambled over to the meat section, back up to the soup aisle, down to the bread, back over to the crackers. Once she had gathered everything, she got into the line with a vengeance. Don't get in her way! But then it happens. In front of her in line is a mother with her baby. When the baby smiled at the lady, she came undone, the anger dissipated, and she smiled back. The secret secreted again. By the time she checked out, the little lady was beaming. "Hi, how are you? You are so cute." Now, if you tried to tell this lady to cheer up, she'd break your knees with her basket! But the contact with the child undoes her. The "face" phenomenon has tremendous humanizing power.

Don't misunderstand my point. We are not talking about sentimentality. For as Bonhoeffer said, if you want to see the evidence of original sin go to the marketplace and stare at people a little too long.[6] The ego's developmental pattern I described is already there in Genesis. In Genesis, the move is from face-to-face awareness into anxiety, then shame and the desire to hide. The fig leaf is not a bad image of repression. Bonhoeffer's argument for our participation in original sin suggests that each one of us recapitulates this Edenic pattern, an argument taken up by thinkers like Kierkegaard and Pannenberg as well. Loss of the self-defining "face" yields up dread or anxiety, which gives way to despair, a deep dichotomy in our selfhood that we persistently conceal from one another, from God, and from ourselves.

This fall into negation, then, reveals why we continually oppose the very love we are made for. At the base of the ego resides an existential

---

6. Bonhoeffer, *Creation*. In *Transforming Moment*, Loder elaborates on this claim that the Genesis account "parallels the ontogenesis of shame." "Genesis (the J writer, at least) may have been working from a similar prototype in moving the woman's face-to-face relationship with God into a felt absence (the woman was 'alone') matched by the environmental negation, God's command ('do not eat'). That the woman responds to this situation and the stranger's (serpent's) face with anxiety is evident in that she overstates God's command ('don't touch' . . .) . . . and finally falls into an incorporation of the negation trap, resulting in an inner division of herself against herself (fig leaf concealment) such that face-to-face interaction could not occur thereafter without shame" (165).

alienation, the ground of our existential guilt before God. As we discussed in connection with Luther and the Holy Spirit in the last chapter, only at this level—not at the level of conscience or socialized ego—does the Holy Spirit convict us. *Mortification* takes place here, in and behind and underneath the ego's defenses. Upon this general foundation of the ego's structure, all particular distortions of lifestyle—obsessive achievement, authoritarian, protean, and oppressive) are built and maintained. Therefore, to this condition, to the deep structure of ego, we must turn if the destructive course of our lives built upon ego is to be altered. We must realize there is no way to put the power of the Spirit of God into this old wineskin of the human ego.

## (B) Ego Transformation Biblically Narrated

This "triumph of negation in ego development" is, then, why it is so hard to say "I love you" and really mean it.[7] However, it is precisely from this condition that Jesus, through the presence and power of his Spirit, proposes to transform us, so that our human spirits are released in the Spirit's power and are enabled to give love sacrificially with integrity. To gain some insight into precisely how the Spirit accomplishes this transformation of the ego and release of the human spirit, let us turn to the familiar conversation between Nicodemus and Jesus in the third chapter of John's Gospel. I am going to read this passage through a kind of Kierkegaardian lens or hermeneutic.

> *Now there was a man, out of the Pharisees, named Nicodemus, a ruler of the Jews. This man came to Jesus by night and said to him, "Rabbi, we know that you are a teacher come from God; for no one can do these signs that you do, unless God is with him." Jesus answered him, "Truly, truly, I say to you, unless one is born anew, he cannot see the kingdom of God." Nicodemus said to him, "How can a man be born when he is old? Can he enter a second time into his mother's womb and be born?" Jesus answered, "Truly, truly I say to you, unless one is born of water and the Spirit, he cannot enter the kingdom of God. That which is born of the flesh is flesh and that which is born of the Spirit is spirit. Do not marvel that I said to you, 'You must be born anew.' The wind blows where it wills, and you hear the sound of it, but you do not know whence it comes or whither it goes; so it is with every one who is born of the Spirit." Nicodemus said to him, "How can this be?" Jesus answered him, "Are you a teacher of Israel, and you do not understand this?*

7. Editor's Note: This phrase "triumph of negation in ego development" summarizes Loder's discussions of the results of ego formation in human development. The second part of Loder, *Transforming Moment* (81–126) is titled "Triumph of Negation."

*Truly, truly I say to you, we speak of what we know, and bear wit-
ness to what we have seen; but you do not receive our testimony.
If I have told you earthly things and you do not believe, how can
you believe if I tell you heavenly things? No one has ascended into
heaven but he who descended from heaven, the Son of man. And
as Moses lifted up the serpent in the wilderness, so must the Son of
man be lifted up, that whoever believes in him may have eternal
life.*

*For God so loved the world that he gave his only Son, that
whoever believes in him should not perish but have eternal life.
For God sent the Son into the world, not to condemn the world,
but that the world might be saved through him.* (John 3:1–17
RSV)

In this encounter Jesus links his counsel to be born of the Spirit directly with his proclamation of the Son of Man being lifted up. And he takes
the lifting up of the Son of Man to be analogous to Moses lifting up the
bronze serpent on the tree in the wilderness recorded in Numbers 21. Let us
read this passage as well.

*From Mount Hor they set out by way of the Red Sea, to go around
the land of Edom; and the people became impatient on the way.
And the people spoke against God and against Moses, "Why have
you brought us up out of Egypt to die in the wilderness? For there
is no food and no water, and we loathe this worthless food." Then
the LORD sent fiery serpents among the people, and they bit the
people, so that many people of Israel died. And the people came to
Moses and said, "We have sinned for we have spoken against the
LORD and against you; pray to the LORD, that he take away the
serpents from us." So Moses prayed for the people. And the LORD
said to Moses, "Make a fiery serpent, and set it on a pole; and
every one who is bitten, when he sees it, shall live." So Moses made
a bronze serpent and set it on a pole; and if a serpent bit any man,
he would look at the bronze serpent and live.* (Num 21:4–9 RSV)

While I am aware of the many critical considerations that could have a bearing on this text, I want to focus on the central dynamic of transformation
here and in Jesus's use of this text. Then I want to specifically take up the
transformation of the achievement-oriented personality.

So what is going on here in Numbers? Why doesn't God just wipe
out the serpents or have Moses put an angel on the pole? We might begin
by noting that this complaining by the people of God is symptomatic of a
deeper separation from, and rejection of, God. Complaining reveals an inner condition, a condition of the heart. Had Moses taken away the serpents,

or put up a positive image before Israel, God would merely offer a situational cure or an inducement to positive thinking. Instead, God purposes to get at the heart of things and to deal with the unconscious depths of the internal condition. The solution must fit both the internal and the external nature of the problem. If condemnation is to be condemned and freedom restored, then the cure must expose the depth of the *curse*, and at the same time provide the *cure*, not for the symptom but for the root condition.

The Israelites took the curse of the serpent into themselves as judgment against their complaining. But only gradually did they grasp that the root of their complaining was death-dealing self-destruction, because it was at heart hostility to God, from whom alone their life depended. So as serpent the bronze image both embodies the *curse* (i.e., the serpent-sin connection) and also pushes the curse as deep as possible into the heart of the people (*mortification*). The narrative never lets us forget that our relation to God is a similar matter of life and death. But as the bronze image is lifted up and placed on a pole by the command of God for healing, it embodies the *cure*, providing a way for the Israelites to turn fully back to God and so to live (*vivification*). The narrative never lets us forget that God alone has overcome death by the power of God's life.

The process depicted in this story resembles how transference works in a psychiatric setting. The psychiatrist receives the transference of hostile feelings from the patient, which the patient actually, but unconsciously, feels toward the parent, perhaps the father. The psychiatrist, by *not* responding like the father, enables the patient to see that the hostility resides in him, the patient. He is doing this to himself. He is condemned in the sense that he is compelled to see how deeply he has been embedded in hostility without knowing it. But because the psychiatrist mirrors the patient's condition and does not react like an angry father, the patient can now recognize the hostility as something he *has*, not something he *is*. Hostility is "out there" now, and he can be freed, perhaps for the first time, to choose for or against it.

In the John passage, Jesus likens himself to the bronze serpent. He becomes a mirror reflecting back on us the internalized infliction of the repression we place upon our deepest longing to see God Face-to-face. Further, he shows us, as in a mirror, not only what we do to ourselves, but what we do, and would still do—kill God rather than receive the love God offers. If you doubt that you would ignore or even deny Christ, consider your relation to the spiritual presence of Christ. How open are any of us to that love relationship? Hanging on the cross, the message in the mirror is, why do you reject perfect love? Why do you keep doing this to yourself?

So the cross is the wrath of God, worse than any flood, expressing what is in the hearts of human beings. At the same time, the cross is the redemptive act of God on our behalf that sets us free to receive perfect love. If you look long enough at the cross you will see behind the mortification to the love that would go to such extremes to give you a chance to change your mind. Jesus became fully and completely the bearer of the curse so as to be fully and completely the bearer of the cure. "*For our sake he made him to be sin who knew no sin, so that in him we might become the righteousness of God*" (2 Cor 5: 21 RSV). Only through Christ as victim can we appropriate the depth of our self-victimization and so participate in the victory of the resurrection.

## (C) A Parable of Negation

To get a parabolic grasp of the dynamics here let us take up the case of the Princeton achiever again. Let us imagine this decent but hard-driven fellow who lives over on Library Place. He gets up at five thirty in the morning, marches across the Seminary campus at 5:55 to catch the shuttle to Princeton Junction. He comes back routinely at eight thirty or nine o'clock at night. Now let's just say for the sake of the story that he has a little boy who is virtually perfect. The little boy is without sin. Thus, what we have here is a hard-pressed, hard-driving Princeton achiever doing the best he can for his kid. He is not a bad person. He obeys the law. He wants in fact to keep the whole law. If he can keep the whole law, perhaps someday Israel will be saved. In other word, he is achieving also for the sake of the society.

But the pressure is getting to him. He has one or two drinks on the train. At home, he has one or two more, just one or two. Now his little boy stands there and says to this father, "I wish you wouldn't do that, Daddy. Mommy says that's not good for you."

"Be quiet! Be quiet! We'll play together a little later." He comes home the next night, after surviving another hard day. Bear market. He has two or three on the train.

"Daddy, it worries me that you are doing that."

"Didn't I tell you to be quiet?!"

The third night . . . same thing . . . a hard day . . . three or four on the way home.

"Daddy, please . . ."

"Shut up!"

The achiever then hits the boy right in the mouth, knocks him down; knocks him out. Looking at the boy lying on the floor, he says, "Oh my God. What have I done?"

The child is innocent. He has no fault in him. The innocence of the child exposes what's in the achiever's heart—it exposes externally what he is unconsciously doing to himself internally. Every obsessive act to keep achievement front and center buries further and further down his deepest longing to give and receive love. He doesn't see the self-destructive quality of his own goodness until he sees the innocent victim of his achievement-oriented virtue.

This self-destructive quality of our ego-oriented existence spawns the defensive lifestyles (achievement obsession, authoritarianism, proteanism, oppression) that in light of the cross are exposed as the very means for denying the life we long to share. Why do you do this to yourself? Why? You want the presence of God. You long for it. You are made for it. Its prototype in the face phenomenon was set down in you before you were three-months old. So why do you kill it when it shows up? The cross is a mirror: the wrath of God showing us what we do to ourselves. As I have said, if you look long enough at the cross, then you can see what love is. Love will go to any extreme to show you what you are doing to yourself so you can change your mind. Nothing affords you motivation to change like seeing a victim of your virtue when you think you are compulsively doing your best.

If the appropriation of Christ takes place, then the crucified Jesus becomes the Face of God for us. In him is the *Logos*, "the cosmic ordering, self-confirming presence of the loving Other."[8] In him we encounter satisfaction for our cosmic longing for a face that will not go away. His presence and identity reach in behind our defenses. They cut deeper than the ego's fundamental negation, because his presence passes through and surpasses the annihilation and death that the ego is designed to prevent us from facing or even noticing. Once we experience his presence as satisfaction of that longing for a Face that does not go away—note the Greek word *prosopon* and the Hebrew word *panim* can both be translated "presence" and "face"—then the ego's defenses become fundamentally unnecessary to our true identity. We will need and use those defenses in some situations, but they are no longer fundamental to all the ego does. Our defenses become reversible, and so we can now choose for or against them without fear of falling into nothingness and despair. This liberation is the key to ego transformation.

---

8. Editor's Note: See Loder, *Logic of the Spirit*, 90. Loder used this phrase often in his lectures and writings, almost as a technical term for the impact of Christ on the human spirit in convictional experiences.

## (III) FROM NEGATION TO LOVE

Let us consider now how ego transformation enables the restoration of relationships with others, the ability to give and receive love.

## (A) Negation Negated: A Case of Defense Reversibility

Here is an example of a woman who lived in a problematic family. As you know from family systems theory, families develop role structures. This woman had a sister who played the role of the bad sister while she herself retained the role of the good sister. The bad sister always engaged in passive-aggressive behavior, having in clinical terms a kind of anal personality. She always made everyone in the family or her circle of friends feel slightly guilty because they couldn't make her feel happy. But at one point, the so-called good sister had a spiritual experience in which she realized her so-called virtue was really vice. She decided out of the strength of her new spiritual life that she needed to try to be reconciled to her bad sister, who was now living in Hawaii. So she invited and paid for her sister to come and visit her.

The first miracle is that the sister came. The second followed. When the sister came, she was still this anal-retentive, passive-aggressive person. The newly converted sister said to herself, "Oh, no! She's doing it again." And her old defenses came to attention. But instead of lashing out, now she prayed and received a spiritual insight: "Your sister is giving you the backside of her pain. She cannot give you the other side. It hurts too much." Freed by the insight, the converted sister no longer *had* to react to the passive-aggressive behavior of her sister. The hold of her sister's manipulative, controlling, or guilt-engendering behavior was broken. She could instead react to the pain behind the defense, because her defenses had become reversible.

Not only can you reverse your own defenses—i.e., take them off or put them on in order to be present to another—but you can also reverse somebody else's defensiveness when they cannot reverse defenses for themselves. In this case, the woman reversed her sister's defenses by talking to her about times of shared pain—addressing the pain rather than the defenses that buried the pain. So they talked intimately as sisters for the very first time. She initiated what could be considered a very tangible, everyday experience of what it means to love what appears to be your enemy, to love the one who has always made life miserable for you and your family. You can "love your enemy" only when and because in the aftermath of ego transformation you gain the capacity to reverse your defenses. Instead of addressing the defense, the transformed ego is free to address the inner source of the defense—the fear, the hurt, the real need behind the symptom.

## (B) Transformation of the Fear of Love

Most important and most powerful, ego transformation frees us to say "I love you!" and really mean it. Why is this so? In terms of this analysis, there are two great enemies of love: the fear of *absorption* and the fear of *abandonment*. These two great fears come from opposite ends of the life span. Absorption is the fear of being sucked back into one's origins and losing independence and the sound of one's own voice. Abandonment is the fear of being deserted or sent off and left to die.

Subliminal longing for the "face" leads, on the one hand, into absorption because you want the other one to be the "face" for you that will not go away—or you want to be the "face" for them. On the other hand, the ego's drive for survival against this fear of negation and annihilation means it cannot surrender its defenses, its objectivity and repressive dynamic without collapse into an abyss—the fear of abandonment. Torn between these fears, one finds that love becomes almost impossible. But once one has convictionally experienced the presence and power of God bestowing the Face of God in Jesus Christ (2 Cor 4:6), the longing for the "face" in human developmental experience is forever satisfied. Neither absorption nor abandonment threatens the convicted person because in Christ one has already died, undergone the death the ego so desperately fears. When conviction transforms ego, we become free to give love sacrificially with integrity.

But what is love? I define Christ's love, *agape* love, as *the nonpossessive delight in the particularity of the other one*. In this kind of love you are not only free to be present to the other one. You also delight in the other one. You are further liberated from your need to make that other one into the missing "face" for you. You can care for them nonpossessively in their particularity primarily because deep caring is how you have experienced Christ's love yourself when he became the "Face." Your particularity has been confirmed, and you are free to be present for the other one. Now you can learn to practice what I call the laws of presence and suffering.

## (C) The Laws of Presence and Suffering

The law of presence is a fierce but uncodifiable law. I go home after lecture and sit down in the kitchen to talk to my wife, Arlene. I say, "I lectured today about this and that and this."

And she says, "Oh, what about this and that?" Pretty soon she stops talking and says, "Hey, where are you?"

I say, "I'm here talking to you. I'm telling you about . . ."

"No, no," she responds, "Where *are* you?" Now we're back to Genesis again, right? "Where are you?" What does my wife want? She wants just ten seconds of real presence: Be there for me. Recognize who I am, your particularity to my particularity. My formula is—thirty seconds of real presence daily is worth six months of marriage counseling. Be there!

We must know, however, that real presence entails *suffering*, since the liberated spirit all the more meets rejection, hostility, and all sorts of misunderstanding—perhaps more than ever before. The law of suffering means that the spiritual task amid broken relations is to embrace such conflict expectantly. The power of the Spirit enables persons to indwell the brokenness around them with the anticipation of new prototypes emerging, new insights erupting, and new relationships unfolding—relationships liberated through suffering to experience mutual participation in the sacred repetition of God's nonpossessive delight in the particularity of each one and all. Such suffering with and for the other is central to the liberated spirit's love. In such suffering we know the fellowship of Christ's suffering (Phil 3:10).

Both real presence with the other and suffering on behalf of the other express redemptive transformation of the ego. Hitherto the ego was the center of the personality, which meant survival and satisfaction—the dominant aims of adaptation. Now, in convictional experience, the negation—the implicit self-destructive quality of the ego—is itself negated. The underlying reality of the personality is no longer the slave to no but to the liberated yes. Jesus Christ as the Face of God is the Yes in us to all of God's promises, which extend far beyond us. This Yes replaces the ego at the center of the personality—creating a dialectical identity: "I, yet not I, but Christ." Notice that this dialectical identity implies a reversible structure: "Christ, yet not Christ, but I." This new identity, resulting from the redemptive transformation of the ego from two- to four-dimensional existence now resonates to and reflects the four dimensions of divine-human experience communicated in Scripture, the Christian tradition, and the liturgy.

I am not just picking on an isolated structure here. Some of you know Ricoeur's hermeneutical treatment of Scripture wherein he takes this basic structure as foundational for understanding the texts of all genres. For example, Ricoeur takes prophetic structure, "the voice behind the voice," and argues that this dialectical identity enters into every textual form.[9] Scripture thus confirms that the transformational ego can now appreciate and par-

---

9. Ricoeur, "Toward a Hermeneutic," 1–37.

ticipate in the world with this kind of dialectical identity. In narration, God is the ultimate Actant who acts within and beyond the story. In wisdom, the sage knows wisdom precedes him. So this knowledge also repeats the dialectic of "a voice behind a voice." The point here is that only as ego is transformed into a dialectical identity does it become congruent with the biblical understanding of selfhood. So when Jesus Christ becomes the Face of God, the transformed ego becomes the agent of our deepest vocation, which is to give love and to give it sacrificially. When Christ becomes for us the Face that will not go away, then the two great enemies of giving and receiving love—the fear of abandonment and the fear of absorption—are defeated. Then we are liberated to give love as we have received the love of God.

## (D) Transformations of Achievement-Oriented Egos: Two Stories

Let us consider two true stories of redemptive transformation of the ego from my counseling experience. Both name are, of course, fictitious but both true stories belong to the church.

### (1) Michael's Story

Michael was a forty-five year old white Episcopalian male who became president of a New York bank by the time he was thirty-five. His passion was the obsession with achievement that enslaves a large portion of our society. The double bind inherent in his lifestyle was that he had replaced personal worth and meaningful relations with others with a culturally defined, culturally driven need to succeed. Thus, he trusted success to do for him what deep personal worth before God and meaningful relations with others are supposed to do—give purpose to his life. The consequence of this substitution was, of course, disastrous, since socially constructed versions of success never can carry the weight that only the divine presence can bear.

Michael's symptoms were typical. At night, he could often get to sleep *only* by thinking of his next promotion. He did not want any more love than he deserved. But by the time he was forty-five, all of his successes simply meant nothing to him anymore. This despair crystallized for him in different ways. For example, once he invited his father, who was a good Midwestern farmer, to come visit him in his New York office. Now if you are an achiever, you have a clean desk, in which everything has a place and there is a place for everything. The father walked in and looked around, but wasn't impressed. So he remarked, "You don't do much work, do you?" Michael began to realize that success wasn't doing for him what it was supposed to do.

But what really got to him was when he caught himself crying during the Eucharist one Sunday. Somehow the presence of Christ in the Eucharist revealed to him, achievement isn't doing what you thought it would. It's not so good. Find out what's going on. So he came to talk. Michael had come under the conviction that his obsession to achieve was self-defeating, self-destructive, and self-emptying. Consequently, he didn't want to incorporate his Eucharist experience into that despair. He didn't want it too emptied of meaning. That's what he couldn't stand—the gutting of meaning from everything in his life. So once he was wised up, he couldn't wise down. And he remembered a time in childhood when he had had a sense of God's presence. Wising up, he wanted to get back to that reality.

In the counseling that I do, where it is appropriate, I combine prayer with the more conventional psychotherapy. During prayer, Michael and I began to discover the passion attached to his original childhood vision. He began to feel what he described as the presence of God's Spirit in his life, even when he prayed alone. We also kept a close watch on the parts of his personality that he could not achieve, like his dreams. He had one dream that was so overpowering that he could only describe it as "like Moses and the burning bush. I saw this inexpressible Light." But his actual hesitation to speak of this "Light" said more than any of his words could have, because it revealed his socialized state. As a result, he felt as if he simply had to take the Eucharist regularly and live out its meaning. So he left the bank president's position to work part-time as a financial consultant in New York. But he spent most of his time at the Cathedral of Saint John the Divine in New York, counseling and helping the street people who came there for refuge. He found the meaning he was looking for. His future became an unfolding of the presence and power of God that he experienced and envisioned in the Eucharist.

## (2) Helen's Story

The second case history concerns a very bright young woman named Helen, a Lutheran, about twenty-six years old, who came into the PhD program at Princeton University. Viciously competitive with everyone in her program, she came to my office promising to kill one of her equally cutthroat male colleagues. Sitting on the couch, she dug into her arm with an open paper clip, in effect, telling me in blood that she meant what she said, and defying me to stop her. Her lifestyle evolved from the oppression she suffered from the moment of birth. Her mother had previously lost a son in childbirth. This devastating experience traumatized the mother, but she tried again. As a result, Helen was born. But of course, Helen was the wrong sex. From the very beginning something was wrong with Helen.

Her double bind was profound. There was nothing she could do to get out of it, because the pervasive sense of being fundamentally wrong plagued every attempted corrective and every assurance to the contrary. She could try to be the indisputably best student, as tough as any male. She could dress, act, and walk as much like a man as possible. But the result of every effort was incessant anxiety and a bad case of bruxism (grinding one's teeth during sleep). Helen was inherently embedded in a double-binding obsession to achieve her way to an acceptance that she could never attain because she had been born wrong.

In the course of counseling, Helen discovered the significance of prayer as passion, as when the life of God takes over and prayer takes on a direction and vitality of its own. Eventually, she had an experience of "baptism in the Holy Spirit" in which she described how in the midst of a fit of self-destruction—destroying her room as a prelude to destroying herself—she was, in her terms, "thrown to her knees" by the spiritual presence of Christ. Subsequently, on the strength of that experience and through the three years of our work together, she was able to reconstruct her personal history even back to the time of birth. In a striking image that came to her during therapy, she saw Jesus taking her place as an infant, suffering in her stead to set her free. After that vision, which came in the midst of our prayer together, the anxiety and the bruxism lessened dramatically. What was the net effect of her spiritual awakening? She now teaches history at a U.S. college—the first woman ever hired for that all-male faculty in its entire one-hundred year history.[10]

The logic of Helen's transformation is clear. There is no insight or relationship within Helen's untransformed, oppressive lifestyle that could correct it without reinstating it. Since there was something fundamentally wrong with her, there was also something fundamentally wrong with whatever she did to make it right. She had to stand somehow outside the whole course of her development from birth on. Through the divine presence, Christ as the Face of God, she received this leverage. Developmental negation was reversed, and she was liberated to reconstruct her personal history, even to the point of physical healing.

---

10. Editor's Note: An expanded version of this story is found in Loder, *Logic of the Spirit*, 46–77.

In both of these cases, the visions reveal a *suffering* Christ. Christ not only resolves the dichotomy between the divine and the human, but he also nullifies the person's suffering by taking it into his own passion for life. Thus, the vision of Christ gives death to death at the same time that it conveys the wholeness and healing always implicit in the divine presence. The vision then breaks the double bind through a double negation and divine disclosure. Through these kinds of redemptive transformations of the ego, persons undergo restoration to their true humanity grounded in Christ through the redemptive power of the Holy Spirit of God.

## (IV) CONCLUSION

Faith, then, is the grounding of the transformed ego in the power of the Holy One, the Face that will not go away. Therefore, faith gives certainty to existence against fear, doubt, delusions, and despair, and frees persons to give love sacrificially with integrity after the pattern of Christ. We now turn to the Spirit's action in social existence, where we will see the same pattern at work in the transformation of role structures and communal existence.

# 7

# Society
## Koinonia *and Societal Transformation*

## (I) INTRODUCTION: PERSONAL TRANSFORMATION
## IN SEARCH OF A CONTEXT

WE NOW MOVE FROM personal to corporate transformation in our effort to describe the necessary and fundamental dimensions of the Christian style of life. A Christian style of life, we have argued, requires the redemptive transformation of one's basic ego posture by the Spirit of God, transfiguring the autonomous and defensive executive power of ego according to power of Christ's nature, resulting in the dialectical identity, *"I, yet not I, but Christ."* But this transformation of the ego puts us more deeply into human experience, including especially our experience with other human beings. Therefore, redemptive transformation of the corporate life is of equal importance to transformation of the ego, and should always be kept in a reciprocal relationship with such experiences. Put theoretically the question we now pose is, how does the Holy Spirit work in a corporate context to effect the four-dimensional, transformational, and christocentric pattern of Christian education that we saw operative in the individual?

Let me begin this theme with a story that comes out of the late sixties, when we would sit around having eyeball-to-eyeball sessions challenging each other with the questions like, why go into the ministry in these turbulent times? One day as we went around the circle, a student named

Jerry spoke up. "The reason I have to go into the ministry is because I had this WOW!!! experience." ("WOW" was sixties' language for a conversion experience.) He went on to explain that when he was fifteen or sixteen, he would frequently go down to the church building near his home and talk to the local minister there. He would talk to the minister mainly because the minister was the only person he could talk to about what he wanted to talk about—life. He couldn't understand what the minister said, but he enjoyed their talks. Actually, these times were respites for Jerry, better than being at home since his home life was fraught with continual conflict and abuse. Jerry's father had succumbed to alcoholism and his mother to serious and constant depression. Eventually, however, Jerry became frustrated with his talks with the minister because of his lack of understanding, and he stopped going there.

Then one night he was awakened in the middle of the night by an argument going on downstairs. He got up and went down into the living room. There he saw his drunken father standing at the other end of the room swaying back and forth about ready to take a swing at his mother. His mother was hovering in trepidation in the corner. At that point, Jerry did something that he had never done before. He walked around and stood in front of his mother, looked his father in the eye, and said, "You leave her alone!" The boy's father responded by stomping out of the house in a rage. With his mission accomplished, Jerry didn't stop to speak to his mother. He simply went upstairs, got back into bed, and went to sleep. Without quite realizing it, however, he had broken out of the oppressive spiritual paralysis of his home life. When he awoke in the morning, he felt so full of new life that he could hardly wait to get to Scripture. He could hardly wait to talk to the minister again. That was his "WOW!" experience. And it was out of this experience that he had come to seminary to become a minister.

The point of this story is that convictional experiences (personal transformations) inevitably go in search of a context that supports, sustains, and continues to deepen the transformational impact according to the new life inherent in it. As Karl Barth said somewhere, "The church is already in the conversion."

Today's spiritual unrest, from the proliferation of literally hundreds of support groups to the New Age movement, is the passionate quest in a worldwide breakdown and fragmentation of Western culture to find a context that calls forth conviction and deepens spiritual communion. Spiritual unrest and the search for meaning, coherence, and transcendence reach far into every segment of society and every cultural context. According to David Burrell, philosopher at Notre Dame, today's spiritual quest for meaning and community has replaced the desperate search in the sixties for relevance.

The longing to get into something that grips you deeply, something that also has social, political, and institutional meaning, reigns in the hearts of many people.

I see this situation of spiritual unrest filled with more promise than danger. I recall an image that Harvey Cox used in his book *Religion and the Secular City*. The pope had arrived in Mexico City, which by law remains the most secular city in the world. (There it is even against the law to wear a clerical collar in the streets!) Getting off the plane, the pope knelt down on the runway and kissed the tarmac.[1] Cox saw in this image a calling forth of the buried spiritual life—the life that has the power to transform not just individuals, but institutions, cities, and nations from Berlin to Beijing. Since then the Berlin Wall has fallen, the back of apartheid in South Africa was broken, and some strides toward peace have been made in the Middle East. When I was in Mexico City not too long ago, I could see that the heavy oppression of the people was being addressed primarily by a shared spiritual life in marginalized church groups and house meetings. In these contexts, socioeconomic and educational differences were being transcended and the life of Christ shared across boundaries. The spiritual life is irrepressible, but it desperately needs direction if it is to flourish. The spiritual life needs a rich and vital communal context that does not distort or quench the impact that the Spirit seeks to inspire and enable in persons and communities.

With this in mind, let me suggest that the current impoverishment of the spiritual life in many mainline Protestant churches is not hidden under the concrete of their spacious but empty parking lots, but rather under the fears and anxieties about the spiritual life and its abuses. The plethora of televangelist scandals dramatizes this fear, but we ought to know better than anyone that corruption in the clergy is an old story. I am not so concerned about Jimmy or Jimmy and Tammy, or their mythical predecessor Elmer Gantry, as I am about the thousands of people who were awakened spiritually over the past several decades, but who found enthusiasm for their experiences largely in communal contexts that were manipulative, rigid in language, authoritarian in spirit, and unable to foster a truly profound response to the guidance of the Spirit.

I want to ask hard questions here: where were *mainline* Protestants when these people awakened one morning to their spiritual freedom and sought the historical richness of the communion of saints for nurture? Where were we when these people needed the benefit of centuries of thoughtful interpretation of Scripture, and the theological language of the church to give voice to the Spirit seeking to gain expression in their lives?

---

1. See Cox, *Religion*, 12–13.

Why were we unable to supply the vital context within which the impact of their conversion experiences could thrive? Why do so many people longing for spiritual reality not find their home and inspiration and sanctification with us?

Spiritual awakening *is* taking place, and it *is* having social, political, and institutional consequences, both in the United States and around the world, for good or ill. Therefore, it behooves us to examine why it is so difficult for us who are supposed to be leaders of the mainline church to get on board with what the Spirit of God is doing—i.e., to supply the context for convictional experience to flourish and deepen. Are we too theologically sophisticated to get into the vitality of the spiritual life? Or, perhaps more to the point, are we are not sophisticated enough? Are we too mature to allow the spontaneity of our convictions to come to passionate expression in our worship or fellowship? Or is it that we aren't mature enough? Are we perhaps afraid that Jesus Christ—his grace, mercy, and peace—is too holy for us: so holy that we fear it will tear apart our carefully maintained two-dimensional empirical church systems?

My concern is not to do away with maturity or the integrity of theology or any of the central doctrines. In fact, it is precisely because we have the benefit of centuries of labor cultivating language about God that we ought to be most concerned with the power of the Spirit that gave rise to that language and continues to give it life. I do not want to sacrifice theological integrity on the altar of enthusiasm, which is a major danger in charismatic movements. On the other hand, I do not want to sacrifice the church in the power of the Spirit on the altar of theological or doctrinal rectitude, which is why I resist every way I can from becoming an enculturated Presbyterian. Fundamentally, the real question is, why won't the church be the church?

I think the current situation calls for a radical reexamination of our patterns of socialization and our tendency to allow them to gain ascendancy over transformation in the Spirit of Christ. So what I want to do here is to examine how the corporate life and the ego form analogously. We seek to uncover the underlying conflict that prevents the church from being true to itself. In light of such an examination, I think we can see why a church immersed in socialization and adaptation to mainstream society is foredoomed to extinction. At the same time, we may discover the inherent sources of renewal.

## (II) THE TRAGEDY OF SOCIAL DEVELOPMENT UNTRANSFORMED

To begin with, let me say in general terms why such extinction now seems inevitable. My conviction is that the underlying Void and emptiness of human existence cannot be put off or contained or controlled by social life and society any more than it can be repressed in individual existence. Other people or institutions have no power against the Void and in view of the inevitable annihilation that faces us corporately as well as individually. Social interactions may be a temporary antidote, a diversion, or an illusion of meaning. But given the universally broken condition of human existence, those most truly aware of the third dimension, the Void, will often agree with Jean-Paul Sartre when he said, "hell is other people." Whether nice people or evil people, there is always the Void that stands between the other's freedom and your freedom. Each one's ego is principally concerned with survival and satisfaction, and each one is caught in the irony that ultimately we get neither. But through institutionalized patterns of socialization, we compose out this realization and the knowledge that others have no power to alter this existential condition. More often than not other persons exercise the power to hurt, shame, depress, oppress, and destroy us. In the natural course of things human life is sickeningly tragic. But usually persons try to live without noticing the existential nothingness that infuses our social constructions of reality. And that inattention to the truly tragic human condition we share may be the truest tragedy of all.

We first become aware of the social dimension of the tragedy of human existence and the possibility of institutionally concealing it from our awareness somewhere between the ages of three and five. Developmentally during this period children normally begin to move out into society, and they learn to conduct their lives in socially constructed roles established for them by the social order. We now turn to this social aspect of human development because here we may begin to see the longing of the human spirit for a higher corporate life.

## (A) Role Structure Development

Let us examine how after early ego formation at about two years of age, we move from ego to family and from family to the larger society. In what respect is this developmental expansion constructive, and in what respect is it destructive? We assert here simply that the social equivalent of ego repression is the creation of *role structure*. Role structure is built up out of the dynamics of social interaction. These dynamics basically extend the phenomena of repression into the social milieu and become the means by which transcendent experiences are muted and transmuted into socially acceptable patterns of interaction.

What exactly is role? By formal definition a role is *a set sequence of learned actions (i.e., personal qualities and attitudes) performed by a person in an interactional situation that is observed and evaluated by others.*[2] What motivates us to develop the competencies that make role-structured social interaction possible? The classical Oedipal or Electra period, which I spelled out earlier in our discussion of the authoritarian lifestyle, extends from age three to five. During this period the child temporarily resolves losing out in the family romance situation. She both surrenders the desire for intimacy with the parent of the opposite sex and represses the desire to do away with the parent of the same sex. Literally rejected and overpowered, the child identifies with the parent of the same sex, resolving temporarily the problem of guilt (through identification with the aggressor) and intimacy (which is attained now indirectly through identification with the one who *is* intimate with the desired parent).

What happens at age three to five must all be reworked again in adolescence at a more complex level. But the basic effect for socialization is that at this early period the child is thrown into another double bind. She can't be too close to others for fear of guilt and punishment; she can't move too far away for fear of isolation and abandonment (see chapter 6). As a result, the child is thrust out of the most intimate dimension of family life to find a way into the world. Thus, role structures are the ingenious yet tragic functional solution to an existential crisis. Roles provisionally solve the double bind by institutionalizing it, making it institutionally normative. But the attendant loss of intimacy, as we shall see, diminishes and even dehumanizes the quality of relationships within corporate existence.

The development of role structure, then, is partly accomplished by virtue of the process of identification. The child learns to imitate the parent of the same sex and so to play that role in society until the child can construct a version of what it means to be a man or woman in society. But the child's emerging cognitive competency at the age of six or seven makes an important contribution to this process of identification. As you may recall, in a classic experiment done by Piaget, a little girl of six or seven is seated at a square table with dolls on the other three chairs. The little girl at this age is able for the first time to identify from her position how the papier-mache mountains at the center of the table look to each of the other dolls. Here the

---

2. Editor's Note: This definition is apparently Loder's own.

child begins to develop the capacity to establish a role on the basis of *how others see her from where they are.* As this capacity generalizes through the prepubertal years, the child eventually learns to conduct life according to what George Herbert Mead called "the generalized other."[3]

Thus, as our socially constrained desire to be intimate with another combines with our recognition of where this other is coming from (his or her motivation), our basic construction of role structure emerges. As Berger and Luckman put it—

> A watches B's action. A attributes motives to B's actions, and seeing the actions recur, typifies the motives as recurrent. As B goes on performing, A is soon able to say to himself, "Aha, there it is again . . ." In this way, specific, reciprocal patterns of conduct develop. That is, A and B will begin to play roles vis-à-vis each other. Their actions become predictable, and they become aware of how they condition each other. Thus, the shared life-world of a given institution emerges.[4]

Role then is the basic unit of social organization. Roles make the difference between a *random* gathering (say, a spontaneous meeting at a streetlight) and an *intentional* group. Note that the word *group* comes from the German, *Gruppe,* meaning, "knot." Groups tie the common knot of mutually assigned, mutually approved, regulative roles. In other words, institutional life depends upon role structures, and role structures depend upon reciprocal understandings of mutual expectations developed in societies over time.

Let us understand that this condition, like the ego, is both a gracious thing and a tragic thing—what I call a "truth-producing error" in human existence. On the one hand, roles allow us to work together for common goals and ends with minimum tension. On the other hand, they enshrine in institutional life the double-bind condition that prevents us from being together in any more fundamental or genuinely intimate or human way. Thus, roles structure social behavior at the same time they diminish human contact. Ironically, they embody values and establish institutions in ways that actually conceal the ultimate tragedy of their own condition.

## (B) The Tragedy of Role-Based Social Interaction

The tragedy of role interaction, or of role relationship, is that as long as we are in our roles, we cannot be present to each other in any way that is more

---

3. Mead, *Mind,* 175.

4. Berger and Luckman. *Social Construction,* 56–57 (text slightly altered).

profound than our roles will allow. We cannot engage the loss or the emptiness of another with our own sense of loss and emptiness. In other words,
we cannot enter with love into the suffering of someone else unless we break
role. But when we break role, we always risk either the agonies of mutually
destructive intimacy (absorption) or the pain of rejection (abandonment)—
both of which drive us back into our defenses. We must admit, then, that
roles and their systemic governance of society and institutions are inevitable but not sufficient from a theological point of view. On the one hand,
because they serve corporate survival and satisfaction needs much the way
ego serves the individual, they become an inevitable feature of the pattern-
maintenance, tension-reduction drive of socialized existence. But analogous
to the ego's defensive relationship to the individual, role structures perpetuate destruction in institutional life under the guise of extending satisfaction
and survival. They are insufficient mediators of human social existence. Let
me spell out a bit further some instances of the tragic side of the making and
taking of roles.

First, I remind you of what is commonly called "ministerial
syndrome"—i.e., the tendency to play the role of the minister as a substitute
for real presence with the other. Perhaps we play the role because we have
been hurt so many times that we can't risk being known any longer. Or
perhaps we have lost sight of our calling in relation to the Real Presence
that called us into ministry in the first place. Whatever the case, in the institutional church, we get into and oftentimes play out our roles without the
awareness that we are doing the very thing against which we are constantly
preaching. We become very capable in the practices of balanced distance
and perpetual niceness. We even may come to believe that these socialized
role characteristics constitute intimacy in the power and Spirit of Christ.

So we practice the *tragedy* as if it were somehow the *solution*. But no
matter how effective the church might be, or how great a time we have in the
youth group, most of us eventually get fed up with role gamesmanship and
demand something deeper. Even when the roles seem socially vital, as when
we are espousing some cause, after a while we realize that something is
missing, something very crucial amid all our activity. We indeed sense that
institutional life based upon role structure is simply an extension of ego—a
kind of negation incorporated riven into the social existence. As long as we
practice role-determined behavior as an extension of the organized church,
we grieve, hinder, and quench the transcendent presence and power of the
Spirit.

For example, the Spirit's work may be obstructed when someone in
your family dies. The minister comes to make funeral and memorial service
arrangements but doesn't break role. She conducts the session very well,

covers all the ground, says all the right things, gets into your internal frame of reference by understanding what you are saying. But still there is this deep sense that she doesn't really know what is going on with the family. The grief in your hearts finds no resonance with her professionalism.

Or, suppose you experience the loss of a loved one and the Spirit of God heals your sense of grief and loss, such that you are ready to go into the funeral utterly joyful. The minster comes and she still doesn't know what's going on. She thinks you may be in a state of denial. Why? Because her professionalism, deeply embedded in role-structure dynamics, has no ability to recognize the Real Presence of grace active and powerful to the human spirit in time of need. Thus, ministerial syndrome occludes recognition of the very grace that is being called upon to meet these situations of loss, grief, guilt, or joy in the Spirit. Ministers and all others who cannot break role have quenched the Spirit at the very time when the Spirit is most needed.

A second example of dehumanizing situations is the retirement dinner. Perhaps no situation may reveal the irony of role systems more than these common events. Retirement dinners tend to function as the ironic celebration of a person being disposed of by an institution. For even as the retiree is being roasted and toasted in his or her departure, the institution is actually claiming its power to do without the contribution the retiree has made. Perhaps such dinners are less an effort to honor the departing members and more an effort on the part of the institutions to assuage guilt and cover over the negation that retirement exposes throughout the structure of the institution. Not only does each current member know the time to celebrate one's own dispensability is coming, but the ultimately depersonalizing significance of socialized institutional reality becomes very evident in the retirement ritual.

Third, even as institutional life endures, over a period of several decades institutions bring about their own destruction. Institutional structures that are built up out of our capacity to construct and interrelate roles and role patterns have their own intrinsic patterns of decline and destructiveness. Similar to how ego structures build up but then gradually decline into death, so also do role patterns and institutions move toward alienation and ironic dysfunctionality. Ivan Illich, in his book *Tools for Conviviality*, charted this phenomenon. According to Illich, institutional life moves through four phases in response to problems that arise needing technological solutions.

(1) Tools or means are brought to bear upon a problem that has been identified.

(2) The effectiveness of the tools becomes a preoccupation and a project in itself as complications arise.

(3) Institutions build themselves up around the technological development of these tools to the extent to which they actually begin to exploit society as a whole. Taking on a life of its own, this institutionalized technology begins to define society in *its* terms rather than serving society in the way originally conceived.

(4) A whole new set of problems and difficulties greater than those tools were designed to solve in the first place now arise.[5]

Examples of Illich's thesis abound. Why, for instance, has the automobile, a tool designed to solve a transportation problem, come in less than a century to enslave major portions of our society, to put it cryptically? Why does a highway system designed to bring people together often separate them? Why do these systems, designed to elevate efficiency of movement develop unending gridlock? Why do labor-saving devices inevitably create more housework? Why are simplified tax regulations harder to follow? Why do paperback books cost what clothbound books used to cost?

Some scholars call this tendency toward institutional alienation the "revenge effect" in socially constructed self-repair. My favorite example comes from the mental health industry. Years ago people were having all kinds of strange, pathological manifestations and being dumped blindly into institutions like cattle. What was going on? We don't know. What we need is a classification system to help us understand the forms of mental illness that are all around us. So, following Freud, Will Menninger, one of the greatest originators of the nosological categories in American mental health, developed for the Army in World War I a whole classification system of mental illness. Here was a real solution to a real problem. Eventually all kinds of people would go to the Menninger Foundation to learn more and more about the intricacies and implications of all of these problems.

The Menninger Foundation even developed an educational program that involved other types of professionals—e.g., ministers, chaplains, and social workers. Pretty soon the Menninger Clinic developed a full range of ideas, theologies, and understandings of nosological categories. Eventually, the categories reached the public arena. Popular psychology began to tell us all about neurosis, psychosis, anxiety, depression, syndromes, and hysteria. As a result, we now have all kinds of books telling us how to get sick when and if we want to! The institution created to solve a problem in mental health thus exacerbated the problem as overcrowded hospitals sent

5. Editor's Note: The schematization of Illich's four phases is Loder's summary of Illich's basic understanding of the problematic underlying modern society, which Illich argued in chapter 1 of *Tools*, "Two Watersheds," 1–9. Loder had earlier elaborated Illich thesis in chapter 1, 15n17, above.

half-sane and disturbed persons into the streets without the care that the original diagnostic categories were designed to engender.

The same thing happened with our school system. There are important things we wanted our children to learn, so we sought the best ways to teach them. Since many of these things were important for all our children to learn in order to assure they could function well in our society, we set up a national system of schools. We reasoned that it was more efficient to teach children in groups with prescribed curriculum. But the institutional structure expanded beyond our control, so that today we have this unwieldy American public education system that often not only fails to deliver on its stated intention but often creates even more intractable problems requiring increasingly desperate measures that seem unsolvable. Illich argued that we have a *schooled* society as a result. As concerns for effective education give way to stereotyped learning, testing scores, and oppression of the marginalized supposedly being served, we keep looking to more schooling as a solution to education not as the problem. As a consequence, Illich wanted to de-school our society.

I suspect Illich's model is dangerously applicable to mainline denominations in their tendency to preserve denominational identity at the expense of spiritual vitality. Consider the case of a young boy, Lutheran by denomination, who went on a retreat, probably sponsored by some charismatic group. He had a powerful experience of God's presence there, which reconnected him to his parents and gave him courage to break off potentially destructive relations with some of his peers. But when he told the minister of his experience, the minister replied, "You came first in your catechism class. Forget the emotional experience." Where did the minister think the catechism came from? True Christian language arises from evangelical and doxological enthusiasm borne out of transformative experiences of the living God.

This anecdote sadly represents a classic example of the tool becoming the source such that, in rejecting the source, one keeps the tool as if it were the source. When the source of life in the Spirit is rejected, denominational identity becomes a fierce preoccupation for institutionalizing the preservation of the tools, occluding the Spirit. The institutional response of the Lutheran minister to the conversion experience of the boy illustrates why socialization into the role-structured life of the institutional church is not the spirit in which to enable the life of the Spirit. Neither can it be the spiritual basis for education in the church.

But this raises the question: "If the institutional church normally enshrines negation incorporated, then what *is* the solution to corporate vitality?" In one word, the answer is *koinonia*. I am talking here about *koinonia* as the intimate relational side of *ecclesia*, as suggested by Paul Lehmann. In his book *Ethics in Christian Context*, Lehmann wrote: "The hidden (*koinonia*) character of the church and the empirical (*ecclesia*) character of the church are dynamically and dialectically related in and through God's action in Christ, whose headship of the church makes the church at once the context and the custodian of the secret of the maturity of humanity."[6] So, to talk about *koinonia* is to focus on the main interests and participatory aspects of the church in the Spirit rather than the institutional church as Nelson spoke of it.

## (III) *KOINONIA* AS THE SOLUTION TO NEGATION INCORPORATED

Let us expand on the meaning of *koinonia*. To begin, I think that it is not sufficiently appreciated how *koinonia* depends upon *perichoresis*. Gregory of Naziansus first used this doctrine of the Cappadocian Church Fathers in theological discourse in the fourth century.[7] *Perichoresis* refers to the inner life of the Trinity. The prefix *peri*, "around," means here "at all points," and the root word *chora* ("space") and its cognate verb *chorea* ("to proceed") combine to signify "mutual penetration at all points," suggesting a kind of dance. We get our word *choreography* from this noun. According to this doctrine, the persons of the Trinity mutually indwell each other in a kind of dance. Each person contains the whole, and each person takes up the task of the other without loss of identity. That is, the persons instantly change places even as identity and mutuality are simultaneously affirmed.[8]

Some scholars have argued that the unity of the Trinity *is* this perichoretic relationality, while the mutuality of the relationality nevertheless heightens the individual distinctiveness of each of the divine persons. Significantly, as T. F. Torrance pointed out, there were times when the early church spoke of the inner perichoretic life of the Trinity as *koinonia*.[9]

6. Lehmann, *Ethics*, 72. Text slightly emended.

7. See Wolfson, *Philosophy*, 418–30.

8. Editor's Note: See the discussion of *perichoresis* in Loder and Neidhardt, *Knight's Move*, 201–2: "Other ways of relating the mutual indwelling of God and humanity in Christ use the notion of 'coinherence,' with the dynamic connotation of a mutual act, analogous to a well-*chore*ographed dance" (ibid., 202; italics original). See also Loder, *Logic of the Spirit*, 195.

9. Editor's Note: See Loder and Neidhardt, *Knight's Move*, 305. There the authors retain an important distinction between the *koinonia* of the Trinity and the *koinonia* relationality that creates the church in Christ. "Mutual interpenetration at all points is revealed to us as definitive in the nature of Jesus Christ, but its ultimate expression

Paul Lehmann discusses *koinonia* as he describes the Reformation doctrine of the communion of saints.[10] As he presents it, the doctrine has two aspects. On the one hand, to be in communion is to communicate the love of God. On the other hand, communion partakes in a miracle of transubstantiation, not so much of the elements but of the people. As Luther put it, "through love we are being changed into each other." Thus, "Let us be what we are, for each other." *Koinonia* is shared human participation in the very life of God. Moreover, in this kind of perichoretic mutuality Christ becomes a living presence shaping communal existence. The spiritual presence of Christ indwells and constitutes the relationality among the members of his body, the *koinonia*. Recall the two disciples rushing back to Jerusalem in the Emmaus Road account finding *koinonia* with the other disciples in response to the presence of the risen Jesus.

Lehmann defines *koinonia* as "the fellowship-creating reality of Christ's presence in the world."[11] T. F. Torrance perhaps improves this a bit when he discusses *koinonia* in terms of "the *communion*-creating reality of Jesus Christ."[12] Both definitions imply that the church as the *koinonia* or the body of Christ must be understood to be in dialectical relationship with the church as an institution (*ecclesia*). On the one hand, *koinonia* can never be identified with the institution. On the other, the *koinonia* can never be entirely separated from the institution. The church as institution and the church as *koinonia* are in a mutually reciprocal relationship. However, the *koinonia* is by far the greater, more vital, constituting and sustaining reality of the dialectic relation.

By implication, we must note that this dialectical relationship means that we can never identify the *koinonia* with that core group of people in our congregations that every minister seems to count on, those who are faithful to the end. Blessed as these people may be, they may also be so well socialized into their church roles that they actually quench the Spirit. *Koinonia* is constituted by the Holy Spirit and includes the enemy and the stranger as well as the cordial and the compliant. Although the *koinonia* is thoroughly social, there is no direct equivalence between a social entity and the *koinonia* because the invisible presence of Christ is the sine qua non of congregational existence. Karl Barth helpfully spells out this distinction in

---

resides in the trinitarian life of God" (ibid., 202).

10. Lehmann, *Ethics*, 63.

11. Ibid, 59.

12. Loder and Neidhardt, *Knight's Move*, 305 (italics added). See also Loder, *Logic of the Spirit*, 194–95.

terms of how the Holy Spirit creates and maintains the dialectic between *koinonia* and the institutional dimensions of church.

> The work of the Holy Spirit . . . is to bring and to hold together that which is different and therefore, as it would seem, necessarily and irresistibly disruptive in the relationship of Jesus Christ to His community, namely, the divine working, being and action on the one side and the human on the other, the creative freedom and act on the one side and the creaturely on the other, the eternal reality and possibility on the one side and the temporal on the other. His work is to bring and hold them together, not to identify, intermingle nor confound them, not to change the one into the other, not to merge the one into the other, but to co-ordinate them, to make them parallel, to bring them into harmony and therefore to bind them into a true unity (which is the unity of the church as the body of Christ).[13]

Thus, the work of the Holy Spirit can be seen as the corporate self-consciousness of the church bringing the socialization reality of the church into conformity with Jesus's humanity, even as it transcends and transforms our humanity by its nature as the power and presence of God.

This christomorphic conception of the church retains the relationality of the humanity and divinity of Christ. In this christomorphic relational reality Christ's humanity is not permitted to define or diminish his divinity, and Christ's divinity is not allowed to swallow up and absorb his humanity. The key here involves preserving the integrity of the relationality that pertains to the inner life of God and to the inner nature of Christ so as to illumine and enable the integrity of the inner nature of the communion of saints embodied in the *koinonia*. In every case, the tension must be preserved. Notice then that a Christian education that takes place within the limits of the institutional church via socialization actually cuts the church off from the very the ground of her existence in Christ and thereby forfeits her nature as the body of Christ.

The great immediate gift here is that the communion-creating reality of Jesus Christ, the *koinonia*, frees congregations from the double-binding condition that role structure places upon them. Liberation becomes possible because the *koinonia* relationship is grounded in and secured by the spiritual presence of Christ. So, as Lehmann understands it, *koinonia* is a four-dimensional phenomenon only because the power of Christ as the

---

13. Karl Barth, *CD* IV/3.2, 761. Editor's Note: Loder added this final parenthetical phrase to emphasize the ecclesial implications of the Spirit's work. It is not part of Barth's quote.

fourth dimension creates and sustains a set of relationships among us that shares in the vitality of his life. By love, the Holy Spirit transforms us into each other, all the while building up in us a corporate awareness of Christ's presence as our essential unity. The fourth dimension (the Holy) here works through the Spirit to transform the other three dimensions (Self, World, and Void), sanctifying the community in the *imago Christi*. By making us aware of the inherent negation in role-structured and role-determined institutional life, the Spirit redemptively transforms our two-dimensional constructs into a four-dimensional experience through which we mutually create one other in Christ. As one of my students suggested, we can now communicate our dialectical identity in Christ as a corporate identity—"We, yet not we, but *koinonia*."

You remember at the outset of this book we talked about Margaret Mead and Talcott Parsons's contention that prophet, priest, and king no longer belong to the church but to key figures in our socialized society. As we said, these are social science interpretations for all we do in the church. But this dialectical version of the church, whose spiritual center resides in the *koinonia*, gives us another way to think about and embody life in the church. Let us reclaim these offices of Christ as we examine how the Spirit of Christ works four-dimensional transformation in the institutional life of church and society.

## (IV) RECLAIMING THE OFFICES OF CHRIST IN THE *KOINONIA*: PROPHET, KING, AND PRIEST

## (A) Christ the Prophet: Seeing Reality through the Light of Christ

The difficulty with using the social sciences to understand Christian education and the life of the church is that they are still trapped in a Newtonian world. Thus, virtually all of their analyses of how the church functions are strictly contained in Euclidean space, clock time, and cause-effect relationships. But, in 1905 Einstein's first paper on special relativity showed that space, time, and mass are not absolute qualities. In fact, these are related to (relative to) the universal constant—the speed of light. *Light* is the invariant factor. Space, time, and mass are what they are at any given point, depending on their relationship to the speed of light. Space condenses and time slows down as they approach the speed of light.

Now relativity as the underlying intelligibility of the world is counter-intuitive—not the way we ordinarily think. But it is demonstratively more accurate about the nature of the physical order of creation than the common sense of Newton's world—and more accurate than the human sciences that are bound to that world. And relativity is far more than an analogy, as we tried to spell it out in *The Knight's Move*.[14] But for the moment, let us simply stick with the analogy and recall Jesus's use of light, especially in John's Gospel, to define his own person. His presence in the power of the Spirit is the invariant, the constant with respect to which time and space are relative. To be in Christ is to be, so to speak, in "the promised land"—i.e., to be at home wherever you are. Furthermore, to be in Christ is to be in communion with the saints everywhere in the world and throughout all time. In Christ we participate already in the end of time. All space and time are relative to him. He radicalizes space and time. And we need to let the prophetic Christ awaken us from our Newtonian slumber.

More specifically, consider what it means to lay hands on the sick and have them recover. If you have ever experienced this kind of event, on either side of the healing arts, you know the difference between medical healing and healing by the grace of God. Medical healing is a technology that seeks to return you to a norm that you enjoyed in the past. This mode of healing should certainly not to be denigrated. But medical healing needs to be distinguished from healing by the Spirit of God. Healing by God's Spirit allows the future to come in upon the present to redefine it in terms of his future because Christ reigns over all. Proleptically in spiritual healing, we are moved into the future, as if there were a wrinkle in time—moved into the future where the body becomes a spiritual body, and the wholeness of our nature is transparently established in the very life of God. Healing is a prophetic sign of the presence of God in human existence.

## (B) Christ the King

Jesus Christ is the Light of the world. To be in Christ is to experience his power to sustain, order, and reorder the spatiotemporal fabric of his creation as we experience it. Such miracles signify the presence of the kingdom of God performed by the spiritual presence of Christ as Creator and Ruler over all creation, which is the ultimate miracle. Thus, the Spirit of Christ

---

14. Editor's Note: Loder and Neidhardt argued in *Knight's Move* that relationality, especially as revealed in Chalcedonian Christology, has ontological priority in the universe. Reality is neither "out there" in the object nor "in here" in the subject but lies in the relationality that permeates and gives order to reality after the pattern of Christ.

reigns, and every miracle is a prophetic word or sign that proclaims the gospel of God. Specifically, his Spirit effects a four-dimensional transformation of the social and institutional order, as we have said. For example, Christ transforms the presumably inevitable order of social hierarchy. Social scientists will all claim that socially constructed hierarchy is inevitable. But is it? In all social organization from the chicken yard to the United States Congress we presume there is a pecking order. Even the chickens know that this power structure must be respected if social order is to be maintained. The social scientists study this order that socialization creates and sustains. We Presbyterians preserve this socialized order with the clerical paradigm and the conduct of the church according to the *Book of Order*. There must be human order in the church, and we determine to do things "decently and in order" to our dying day.

But from the standpoint of the kingdom of God, and the *koinonia* that arises in response to the gospel, even if hierarchy is inevitable it is no longer definitive. In the Spirit, socialized order becomes reversible, and the congregation's identity becomes dynamic and dialectical. I am reminded of the box in the railway station platform I saw that had the following note attached to it: "This box must be kept bottom up. I have labeled the top 'bottom' in order to avoid confusion." Something like that occurs in the ecclesiastical power system with the *koinonia*. Thus, in Christ, there is a transvaluation of values commensurate with the kingdom. We learn to commend churches of smaller size, in marginalized communities, that commit themselves to doing a more effective mission of being the body of Christ in witness to the neighborhood. We commend congregations that find profound ministry in menial tasks, because they understand that Christ has redefined what is menial.

On the other hand, we realize in Christ that socially powerful congregations are only commendable to Christ if they make the interests of the little ones more important than their own preservation and reputation (Matt 25). We discern in Christ that the church does not exist for itself but to be the servant of all persons in need for the sake of making and keeping human life human. From this theological vantage we also know that congregations that do not conform their ordering of life to the light of Christ will inevitably contribute to the decline that Illich described. Jesus the Servant King labeled the top "bottom" in order to avoid the confusion created by socialization between us and the chickens! In the *koinonia*, the hierarchical structures of socialized order become reversible as the power of transformation through the Spirit gains and maintains marginal control over socialization dynamics.

The Spirit of Christ also affects four-dimensional transformation of territory. Social science maintains that physical space is definitive of our humanness and essential to survival. Robert Ardrey's book *The Territorial Imperative* remains a classic on this topic that argues for the primal significance of territory. One illustration of the phenomena he described had to do with a naturalist's effort to mate two leopards. When he opened the male's cage to the female, the male leopard struck and killed the female straightaway because she got into his territory. Biblically and corporately, the power of space is also well known. In the biblical theology, the themes of the promised land and the promise of the visible peaceable kingdom established at the end of time, re-created by and in Christ, emphasize this concern for space.

Recall W. D. Davies's persuasive argument in his book *The Gospel and the Land* that Jesus Christ is himself the Promised Land.[15] Thus, in Christ we abandon in a concrete sense all necessity for sacralizing promised lands of our own making—personal, national, or international. In Christ, the holy one, you no longer need a place. You don't need a particular building. No place is more holy than some other place when Christ is present. No group is per se more holy than some other group. Jesus is the Promised Land. He is also the Vine and the Bread of Life, the one who gives you all the nourishment that you need. He is the one whose reign protects and delivers, like a Good Shepherd. As King, Jesus is the one who gives to us everything that the land is supposed to give us, and more.

## (C) Christ the Priest

And this christological conviction involves also an ecclesiological conviction. Where is our space as the people of God? The relational quality of the *koinonia* is our space. Where are we at home? The *koinonia* is home. The *koinonia* is our land. The *koinonia* is our place. The *koinonia* frees us from having to set out the boundaries of our territories according to the dictates of unredeemed socialization, so we can welcome the stranger, do good to those who persecute us, and overcome tribalism and prejudice.

As Priest, Jesus supplies the *koinonia* with the sacraments for its edification and nurturance. To be sure, the anthropologists and sociologists have their own definitions of sacraments as rites of passages (baptism) or rites of intensification (communion). But the Spirit of Jesus Christ as Priest transforms these socialized practices so they bear new life. For instance,

15. Loder, *Logic of the Spirit*, 210. See also Loder and Neidhardt, *Knight's Move*, 305.

take the rite of identity. According to psychoanalyst and anthropologist Bruno Bettelheim, rites of identity enact mock births.[16] Thus, in the Christian tradition, he would say baptism is an identity rite. But for the *koinonia* in the power of the Spirit, baptism is a transformation of the socialization version of rites of identity. In reality, baptism—theologically considered—is the toughest critique possible of a socialized rite of identity. Despite our appreciation of cultic practices, baptism is anything but a cultic act.

Think for example, of our common practice of baptism. The minister read the words from the handbook. We stretch our necks to watch what is about to unfold, and we forget to listen to what is being said. But still, we know the right words. (If someone read the wrong words, we would know!). The parents bring the baby up to the front of the sanctuary. Everybody hopes he doesn't cry, especially the pastor. "Henry Murgatroyd Jones," she says. "I baptize you in the name of the Father, the Son, and the Holy Spirit. Amen." Everything's fine, wonderful. "Here is your certificate." Socialization has taken hold of baptism to give it acceptability in a socialized world, and we all clap.

But baptism, theologically considered, is actually just the opposite of this socialized rite. Baptism is a judgment on socialization. You cannot get into this community except by an act of God. In baptism, God acts. There is no way to enter this communal order, except God acts. When we turn baptism into a socialized cultic act, we miss the whole point. Baptism is a sign and a demonstration of the truth that we do not create this social unit, the church. We do not perpetuate the communion of saints. The inherent life of the *koinonia* has nothing to do with our initiative apart from the communion-creating power of the Spirit.

Similarly, from a socialization standpoint, the Lord's Supper is a rite of intensification of membership. But from the standpoint of the *koinonia* it is a rite transformed by an act of the Spirit. At the Lord's Supper, we drink the blood of Christ in response to Christ's invitation and action. Christ has put us into a new bloodline. This bloodline is a judgment on all kinship and socialized orders we create and maintain. Your true identity and allegiance no longer belong to your family, or to your tribe or to your country. You do not belong to these social constructions any more. You belong to Christ. Christ separates you from your family, your tribe, and your nation. Why? Because Christ wants to liberate you from your embeddedness in socialized existence to really love your family and tribe and country freely and without

16. Bettelheim. *Symbolic*, 133–34, 214–26.

manipulation, without fear of absorption or fear of abandonment.[17] Let me expand on this claim.

The reason you have to be separated from your primary social order, the family, is because family is where you learned ego patterns and role structures in the first place. And the secondary socialization that reinforced these patterns and structures call for liberation through the Spirit. As long as the practice of the Lord's Supper sacralizes ego patterns and role structures, it is taken to your condemnation. Communion ends up sacralizing self-destruction in the name of Christ. So, communion rightly administered, taken, and thought about separates you from the family, from kinship ties, from all other public allegiances, so that you can reappropriate those relational allegiances on the strength of who Christ is. Christ is a communion-creating reality that transcends and condemns the sacralization of socialization and role structures in order to redemptively transform social life according to Christ's nature. The Lord's Supper is fundamentally misappropriated when it serves to sacralize ways of ordering human life according to the alienation revealed as original sin. True communion does just the opposite. It exposes socialized alienation as utterly sinful so that the community can be liberated to embody its holy vocation as the people of God.

I recall the story of a woman who had been in counseling for some time to overcome what she felt were the deleterious effects of the emotional violence that she experienced in relation with her parents as a child. Then one day in the course of taking the Eucharist, the overwhelming presence of God presented to her in the wafer and the cup hit her with such force that she came to a profoundly new realization of herself in relation to others. She realized, "I am responsible for my life." In other words, she realized that to be fully forgiven, she had to take full responsibility for her actions. Thus, the Eucharist set her apart and brought her to conviction in order to set her free by an illumination that put her into a new relationship with her parents, which no therapy could have achieved.

Christ is the Light of the world. In reclaiming him as Prophet, Priest, and Ruler through the power of his Spirit, I have tried to help us reflect about the ways his Spirit operates within the institutional context, transforming conventional socialization patterns for the sake of the communion-creating reality of Jesus Christ.

---

17. Editor's Note: See Loder and Neidhardt, *Knight's Move*, 287–306 for their extended discussion of the perichoretic impact of the Spirit on corporate existence.

## (V) THE HOLY SPIRIT, COMMUNAL VITALITY, AND SOCIAL FORM[18]

Let me return here to our original observation about a worldwide spiritual awakening and the need for an authentic context that supports life in the Spirit. In response to this awakening we do not want to advocate spiritual enthusiasm that disintegrates the important need for social form. The elimination of social form is impossible in any case, for all spiritual passion seeks some kind of social form, even if it is ushered in covertly. In point of fact, the spiritual enthusiast very often supports an authoritarian social context in order to support a futile attempt to stay true to the Spirit. Rather, we are trying here to recover and reclaim the spiritual vitality inherent in the forms we already inhabit so that we can become the holy people we are called to be. The Holy Spirit endows us with the capacity to know far more than we can tell. Through Christ, the Spirit establishes us in a communion with the Creator and Ground of all that is, embodied in concrete communities of faith. In the Spirit we become immeasurably greater than we are in ourselves, so that the fullness of the community manifests far greater integrity than the sum of the parts, even as the parts are also enhanced.

Corporate life always enlarges the human spirit, but we must say, not always in the right direction. At a professional basketball game in Madison Square Garden, I watched the beer-drinking crowd become a large corporate beast, roaring for victory, despising the enemy, rising up to drink it in when blood was shed on the court. Unless this kind of corporate unconscious is transformed, it will ultimately embody the alienation that inevitably takes hold of every unredeemed social construction of reality. Only as we let that which is ultimately greater than our social constructions—the spiritual presence of Christ—define and give order to our corporate life will our social contexts embody the redeemed life in the service of Christ.

The sociality empowered by the Spirit also heightens the individual particularity and uniqueness of each person in the community. As a result, the Spirit enables communities to transcend the defensiveness of socialization or tribalism, which breeds the absorption or abandonment of individuals, so that the whole community, and each member of the community, is liberated by mutual participation in the perichoretic life of God. From this posture, socialization through role structures must undergo a

---

18. Editor's Note: In one version of the manuscript Loder had inserted five asterisks prior to the start of this section, for an unknown reason. Since this breaks with the rest of the structure of the manuscript, I gave a title to this division that seems to anticipate the next section.

transformation that breaks out of the double bind of institutional life to enable the corporate and individual practice of freedom of the Spirit.

In the New Testament, we glimpse this transformation in Luke's portrayal of the pentecostal experience that gave birth to the church in Acts 2. This narrative, which we mentioned earlier, is very instructive because here the Spirit breaks through all cultural barriers and redefines all norms and rules in terms of the power of the Spirit to convey the true identity of Jesus Christ. The Spirit transcends anything that ever happens in Madison Square Garden. Note again in particular that the event of Pentecost comes on the day on which the Jews would otherwise have celebrated the giving of the law to Moses on Mount Sinai. Luke imagines here that a transformation of the law of Moses has occurred such that the norms and values of Israel are taken up and transformed by the "*law of the Spirit of Christ*," which is *life* in Christ Jesus (cf. Rom 8:2).

Notice first how the unity created by the Spirit that day, uniting the diverse tongues of people from all over the world, reversed the cultural and linguistic confusion and animosity characterized by the judgment on Babel in the Genesis account (what we argued earlier was a judgment on socialization dynamics). Second, the new law of the Spirit of Christ transcended the diversity of humanity without obliterating differences. When Christ reigns in the heart of the community, those who hear the roar of the Spirit exist as a harbinger of the new Jerusalem, the new Israel, the holy people of God, gathered not by the power of socialization or enculturation but by the definitive act of God's Spirit, creating unity in diversity and diversity in unity.

Let us now turn to consider how the Spirit's transformation of role structures impinges on other relational contexts or situations in which new behaviors become warranted.

## (A) Behavioral Manifestations of *Koinonia*

How does the communion-creating activity of the Spirit manifest itself in ordinary human social behavior? Let us consider two actual cases to answer this question: Marriage and loving one's neighbor.

### (1) Thinking Married

One behavioral manifestation of what *koinonia* looks like comes up often in marriage counseling. Consider a couple planning to marry that comes to me to talk. What a happy occasion this is, right? Well, not always. But suppose it is. As we talk, I realize that the couple is not *thinking* married. They are thinking single. They imagine the marriage relationship is something they maintain. Ego structures and role patterns still govern the relationship—even though there are liminal experiences of laughter, sex or aggression. The relationship remains something each one seeks to control from the standpoint of his or her ego or role posture. In other words, they have sort of agreed to help each other get along in their combined singleness, and so to solve some of their personal, emotional, sexual, and spiritual problems by marrying each other. This is a picture of marriage as socialized institution.

Now you can do marriage in this kind of a role-structured sort of way. But as a minister of the gospel of Jesus Christ, I am not going to perform the ceremony for anybody who wants to do that. I am just not interested in that approach to marriage. I am interested in the couple learning to "think married." Learning to think married means learning to let the relationship have a power of its own, to become a positive third term for which roles become secondary. I want couples to think *koinonia*, which is to think about what it means to mutually create each other such that the relationality in Christ actually liberates the individuals to love, rather than the individuals having to perpetuate the role relations. You are really free when you don't have to keep working on the relationship. You are really free when you can trust the relationship to have a life of its own. Even this kind of relational thinking will eventually be distorted in the direction of absorption or manipulation unless the couple learns to trust the Spirit through prayer at every level of inner dialogue. Prayer recognizes that marriage is the creation of the Spirit of Christ. As I tell my students, spiritual heat is hotter than sexual heat, and this heat is the prerogative of all persons, married or not, who participate in the *koinonia*.

## (2) Neighbor Love

Another behavioral manifestation of *koinonia* is the genuine expression of love for one's neighbor engendered by the Spirit. The power of the *koinonia* liberates us to love the neighbor, even when the neighbor is our enemy! Paul's teaching in Rom 12 is very telling.

> Let love be genuine; hate what is evil, hold fast to what is good; love one another with brotherly affection; outdo one another in showing honor. Never flag in zeal, be aglow with the Spirit, serve the Lord.
>
> Rejoice in your hope, be patient in tribulation, be constant in prayer. Contribute to the needs of the saints; practice hospitality.

*Bless those who persecute you; bless and do not curse them. Rejoice with those who rejoice; weep with those who weep. Live in harmony with one another; do not be haughty, but associate with the lowly; never be conceited. Repay no one evil for evil, but take thought for what is noble in the sight of all. If possible, so far as it depends upon you, live peaceably with all. Beloved, never avenge yourselves, but leave it to the wrath of God; for it is written, "'Vengeance is mine, I will repay,' says the Lord." No, "if your enemy is hungry, feed him; if he is thirsty, give him drink; for by so doing you heap burning coals upon his head." Do not be overcome by evil, but overcome evil with good.* (Rom 12:9–21 RSV)

Paul's description here of *koinonia* ethics in the Spirit is remarkable and warrants considerable commentary. But let me limit my comments to his concluding instruction. As you know, this concluding advice to "*heap burning coals upon [your enemy's] head*" is not a matter of killing him or her with kindness. Such action would be a form of revenge or manipulation. Paul counsels against that response in the previous verses. Rather, the practice of "heaping coals" refers instead to an Egyptian rite of penance by the one offended. In essence Paul counsels that if one has done something wrong to you, you should put coals of fire in a pan, put the pan on your head, and walk back and forth in front of your enemy's house to say that you have had a change of mind. If you return evil for evil, vengeance will make it harder for the other one to change their mind. Returning good for evil in this way will maximize the prospect that your enemy may have a change of mind commensurate with yours, and perhaps that reconciliation will result from the mutual repentance!

How is this practice possible? The act only becomes possible as an expression of the *koinonia*—a corporate life that thrives on forgiveness as a response to indwelling the spiritual presence of the forgiving Christ. Do you recall the case of Helen in a previous chapter? Her mother had hated her for being the wrong sex, and her father had abandoned her. They were too ashamed to reach out to her. But then she underwent transformation in the power of the Spirit, and this experience engendered in her a desire to reach out to them and restore the sociality of their relationship. Her act of "placing hot coals on her head" resulted in their change of heart and mind, breaking the back of their socialized defensiveness and resulting in a restoration of relations. Helen's testimony of this experience—"This belongs to the church!"—implied that *koinonia* was already in her conversion, as Karl Barth puts it. I am sure you know similar cases about social transformation. What I am suggesting is that in experiences of the transformation of relationships, the ethical power of the *koinonia* manifests itself.

## (B) Societal Transformation in Oppressive Contexts

In conclusion, let me offer several testimonies that demonstrate the invisible redemptive power of the *koinonia* in the context of *ecclesia* under oppressive conditions. The first testimony comes from Hendrick Kraemer, a well-regarded Dutch theologian and statesman who wrote out of his experience of Nazi Germany's occupation of Holland in World War II. Kraemer, a Nazi resister who deplored the Nazi atrocities and who worked for the reform of the church after the war, asserted that it was under the German occupation that the church became revitalized.[19] Kraemer here celebrates the *koinonia*, the relational presence of Christ engendering the power to reform the institutional church amid the horrors of the Third Reich and to resist accommodation to the socialization patterns of this hostile and dehumanizing force that had come upon the land. As we have noted, this spiritual and social reform of congregations is the corporate analogue to the transforming moment in individual conversion. In the individual, when ego structures are stripped away, the inner vitality must be called upon to re-create the personality. In the church, when socialization structures can no longer protect the people under oppression, the relational reality of Christ reconstitutes and empowers the convicted congregation to be more than they ever were before. Kraemer testifies that oppression is often the catalyst for redemptive transformation of congregational life.

A second testimony of the *koinonia* being revitalized in contexts of oppression comes from Minon Ochinsky, a theologian from Czechoslovakia whom I met at the Center for Theological Inquiry in Princeton some time ago. He knew I was interested in the kinds of things that I have been writing about in this book. So one day he said, "Let me tell you what happened in Czechoslovakia." He explained that after the Communist takeover there, about fourteen years of intense industrialization and indoctrination into Marxist doctrine was instigated to control the Moravian section of the country. The Marxists spared no effort to wipe out or undermine everything

---

19. Editor's Note: Loder gave no reference here. But it seems fairly certain it comes from Kraemer's important book *Theology of the Laity*, which highlighted a lay movement in Europe after World War II called the Evangelical Academies. In reference to the depletion of clergy, this lay movement helped the church revive. Kraemer noted, "the rise and growth of Evangelical Academies in Germany must be seen on the background of this desperate situation and the spiritual and moral chaos in which Germany found itself immediately after its defeat . . . So the Evangelical Academies intended to be meeting places for a dialogue between Church and World. After the experiences of the Hitler regime when all free meeting of minds was impossible, this was quite a new beginning, and it was of great importance that Christians took the initiative (Kraemer, *Theology of the Laity*, 38).

that had to do with the church. Eventually, the government commissioned the Department of Culture to study this forced enculturation to see if the regime had, in fact, brought the people to conviction about dialectical materialism and the destiny of history according to Karl Marx, not Jesus Christ.

To the dismay and embarrassment of the Communist leadership, the Department of Culture discovered that religious conviction had actually grown during the time of the industrialization and indoctrination. That is, religious conviction had grown *stronger* in response to the oppression. Certain religious leaders, who had previously not been taken seriously because they had always played out their religious roles, came into a kind of purified sense of conviction. People began to respect these clergy in their newly found courage. Furthermore, government officials told parents that their children could have some religious instruction from a certified religious teacher if they so wished. But they were warned in no uncertain terms that such instruction would go on their permanent record and make it very difficult for them to get a job when they entered adulthood. Despite these dire consequences, more parents than ever before wanted religious instruction for themselves and their children. "I don't care what the consequences are," they said. "We want the religious instruction."

As an aside, you would think that in a society like the United States, in which we are perfectly free to socialize everybody and anybody into Christianity, the church would enjoy a growing and dominant place in society. Yet by most accounts, many mainline churches are not only *not* flourishing, but they are moribund. And we all wonder why the church languishes when it seems so free. Why can't the church be the church? What the Czechoslovakian and Hollander stories suggests is that there may very well be an inverse relationship between socialization and the freedom to socialize, on the one hand, and the inner vitality of the Christian community on the other. In this inverse relationship, the more that Christian socialization is attacked, made difficult, or stripped away, the more persons may draw upon a their inner depth of conviction so as to release the communion-creating power of the Spirit. I do not advocate oppression and suffering. But these testimonies suggest that in the Spirit we can be grateful in our suffering because, as the author of Hebrews put it, Jesus Christ himself was made "*perfect through suffering*" (Heb 2:10), and as the apostle Paul put it, the church "*may share his sufferings*" (Phil 3:10), and Paul himself may even "*complete what is lacking in Christ's afflictions*" (Col 1:24).

Finally, let me offer a third testimony of social transformation amid suffering, the story of Timothy Njoya of Kenya. I met Timothy while he was a student at Princeton Seminary. He got so turned on to the power of transformation that he wrote a four-hundred-page term paper about it.

Eventually, he earned his PhD, writing his dissertation on authoritarianism and transformation in authoritarian missionary contexts.[20] Timothy noted that when individual conversions to Christ were experienced in these authoritarian contexts, nothing really changed. The usual result was simply that the authoritarian tribal language and expectations that ruled the person prior to conversion were simply appropriated as an authoritarian Christian language and set of expectations. You could even convert the whole tribe, Njoya noticed, but nothing changed in terms of the social structure. Njoya argued that the authoritarian spirit of the culture eventually corrupted the potential social impact of the conversions. So he committed himself to go back to re-awaken the transformational potential for social experience that was already in these people because of their conversions.

So Timothy returned to Kenya to pursue transformation. But his efforts to unlock this social potential came up against an authoritarian and oppressive government determined not let the people or the church gain any real power. Yet change did begin to take place. Feeling more self-assured and self-sufficient, the people started questioning the authority of the government. In response, the officials of the government decided to kill Timothy. One day on his way to a Presbyterian meeting, he was driving up a hill where there was a sharp drop-off. The government contrived to have a car pull out right in front of him. By reflex action Timothy turned the wheel to avoid the crash. His car plunged off the edge of the cliff and rolled down the steep incline. He thought to himself, "This must be what it is like to die." Finally, he landed at the bottom of the cliff. The car stopped rolling. He felt himself. Nothing wrong. So he got out of the car, climbed the hill, secured another car, and went on to the presbytery meeting!

The government was undeterred. They hired assassins, who, unbeknownst to them, had actually benefited from Timothy's ministry. These people entered his home to kill him with knives. As they confronted him, Timothy said, "Look, you don't have to do this."

But they needed the money desperately. "Yes, we have to do this." And so they thrust their knives at him. They cut him again and again in the hands, which he used to signal them to stop. But they couldn't kill him.

---

20. Editor's Note: The reference in quotes, "authoritarianism and transformation . . . contexts," originally appeared to be a title in Loder's manuscript. But the research librarian at Princeton Theological Seminary could find no reference to anything written by Njoya with this title. Thus, the "title" actually seems to be Loder's recollection of the substance of Njoya's 1971 dissertation rather than its proper title. Njoya's dissertation was called "Dynamics of Change." Efforts to contact Dr. Njoya to clarify the situation failed.

"No, you don't have to do this. I forgive you," he said. Finally, they left him to bleed to death. But before he did, his wife found him and drove him to the hospital.

The thing that prompted him to tell me this story was my inquiry into the big scars across his hands. He was in the hospital for a whole year recovering from the wounds. The amazing thing was that the people of the church paid every penny of that hospital bill. These people were desperately poor, like the assassins. But because of the hope he had given to them, they gladly paid his bills. Do you know what their actions represent? The *koinonia*! Life in the Spirit overcomes all the authoritarian role structures, all the rigidity, and all the defensiveness that prevents us from loving one another. In the end, the government in Kenya changed. Officials noticed the great good that Timothy was doing, and they liked what they saw. So today, as far as I know, Timothy still administers a pastoral institute in Kenya, and the government sends professors from the university to participate in his school and to learn about transformation.[21]

## (VI) CONCLUSION

In this chapter we have described and illustrated what life in the Spirit of Christ means in the social realm, the *koinonia*, and how the life of Christ challenges socialized existence to undergo redemptive transformation for the benefit of all. We have elaborated Paul Lehmann's insight that the *koinonia* represents a four-dimensional transformation of the corporate life, which corresponds to four-dimensional transformation of conscience (ordered by ego) in the individual. Lehmann once averred, "*Koinonia* is the price we pay for the progress of conscience."[22] *Koinonia* is the corporate embodiment of the Christian style of life. From a theological point of view, any sustained renewal of the church today requires that we learn to live in the Spirit. But sociality is only one crucial dimension of corporate existence that needs transformation. Redemptive transformation must also occur in the cultural realm—the realm of language, metaphor, and symbol—which is the concern of the next chapter.

---

21. Editor's Note: Rev. Dr. Timothy Njoya has served for many years as a pastor, scholar, and social activist in Kenya. I believe he has retired. My efforts to contact him failed.

22. Editor's Note: Loder is paraphrasing Paul Lehmann's trope on Freud in *Ethics in a Christian Context*, 361. There Lehmann writes: "To paraphrase the Freudian epigram . . . *if 'conscience is the price to be paid for the progress of civilization,' the* koinonia *is 'the price to be paid for the progress of conscience*" (italics original).

# 8

# Culture
## The Word and Cultural Transformation

## (I) INTRODUCTION: THE IRREPARABLE DISJUNCTION BETWEEN LANGUAGE AND REALITY

WE MOVE NOW TO the question of culture (the latency box in Parsons's scheme), and its transformation in Christ. Culture is simply *the power of the human imagination crystallized into repeatable public forms*. In view here is the whole range of images, signs, metaphors, symbols, and symbol systems together with their power to state, secure, establish, and legitimate core values and styles of life deemed important for a society. Culture constitutes the staying power of a socialized, enculturated society.

However, as with all dimensions of human action, culture is caught in its own version of a double bind. Cultural critics have repeatedly pointed out that throughout history cultures suffer from an implacable problem— i.e., that it is extremely difficult, if not impossible, for language to tell the truth. Practitioners of what is now called the hermeneutics of suspicion have also maintained from ancient times—from the Cynics to the Epicureans, from Nietzsche to Freud, from existentialism to deconstructionism—that it is extremely difficult, if not impossible, for language to tell the truth. Note that the seemingly irreparable barrier between language and reality need not be the case only in arcane philosophical conversations of academics cloistered in ivory towers. Every child comes to the alarming and disillusioning realization that lying is possible, even normative, in everyday experience. Alongside this realization comes the gradual recognition, as the child matures into adulthood, of the many, perhaps inexhaustible, aspects of what is involved in trying to tell "the truth, the whole truth, and nothing but the truth."

This legal litany is something of a paradox since it has traditionally been concluded, "so help me God." The paradox lies in the fact that it is really only God who can tell the truth. Indeed. God's Word and God's nature are one and the same. By contrast, human language, and by extension all human culture, always and inevitably bear in some measure, the irreparable disjunction between language and reality. This disjunction, it must be noted, is the crux of the double bind at the heart of Christian culture as well, borne by the church. Why is it so hard to tell the truth even when, through Christ's Spirit, we live and move and have our being in him who is the truth? At the risk of only further exemplifying the problem, I will now attempt to answer the question in terms of what must be present and what obstacles must be overcome for the truth to be told with integrity.

To begin, I want to focus on what may be the most powerful influence upon the formation of culture, namely, the *master image* (Gibson Winter), also called *root metaphor* (Paul Ricoeur) or *root image* (David Tracy). Master images are deeper and more powerful than language, doctrine, or even the words of Scripture, because master images determine how language, doctrine, and Scripture are interpreted and how they shape our lives. Master images profoundly establish the dominant values and vision of our lives with the same kind of subtle, unobserved power by which Euclidean space supposedly established the three-dimensional container in which we move bodily. We know this image is false, but we continue to live in a Newtonian world anyway. Similarly unexamined and naively taken for granted as "the way things are," these root metaphors of human existence set the boundaries or outer limits for what we will permit ourselves to believe or think possible. Though they generate many and varied surface expressions, master images establish the grounds for consistency and normality—"the way things ought to be" both in life and in death.

## (II) MASTER IMAGE DEFINED AND DESCRIBED

So let us proceed to define root metaphor more carefully. Root metaphor is *the shared imaginative construction of the world that shapes our lives at the level of corporate, preconscious awareness.* Note two elements in this definition. *First,* by *preconscious* I mean that root metaphors work for us and on us at a level beneath consciousness. But unlike the unconscious, master images are subject to conscious examination. They can be drawn up and pondered, mulled over and critiqued. Most of the time we are not aware of our master or root images and how they influence and even determine our thoughts and actions. Nevertheless, we *can* become aware of them.

*Second*, the master image is corporate in that it has been learned and imbibed from personal, social, and cultural environments. Root images are the powerful product of socialization by which the core values of one's dominant society take up residence in the roles and egos of the members of that society. Since one may participate in a master image with others without thinking much about it, whole groups, families, and societies may be drawn together and governed by one or two master images without recognizing why they feel a commonality.

All of this discussion is rather abstract. So now I want to give you an extended personal illustration of a master image—how it worked and how the spiritual presence of Christ transformed it. But first I want you to notice that what ego defenses are to personality and what role is to social organization, the master image is to culture. Culture is an inevitable, but not necessary, double-bind phenomenon that must undergo redemptive transformation if it is to participate in and support a Christian style of life.

## (A) The "Loder Mystique":
## The Power of the Familial Master Image

I am going to take some personal privilege and use a homely example of a master image. That is, when I was growing up I was dimly aware of a master image that ruled our family, embodying what it meant to be a Loder. Now there was a territorial origin here. We lived in a small town set in the midst of the Nebraskan plains. My grandfather owned the only grocery store in town. He was also the mayor of the town. He had four sons who were known as the Loder boys. One of these boys was my father. The Loder boys were always on top, full of mischief, full of fun, always superachievers.

In the Loder clan, men were the center of importance, energy, and talk. The women whom they married were supposed to be attractive, charming, and faithful, and to admire their men. But they and their families were clearly of secondary significance. Their task was to bear children and be good wives and mothers. Loders, like Kennedys, did not cry or complain. Such behavior was called bellyaching. Loder men were gutsy, honest, religious—but not overly so—and in one way or the other they always came out on top. Cultural activity occurred at holidays and family reunions for whatever occasion—births, deaths, marriages, and so on. The Loder master image was not any one person. It summed up the unity of the whole Loder family, which was intensified at these not infrequent gatherings.

The Loder image was variously embodied in each of the four sons. And it functioned as a kind of sublimated stimulus and control mechanism over the behavior of all who were present at any of the cultic gatherings. The master image was ritually reinforced by the horseplay, by the retelling of old stories, and by the celebration of cultic heroes. For instance, old Uncle Lou Loder was so tough when he first went out to Nebraska that he beat off three Indians from his land single-handedly with nothing but a log in his right hand. To notice, or to ask, how the Indians might have felt about the story was to miss the point, and to be kind of a nerd. Everyone just knew that there were certain things that were okay and other things that weren't. Thus, the master image embodied a core value without even being articulated as such.

Women were not to be more articulate or clever than the men, at least not for long in any given conversation. Single-minded devotion to a cause or a research project that could not be explained fully to the others or shown to have clear and immediate pragmatic significance was arrogant and presumptuous. To be deep and quiet as a person, such that one might not easily join in the cultic play, was to be suspect, and would bring charges that you were depressed about some hidden problem. Genuine self-sacrifice was considered weak if it could not also be considered prudent. Too much individualistic self-assertion was immediately cut down to size. Failure to appreciate the off-color humor was considered prudery. Drinking was absolutely forbidden. Smoking was thought manly and permitted for men, but women never should. The Loders were tough competitors who never gave up until it was over. Actually the Loders went one up on Yogi Berra: "Even when it was over, it wasn't over."

I could go on describing the various expressions of this master image, but you can see how it functions, how it is perpetuated, and how it controlled affect, thought, and value. So absorbing was it for a child raised in the cult that it seemed to embody the ultimate meaning of how to be in the world. Whether with the Loders or alone or with some other group, one always felt constrained to act like a Loder. This master image ordered the universe and everything in it. The image even came with totems. One of the totems was a Loder nose. Even our genes cooperated with the cult! I have a Loder nose. You don't know what that is, but I know what it is, and that is one thing, short of surgery, that I cannot change!

Thus, a master image or root metaphor creates this kind of life-determining ethos. The ethos is elusive and very difficult to get hold of, since it is embodied differently in different individuals. Still it has tremendous power to restrain and determine the whole of one's life. Perhaps you can see in this analysis how families can recapitulate the thesis, developed by Pannenberg and others, that in the cult and in cultic practices of religion, we find the origins of culture and culture's claims to foster ultimate meaning for members of society.[1] From generation to generation, symbols and values emerge and become the intentional basis for individuals belonging to the corporate unit in question—or the basis for their marginalization or exclusion.

## (B) The "Loder Mystique" Transformed: The Power of Convictional Experience

For all of its subtle power, however, there are ways in which the master image can be changed, modified, or transformed. Let me mention three ways. *First*, root images can be modified peripherally by encountering what we might call an antienvironment. That is, a self-image is modified as one encounters powerful countervailing circumstances. In the illustration that I gave you, my college experience as a philosophy major chipped away significantly at the Loder image. I began to be increasingly conscious of the underlying biases and limits implicit in the image as I experienced a liberal education. *Second*, cultic master images are naturally modified from within, as when one ages or matures. Again, within the Loder illustration, one of the Loder women finally outgrew the limits of the image and refused to take part in the cult. To everyone's consternation, she just wouldn't play the game anymore.

*Third*, and most significantly, master images are altered radically if some major conflict emerging from within or from without touches the nucleus of the image to place it under question. On the negative side, experiences of death or some disaster that confronts the heart of the image may educe a radical reconsideration of the image's power. More constructively, some in-depth form of therapy or a life-altering religious conversion may expose the negation bound up in the image to bring it under critique and reassessment. To give you an illustration of how a master image can be transformed, let me tell you what happened to my version of the Loder image.

After I had gone through college and had come to Princeton Seminary, the Loder image was already weakening, lessoning its hold. But I still lived my life as a Loder. My family respected my decision to attend seminary so long as I really thought things through and determined prudently to make a pragmatic difference in the world. After my first quarter, my father was

1. Pannenberg, *Anthropology*, 338–39.

diagnosed with brain cancer, and I was called home. For about nine months, we called on the ministers of the city, and the Loder boys came and went. But over the course of nine months, my father died.

After he died, I became very depressed and developed a glandular illness, which I am pretty sure was directly associated with his death. I was lying there in bed thinking, Here I am, at the end of my first quarter at Princeton Seminary, and I really ought to pray about this terrible experience. So I began to write out my prayers to make sure that I was speaking coherently. After all, Loders are *never* incoherent. So I wrote and rewrote my prayers. But nothing happened. Finally I got angry. I doubled up my fist and smashed it into the pillow. "God! If you're there, *do* something!" Astonishingly, God *did* something. But what God did wasn't what I thought I wanted. And it certainly wasn't what a "Loder" was supposed to want. Something like liquid heat began at the bottom of my feet and shot through my body and practically threw me out of my bed. I jumped up and sang what I, as a philosophy major, would never think to sing: "Blessed Assurance, Jesus Is Mine." Next, I immediately picked up Emil Brunner's little book, *The Scandal of Christianity*. I started to read it. But I didn't so much read it as I just *recognized* it as testimony! In the heat of convictional experience, the theological language Brunner had written became transparent to the meaning of my experience. Brunner's words pointed unfailingly to Jesus the Word, who was now present to me in my pain and anguish.

When I told people—especially members of the Loder family—what had happened, they said, "Oh, that's nice. I'm glad that happened to you." I know they were waiting to see if the experience fit the Loder image. But now, the mystique, the mythic force of the master image that had held me in thrall was broken. Although I retained many of the Loder characteristics, according to my family's master image I was no longer a Loder anymore.

I am telling you this experience as a parable of how the Spirit breaks through and transforms master images. The myth was broken. The master image no longer really had control over me. I didn't belong to anyone's system anymore, not even my family system. I belonged to something else, the transparent presence of Christ. The problem I then faced was to reconstruct what happened to me on the basis of this radical alteration and displacement of the master image, and to do this reconstructive work on the basis of indwelling the spiritual presence of Christ.

When I came back to seminary, I remember being so peaceful about everything. Gone was the obsession with competition, my need to be on top as Loders had to be. I remember interviewing over and over again for a required field education position. Positions would get down to two people, and I was one of them, but they always took the other person. The kindly woman who was at the field education office said, "I'm sorry that none of these positions is working out for you. Are you feeling bad?"

"No," I said, "It's okay with me." And I meant it. I was completely reoriented according to something else, a different order of meaning and value more powerful than the master image that nurtured me.

What I have just set before you is a paradigm, an outline in narrative form, of a Christian critique of culture that I now want to develop more fully as a guide to our approach to Christian education, as seen from a cultural perspective.

## (III) THE TRANSFORMATION OF CULTURE

## (A) The Double Bind of Two-Dimensional Culture

Earlier I said that a master image is to culture as ego is to psyche and role is to society. Remember that although the ego presents us a way of adapting to the world, it is a double binding phenomenon that has to be transformed. Similarly, the role structure that allows us to enter into balanced-distanced social relationships is a double binding phenomenon that needs to be transformed in the context of *koinonia*. I am arguing here that the master image has this same double binding quality. Master images establish the matrix within and by which we generate culture, but they remain largely unexamined phenomena that need to be transformed.

What is the double bind inherent in the master image? I would answer that the master image supplies a context of meaning and support that we all need, while stifling the deeper longing in us for a transparent Face—to-face relationship with the divine presence. But once it is transformed, the master image of the cult is something you *have*, no longer something that *has* you. It no longer defines you. Moreover, since no other cultic image can define you either, there is no need to search for an alternative. The glorious freedom of being in communion with the living presence of Christ defines your freedom. Tragically, the double binding character of master image prevents such communion. Instead of living in freedom, we live in fear. We fear that without some two-dimensional cultic order to belong to we will be cut adrift into cosmic loneliness or absorbed into some totality and lose our individuality. Thus, caught between the fear of abandonment and the threat of absorption, we are inextricably bound until the liberating presence of Christ breaks the image's hold on us.

In my case, the experience of the spiritual presence of Christ exposed the double binding character of the Loder master image. Please understand that this master image wasn't without importance, any more than ego and social roles have some importance in a Christian style of life. It had value for me then, and it has value for me now—but only relative value. But it needed to be transformed, to be put into a radically different frame of reference. It needed to be radically relativized by the transparent sense of Christ's presence. Indeed, a transparent relationship with the divine presence exposes and transforms all types of imagery and places them in the service of Christ.

Thus, what pertained in this family cult pertains also in the case of explicitly religious images. Such images are also double binding until transformed. As a paradigm of the relation of religious culture to the reality it signifies, think of Peter on Mount Tabor, the Mount of Transfiguration (Matt 17:1–8; Mark 9:2–7; Luke 8:28–36). Jesus was transfigured right before Peter's eyes in an incredible theophany. But the experience confused Peter. Why? No doubt the unmediated presence of the Holy shattered his religiocultural reality, his Judaic master images. So he said, without knowing what he was saying, *"Let us build a booth for you and Moses and Elijah here."* There is real irony in Peter's suggestion, because booths appeared on Israel's historical scene only after it was evident that God did not dwell openly among the people anymore. A booth was a special place to be with God. But it was a cultural response to the *absence*, not the presence, of God. So God responded to Peter's suggestion by ignoring it. God drew attention to the presence of God in the Son. *"This is my beloved Son. Listen to him."* When the divine reality is present, you don't create culture. You listen! Mircea Eliade, the great historian of religion said, "When the gods depart, that is when religion as culture begins." When the gods depart, then we put "God" into cultural forms, call it religion, and teach faith through enculturation.

What we have in our theological culture is a very fragile—necessary but fragile—language and set of symbols that needs repeatedly to be made reversible, undone as two-dimensional culture and made transparent to the divine presence through the Spirit. We tend to resist this transformation, however, just as God's people have always resisted coming into the presence of a holy God. Consequently, Seward Hiltner could speak of liturgy as an ingenious pattern of defense. He argued that we design the liturgy to get us close enough to the holy to ease our conscience, yet keep us far enough away so it won't make any real difference in our lives.[2] We draw into the presence of the God and we say, "What a wonderful experience that was!"

2. Editor's Note: Loder does not give the source of Hiltner's observation. But it may have come from Hiltner, *Religion and Health*, 160–61.

But we go away from the service before anything really happens, because if something *really* happened, it might even mess up the beautiful experience of the liturgy.

We want "decency and order" in all things, don't we? That is an important dictum, especially for us Presbyterians. But the impetus for order can become deeply ironic—even demonic—if the image of decency and order remains resistant and closed to the transparent movement of God's Spirit. For example, a woman who had an effective ministry that included healing was asked to preach in a Presbyterian church. She accepted the invitation. During the service she participated fully in the liturgy until she started to preach. Then she stopped and said, "There is someone here who is right now being healed of cancer." She specified the place in the body. At first nobody responded to her call. She repeated, "You can come; please come." The person finally did come, and was healed in the service. Do you know what the reaction was afterwards? "Who does she think she is! Messing up the liturgy! What right does she have to mess up *our* worship service!" Is not this anecdote painfully familiar?

Tragically, religious symbols, liturgies, and images can double-bind us against both the expression and the experience of the divine presence. Searching for how religious language, symbols, and images might be transformed so as to invite rather than occlude the divine presence, we can learn an important lesson from Eastern Orthodoxy's use of the icon.

## (B) Icons and the Word of God

Several years ago in Geneva, I heard a lecture on icons given by Eastern Orthodox theologian Nikos Nissiotis.[3] He described how icons are intentionally made to be different from realistic or Renaissance art, and, of course, should in no way serve as a commercial art form. The apparent distortions of perspective and the statuesque posture of the figures are precisely designed as an aid to concentration on the divine presence. That is, they are designed so as to focus the viewers' attention *beyond* the icon to the reality they signify. As self-mitigating symbols and images, icons vanish as three-dimensional objects when the divine appears. As pictures, they become open windows to the divine presence. Thus, contemplatives attend to an icon until they are met from the others side by the divine presence. Drawn

---

3. Editor's Note: Loder only used the title "Professor Nissiotis" here. But he is no doubt referring to Nikos A. Nissiotis, a well-respected theologian and philosopher who focused on the work of the Holy Spirit and who encouraged interfaith dialogue in the World Council of Churches.

behind the image at that point, they begin to turn and see the world through the lenses of the icon. In this way, icon as picture or image vanishes and becomes a lens for reenvisioning one's self and one's world.

The power of this iconic reenvisioning is immense. For example, a student from the Near East described to me in the course of our counseling a remarkable experience of transformation. As a response to a broken love affair here and death and a broken home in Taiwan, she decided that she could not go on living. She decided to take her life, but, interestingly, she wanted to clean her room first. As she did so, she came across an icon—an image of the face of Christ before which the devotee burns incense. Struck by the presence of the forgotten icon, she decided to pray and ask God's forgiveness before she took the overdose of sleeping pills. But as she performed the ritual on her knees, she began to contemplate the face of Christ behind the wisps of smoke that rose from the incense. Soon the image vanished and she found herself once again *in Christ*—that is, viewing herself as Christ viewed her, valuing her from the standpoint of his love for her. When she finished, she rose up feeling joy in her heart and a desire to live. Moved in this way by Christ's Spirit, she dumped out the pills. The iconic image had become transparent, an imageless image, and now instead of seeing the little icon as a part of her despairing world she saw the world through Christ's eyes. His vision of the world had become her own vision.

In terms of the material that I have discussed earlier, recall that the Emmaus Road story culminates in a similar analogous turn, whereby the visible but unrecognized Christ vanishes. Once he is gone, the disciples "see more" because they now see the world and themselves through the lens of his nature. Thus, when the human imagination yields to the divine presence, a critical turning point occurs in cultural experience. A similar pattern of transformation occurs in the practice of spirituality according to the classic fourfold pattern. The pattern is, (1) Awakening, (2) Purgation, (3) Illumination, and (4) Unification. The basic move I am describing here takes place most decisively between purgation and illumination. According to the pattern, then, we can expand a bit on the steps as follows.

(1) *Awakening*. Here is the awakening to God's presence, leading to seeking God in prayer.

(2) *Purgation*. The effort to purify oneself reaches its limit. That is, here one is brought to an extremity where one's limits are reached and one's resources exhausted. Then and there one may anticipate being met from "the other side."

(3) *Illumination.* Here the shift occurs from praying to being prayed, leading to an illumination of one's true situation.

(4) *Unification.* One learns to live in the relationality revealed in the presence of God.

To become the iconic bearer of the divine presence that it is intended to be,
Christian culture (e.g., biblical and theological language in the context of
the *koinonia*) needs to be repeatedly transformed, made transparent to the
reality to which it bears witness.

## (C) Theological Culture as Four-Dimensional

There are, however, many powerful socialization and enculturation forces
working against such cultural transformation. These cultural forces enter
the church, pervade the life of the *koinonia*, and reduce it to a cultural by-
product of the larger, unredeemed social system. As we have described it
earlier, if the master image at work in your particular congregation implicitly applauds an achievement-oriented obsession, then, if you are susceptible
to this lifestyle, two-dimensional socialization forces that have created and
now maintain the achievement obsession in the first place will ironically
control your use of theology and Scripture. In this case, teaching the Bible
and Christian faithfulness becomes a two-dimensional practice that frus-
trates and grieves the power of God that longs to love us Spirit-to-spirit and
to infuse our lives with the transcendent meaning and purpose revealed in
Christ.

Therefore, we now must look more closely at theological and biblical
language in light of this iconic model. Of course, volumes have been written on the uniqueness of theological language. But the core of the issue so
far as it focuses on great theological themes and the content of the faith
embodied in this language is this: *The major themes and dominant symbols
of the theological lexicon are inherently four-dimensional.* That is, they embody the four dimensions—Self, World, Void, and Holy—in single semantic
forms. They signify and bear four-dimensional meaning because they have
evolved through revision and refinement over centuries to express the dialectical identity of persons in the Spirit. Persons who confess, "*I, yet not I,
but Christ,*" and communities that confess, "*We, yet not we, but the koinonia,
the body of Christ,*" embody the dialectical identity that Christ has called
forth. Thus, they require a language commensurate with the same dialectic
transposed into cultural terms. This theological culture has in turn fed back
into the lives of individuals and society, calling forth that dialectic wherever

it may be latent in those who need awakening or wherever the desire to worship needs expression.

We can discern the dialectical structure of this language by simply reflecting on such common terms used both in the society and the church, like "grace," "love," and "peace." All of these terms appear in ordinary two-dimensional speech. However, theological grace cannot be equated with ordinary human grace. Theological grace is ordinary grace negated and re-created to bear four-dimensional meaning. Theological grace is grace, but not like any grace you ever heard of or imagined! Heavenly grace, God's grace! What about love? Theological love is love, but not like any ordinary love. God's love! *Agape* love! And what about peace? Theological peace is peace, but not as the world gives. Theological peace is "*the peace that passes understanding.*" One of my students once gave this description of the theological semantic: "It is like making a Maraschino cherry. You take an ordinary cherry, bleach it white and colorless (negate it), then you dip it into bright red dye. What results is an extraordinary red cherry, magnified beyond any ordinary redness, re-created!

In more sophisticated terms, Austin Farrar (*Finite and Infinite*) developed his notion of the "negative analogical dialectic" of theological language; Langdon Gilkey (*Naming the Whirlwind*) called attention to "the dual intentionality of theological symbols"; and Ian Ramsey, (*Religion and Language*) drew attention to "the logical oddity" of theological language.[4] Moreover, Wolfhart Pannenberg called theological language "doxological language" because it has its most appropriate use in the context of its origin in worship.[5] Theological symbols are intrinsically four-dimensional because they take in negation and make it the occasion for a higher order of speech. Thus, semantic transformation in thought or imagination corresponds to redemptive transformation in other arenas of human action.

---

4. Editor's Note: Loder discusses the theological semantics of Gilkey (*Naming the Whirlwind*), Farrar (*Finite and Infinite*), and Ramsey (*Religious Language*) in Loder, "Fashioning of Power," 198–200—all in relation to Paul Lehmann's convictional style of writing, which conforms to his convictional theological ethics. Loder notes that theological language is "logically odd" (Ramsey) because "under conviction we try to express in symbolic form the odd situation that God has revealed himself. The result is a set of logically improper word pictures that by their very impropriety are designed to awaken conviction."

5. Editor's Note: Loder did not give the reference for Pannenberg's assertion. But he seems be referring to Pannenberg's *Jesus, God and Man*. In an excursus on the structure of language regarding Jesus's divinity, Pannenberg distinguishes kerygmatic language (focused on God's actions in history) from doxological language (focused on God's essence) and asserts, "All theological language about God has such doxological character; it is essentially characterized by the structure of devotion and worship . . . in the doxological statement the 'I' who speaks disappears" (184).

However, as we said above, even though the semantic structure of theological language at the heart of our tradition is inherently four-dimensional, carefully constructed to be the language of the Spirit of Christ, two-dimensional master images or root metaphors that surround us and that dwell in us through socialization still largely domesticate our actual use of theological language and symbols. This domestication of language serves the interests of pattern-maintenance, tension-reduction socialization forces that serve negation incorporated. When socialization rules, theological language is impoverished and rendered impotent to create, compose, or express the true four-dimensional nature of the *koinonia*. The dominance of socialization prevents the *koinonia* from performing its appointed vocation, which is to call the people of God to embrace a transparent relationship with the divine presence in witness to the world. Socialization prevents the congregation from bearing transparent witness to the Word of God as the church's ministry effectively imbibes two-dimensional pronouncements as if they came from the mouth of God. The Word of God is distorted and even silenced.

In this context, congregations lose their prophetic witness as well. Four-dimensional theological language and symbols always stand in judgment of any two-dimensional usage, just as "the world is round" stood in judgment of Kierkegaard's madman. Yet the church continues to practice this idolatrous use of her theological heritage, destroying the integrity and credibility of her witness. We will return to the *koinonia's* iconic participation in theological language at the end of this discussion so as to recognize more fully the theological critique of culture and the iconic usage of theological culture itself as intrinsic to the church's life, education, and witness.

## (IV) THE MASTER IMAGES OF AMERICAN CULTURE

But now let us examine how this critique of theological culture might apply to the context of our wider society. With the help of Gibson Winter's book, *Liberating Creation*, I want to ask, what are the major threats coming from our culture to our proper use of theological language? What are the two-dimensional root metaphors that pervade our society and culture, such that their power prevails in congregational contexts and tends to subvert the life, educational practices, and witness of the church? What are these master images and how can we undo their double binding nature?

We must first emphasize, of course, that master images don't know anything about the supposed boundaries we make and try to uphold between church and society. These powerful images colonize the consciousness of the church just as much as they colonize the consciousness of the larger society. They intervene, and they impose upon church life the same kind of behavior that they impose in the secular order. Master images could care less about what reality the church is called to witness, so these master images function like subliminal forces that enter in and take control of ecclesiastical life. They turn all the things we say about God, Christ, character, virtue, and learning into the service of their values and purposes, which, as we have argued, bear the triumph of negation not the Word of Life.

## (A) The Machine

Winter claims that in our society we have two great master images that control most of the others. He calls them "root metaphors." One is the Machine and the other is the Organism.[6] The master image of the Machine, I think, can be summed up in a little ditty that we recited at the onset of the present era, in the early sixties: "The bomb, the box, the pill, and the mechanical brain." We thought then that "the bomb, the box, the pill, and the mechanical brain" would eventually shape the future of American culture. In effect, we were partially correct. Today we would include nuclear power, video satellite communication, genetic engineering, the computer, and artificial intelligence to assess the hold of this master image on American society.

The real problem, of course, comes not from just these or other technological products that fill our lives today. These products all point back to the deeper cultural vision of ourselves generated through the master image—an attitude toward life, a pervasive mentality, implicit values—that in turn funds the imaginative energy that goes into making nuclear power, genetic engineering, the computer, and artificial intelligence essential to our way of life. The major cultural issue is the power of the master image of the Machine to create and shape the consciousness that funds our way of life. This image, for example, underlies and confirms our obsession with achievement as a central motivating force in American society. The A-type personality, obsessed with achievement, is compelled under the power of the Machine image to get the most done in the shortest among of time possible, with little attention to the quality of relations or communal formation that take so much time and personal presence to develop. In an achievement culture, efficiency is of the essence. If it is faster, it is better. What is new always trumps what is old.

And so, in the achievement-oriented personality, this mechanistic mentality also designs and determines meaning and value over the course of

6. Winter, *Liberating*, 1–8.

a lifetime in our society. Think, for example, how achievement determines the meaning that aging itself takes in our society. Note the kind of bell-shaped curve that represents a scale of value that only depends on productivity.

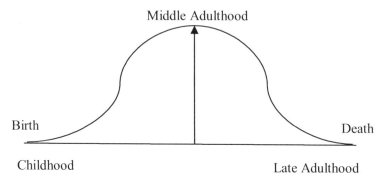

*The Bell Curve of Aging*

According to this measure, you are most valuable in middle adulthood at the point of maximum productivity. Your worth to society is not built on your character or your wisdom (slowly acquired values). Your worth is controlled by the core values of our society, which is largely governed by the master image of the Machine as it assigns human worth according to that bell-shaped curve.

The Machine image intrudes into corporate culture to impact interpersonal relationships, despite efforts that businesses might take to make their culture people-friendly. For example, when Roy Fairchild delivered the Warfield Lectures on spirituality a few years ago, he cited the example of a highly computerized corporation that had to hire therapists for employees because they began to treat each other with computer-type expectations.[7] In this corporate culture, short, snappy, low-affect responses were the only ones considered acceptable. When those kinds of responses weren't given, frustration mounted and relationships disintegrated. The reason corporate leadership considered this situation dire and not ridiculous, and sought to remedy it by hiring new technicians (psychotherapists), is they too had fully submitted to the power of the Machine image.

Of course, the Machine image also thrives in the church. In Christian education, for example, the Machine image may take the form of a national

7. Editor's Note: Loder probably has in mind Fairchild's 1987 Warfield series, Issues in Contemporary Spirituality. The theme that Loder cites comes in lecture 1, "The Upsurge of Spiritual Movements," recorded on March 23, 1987.

uniform curriculum design complete with step-by-step instructions on how to use it with minimum preparation (and almost no theological reflection needed!). The Machine image may also manifest itself structurally by determining the underlying organization of staff expectations. For example in a large church in the Midwest that is heavily supported by a major machine industry, the organization of the staff was literally impeccable right down to the last pencil. The Christian education director in charge of the department required the pastor's wife to fill out a requisition form for a pencil she wanted to take from the office. Now this absurdly laughable situation may be extreme. But this extremity allows us to see clearly how the mechanistic metaphor inserted itself into the organizational life in the church as a reflection of the town's industrialized culture. And when we learn that this head of the Christian education department was the most appreciated and valued person in the church, lauded for his powers of organization, we may not laugh at all. So the mechanistic metaphor indeed has the power to overwhelm and determine the educational life and ministry of the church.

## (B) The Organism

Over against this Machine metaphor, and functioning in opposition to it in our own country, is Winter's second great master image—the Organism. The characteristics of the Organism refer back to themes discussed in our last chapter on social organization—territoriality and kinship systems, intensification rituals, developmental ideals, having our space, and the family and its hierarchical structure.[8] These factors all tend toward a tacit sense of what some observers call "tribalism." Scholars have documented that tribalism pervades contemporary society in the explosion of support groups springing up like mushrooms throughout our country. Recall Robert Withnow, a well-known sociologist from Princeton University, who published a study of this phenomenon he called, *Sharing the Journey*. The *New York Times* caught the essence of his findings when it reviewed the book under the title "In Groups We Trust."[9]

Let me tell you a story to illustrate the power of tribalism that was told by George MacLeod, the missionary founder of the Iona Community.[10]

---

8. Editor's Note: Loder's trope on the "Loder mystique" earlier in this chapter is an example of the power of the organic image to exercise a conformist force on family members.

9. Swidler, "Groups," 13.

10. Editor's Note: George MacLeod founded the Iona Community in Glasgow and Iona in 1938, during the worldwide depression. The "antimissionary tone" to which

Although somewhat antimissionary in tone, his tale is very instructive for our theme. McLeod spoke of a young missionary, full of zeal for the gospel, who went off to preach Jesus to an aboriginal community. He learned that one ritual of this particular tribe involved a big celebration, like a harvest or spring festival. The villagers danced and drank to excess. They got so drunk, in fact, that they abandoned all the mores of their society by ending the festival with a licentious free-for-all out in the woods. But right before running off into the woods, the final communal act was a period of silence during which everybody stood in a large circle in the middle of the celebration grounds.

Now this young missionary, in his effort to prevent these pagans from doing the immoral things they wanted to do out in the woods, thought he would take advantage of this period of silence. When the moment of silence came, he jumped into the middle of the circle and started to preach Christ. The stunned pagans stood there for a little while staring at him. Then off they went into the woods to conduct their orgy. The missionary was undaunted. The next year he came back and did the same thing. In fact for the next twelve years, he jumped into the middle of the circle and preached Christ to them during the ritual silence. But every year without fail the aborigines ran off into the woods right after the sermon. Sometime during the thirteenth year, the missionary became so ill that the agency removed him from the mission field. When the chief of the tribe learned of his departure, he went straightaway to the missionary compound with a request. "Could you please send us another missionary for the festival?" Amazingly, the preacher had become part of the aborigines' ritual![11]

Now put yourself into this story, not in the role of the missionary but in the role of one of the tribal members. Try to feel the power of tribalism if you can. No matter how many times the minister stood up and preached Christ—no doubt effectively, brilliantly, and/or movingly—for a tribal member he had simply become a part of the ritual! This story should sound quite familiar to church people who have heard updated versions of the story. "Hey! We have a great new minister. She's a great preacher She's got us organized and is doing good things for our young people." Like the

Loder refers may be understood as MacLeod's criticism of a Christianity disconnected from, and unconcerned about, the plight of the poor and the rebuilding of society. Like the pagans in the story who just kept doing what they did in the festival with no ear attuned to the gospel preached by the missionary, MacLeod was concerned about the "paganism" of an church unattuned to the gospel's call to work for the transformation of society.

11. Editor's Note: Loder did not disclose where he heard or found McLeod's story.

missionary, she's been absorbed right into the "tribal" system. She's great because she's sacralizing what the "tribe" wants to do anyway.

The tribalistic impact of the Organic master image is so powerful that it can absorb almost anything. Many of our churches are as reluctant to receive the power of the gospel as those natives caught up in their drunken stupor. The further irony of this reluctance is that we Christian educators very often become avid purveyors of something called "group-think." That is, we believe in group dynamics and groups for all ages. There are buzz groups, study groups, youth groups, sharing groups, work groups, and countless committees. In our commitment to "group-think" we tacitly capitulate to the idea that a good group increasingly approaches the highest good automatically. We work hard to develop group spirit, an all-important special little feeling about *our* group. The essential hope is always that everyone leaves the group feeling better about themselves. What we seem to want is a kind of conflict-free interfluence in which everybody merely "moves and grooves" together, exchanging meaningful looks and comforting thoughts.

Part of the power of group-think for us is its promise to counteract the loneliness and all of the detrimental influences the Machine master image has brought us. Thus, much of what we do to perpetuate the Organism in terms of restoring community and mutuality, and fostering development, we do to counteract the Machine's hold on us. Ironically, the Machine image was itself created to counteract the weaknesses of the Organism. To reiterate, the implicit danger with the Organism is that we tend to perpetuate a church tribalism that resists and subverts any claims that the gospel makes on us that would subvert the tribe's concern for self-preservation. To put it differently, we are in grave danger of domesticating the church's very reason for being. The organismic spirit nostalgically desired in our churches usurps and arrests the prerogatives of the transforming work of the Holy Spirit. In-group equilibration drifts toward stagnation, because the negation-bearing power of group-think functions like an opiate on the spirit of the church (Marx). Deadened to the Spirit's presence, the church degenerates into a sacred organism obsessed with its own survival, abandoning its missionary call to exist for the sake of the salvation of the world.

## (C) The Artist

So, whether we serve the Machine or the Organism, the unexamined and untransformed master images that capture us destroy the human spirit by compromising the transforming work of the Holy Spirit. Winter recognizes this destructive tendency. So he proposes as an alternative, third image, the

Artistic master metaphor. He argues that this root metaphor works transformation because the Artist image combines the technical discipline required of the Machine image with the naturalistic, generative, and holistic requirements of the Organismic metaphor. Moreover, since artists are open in their creativity to the deepest orders of creation, the Artist image transcends both the Machine and the Organism metaphors. Thus, for Winter, the Artist is a kind of a generative master image that resolves the difficulties of the two other master images in the direction of liberation and spiritual renewal.[12]

If I were to make a case for what Gibson Winter says, I would argue that the reason for this shift to the imagery of the Artist is that *creativity*, as the essential dynamic of the human spirit, catches the transforming work of the imagination in flight, so to speak. Thus, instead of focusing on a particular image, the alternative metaphor of the Artist emphasizes the *process* implicit in representational play, which is the very dynamic process by means of which master images are generated. This shift from image to process is crucial. By adopting this focus Winter assumes that no single image—Machine or Organism—will be able to captivate and subdue the creative work of the human spirit. In this way, according to Winter, the human spirit saves itself from false consciousness, from ideological entrapment. By implication, then, the Artist root metaphor does not eliminate the Machine or the Organism, but makes creative use of both. So far so good, I would say.

But if Winter stops there, then I have to object to his alternative, because the double-binding dilemma inherent in the human creation and use of the images remains. That is, the inherent bondage of the human spirit to the structures of the ego, and the need to maximize satisfaction and insure survival, remains. Both the creativity of the human spirit and the images created by the human spirit must themselves be transformed—created, negated, and re-created—and not merely perpetuated. If they are merely perpetuated, the human spirit's attempts to be true to its creative intelligence repeatedly generate new images and metaphors that inevitably serve the negation inherent in socialization itself. Without even realizing it, the creator falls prey to the creations. The human spirit either falls in love with what it creates, or it falls in love with its own power to be creative. In other words, what you really like about being creative is that you can enjoy creating and re-creating yourself. You fall in love with creativity for its own sake. I know someone who says he loves to write Christian education curriculum. But after he creates it, he loses all interest in it. This Christian educator suffers from a narcissistic attachment to the creative act itself. If you know anything about Kierkegaard, you will recognize here the false consciousness of the

12. Winter, *Liberating*, 10–28.

Aesthetic personality. As Kierkegaard illustrates it, this educator was learning to sew without ever tying a knot in the thread! He doesn't tie anything down. He's very creative, but ultimately he becomes bored and disillusioned. Even artistic creativity, taken as an end in itself, fails as a master image.

## (D) The Protean Lifestyle

Here, to illustrate the point, I will make a brief reference to the protean lifestyle that I discussed earlier. Robert Jay Lifton continued his work on the protean personality most recently in *The Protean Self*, in which he affirmed this lifestyle as a viable way to live in our postmodern society. Recall that he named the lifestyle after the Greek god Proteus, who continually changed his shape and nature—from a wild boar to a lion to fire to blood—all to avoid assuming his proper identity and calling, which was to prophesy.

The increasing fragmentation of contemporary culture generates a lifestyle that distrusts all order and stability and stresses as its theme, "dying and rising." Ironically, Winter may be correct when he sees open-ended creativity of the artist as a real alternative to the other two metaphors. The artist metaphor generates just this kind of creative personality type. Indeed, the protean self studies computer technology for a while, then transfers into counseling. S/he gets into group therapy for a time, then learns investments. Increasingly bored, the protean then perhaps goes to seminary or moves into social work. Thus, the protean personality moves across the schemas set by the Machine and the Organism, all with the rationale: "I am growing and developing my sense of myself." Unfortunately, this constant search to establish personal and professional identity generates a longing for nurturance but a rejection of commitment; a deep ideological hunger to know yet an attendant cynicism about all available ideologies. Here, creativity runs amuck as the protean person searches endlessly for a transcendent center that can tie a knot in the thread of self-evasion parading as self-discovery.

As much as I want to affirm creativity as the underlying dynamic of the human spirit, if left to itself this creativity is also destructive of spirit. Perhaps Winter's Artist image may be more a product of this emerging postmodern protean ethos than a genuine antidote to the Machine and the Organism. If we are hoping to return human creativity to its appropriate ground, then we must call creativity to regain and live out of its analogical relation with *Spiritus Creator*. Theology provides a four-dimensional alternative cultural solution that moves beyond the two-dimensional solution Winter suggests.

## (V) THE WORD OF GOD AS TRANSFORMED
## MASTER IMAGE

Walter Wink provides us with a starting point for considering a theological alternative to Winter in his book, *The Bible and Human Transformation*. Here, in a popularized treatment, Wink shows how the clash of master images works itself into our study of Scripture. He claims first of all that normative methodology of historical biblical criticism is "bankrupt."[13] Such a critical approach is, in Winter's terms, the outworking of the master image of the Machine in the context of biblical study. Thomas F. Torrance also makes this same criticism in *Space, Time and Resurrection*. He argues that biblical criticism as the quest for truth, especially in extreme cases such as the quest for the historical Jesus, simply reflects the Enlightenment mechanistic worldview. Torrance points out in this book (and indeed in all of his *oeuvre*), that postmodern science has fully discredited as untenable this mechanistic view of reality.[14] Biblical scholars functioning like technologists may not know we live in a postmodern world, but theoretical physicists and theologians such as Torrance know it very well.

Thus, this analytical, critical, reductionistic approach to Scripture can hardly be the search for truth that its supporters claim. This approach more accurately signifies capitulation to a powerful master cultural image—the Machine—that inevitably occludes the full meaning of what can be observed. Those who would attempt to establish the truth or falsity of Christianity by taking up a quest for the historical Jesus don't know that the Enlightenment is over. So, historical and critical studies require a larger and more dynamic context of meaning than the Machine can give.

Of course, the master image of the Organism, the antithesis of the Machine, is equally denigrating to scriptural interpretation and to faith. The efforts to domesticate the Scripture—i.e., to make the Bible itself holy ground and to treat it as the ark of the covenant—is essentially cultic, tribal, and regressive.

So Walter Wink wants to remedy this situation of spiritual impoverishment by introducing a "dialectical hermeneutic," a paradigm of creativity and transformation to guide the study of the Bible. His three-step paradigm, influenced by Carl Jung, Hegel, and the structure of argumentation found in philosophy, offers a schema of "fusion, distance, and communion." Wink outlined the model as follows:

I. Fusion with the Cultural Horizon of the Text—

13. Wink, *Bible*, 1–15.
14. Torrance, *Space*, 1–26.

N 1: Negation of fusion, suspicion of the object (biblical critical material brought to bear upon the text)

II. Distance—

N 2: Negation of the negation through suspicion of the subject (Jungian analysis of Self)

III. Communion—

Archetype of the Self corresponding to the figure in the text[15]

Thus, according to Wink, there is an archetypical pattern of Levite, priest, robber, and Good Samaritan in each of us. As we engage the Bible, Wink asks us to establish a kind of communion with the images narrated in the text that goes far deeper than ego knowledge or technical grasp would take us. His approach seems to me to be on the right track. But the problem is that this creative interaction with the text retains the same difficulty with images that Winter's approach offered. The images remain opaque, not iconic. That is, Wink's method can't account for how these images themselves must become transparent to the presence of God, who alone is the ground of human creativity. The Jungian archetype is creative. But the archetype has no power to ground the self transparently in the life of God. Instead, it grounds the human self in the primordial archetypical history of the race, a distinctively human creation that lacks the dynamism of a liberating relationality that the transparent presence of Christ enables.

The alternative approach to Scripture, and so to the repeated transformation of Christian theological culture (language and symbol) begins with an assumption much like Karl Barth's when he said that he really had no system for interpretation of Scripture. But if he did have one—

> then it consists in the fact that I persistently keep in view what Kierkegaard called the "infinite qualitative difference" between time and eternity, in its negative and its positive significance. God is in heaven and you are on earth. The relation of *this* God to *this* human, the relation of *this* human being to *this* God, is for me the theme of the Bible.[16]

15. Editor's Note: Loder added comments to Wink's schema for clarity sake. The schema is presented in Wink, *Bible*, 19.

16. Barth, *Römerbrief*, 13. Editor's Note: While Loder quoted the English translation of this passage, his footnote indicates he was also using the German text. This German quote occurs within the "Vorwort zur zweiten Auflage" of *Der Romerbrief*. The principle articulated in this quote represents the "early" Barth influenced by Kierkegaard. Of course, Loder and Neidhardt develop this Kierkegaardian position in exhaustive detail in *Knight's Move*, and it continued to shape Loder's neo-Chalcedonian practical theological science. Loder actually restated this Barthian sensibility in terms of what he called "the core generative problematic" of practical theology. In his 2000 essay "Place

In other words, the frame of reference by which Barth approaches the text is the christomorphic relationality, the Chalcedonian model that we have discussed at length in previous chapters. Starting with such a christomorphic frame of reference, a biblical text can be indwelt until it yields up the source of the divine Wisdom that gave rise to it. In other words, if we are to recover the life of the Spirit by which the Scriptures becomes the Word of God, then the iconic approach I suggested earlier must pertain. A model for doing this begins with Barth's christological frame of reference:

I. *Awakening*: Come to the text in faith and trust Scripture to communicate God.

II. *Indwelling*: Let Scripture itself disclose the way it should be read and known.

(A) Negation of text by exegetical and critical methods (N1): *Purgation*.

(B) Negation of negation—(N2): text incorporates the negation of (A), becomes critical of the self as interpreter (subject).[17]

III. *Illumination*: Scripture becomes iconic to the divine presence

IV. *Intimacy*: Movement into the inner life of God as the spiritual presence of Christ makes the text an "imageless image" allowing entry into the "Strange New World of the Bible" (Barth).

V. *Unification*: Return to the world in the passion that *God* has *for* the world, though infinitely distant from the world. The world's longing for God, and God's compassion for the world, become a differentiated unity. The measure of the difference, accordingly, is the measure of the power of the unity.[18]

---

of Science," Loder stated: "[All issues related to practical theology] *require that two ontologically-distinct realities, the divine and the human, be brought together in a unified form of action that preserves the integrity of both and yet gives rise to coherent behavior*" (23, italics original). See also Wright, "*Homo Testans*," 22. This volume, then, represents Loder's most straightforward effort to envision how theories of interdisciplinary practical theological science emerge in response to indwelling this core problematic so as to inform and guide life in the Spirit, a Christian style of life in every dimension of human action. Loder's work responds to H. Shelton Smith's imperative from 1934: "Let religious educators reckon with Barthians." Yes indeed! And one has!

17. Here the interpreter asks, "Who am I that I can grasp the Word of God?" It says to me, "You can do nothing" and yet "I must do this." The depth of the negation is the measure of the height of the inspiration that will follow. Shallow negative yields shallow inspiration.

18. The reference here is to the classic typology of the dynamics of transformation, cited in chapter 5. The connection I seek to make here is the integrity between the pattern of transformation and the pattern of iconic Bible study, signifying the redemptive transformation of the interpreter's imagination taking hold of interpretation.

Thus, the Scripture, the central culture of our faith—and, by implication, all culture—is transformed by a transparent relationship between the Holy Spirit (Barth's "this God") and the human spirit (Barth's "this human being"). The words and images of the Bible become the Word of God, revealing to the interpretative community the transparent unity of God and humanity achieved through Jesus Christ.

Transparency in relation to God through the Scripture, moreover, becomes transparency in relation to the world and to all the actualities of one's life. The conversion of C. S. Lewis to Christianity illustrates this point paradigmatically. As is well known, Lewis's first conversion was to theism before he became a Christian. Converted from atheism, he believed in God, but not yet in Christ. An account of how he came to believe in Christ comes in a letter he wrote to his lifelong friend Arthur Greeves. Secondarily, this account offers us a very succinct portrayal of the christological transformation of mythic imagery—i.e., of how non-Christian culture comes to be transformed by the reality of Christ's presence. Lewis testified to Greeves—

> What Dyson and Tolkien showed me was this: that if I met the idea of sacrifice in a pagan story I didn't mind it at all: again, if I met the idea of a God sacrificing himself to himself . . . I liked it very much and was mysteriously moved by it: again, that the idea of the dying and reviving God (Balder, Adonis, Bacchus) similarly moved me provided I met it anywhere *except* in the Gospels. The reason was that in Pagan stories I was prepared to feel the myth as profound and suggestive of meaning beyond my grasp even tho' I could not say in cold prose "What it meant."
>
> Now the story of Christ is simply a true myth: a myth working on us in the same way as the others, but with the tremendous difference that *it really happened*: and one must be content to accept it in the same way, remembering that it is God's myth where the others are human myths; i.e., the Pagan stories are God expressing Himself through the minds of the poets, using such images as He found there while Christianity is God expressing Himself through what we call "real things." Therefore, it is true, not in the sense of being a "description" of God (that no finite mind can take in) but in a sense of being the way in which God chooses to (or can) appear to our faculties. The "doctrines" we *get out* of the true myth are, of course, less true: they are translations into *concepts* and *ideas* of that which God has already expressed in a "language" more adequate, namely, the actual incarnation, crucifixion, and resurrection.[19]

19. Green and Hooper, *C. S. Lewis*, 116–18. Editor's Note: See also Loder's discussion

Here we follow the transformation of Lewis's mind that allows him to reenvision transformations in culture as representations of God's transformation of real things—i.e., God's transformation of real things issuing in the transformation of culture. Languages, images and myths all become relative to God's Word communicated in real things, the "actual incarnation, crucifixion and resurrection." The key, I think, is Lewis's sensibility that the master image, the typology, the myth, the archetype—all of them—vanish as cultic phenomena. When consciousness awakens to the fullness of the reality of the spiritual presence of God, Christ becomes an "imageless image," revealing one's *entre* into the inner life of God.

This experience makes Lewis, in turning back to the world, transparent to the created order. He reenvisions culture through the lens of the imageless Christ. By comparison to this spiritual presence, all cultic type images are in a fundamental sense, no more than poetry, or, at worst, occult. In either case, they *occlude* the vision. Accordingly, the impact of Christ as the "real thing" renders the Self, World, and Void dimensions of culture transparent to the Holy, even as the Holy exposes the Self, World, and Void to the continual critique of culture. Lewis moves through culture to Spirit and, in turn, critically reappropriates culture according to Christ's nature.

## (VI) CONCLUSION

In conclusion let us return to our point of departure. We began with the difficulty of telling the truth, which grows out of the barrier between language and reality. We are not unaware of the inevitable entanglements this issue raises for our postmodern context. But we have attempted in several ways to point beyond the philosophical debate to assert the theological conviction that only through the redemptive transformation of our language by the transparent presence of Word of God can we hope to come close to telling and living the truth. We concluded that C. S. Lewis, in his letter to Arthur Greeves, gave evidence of the transformation of culture at its very roots. Lewis's letter functions as a large-scale variation on the experience I went through following my father's death. I was released, put into relation with the Spirit of Christ, and given a new consciousness. Through this experience I became potentially four-dimensionally transparent and able to assimilate the critique of culture implicit in theological language and explicit in the spiritual presence of Christ. In a word, the effective presence of the Spirit of Christ replaces the master image in convictional experience. The effect of that presence is that everything that appears in a cultic context—regarding

_of Lewis's conversion in Loder, *Transforming Moment*, 149–50._

the Self, the World, and the Void—becomes symbolic as all mythic systems become transparent to the Holy. The transformation of culture, then, does not eliminate culture but makes it iconic, a visible and tangible occasion for entering into the invisible and intangible presence of God.

Our pervasive difficulty in telling the truth, then, is only overcome by the One whose nature and revelation are essentially the same. Only the living Christ can finally provide the bridge between language and reality. The bipolarity between human words and God's Word covers an infinite distance, which is the vast scope of the difference, embraced within, but not dissolved by, the singular person of Jesus Christ.

# Human Participation in Divine Action

*The Claims of the Theory*

# 9 [1]

# Theory

*Structuring the Vision, Part I*

## (I) INTRODUCTION: REASSERTING THE PRIORITY OF THEORY

As WE TURN NOW to the explicit formulation of the theory we have been building, let me recall for you our background discussion of the priority of theory. From Gadamer's work we learned that *theoria* was originally used not merely in the sense of the process of "seeing" as aesthetic, but also of the context of what is being seen, that is, by the gods. *Theoria* involved participation in a festival celebration of the gods and so in some regard meant taking the gods' values upon oneself. This etymological rootage is important for three reasons. *First*, although theory may be stated explicitly in propositions, its real significance is tacit or implicit. One might recount the festival or speak of the gods specifically. But the reasons they are significant reside in the tacit implications of that significance. These implications are deeply

---

1. Editor's Note: The ED 105 class, "Education Ministry" upon which this book is based, originally consisted of twelve lectures. During my time at Princeton Seminary Loder delivered eleven of them. One lecture, the eleventh, dealing with curriculum, was delivered by one of Loder's students. The ninth and tenth lectures were called "Theory: Structuring the Vision, Part I" and "Theory: Structuring the Vision, Part II." I believe that one manuscript edition combined these two lectures into one chapter. I decided to include the original two lectures here, knowing that even if there is some overlap, the two chapters provide an added richness to this book as a whole.

participatory, voiceless but expressive in multiple ways, and they continue to unfold in one's life. So it is with good theory. Just as $E=mc^2$ is simple to say, its tacit implications stretch all the way from Einstein's sixteen-year-old imaginative journey at the speed of light, when he first intuited the theory of relativity, up to the countless contemporary confirmations of its explanatory powers, and its introduction of the nuclear age. Thus, even though the theory's terms may be explicitly simple, its real significance is tacit and, so, widely implicative.

*Second*, in order for theory to do its work, it must be indwelt. Theory must be lived in, so that its tacit implications may become generative of focal or explicit forms of practice. Furthermore, theory must, if it is good theory, continually provoke even deeper indwelling of the phenomena in question over time That is, the reason for indwelling the theory is not to *have* the theory, but to allow the theory to become increasingly disclosive of its hidden potential in the full scope of the educational environment.

In Aristotle's classical categories of active reason, *theoria* stood above the *poiesis* of craftsmanship, the *praxis* of reflective political activity, and the *phronesis* of sound judgment. *Theoria* drew all of these into their proper place and position with respect to each other, so that each, informed by *theoria*, could fulfill its purpose of contributing to wisdom or *Sophia*, the fruit of *theoria*—i.e., the wishless absorption in the divine nature (Windelband). Thus, to indwell the theory means just the opposite of what trivializers of theory think. Theory is just the opposite of an abstract, manipulative or irrelevant system. By design, good theory creates the most profound reciprocity possible between cognition and experience, between understanding and action, between the life of the mind of the theorist and the life of the mind of God. Theory calls for indwelling, so that both the "Christian" and the "education" of Christian education may disclose their deepest meaning in relation to each other.

This concern to indwell theory leads to the *third* implication for privileging theory. The ultimate claim for theory is not that it connects theory and practice with coherence, but that it actually discloses in continually deeper ways the hidden intelligibility that underlies the particular concerns of theory. $E=mc^2$ discloses the hidden rational and mathematical intelligibility of the universe. By analogy, Christian education theory should be designed to disclose in every facet of its expression the underlying intelligibility of all things, hidden in the nature of Christ. Much of his nature, as with the rational nature of the universe, must remain tacit. But it should be clear that the underlying intelligibility of Christian education theory is neither the logic of the human sciences, nor the ordered systematic development of one's theology, nor anything that science or the philosophy of science could come up with. The ultimate intelligible order on which Christian education theory is based is the inner logic of Christ's nature witnessed to in Scripture and developed for the church especially in the Chalcedonian formula. This affirmation does not reduce itself to a monotheism of the second person of the Trinity, because the whole of the Trinitarian life is present in each of its persons (*perichoresis*). But through the incarnation of God in history in the Son, communicated through the Spirit in every age, the inner life of God is and continues to be disclosed to us in terms most like our own.

Looking through the lens of Christ's dual nature, we have argued that the crux of Christian education is the interplay between socialization and transformation. Christologically, socialization is as essential to the enterprise of Christian education as the humanity of Jesus Christ is essential to his nature. We must take socialization that seriously. But we must not take it more seriously than we take transformation. For by the same christological analogy, transformation is as essential to Christian education as divinity is to the nature of Jesus Christ.

Thus, as we plan and enact educational strategies and activities in the life of the church as the body of Christ, we must deal always with both sides of this interplay, both sides of his nature. In the body of Christ, we cannot act educationally as if only his humanity mattered, reducing Christian faith to some form of mere humanism. Nor can we act as if only his divinity mattered, rendering faith into some form of irrelevant docetism. In their dynamic, christomorphic relationality, socialization and transformation must be held together and apart with the predominant significance of transformation setting the source and destiny for socialization. Thus it was for Jesus. Even as he laid down his life of his own free will, he did nothing but what he saw the Father doing. The Chalcedonian interplay between socialization and transformation is the crux of Christian education and it embodies the ultimate intelligibility in which the theory of Christian education must be grounded.

From our knowledge of Christ, we can see that the hidden structure and dynamics of human existence are four-dimensional and transformational. Thus, we clearly cannot be satisfied in our educational work with less than four-dimensional transformation if it is to be true to the full scope of our humanity, as revealed in Christ's nature by his Spirit. In answer to the obvious next question—what does it mean to say that the full scope of our humanity is potentially four-dimensional and transformational?—I have tried in the foregoing chapters to explicate what is tacit and implicit in this claim. Namely, the dynamics of four-dimensional transformation are potentially operative at the core of every major arena of human action. Although I have described all this explicitly, it should be indwelt by now so that a tacit reservoir of resources and meanings is effectively in place and available for the construction of theory.

Recall, for instance, that in personality we have seen that the psyche is fundamentally four-dimensional but that the double-binding nature of the ego itself needs to be transformed before this four-dimensionality can be appropriated. In social and corporate life, I have tried to show that the fundamental constituents of institutional and corporate existence (role structures and communal networks) are also double-binding, two-dimensional phenomenon, which conceal the four-dimensional potential in corporate life for *koinonia*, the communion created uniquely by the spiritual presence of Jesus Christ. I have tried to show further that in cultural life a similar situation occurs. The symbol and value systems carried forward from generation to generation by master images and root metaphors are two-dimensional until they become transparent bearers of the spiritual presence of Christ through the work of the Spirit. Recall that we used as paradigmatic the theology of iconic transformation in Eastern Orthodoxy to argue that Scripture becomes the Word of God in an analogous iconic, hermeneutical process.

Because we are here concerned to educate for a Christian style of life that engages with coherence all of these arenas of human action, no one arena of action can finally be separated from the others. These arenas of human action are not discrete arenas disconnected from each other, but aspects of a whole. Subsequently, attention to one or two of the arenas apart from the others creates a distortion in faith and life, resulting in disillusionment, confusion, apostasy, and self-destructive forms of human interaction. For example, individual conversion without a context of *koinonia* becomes privatistic, impotent, directionless, and perhaps authoritarian. *Koinonia* and conversion without appropriate language and meaning (confessional language, sacred texts, and sacrament) lose critical self-awareness, often succumbing to conformity by manipulative or authoritarian leadership. Corporate life and Christian culture without conversion lead to lifeless and empty forms of religion that signify at most that something vital has been lost. Where the transforming power of God is absent, empty enculturated religion reigns.

## EXCURSUS ON BODILY TRANSFORMATION

Admittedly I have not said much about is the *organic* arena of existence, which is the recipient of legitimated action by the other three aspects of the Christian style of life. I must therefore insert a brief note here in anticipation of a longer treatment in some future time. What the Spirit seeks here is the transformation of organic existence into the service of a Christian style of life. Transformation means that a fearful preoccupation with survival and security, which are the elementary drives of the organism, becomes rather a passionate love of life that paradoxically finds expression in self-sacrifice and self-giving. Under conviction by the Spirit of Christ one may now suffer bodily, even be crucified, not out of despair, but out of the sheer love of life that is too large for the two-dimensional structure of untransformed culture to contain or appreciate. We must not forget that the empty form of religion, concerned only with its own self-preservation, crucified the Lord of life, even as the Lord of life, in that same event, gave himself up for us all so that our embodied existence might be filled with the life of the Spirit.

Transformation of the body into the service of Christ may also take other forms, like overcoming suffering instead of enduring suffering. One may, for example, be healed physically by the grace of God and restored to Christ's service. Not to acknowledge healing as a real possibility for life in the Spirit surely tends toward our becoming ascetic or gnostic! Yet healing must not be presumed as the only sign of faith. How God works bodily transformation may be different for different people, or for the same people in different circumstances. One may fast or give one's body to be burned in response to the Spirit's call to service. Or, facing total exhaustion or debilitation, one may find in the Spirit physical resources that supply abundant energy to the body to continue service. Or again, one may deny oneself sexually for the sake of devotion to Christ amid a promiscuous culture. Or one may affirm sexual union in the marriage covenant as a testimony of the power of Christ amid a protean culture. One may enjoy eating and celebration of life (cf. "The Feast at Cana"). Or one may "fast for forty days in the wilderness" to clarify one's mission

In its transformation, organic life, the body and its functions become thereby the wonderful and necessary, but not definitive, vehicle of the Christian style of life. Concerns for survival and satisfaction no longer remain preeminent values, but they are placed in the service of the Truth that mediates the transformation. The decisive text for this aspect of the Christian life is Rom 12:1–2.

> *I appeal to you, therefore, brethren, by the mercies of God, to present your bodies as a living sacrifice, holy and acceptable to God, which is your spiritual worship. Do not be conformed to this world, but be transformed by the renewal of your minds, that you may prove what is the will of God—what is good and acceptable and perfect.* (RSV)

This text begins with the great *"therefore"* that proclaims, in effect: "Since the merciful God has acted on our behalf, do not let the world conform us to its way of being, but *'be transformed (metamorpheo) by the renewal of your minds.'"* But Paul connects the transformation and the renewing of the mind to the fleshly act of presenting our *"bodies as a living sacrifice"*—not to the world but *"holy and acceptable to God."* The Spirit's transformation is always embodied and must impact the way our bodily existence existentially serves the kingdom of God. There is no such thing as a disembodied spirituality. Spirituality enabled through the Spirit puts us more deeply into our bodily existence, following the grammar of the incarnation. Much more could be said, of course, about the work of the Spirit in the organic dimension. But fundamentally what I have summarized represents a transformation of survival and satisfaction into the joys and sacrifices of the abundant life of Christ's Spirit, lived out bodily in concrete service and devotion.

## (II) THE REPORTER SOURCE: CONNECTING THEORY TO CHRISTIAN EDUCATION PRACTICE

What I want to do now is to bring these understandings derived from the intelligibility of Christ's nature to bear upon the field of Christian education by way of a theory that will be propositionally explicit, but whose real value and power will be tacit and implicit along the lines I have suggested. Independently several of the field's most prominent figures have employed what is sometimes called the "reporter source" as a way of structuring and relating the wide diversity of factors that play into any intentional Christian education endeavor.[2] In a recent dissertation, an "interrogative hermeneutic," made up of a set of questions used for reportage in every culture in the Western world, was used to guide the interpretation and planning of diverse social activities.[3] Specifically, the "reporter source" constitutes the strategic use of a series of interrogatives—Why? What? Where? How? Who? When?—directed towards the purpose of integrating aspects of practice into a strategic whole.[4] We will use a similar hermeneutical strategy below to attain a similar result for our practical theory of Christian education practice.

2. Here I am particularly indebted in this section to the work of D. Campbell Wyckoff, *Theory*, 83–157.

3. Editor's Note: Loder does not reveal the dissertation in question. It is not one of the dissertations Loder supervised.

4. Editor's Note: Wyckoff introduces a section of *Theory* with these six questions, 84–94. Loder surveys Wyckoff's answers to these questions before he answers them in light of his own understanding.

In the field of Christian education, we must, in addition, ask two further questions. *First*: By what integrative strategy are the answers to the reporter source questions to be interrelated? We seek here the *organizing* principle that must show how the persons involved may, within the context, time their use of the process in order that the scope may be covered and the purpose fulfilled.[5] *Second*, since the answers to the reporter source questions presuppose a larger context of meaning, we also need to answer the question that yields the *guiding* principle for our theory: How does the Christian educator perceive him- or herself in relation to the fundamental reality at stake in the enterprise of Christian education?

This approach to theory construction may be schematized as follows:

THEORY:

SET OF PRINCIPLES WHICH ARE A DEPENDABLE
ORIENTATIONS TO PRACTICE

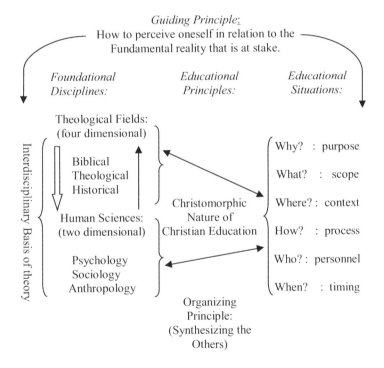

**Schema of Theory Construction**

5. Wyckoff, "Understanding," 77–84. See also Wyckoff, *Theory*, 138–46.

To clarify this schema as a systematic set of flexible perspectives, let me briefly summarize by comparison D. Campbell Wyckoff's very general but substantive answers to these questions.

The *first* question is the *why*, or the *objective* question of Christian education theory: Why do we engage in Christian education? What is its point or purpose? Wyckoff's answer derives from the statement of the National Council of Churches. "The objective of Christian education is that all persons be aware of God's self-disclosure, and especially God's seeking love in Jesus Christ, and that they respond in faith and love, to the end that they may know who they are and what their human situation means, grow as children of God, rooted in the Christian community, live in the Spirit of God in every relationship, fulfill their common discipleship in the world, and abide in Christian hope."[6]

*Second* is the *what*, or *scope* question: What concerns are to be dealt with or covered by the subject matter and experience in Christian education? Here Wyckoff says that the briefest adequate answer is that "the scope of Christian education is the whole field of relationships, God, humankind, nature and history in light of the gospel."[7]

*Third* is the question of *context*: Where may Christian education carry on its work with integrity? What is its proper context, considering its character, rootage, and functions? Wyckoff wants to answer, the church. But he indicates that by the church he also means the larger context of the church. Christian education partakes of the whole objective and mission of the church, leading persons to undertake that mission and ministry intelligently and effectively in the world. So the context of Christian education is the church, but the church as it is continually involved with the world. Wyckoff rightly distinguishes the church in mission from "our little church" supported by "our little education program" on Sunday morning for an hour. For Wyckoff, the church both interpenetrates the world and is interpenetrated by the world.

*Fourth* is the *process* question of Christian education, the question of how. How does Christian education implement its strategies for transformation? With what process are we going to cooperate in the act of teaching

---

6. Wyckoff, "Understanding," 79, and *Theory,* 79, 121–29. One difficulty with this kind of a statement is that it tries to be explicit where tacit knowing must be permitted to generate implications, and so becomes both too specific and too general at the same time.

7. Wyckoff, "Understanding," 79. See also *Theory,* 46 and 129 (texts slightly emended in second and third references). It should be acknowledged here that Wyckoff's structure of this field from "foundations" to "situations" is fundamental to the field as a whole and it endures over time.

and learning? Overall Wyckoff avers that "the methods by which persons 'be and become' in the Christian faith and life are actually the basic ways in which God, humankind, nature, and history interact for educational results." Clarifying the meaning of this general statement, he writes:

> Persons be and become in the Christian faith and life through understanding the learning tasks of listening with growing alertness to the gospel and responding in faith and love. Such listening and responding, requires first that persons undertake the task of assuming personal and social responsibility . . . [and] second that persons engage over and over again in a cycle of learning tasks: exploring the field of relationships in light of the gospel, discovering meaning and value in the field of relationships in light of the gospel, and appropriating that meaning and value personally.[8]

*Fifth* comes the *personnel* question: Who is involved in Christian education? Who are the persons who are partners to the educational transaction, and what are their roles? Wyckoff wants to define the personnel question in terms of the roles of three actors: (1) the *learners* (who are learning in many different settings and in many different ways, most of them not connected with the church); (2) the *teachers* (who are themselves learners, but who in this connection also act as guides who invite learners into educational experiences); and (3) *God* (the Holy Spirit, who is the Teacher, thus requiring that the human learners and teachers conduct the enterprise of Christian education in an atmosphere of prayer and receptivity to the Spirit's leading).

*Sixth* is the question of *timing*, the *when* question. When does Christian education take place? Wyckoff divides this question up into four interrelated times: (1) The *learner's* time, which involves important questions of the learner's readiness, motivation, and plans for learning; (2) *God's* time, which refers to the movement of God's will and actions in the community; (3) *occasional* time, which refers to significant events and trends emerging in one's particular historical period; and finally, (4) the *church's* time, which refers to that "by which it uses the past (tradition) and the future (its anticipation of God's will, emergent environmental factors, and emergent human needs) to determine the steps to be taken now and in the future in order that its response may be faithful."[9] Education takes place relative to these different interlocking understandings of time.

For Wyckoff, the organizing principle by means of which all of these questions are drawn together must show how the persons involved may,

8. Wyckoff, "Understanding," 80.
9. Ibid, 81.

within their context, time their use of the process in order that the scope may be covered and the purpose fulfilled. Wyckoff's basic answer to this concern is the church's experience, which he breaks down into three parts: (1) the church's experience in its life and work, (2) its situational or existential experience, and (3) its historical experience. In other words, he wants to look at the church's experience historically and to interpret current existential situations in light of the overall sweep of the historical account of the church's life. Wyckoff's guiding principle is essentially the gospel, so that any education that does not concern itself with God's redeeming activity in Jesus Christ has to be corrected in light of the gospel.

## (III) TRANSFORMATIONAL PERSPECTIVES ON CHRISTIAN EDUCATION

With Wyckoff's structure in mind, let us move now to the constructive task of articulating in the form of explicit propositions a redemptively *transformational* theory of Christian education in light of the previous chapters. These former chapters will continue to supply the underlying resources and ground for our efforts to make Christian education intelligible according to the logic of the Spirit in Jesus Christ. Of course, to take the Spirit seriously in this way does not permit us to formulate principles that we promise will automatically deliver the Spirit. Rather, what we have in the theory is a systematic integration of perspectives that hopefully attunes us to the Spirit's presence, and thereby permits us to make appropriate responses to whatever educational situations occur, so that the work of the Spirit may prosper. Thus, the following formulations retain an asymmetrical, bipolar structure of Spirit-to-spirit relations and so are meant to serve the divine Spirit's liberation of the human spirit in cooperation with the structure of Christ reflecting the Chalcedonian analogy described above.[10]

## (A) The Guiding Principle

*Question*: How does the educator perceive him-/herself in relation to the fundamental reality that is at stake—i.e., the fundamental assumptive reality behind the educational endeavor?

10. Editor's Note: "Asymmetrical bipolar structure" is Loder's shorthand for the Chalcedonian model of the dual nature of Christ that the Holy Spirit replicates in its ordering of human thought and experience, including in Christian education thought and experience. As I have noted, Loder and Neidhardt spell out the meaning of this Chalcedonian grammar in exhaustive detail in *Knight's Move*.

*Answer*: The guiding principle for our transformational theory of Christian education is rooted and grounded in the very life of God, *Spiritus Creator*.

This assertion means that Christian education is conducted "in the Spirit" and in accordance with the eschatological mission of the Spirit in the world. More specifically it means that Christian education in any social context must become transformational, four-dimensional, and christocentric. Since the grammar of the Holy Spirit is transformational, transformation becomes by analogy the basis for correlating the Holy Spirit and human spirit, the theological and the human sciences. This correlation then is the basis for how I as teacher must perceive myself in relation to the enterprise. *First*, I as teacher am a socialized human being, yet I am nevertheless uniquely and profoundly spirit. This affirmation means that I must seek to fully engage in existence as a four-dimensional creature, participating in and undergoing transformation by the power of the One whose nature is given to us in Jesus Christ. This convictional claim and life of the teacher or theorist is not irrelevant to the practice of Christian education. Conviction by the Spirit is the only way we are enabled to truly "see things whole."

*Second*, as to the enterprise as a whole, *Spiritus Creator* bears a four-dimensional relation to education, even as education bears a two-dimensional socialization relation to transformation. Out of this interplay, transformation as bearer, source, and destiny of socialization, works to reshape all educational acts according to the nature of Jesus Christ in and beyond the institutional church. The church exists in and under the power of the Spirit. The Spirit is not, in any sense, under the power of the church.

This transformational approach does not eliminate alternative notions of the "guiding principle" from other writers in the field, such as "the Bible," "the gospel," "the church," or more extended statements like, "Christ's redeeming activity in the world." These principles are implied, but the above statement first makes the interdisciplinary nature of Christian education explicit via the concept of four-dimensional transformation. Furthermore, this approach makes it clear that Christian education—though tacit in the Hebrew Scriptures—begins explicitly with God's initiative in Jesus Christ in his incarnation and culminates proleptically in the church's relation to Jesus Christ in his glorification. The "already but not yet" nature of that prolepsis is finally to be consummated in the eschatological future when God becomes all in all. The overarching name for this sweeping action of God in and upon human life and history is *Spiritus Creator*.

## (B) Purpose

*Question*: What then is the purpose or aim of Christian education?

*Answer*: The purpose is create for all humankind a Christian style of life, where style is the fashioning of power in all arenas of human action through time.

The tacit dimension of this question reiterates that *Spiritus Creator* is the principal educator whose purpose is the transformation of all things unto the glory of God. Humanly speaking, to create a Christian style of life means nothing less than to intentionally participate in what Christ's Spirit is doing in the whole field of human action—i.e., to bring about in the physical, psychic, social, and cultural dimensions of human existence a four-dimensional awareness of, and response to, what it means to be fully human after the pattern of Christ. More specifically in terms of the four dimensions, there is in every arena of human action both an inherent capacity for self-destruction, corruption, and nonbeing, as well as a potential for regeneration and new being. To live a Christian style of life means that one participates in the second potential for the sake of transforming the first. In every arena of human action, and in all of them taken together, redemptive transformation constitutes a principle of coherence and continuity as the negations inherent in all dimensions of human action are themselves negated and brought into the positive service of Christ and his Spirit.

On the socialization level, for example, ego, roles, master images, and organic survival become reversible. Thus, Saul's authoritarian aggression pursuing the elimination of the church is transformed into Paul's aggressive apostolic service under the nonauthoritarian authority of Christ. The achiever's intensity to grasp and to acquire is transformed as well, not into wimpish conformity but into self-sacrifice and saintliness—from the driven or obsessive intensity of achievement to the deep and centered intensity of a Saint Francis of Assisi. In the case of oppression, self-directed aggression becomes potentially revolutionary such that in Christ, justice is pursued with compassion for both the oppressor and the oppressed. Revolution transformed leads to the radical witness (*marturos*) of a worshiping people in a non-Christian world. With the protean lifestyle, the effectual presence of Christ transforms the myth of dying and rising into historical, covenantal existence, ending ideological hunger and cynicism in favor of transparent relationship with the divine presence (recall C. S. Lewis's conversion from theism to Christ).

But a style of life is not just the concern of individuals. All communal arenas of human action undergo redemptive transformation by the power of Christ's Spirit. Thus, a Christian style of life in the Spirit permeates social, cultural, and organic arenas of human action through time. Indeed, the full scope of human history may take in the spiritual nature of Christ. In summary, whatever the sociological starting point, the aim and purpose of Christian education is to create a Christian style of life in all arenas of human action and history in the power of the Spirit.

## (C) Content

*Question*: What is to be taught and learned in transformational Christian education?

*Answer*: Christian education concerns the four dimensions of whatever may be taught and learned in all four sectors of human action.

Implicitly, this perspective says that all subject matter constructed through socialization will yield to the four-dimensional, transformational perspective of Christ. Thus, the achiever's world only becomes fully intelligible according to the nature of Christ. Within the church, human situations (E. Farley[11]), events (C. E. Nelson), or curriculum materials (D. C. Wyckoff) for each and every age will need to be explored for their four-dimensional potential and taught from that perspective. Let me offer here a paradigm for four-dimensional teaching—the *parable*.

### (1) The Parable as a Paradigm for Four-Dimensional Teaching

A basic paradigm of four-dimensional subject matter is the parable. Structurally, parables violate two-dimensional expectations (Self and World) and expose the third (Void) for the sake of the fourth (Holy). For example, let us look at Jesus's parable of the Pharisee and the Publican in Luke's Gospel.

> *Two men went up into the temple to pray, one a Pharisee and the other a tax collector. The Pharisee stood and prayed thus with himself, "O God, I thank thee that I am not like other men, extortioners, unjust, adulterers, or even like this tax collector. I fast twice a week, I give tithes of all that I get." But the tax collector, standing far off, would not even lift up his eyes to heaven, but beat his breast, saying, "God, be merciful to me a sinner!"* (Luke 18:10–13 RSV)

---

11. Editor's Note: Loder probably refers here to Farley's *Ecclesial Man*.

In the first century, the hearers expected that the Pharisee naturally offered an acceptable prayer, whereas the tax collector (publican) could not, since he was unclean. This normative world of expectation can be diagrammed as follows:

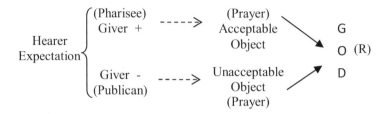

*Conventional Pharisee/Publican Prayer Expectation*

The parable, however, violates those expectations, because in it the tax collector (not the Pharisee) offers the acceptable prayer.

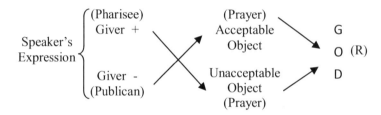

*Transfigured Pharisee/Publican Prayer Expectation*

Violation of the two-dimensional perspective of the hearer's expectation negates the negation implicit in that expectation, and so discloses the presence of Christ—what it means to abide in Christ's nature—in the act of prayer.

Jesus lived and taught parabolically even when he was not telling parables. For instance, let us consider Jesus's encounter with the Syrophoenecian woman in Matthew.

> *And Jesus went away there and withdrew to the district of Tyre and Sidon. And behold, a Canaanite woman from that region came out and cried, "Have mercy on me, O Lord, Son of David; my daughter is severely possessed by a demon." But he did not answer her a word. And his disciples came and begged him, saying, "Send her away, for she is crying after us." He answered, "I was sent only to the lost sheep of the house of Israel." But she came and knelt before him, saying, "Lord, help me." And he answered, "It is not fair to take the children's bread and throw it to the dogs." She answered, "Yes, Lord, yet even the dogs eat the crumbs that fall*

*from their master's table." Then Jesus answered her, "O woman,
great is your faith! Be it done for you as you desire." And her
daughter was healed instantly.* (Matt 15:21–28 RSV)

One may argue here that the text invites us to consider that Jesus experiences
an identity crisis in relation to the pagan woman, who places his supposedly
patriarchal Jewish faith under question. But is this text predominantly concerned with the interruption of socialized male-female interactions? I think
not, since that view would tend to support a two-dimensional interpretation
of a four-dimensional text. Even if there were something to this socialized
notion, the text pushes the interpreter to discern the point of the narrative
in a much larger and more powerful framework than socialized role relations suggest. The pagan woman is compelled to confirm herself in relation
to Jesus—the four-dimensional impact of Christ's presence. Thus, she is
willing to identify (Self-World) with the dispossessed and outcast (Void)
for the sake of Jesus being Savior for her and her daughter (Holy). This
four-dimensional faith mediated by Jesus brings healing for both mother
and daughter from beyond the social construction of reality. Note here that
the iconic reading of Scripture described in chapter 8, though considerably
elaborated, is also structurally parabolic. That is, it is a contemplative effort
to negate the negation (Void) of two-dimensionality (Self and World) in
anticipation of being addressed by the fourth (Holy).

### (2) Other Illustrations of Four-Dimensional Teaching

With the theory in mind, we can see how recognizing the four-dimensional
scope of any teaching situation calls out for transformation in four dimensions. Let us consider the potential of several teaching situations.

The first situation comes from an experimental kindergarten at the
Presbyterian School of Christian Education. Jason is a recalcitrant boy,
destructive of both toys and relations. His mother and teacher decide that
something inside Jason's head is making him think badly of himself. So
instead of punishing him or setting more limits, they agree to try to love
him into changing. They embrace his self-negation with unconditional love.
Their efforts demanded endurance and the mutual support of both mother
and teacher. But at age ten Jason is a respectful, impressive young man with
considerable self-confidence and quite capable of enjoying new situations
with imagination and ingenuity.

A second situation comes from the work of Lynn Gray, who was
asked by the Urban Coalition for Educational Revision in New York City
to study why some schools were surviving urban drought, while others, for

no obvious reasons, were not. He found that something like "spirit," creative life, existed powerfully among the faculties of those schools that were succeeding. In other schools, he would have the faculty and the administration sit around and "historicize"—tell their stories—about their school experiences. He recorded each story on newsprint by going around the room and listening for the emotionally charged words and events, which he would underline. Gray discovered rifts and animosities buried underneath the relationships of these less successful faculties and administrations. The schools that thrived together were the ones that had openly dealt with those underlying problems. They had a kind of gracious corporate understanding of one another that was sufficiently honest and implicitly, if not explicitly, four-dimensional.

A third story comes from the sixties, featuring one of our students who found a summer internship in a California church that was socialized to the last detail. Gary was a very thoughtful and perceptive person, who didn't say a lot, but he saw a lot. Mistakenly, he was introduced to the youth of the congregation as a psychologist from Princeton. Rather than correct the impression, Gary watched to see what impact the label would have as he played out that role.

Every Sunday evening at seven o'clock sharp, a thundering herd of kids descended into this "youth room," all shouting, "Hi, gang!" Gary simply watched as they sat down at tables where Bibles were already set out. The teens went through a routinized course of Bible study, looking up the text, working and talking out their interpretations. When they finished the study, a time of fellowship with refreshments commenced. This predictable routine went on every Sunday. The transformational educational question here is, How do you engage in parabolic teaching with this kind of socialized group? Do you get them to study parables? No! They will just incorporate the parables into their authoritarian routine. What they need is a parabolic experience.

So Gary arrived early one Sunday, took all the tables out of the room, put them in another room, and locked the door. Then he stood at the front of the auditorium and waited for the thundering herd. "What happened to the tables?" they asked. Some adventurous soul found them and said, "Here they are!" But Gary had locked the door. At this point, Gary put his foot up on the platform in front of the room. As soon as he did so, everybody sat down on the floor, just like there was a lever on the platform he controlled—socialization dynamics, *par excellence*! Having their full attention, Gary now held up a sign in front of him that read, "I'm lonely," all the while saying cheerily, "Hi, gang!" He went through a whole series of these contradictory signs and surface messages seeking to expose the underlying loneliness and pain that he sensed filled the group's individual and collective egos, role structures, and images of what congregational life offered.

Next Gary walked over to the leader of the group and said, "I really don't like you, because I don't like the way you manipulate this group. Let's talk." The leader consented. Gary sat down and told the leader exactly what he felt. As soon as they started to talk, other people started to talk about what disquiet lay under the surface of the group. Eventually they began to ask the question, what are we going to do? (Recall Freire.) In answer they decided to try practicing real Christianity. They went out into the town, into the parks, into the bushes to invite and bring people into the group. They brought these lonely, forgotten street people into their youth room. They talked to them about who Christ is. They fed them and sent them on their way. This parabolic action upset the church and created quite a hullabaloo. Fortunately, so the church thought, Gary was only there for the summer. Back in Princeton that fall, Gary received as many as seven letters a day from those kids asking him what had happened. "What's going on? What's this really all about?"

The major factor missing in this last case, which is otherwise very good, is that there isn't a sense of worship. There isn't a more explicit sense of the origin and goal of transformation in the Holy. It ends a bit too much embedded in the conflict posed by the question of reality. The missing fourth dimension could have been easily supplied by worship, so the teen inquiries posed to Gary could go beyond Gary, such that Gary himself became a transparent (iconic) witness to the Holy. Perhaps this omission was the fault of the *Zeitgeist* of the sixties, a time when everything was questioned and when people often lived more easily in the questions than in the answers.

To recap: What is to be taught and learned in transformational Christian education? In relation to the presence of the Spirit, all content is nothing less than the four-dimensional human existence embedded in all four sectors of human action, awaiting transformation.

## (D) Context

*Question*: Where may transformational Christian education carry on its work with integrity?

*Answer*: The context of Christian education is the present and coming reign of God, the proleptic form of which is the dialectic between *koinonia* and *ecclesia*.

Educationally, the context to be preferred is one that fosters the creative process as a key to the human spirit. By "creative process" I do not mean a sense of diffuse gratification of libidinal impulse, or creativity for creativity's sake. Rather, what is envisioned is creativity as the disclosure of hidden orders of meaning and intelligibility seeking to come to experience. To be more specific about this context, a study by Pettigrew and Pajonas delineates eight criteria for contexts that sponsor or enable creativity in this more profound sense.[12]

(1) *Rapport*. Creative processes require *a context of rapport* as the first basic principle. Rapport involves a willingness to enter into the frame of reference of the learner, to let it resonate with one's own, to be instructed by one's sense of the other and by the other's own sense of selfhood. Such a context involves true mutuality.

(2) *Negotiation*. There can be *no absolute human authority* in creative experience. Neither should chaos reign, but chaos is not the only alternative to absolutism. Rather, in the process of creativity all viewpoints must be *negotiable*. Human limits are recognized, but a minimum number of rules should be allowed to contain those limits. Things are negotiable at the learner's level of competence. Note that if an absolute authority governs the transformational dynamics in an educational context, the dynamics will inevitably turn demonic rather than redemptive (recall examples from Jonestown, other personality cults, and terrorism in the name of religion).

(3) *Imagination*. Creative process requires an *affirmation of the imagination as an organ of truth*. There are four basic modes of teacher-learner interaction that can be identified by the key words: *is* (empirical), *ought* (normative), *seems* (subjective), and *means* (meaning).[13] Ironically, the most often neglected educational interaction, but the most common interaction in ordinary experience, is expressed by the word *seems*. *Seems* is just as important a part of seeking truth, theologically speaking, as are *is*, *ought*, or *means*. Learning must be personally appropriated. Thus, there needs to be room to cry, feel, and say, "This is how it seems to me. This is how I feel."

(4) *Stress*. Creative process always places *a positive value on stress or conflict*. Valuing stress does not mean starting fights, taking sides, or fostering acrimony. Creativity requires that we truly learn to entertain a context in which the negation of negation is seriously considered. For example, stress for the achiever arises when the supposed power of achievement to establish ultimate worth comes under question for the achiever. For the authoritarian,

---

12. Pettigrew and Pajonas, "Social Psychology," 87–106. Pettigrew and Pajonas were social psychologists at Harvard who were invited to design an educational program to undercut prejudice in the New York schools in the 1960s.

13. Loder, *Religious*, 126–39.

stress arises when they are confronted by, or sensitized to, ambiguous aspects of their human experience that they may come to realize and accept as essential to their humanity. Rapport, negotiation, and imagination foster this kind of positive valuing of stress, leading to transformation.

(5) *Complexity.* A creative process must enable *a preference for true complexity rather than noncomplex simplicity.* That is, simplistic teaching or simple-minded simplicity should be avoided if creativity is to be released. Persons must learn to embrace complexity and contradiction in the search of the elegant or profound simplicity that masters a wide range of complexity. The formula $E=mc^2$ and the confession "Jesus is Lord" are paradigmatic expressions of profound simplicity in science and faith, and these profound simplicities can only be embraced through continual engagement with their implicit contradictions and complexity.

(6) *Difference.* Creative process requires *the recognition, acceptance, and even delight in, personal differences.* Appreciation of differences does not mean celebrating a live-and-let-live philosophy, which slides rapidly into indifference. Rather, the watchword is more like "live and let [the other] flourish." Creativity requires a recognition, acceptance, examination, and delight in the particularity of the other one.

(7) *Structure.* Creativity needs both *an instrumental and an expressive axis*—i.e., structural dynamics that support a relatively efficient creative exchange and regulation of intragroup dynamics in continuity with the creative objectives of the educational process. Creative process must be essentially open-ended but never formless.

(8) *Self-Liquidation.* All transformational educational groups need to be *self-liquidating* on the principle that repeated role interaction tends toward rigidity and defensiveness. Socialized patterns need to be consciously broken and restructured. Even healthy marriage relations self-liquidate role-structures as they progress according to the standard paradigm. Couples marry. They liquidate (renegotiate) their binary relations when children are born. They renegotiate again when children leave the home . . . and when they return after they have left! And liquidation and restructuring happen again when the couple faces other kinds of loss or death.

Attention to these criteria prepares the human spirit for receptivity to the *Spiritus Creator*. But for this receptivity to be fully encouraged, the creative life of the human spirit must find its proper and true context in worship. Creative group life eventually fragments or collapses into a narcissistic love of its own originality unless it becomes transparently grounded in the creative life of God. Thus, all that is done to foster creativity in the human context must be sustained in prayer and worship if it is to become and remain four-dimensional. The human community can "*prepare the way of the Lord."* We can be awakened to our human capacity to appropriate the communion-creating reality of Jesus Christ. But the transforming fulfillment of that awakened longing and hope remains God's prerogative.

## (E) Timing

*Question:* When does transformational Christian education take place authentically?

*Answer:* Christian education takes place authentically when *kairos* (the fullness of time) transforms *chronos* (sequential time) and implicitly returns all the times of our lives to their source in God.

In transformational education, the stress must always remain on the quality of an event over against quantification, the sequence of a program, the clock-time available, or performance evaluation. There are fundamentally two kinds of time, *chronos* and *kairos*. The two types of time exist in a complementary relationality. By that I mean first of all they always exist together in relation. So as long as we are dealing humanly, we are always dealing with both *kairos* and *chronos*. Yet, while they always exist together, they always exist in an asymmetrical differentiation. To talk or think chronologically is not to talk or think in terms of *kairos*. To talk or think in terms of *kairos* is not to talk or think chronologically. These times are qualitatively differentiated, so that one exercises marginal control over the other.

In their proper asymmetry, *chronos* unfolds sequentially and *kairos* gives the chronology its true meaning. But meaning is building up under the surface of chronological time as its tacit dimension—the fullness of time. Chronology without *kairos* would be pointless succession. *Kairos* without chronology would be purely episodic. As meaning exercises marginal control over mere sequence, *kairos* exercises control over *chronos*. The general perspective of time underlying this study reflects this dialectic. But now let us examine how we live out this dialectical understanding of time in educational terms.

### (1) Developmental (Chronological) Time

*Chronos* or sequential time most commonly enters educational planning in relation to human development. For example, curriculums are constructed to pay attention to readiness for learning according to chronological age. Examples of the importance of developmental readiness are countless. I have already cited in a previous chapter how role structure emerges at about seven. Before this time, the use of structured role-play techniques will probably be ineffectual. Moreover, before the age of six, children do not have a developed sense of plot. Earlier they will listen to stories with great attention to episodes. But they will not recognize plot (how the episodes relate to one another) until after age six. At all ages, learning is always to some extent developmentally determined. For example, the older person over seventy, let's say, is often not able to solve new problems as quickly as a child of seven. But older people can group things in general thematic terms—get the big picture much more readily—perhaps more readily than they could twenty-five years earlier.

For educational reasons, we study development to see what can actually be grasped at what period of time. Concern for developmental readiness does not necessarily limit what can be taught (content), but it does control the form in which it is taught. For instance, according to Jerome Bruner, you can teach any content to a child at any time as long as you adapt its form to their age level. In secular education, this principle was the basis for the so-called new math. Although the new math initiative was not particularly successful, the idea was sound if one could correctly ascertain the structure of the discipline. But why are we interested in readiness to learn transformationally? Aren't we just reflecting on adaptation to the existing culture, and therefore engaging in an exercise of socialized thinking?

I would answer that attainment of the stages makes an indirect contribution to transformation. That is, educators must take account of developmental readiness because the logic of transformation is built into the stage-transition process. Transitions must be made successfully as a way of building up hope into the personality of the developing person. Once Pascal is reported to have said, "It's not the fox, but the hunt that matters to us." Thus, it's not the stages but the dynamics that give rise to the stages that matter. These dynamics allow us to "catch on" at higher levels of complexity and qualify us as intrinsically spiritual in nature. Even if the socializing environment is preoccupied with our stage-level achievement, the transformational contribution is being made indirectly through the dynamics.

## (2) Kairos Time

In counterdistinction to developmental time, there are crucial times that leap out of the sequence of *chronos* and change everything. Here are four such *kairotic* times that are essential to transformational education.

## (A) TEACHABLE MOMENTS

"Teachable moments" are important times educationally because they teach the learner that figure-ground reversals are possible. In such "moments" chronological sequence can be set under the higher order of *kairos* that gives the sequence its meaning. For example, the matrix of socialization sustains itself for the sake of the "moment" because the "moment" is that which gives socialization its meaning. In the teachable moment, the preceding material makes new sense. In this sequence, the "moment" is more important than the planned sequence.

The teachable moment is well illustrated by the case of Elsie. Elsie was a little girl who always sat on the side and never said very much in her church school class. She would go through the routine of the learning and singing, but never really got involved. Then one day as the class started to sing the closing hymn, Elsie came up and just stood in front of the piano and her teacher with her hands folded. Now the teacher knew that this was a teachable moment. It was a teachable moment because Elsie's spirit had grasped what was going on and was, at this point, ready to partake in the class's worship time. However, her gesture, signifying her desire to participate, demanded that the class stop the music and pray. So the teacher said, "Elsie wants to pray. Let's stop the music. We are all going to pray." And so they stopped and prayed. This action was the key to liberating Elsie's spirit, giving her confidence in her power to create meaning in a situation that had been confusing to her.

There are many such teachable moments like these, but no plan guarantees they will occur. As delineated above in the section on context, an environment more suited to transforming moments should be constructed. But readiness is a key to learning in these contexts. There are two kinds of readiness—predictable and unpredictable. The teaching moment is a kind of unpredictable readiness, but the power of that readiness for learning is something that needs to be cherished. Teachers must be ready to take the opportunity to make the most of every teachable moment that comes their way. They must learn the grace of being interrupted.

## (B) CONVERSION EXPERIENCES

Another kind of *kairos* time, the most powerful of all, is the *experience of conversion*. Under the aspect of time, conversions as culminations of one's relation to God are optimal times to learn. Therefore, conversions need to be thought through for their creative impact. As events, they prompt a transformational reenvisioning of the past that opens up the future. Conversions are not ends in themselves, but new beginnings. In conversion there is a culmination of previous events—events not even necessarily recognized as significant before the conversion—and a consequent disembedding from one's chronological, two-dimensional understanding of one's own life, for the purpose of living out the freedom of the Spirit of Christ.

Recall the experience I had after my father died. I hit the pillow in frustration at God's absence, and the Spirit of God came to me in the fullness of presence. I sang and read Emil Brunner to give the experience an articulation of its meaning. Here is an example of the fulfillment of time—a *kairotic* moment. In turn, this moment redefined my past, the qualitative significance of all that led up to it. From the standpoint of that experience, I looked back through chronological time to see the sequence of events in my life in ways I hadn't seen them before. Things that I hadn't thought were particularly significant became significant.

For instance, I remembered a time when I was ten or so. My family didn't attend worship services. But I woke up one Sunday morning, and decided *I* was going to go. So I went. This experience wasn't a particularly memorable episode in general at the time. But from the standpoint of my later conversion experience, this seemingly banal event became very significant. An encounter I had with a Nazarene bishop gained significance for me as well, along with a number of other experiences. Moreover, as I looked back through developmental time, I realized that I was not in relationship to my father, mother, or family as before. After the conversion, the Loder image was something I *had*; it no longer defined who I *was*. I now belonged to Christ, who was really the origin and destiny of my human nature.

So in conversion the *kairotic* moment becomes a time that transcends the developmental sequence and tells you that you no longer *are* your developmental history. Your socialized history becomes something you *have*. The conversion allows you to turn back and reappropriate that history in new ways. In educational settings, we can help people with this reconstructive reenvisioning of past and future by giving them space and the opportunity to indwell their experience of Christ. Conversion reflects the teachable moment *par excellence*.

(c) Historical Events/Crises

A third kind of *kairos* time relates to historical times of crisis. When we were marching during the sixties with Martin Luther King Jr.'s crusade, all the biblical language about the call to *"present your body as a living sacrifice"* took on powerful personal as well as social and cultural meaning. The decade of the nineteen-sixties functioned as a time to reenvision the past in light of a new future—a time to recover "roots" and to dream King's "dream" for the future. Those were teachable days, a time of *kairos* to learn that society's survival must finally to become subordinate to the Truth that perdures through time.

## (D) Transformational Time

Transformation can be understood in terms of these two views of time: The evoking in *chronos* of an undercurrent building toward a *kairotic* moment, the moment of transformation. Thus, one might examine where one is— and where the learner is—in transformational time. That is, where is one in the transformational pattern we have outlined? Here again, the Emmaus Road story reflects the paradigm of four-dimensional transformation. Let's review the grammar in terms of *kairotic* moments.

(1) *Conflict.* Is an individual, a group, or a family primarily in a time of *conflict*? If it is, is the conflict truly four-dimensional? Is it the God of Jesus Christ with whom they struggle?

(2) *Interlude for Scanning.* Are individuals or groups ripe for a rich time of *scanning*? Does learning need to reach back into personal history, find stereotypes, and follow hunches?

(3) *Insight.* Has there been a *breakthrough* in learning, excitement over a wonderful idea? Then perhaps we have the *kairotic* moment in search of a new context of continuity.

(4) *Release.* Sometimes there is a *joyful sense* of the meaning of life in which one is grasped by a new and deeper order of things (e.g., a dream). Learning then needs to indwell this experience with joy, seek its source, and allow the celebration of that joy to teach one how to live in light of the experience.

(5) *Interpretation.* Have individuals or groups entered educationally at the point of the conclusion, *the known result*? Are they seeking to know its foundations, where it came from, and its underlying dynamics involved? Are they indwelling the answer?

We will return to this pattern when we come to process, but one might call this *kairotic* time transformational time. What time is it in your spiritual life?

# (F) Personnel

*Question*: Who educates for transformation? Who teaches and who learns?

*Answer*: The Spirit of Christ is the Teacher who works in all contexts in and for the redemptive transformation of the human spirit.

Accordingly, the human teacher is the *provocateur* of the human spirit. The pattern of transformation may be learned from within and appropriated as the grammar of the Holy Spirit. In this way the human teacher in the power of *Spiritus Creator* "*prepares*" (in two dimensions) "*the way of the Lord*" (in four dimensions)."

## *(1) Family as a Provocateur of the Spirit*

By way of illustration, let me focus first on family education. Families are the front line defense against social scourges like drug abuse and violence. Many families also face the extraordinary difficult task of coping with mental illness in their midst. In meeting these challenges, the family's most powerful offensive resource is communicating to their members the power of the human spirit. The family can foster, albeit at the human level, the self-consciousness of family members as spiritually grounded and creative. What follows are a few examples and paradigms to consider.

(a) *Wonder*. The family enables the human spirit by nurturing the practice of wonder. Parents can demonstrate what it means to be fellow explorers of creation as God's gift to us all. When the child discovers something like, I'm breathing air! the look in the mother's eye that responds with a sense of wonder at the presence of another spirit, free and with a life of its own, communicates nonverbally, Yes! And you're terrific!

(b) *Play*. Play is a propaedeutic of the spirit and the foundation of worship in the child (i.e., it evokes the spirit at an early age).[14] Families should play with the Christian language. When you educate in the Spirit in the family context, you learn not to teach children to parrot exactly what's "right to say." Rather, you get into the conversation and play in the language with them, because playing with language prepares them to experience the transcendence of worship together.

For example, when Tami was four or five, she played sometimes in the basement. One day she came upstairs saying, "Daddy, God is in the basement." Talking with her about her discovery, it turns out that after she heard us say that God was everywhere, she reasoned that God must be in

14. Pannenberg, *Anthropology*, esp. 321–39.

the basement. Now, I didn't say to her, "Now look, that's not how we think about the omnipresence of God. Let me explain to you how we are supposed to think about it." Rather, my response was, "Tell me about it." I'm not so much interested in doctrinal rectitude, as I am speaking spirit to spirit, using language to enter into the faith that we share and worship together. So its not so much right doctrine as right spirit we want to encourage. The Spirit will in turn beget right doctrine as most of our creeds emerged from the act of worship. Play together with the language; it enables the language to become a bearer of the Spirit, and so of the *koinonia*.

(c) *Suffering*. Parents also need to become fellow sufferers with their children. Parents need to cultivate a high tolerance for the unlovely in their children, to struggle in and with the anguish of their children, without trying to "fix things" right away. Parents need to learn to sit beside loneliness, rejection, and maybe engender some kind of conversation with it, and so discover with them that these struggles are not as big as they seemed (even though they fill your body with dread). Suffering with children can be very demanding, but also very fruitful.

Anne Sullivan was a classic illustration of a teacher's sensitive spirit calling forth the spirit of the other. She held on to Helen Keller beyond the limits anyone would have thought possible, until transformation occurred in Helen's spirit. Amid Helen's silent world, when she learned the word "water" from Anne, her spirit exploded with such creative force that the revolution in speech took her through Radcliff College and beyond. Her awakened spirit embraced a fuller experience of reality through speech, so much so that when she was told who Jesus Christ was, she replied, "Oh, I have always known Him." Thus the Holy Spirit testifies with and through the liberated human spirit that we are children of God. The short-term embrace of suffering cannot to be compared to the long-term joy made possible through a transformed life.

(d) *Celebration*. Families should learn to celebrate the presence of Christ. The book of Acts is full of events designed to elicit the wonder and praise of God in us. If you have lost your desire to praise God, you have lost your spirit. We need to treat each other as fellow celebrants of the presence of God in Jesus Christ. We should commit ourselves to really enjoy praying together. Such prayer is not just something we do just before meals because it helps us to remember something. We don't squeeze rote prayers in ahead of our favorite television program. Prayer is not something we do at bedtime because our folks did it with us at bedtime. In the Spirit, prayer is something we *really* like to do! We can't image our life without prayer.

At the age of three or four, Tami had trouble sitting still during family times. So we tried to let her do things that exhibited the joy of worship. She would draw and sing, and eventually she made up her own song: "Oh butterfly, O butterfly. You love Jesus, so do I. O butterfly." Now speaking from personal experience, family devotions do not always go smoothly. But, dearly beloved, this is the right fight to take up if we are to live in the Spirit. The issues that come out in the family's effort to learn to celebrate the presence of Christ *are* the critical issues. We want to pay the price in terms of family dispute, if necessary, to get excited about this most important thing—living in the presence of Christ.

## (2) Teachers as Provocateurs of the Spirit

Let me now turn to formal educational settings. Teachers who succeed in teaching spirit to spirit become spirit in the act of teaching. Teachers repeatedly remember to ask the question: "How am I learning in the act of teaching?" In this regard the Spirit is already operative. To ask the question is to begin to appropriate the transcendence that otherwise gets suppressed, allowing teachers to simply slip into the role and "do the job." Correlative questions are: What questions are implied in my answers? What answers are implied in my questions? What failures are implied in my successes? What successes are implied in my failures? Living with these questions and answers suggest that the teacher's spirit continually attunes itself to the process of reenvisioning the educational enterprise. Two important films bring out these issues vividly and dramatically.

First, a dramatic film that portrays the spiritual power implicit in repeatedly breaking the perceptual set of a strict preparatory school is Robin Williams' compelling performance of master teacher Mr. Keating in *Dead Poet's Society*.[15] You recall from the film that Keating effectively exposes the third dimension (Void) underlying a highly socialized, achievement-obsessed prep school. He shows his students pictures of the alumni of the school now providing nourishment to the daffodils and tells them, *carpe diem*—"seize the day." Keating calls the English textbook's dry, structural analysis of poetry "excrement" and charges his boys to rip it out of the book. He calls them to view their classroom from the top of their desks and he celebrates the release of the human spirit from one oppressed student who cries out with a great barbaric "YALP." All these challenges effectively release the spirit of these students from the achievement-oriented and

---

15. It is well known that this film is not strictly fiction. Tom Shulman, who wrote the screenplay, had a teacher, Samuel Pickering, who did all that Keating did and more. But Pickering cringed from the thought that he had such a powerful impact on his students. However, Shulman and his work are evidence that he did.

authoritarian dynamics into which they are being socialized. Keating taught English literature, but in doing so he sought the liberation of the human spirit. However, the movie ends tragically with great ambiguity culminating in a suicide because the spirits of the boys, having been liberated from the distortions of socialization, never find their grounding in the transcendent and life-affirming Spirit of God.

If one compares *Dead Poets Society* to the Danish film *Babette's Feast*, the tragedy of the former movie becomes heightened by the theological redemption portrayed in the latter. Both filmed stories are transformational narratives, and both Mr. Keating and Babette are *kenotic* figures who empty themselves of the conventional meaning of their social roles in order to give totally of themselves to others. In self-giving they become spirit, and their artistic skills become generative of spirit in others. That is, their sacrifice promises to liberate those nearest at hand—their neighbors—from two-dimensional bondage. But the big difference between the stories lies in these characters' different responses to the third dimension, the Void.

Keating's response to the Void underlying the prep school's authoritarian achievement obsession is basically, "Exercise the human spirit and seize the day." Thus, Keating's call to liberate his charges begins and ends with the human spirit. Such liberation falls short of attaining humanization, and remains conflicted and confusing and ultimately tragic. As the film portrays it, one particularly sensitive boy takes into himself, in a Christ-like image, the oppression of authoritarian parenting and, in despair, ends his life. Thus, *Dead Poets Society* portrays what is at stake when we seek to liberate the power of the human spirit in three-dimensional contexts without the promise of the Holy to mediate the transformation.

The outcome is not redemptive but tragic because the human spirit, however free, cannot by itself grasp the nature of Christ amid the Void, much less take the presence of the Void into itself to negate the negation and enable redemption. Only God's Spirit redeems the human condition. For this God the human spirit cries out. Others may seek to "seize the day" in variations—in violence, romance, and nonconformity—but these efforts end up inevitably leaving the human spirit educated but groundless. There is a form of freedom here, but with no answers as to why be liberated and with no power to be liberated in a way that actually liberates.

On the other hand, *Babette's Feast* is set in the context of a pious Protestant worshiping community on the desolate southern coast of Denmark—albeit a hostile, embittered little community in which "righteousness and bliss" no longer kissed one other (Ps 85:10). The righteousness of the righteous had disintegrated into shame, guilt, and despair, swallowing up all bliss. And the efforts of the unrighteous to pursue bliss as an end in itself swallowed up all hope for a meaningful life. The community embodied the triumph of negation. Then, into this seeming godforsaken world, the foreigner and papist Babette Hersant comes seeking refuge from the wars tearing apart her native France. As an émigré she has lost everything—everything except her ability to cook . . . and a faded lottery ticket. For many years she serves the ascetic community with quiet dignity, preparing meals and doing housework. But Babette has a secret: she had been the celebrated master chef at the world-renown restaurant—the Café Anglais—in Paris.

After a time, Babette wins a huge fortune through that lottery ticket. She then astonishes everyone by offering a parting gift: as her last supper she would prepare an authentic French meal for the edification of the community. The community accepts her offer with gratitude. But as the exotic and extravagant food, wines, and liquors arrive, along with the elegant dishes and crystal stemware, the community becomes traumatized. They suspect the papist heretic is preparing a witch's brew that will damn them all to hell. Staring into the Void, the faithful decide they will keep their word and attend the dinner but save themselves by promising one another not to taste the food (a collective ego's ludicrously futile defense against the Void!).

The fateful day arrives. The faith community and invited guests gathered together to partake of Babette's seduction. As course after course of delectable fare is served, the community keeps a tight rein on their emotions and on their words. But one of the guests, the worldly General Lowenhielm (who had loved Martine, one of the pious daughters of the founder of the community long ago but left her to seek his fame and fortune), no longer can contain himself. He recognizes that the meal they are eating exactly reproduced the signature feast he enjoyed years before at the Café Anglais, in Paris, a restaurant famous for having a woman chef! Lowenhielm, who knows how empty his life has become, finds himself stirred to the depth of his soul. The kenotic sacrifice of Babette's extravagant gift, set against his despair, awakened his spirit to the divine source of all blessedness, the blessedness he had left behind long ago. The meal has become a sacrament, with the source of all righteousness and blessing (Holy) mediating new life through an act of human creativity. Lowenhielm is compelled to speak the Word of God to interpret the miracle.

So he stands up before the parishioners and guests and recites Psalm 85:10: "*Righteousness and bliss have kissed each other.*" He knows that this Scripture is being fulfilled in their hearing. The Word has taken on the flesh of his own testimony, and will soon take on flesh in the lived testimony of the congregation. Babette's feast has been transfigured into an act of worship. In the proclamation of the Word and the sacrament of Babette's feast, the community becomes the *koinonia* as the fruit of the Spirit invades their lives—joy, forgiveness, understanding, reconciliation, love (even romance!), laughter, and singing in the streets. The negation of the Void has been negated by the renewing power of the Spirit (Holy). The redemptive scene ends when one parishioner sums up the experience for everyone with a heartfelt: "Alleluia!"[16]

Both of these films portray a spiritual transformation. But in *Dead Poets Society* the mediator is Keating himself—or Byron, Shelly or other dead poets—who cannot move beyond the third dimension. But in *Babette's Feast*, the mediation clearly comes from beyond Babette, whose act becomes transparent to the God to whom Lowenhielm testifies. The Spirit of God, who far exceeds anybody's expectation, indwells Babette's own actions, resulting in redemptive transformation. Comparing these two films proves useful, I think, because it demonstrates the absolute necessity of becoming spirit in a four-dimensional context and also the potentially tragic consequences of becoming spirit without a sufficient ground in the Spirit of God.

## (IV) CONCLUSION

In terms of the teacher and the learner, we need to stress again that the human spirit is already operative in you and in those with whom you are engaged in a teaching and learning activity. It's already there! You don't have to make somebody be spirit. You don't have to inject spirit. But you do have to recognize how the spirit it is suppressed under often heavy patterns of socialization, bound to two-dimensional or three-dimensional horizons. The point is to awaken spirit, to name it, to affirm it, to celebrate it, and to lead it into the context of worship.

---

16. Editor's Note: I have elaborated a bit on Loder's description of the story portrayed in *Babette's Feast* to aid those who may not know the film or the short story by Karen Blixen (Isak Dinesen) upon which it is based. Loder's theological interpretation of the film goes beyond the intention of both the author of the story and the director of the film, who, similar to Gibson Winter, charge art (writing, cooking, or both) with the power to mediate new life (recall chapter 8). I tried to add details to illuminate the profundity of Loder's four-dimensional interpretation that requires a context of worship to support true transformation (to be elaborated in chapter 11). I should also say that this film has special meaning for me in relation to Dr. Loder. Before I became his student, he came to Seattle in 1988 to teach a course titled, "The Holy Spirit and Human Development." After the first session a group of us went to Seattle's premier arthouse theater, the Harvard Exit, to see the newly released *Babette's Feast*. We were astonished how Loder's insights into redemptive transformation allowed us view the film theologically. The Spirit had sanctified art and scholarship as acts of praise and worship, without diminishing the art or the scholarship in the process.

Very likely the teacher who teaches this way has learned to empty herself of her enslavement to socialization and who, out of that *kenosis*, enables the spiritual life of her students to flourish at a human level for the sake of participation in the transformational work of the Holy Spirit. Teachers who teach in the Spirit are not just concerned with intellect, or with conscience, or with behavior. They want to liberate that distinctly human capacity to create and compose worlds of meaning in a way that opens others to redemptive transformation, the communion-creating power of the Spirit in accordance with the nature and person of Christ, creating and sustaining the *koinonia* within every destitute place and time.

# 10

# Theory
*Structuring the Vision, Part II*

## (I) INTRODUCTION

We continue our emphasis on how to structure the vision of our theory of Christian education as a work of the Holy Spirit transforming the human spirit. To do so we will develop more fully our emphasis on the process of transformational learning.

## (II) TRANSFORMATIONAL PROCESS

*Question*: What is the process of transformational Christian education?

*Answer*: The process of Christian education is intentional participation in the dynamics of transformation as portrayed in the analogy of the Spirit.

Recall the five-step pattern illustrated by the nine-dot problem and Archimedes's discovery of the first principle of hydrostatics:

(0) Context

(1) Conflict in context

(2) Interlude for scanning

(3) Insight felt with intuitive force

(4) Release of tension—restoration of phenomenon

(5) Confirmation or verification and interpretation

Intentional participation in these dynamics means that we learn in some depth what each step requires in order to be able to enter into the knowing process with learners at any step depending on where they may be in transformational time. Thus, each of the steps constitutes a teaching-learning task, but an implicit drive toward continuity among them integrates the process. We must note how vitally important it is that no single learning task gets separated from its larger context of transformation in Christ's Spirit. Christian learning tasks are by definition intentionally fostered forms of attention, practice, and reflection by which one comes to participate in the ongoing transformational Spirit of Christ. I want to briefly specify the five learning tasks, in terms of both their positive form and their most common perversion. In this way we become clearer about why these tasks need each other and move toward mutual support and continuity in Christ's Spirit. These tasks of course are subject to further analysis and specification. But here they will nevertheless serve to make transformation in the Spirit more educationally concrete.

## (A) Learning Tasks

To aid this concern for concreteness, the five learning tasks that correspond to the grammar of the human spirit can be ordered, not according to the order given above, but corresponding to the order in which they represent how we most commonly think of and practice Christian education.

### (1) Interpretative Learning

The first type of learning is *learning interpretation and responsible action*. I put the matter this way because interpretation and action should be seen as mutually informing the practice of a Christian style of life. In the paradigm case of Archimedes, accounting for his "Eureka!" and his "streaking" response in principle and verification—i.e., in his interpretation and responsible action—was extremely important. This fifth step in the sequence generated by transformation usually serves as our most common, and sometimes our only, point of intentional entrance into the practice of education. Where education is concerned, we tend to begin at the end of the creative act of learning as if interpretation is everything. Interpretation and action are the concerns that we most commonly associate with education.

Who does not ask his/her child, what did you learn? and, what did you learn to do?—thus assuming that interpretation and application is the point of all education. In more sophisticated terms this task is associated with the best sense of the term "professional"—i.e., one who professes and practices in accordance with the knowledge s/he professes. We are most familiar with this task so I will not say more about the positive aspects.

However, focus on this task alone creates an educational perversity. Emphasis on interpretation and action easily becomes an activity that does not reach back into the history of the intense struggles and redeeming insights that gave rise to the knowledge being professed. This omission is an especially serious one when theological content is at stake. Interpretation under the increasingly powerful social influences of the Machine metaphor slips into becoming a mere commodity, the *answer*. Similarly the learner's action becomes *imitative*, not a personally appropriated engagement that generates further insight vis-a-vis the demanding claims of the content Christianity teaches. One supposedly becomes a good learner, learning how to study and pass exams. But one never learns to learn. One never learns to know how to generate one's own thought. One becomes a good practitioner by means of adopting techniques, but without thinking about the meaning of practice. In essence under the influence of the Machine, education becomes perverse as *interpretation* reduces itself to having *answers*, albeit "good" ones, and *practice* reduces itself to *imitation*, albeit following "good" advice. The end result is the false education under the guise of *professionalism* that merges efficiency and results to cover the wake of stagnant ideas and empty jargon.

Instead, learning interpretation in correlation with responsible action ought to be kept alive and responsive to the full range of the transforming work of the Spirit of God. The Spirit continually awakens and gives rise to deeper roots of biblical, theological, and historical meanings in the very midst of, and in response to, current human action. For example, the theme of Jesus and the land becomes more profoundly significant as social uprootedness and the current search for roots becomes significant. The maternal metaphor for God becomes more profoundly significant as feminist interests and concerns become prominent in the educational curriculum. Interpretation and action must be kept in the larger context of Christ's transforming Spirit if learning is to remain redemptive and alive.

## (2) Conflictual Learning

The second type of learning most common to us starts at the opening end of the sequence of transformation—our engagement with real conflict. In response to conflict, our task is first of all to learn *to face and embrace appropriate conflict with perseverance*. Such embrace of conflict is a complex matter. Diagnosing critical conflicts with care requires considerable sensitivity, as Paulo Freire and the advocates of *conscientization* make plain. Learning at this stage requires indwelling the context in both its positive and destructive aspects. Taking care in this respect—i.e., caring about resolving conflict—is as important as perseverance. One cannot create what one does not care about and persist in. Difficult as it is to face and embrace conflict, transformation requires this kind of courage, whether the conflict occurs in relation to the social issues of oppression and justice or focuses on more clinically oriented educational experiences.

The perversity that underlies this learning task, when separated from the guiding principle of transformation, is for learners to become narcissistically preoccupied with the *human* struggle, and the conflict fails to heighten consciousness of *God's* action in the world. This failure occurs often because the learner does not clarify from the outset that the ultimate and decisive conflict is not "my suffering," "their suffering," or "our suffering." The redemptive question is, what is God doing in this world to create a people who are truly human according to the humanity of Christ? This theological and christological conflict underlies all the others and is signified by them, so that to engage in all forms of suffering we must come to face and embrace with perseverance this underlying, ultimate conflict. Only when all human suffering is seen in the four-dimensional context of Christ's work and presence will human conflicts find redemptive transformation in Christ, the living answer.

From this convictional standpoint, the modern myth that to "live the question" as some sort of legitimate answer to conflict is a cop-out. If you do live the question, do not live in it for its own sake. Live it for the sake of providing the context in which the spiritual presence of Christ can act and be received, and the human spirit liberated. Then, living the question may provide a sacred space within which to live the answers. An unwillingness to receive the spiritual presence of Christ may reveal an unwillingness to allow the Spirit of Christ to determine what one will suffer for his sake.

## (3) Learning through Celebration

Third in the order of learning tasks familiar to us and inherent in the sequence of transformation is *learning to celebrate*. "Learning" and "celebrate" may sound like a contradiction in terms, since some associate celebration with what you do *after* learning is over and done with! But this very idea precisely perverts the place of celebration in relation to learning and calls us to rethink the importance of celebration for learning anything according to the logic of transformation. In the paradigm case of Archimedes's discovery, he does not celebrate disorder but the discovery of the hidden order of things. Celebration in transformation is neither an isolated outburst, nor a temporary self-indulgence, nor a random selection of instinct gratification. Celebration is the repeated awakening to, and profound appreciation of, the fundamental but hidden order of all things undergoing transformation unto the glory of God.

The distinguished geneticist Barbara McClintoch won the Nobel Prize in 1983 for observing corn plants. "The important thing," she said, "is to see one kernel that is different and make that understandable. If it doesn't fit, there is a reason for it."[1] What was she doing? She was looking for the hidden order underlying corn plants, and when she found it, she, in replication of Archimedes, went out into her cornfields and shouted "Eureka!"

What about the Christian context? Imagine a woman is miraculously healed of AIDS, a blind man's sight restored, a hearing problem healed. What do we celebrate? None of these miracles in themselves warrants theological celebration unless we understand them in terms of the hidden order of Christ being revealed. Celebration comes not from the healing event itself but from the discovery of the hidden order of Christ's nature *behind* these events. Now *that* discovery is worthy of celebrating! In this particular learning task there is an important corollary. One tends to learn what one celebrates—namely, the things that generate energy and enthusiasm deep in one's spirit. Hence, *what* order or *whose* order one celebrates under the surface is the all-important consideration, because that is the order that will be learned and driven deeper into the learner with every repetition. In cryptic terms, you become what you celebrate.

1. Editor's Note: Loder does not cite the source of this quotation. But in *Knight's Move*, 230, the quote is revealed to be in Keller, *Feeling*, xiii.

## (4) Contemplative Wondering

The fourth type of learning task I will call *contemplative wondering*. Learning in this way leads one to enter the transformational sequence at the second stage we called interlude and scanning. Here the learner is encouraged and supported to enter into a state of expectant searching. S/he immerses her-/himself in the exploration of connections and combinations of meaning for which both the basic problem and the redeeming conflict may still be obscure. S/he has only a strong hunch, or rather I should say, the hunch has him or her. Contemplative wondering imagines that one follows an inner voice or carries on an internal dialogue with the unseen teacher as Augustine and Calvin suggested.[2] Most of us visible teachers have a great deal of trouble with learners who do not know exactly what they want to learn, and we don't seem to be able to handle their efforts to be faithful to an unseen voice that they trust implicitly.

Carl Rogers has been especially instructive in showing us that a context of persons who supply the "freedom to learn." His emphasis on supporting and refocusing the inner guidance of the human spirit rather than supplying answers or interpretations expresses a vital part of the overall process of learning anything.[3] All learning in depth according to the human spirit obviously requires as a crucial element this ability to contemplate and wonder. Without enablement and support for contemplative wondering, insights will be proportionally shallow and governed by expediency rather than by satisfying the deeper longings of the human spirit for meaning. For example, one may learn the language and thought of Karl Barth (or anyone's favorite theologian) even to the point of knowing what Barth might say next. But without the capacity for contemplative wonder one will never come to an intuition of the Source that a gave rise to Barth's language and thought in the first place. Scanning reveals the deeper longing of the human spirit to "know things whole" in relation to the One who created all things. That is, contemplative wonder is the spirit's inner movement toward ever more comprehensive or universally valid understandings, in response to the Reality that transforms all things.

The perversity of wondering, of course, is subjectivism and the dark love of "inscape"—i.e., enjoying the suspended animation of living in the despair of possibility with no end in sight. However, let me emphasize that the chronic embrace of subjectivism or self-absorption is as antithetical to transformation as its opposite, the embrace of shallow false certitudes. The

2. Calvin, *Institutes* 3.1.4, 541–42.
3. Rogers titled one of his books *Freedom to Learn*.

first tendency perverts contemplative wondering by turning it into a self-indulgent preoccupation with complexity for complexity's sake. The second tendency perverts contemplative wondering by denying the true complexity of thought and existence.

## (5) Convictional Learning

The form of learning I believe we understand least is perhaps most crucial to the transformational process. I call this form *learning from convictional experiences or from insights that reach the proportions of convictional significance.*[4] Those numinous experiences that have overwhelming convictional force often seem to be threatening aberrations from the ordinary course of life because they bear the discontinuity of grace that disrupts socialization. Yet they have a profound significance upon the lives of those who experience them. Some studies show that 75 percent of Presbyterian clergy (PCU-SA), 45 percent of Presbyterian laity, and about 40 percent of the American population have had experiences of sudden spiritual awakening.[5]

I am not arguing that everyone must be induced into having such an experience. Nor am I arguing that we should worship convicting experiences. Nor should we gather into groups for which the membership ticket is having had an experience or being able to have one on a weekly basis. These kinds of perverse responses or attitudes to the significance of convictional experiences distort the great learning potential bound up in these experiences. We must not allow our animus toward these perversions blind us to the reality of convictional experiences as profoundly educational. Indeed, when such experiences lead to true convictional power, they serve a prophetic calling of the church. Symbolically and substantively they preserve the profound sense of the reality of "uncreated grace" that surrounds us. And they encourage the decisive break with the socialized order that liberates the human spirit for life in the Spirit and that undergirds all legitimate prophetic protest against unjust systems. These experiences declare that redemptive grace is God's alone to give. These experiences move one through the pattern of transformation into the worship and glorification of God, the supreme end of the transforming work of Christ's Spirit. As such, they are signs of the presence and power of the kingdom of God. They belong not to

4. Editor's Note: The book that set the trajectory for Loder's scholarly efforts for decades following his "convictional experience" in 1970, *Transforming Moment*, was dedicated to helping make such experiences the subject of scientific investigation. Loder's experience of the Spirit moved him more deeply into scientific culture to generate real knowledge of the human situation.

5. See Presbyterian Panel, *Questionnaire*, 16–20. See also Greely, *Sociology*.

the convicted person but to God's people, the church. They expose, however momentarily and partially, the nature of the reality into which all of life is being integrated.

## (B) Completing the Transformational Process

Each of the five types of learning needs the others to complete the overall theme of transformation as the guiding principle of intentional Christian education. However, no one person will be equally competent in all types of learning. All of us together as the body of Christ, under his Spirit's unifying intention, constitute the learning community of faith that exhibits the transforming life of Christ in and for the world. Deepening or intensifying the transformational process at any one of these points tends to deepen all the others. For example, pushing deeper into an interpretation will soon present a conflict, which if embraced will yield new scanning, insight, and release of tension toward a deeper interpretation. Consequently, teachers must learn to take themselves and their students into and through all five movements of the transformational pattern as the Spirit guides the teaching-learning event into truth. Teachers at all levels are called to enable and encourage their learners to enter into the transformational process at whatever stage connects them to it, but from there to complete the transformational sequence because the transformational pattern is already in them. They already know the whole pattern. More importantly, teaching-learning experiences governed by the Holy Spirit affirm both the spiritual power that is already at work in learners and teachers but also the need for the human spirit to continue to find its true creative energy in the Spirit working in concert with their human spirit toward redemptive transformation.

## (III) TRANSPOSITIONS OF TRANSFORMATIONAL LEARNING

The theoretical assumption at work in our discussion of process is that the five-step transformation paradigm lies at the core of a great deal of good teaching that is already taking place. But the theories underlying much of our thinking and practice in the field of Christian education may not fully express this transformational dynamism as a work of the Holy Spirit. This possibility suggests the need to use the transformational model we are developing here as a critical lens to challenge extant theories of Christian education with regard to their understanding of the Spirit's action in educational ministry. With this concern in mind, let us turn now to the transpositions of this transformational paradigm as it is expressed in certain, already existent theories of educational process.

## (A) Broken Narrative: Margaret Krych on Teaching Justification by Grace to Children

In her marvelous dissertation connecting Paul Tillich's theology of correlation with transformational narrative, Margaret Krych developed a narrative approach to learning in the church school. She offered a popularization of her model in her book, *Teaching the Gospel Today*. Using Tillich's understanding of correlation, in which existential questions interact critically with theological answers—she developed a pedagogical process in which learners entered reflectively into the questions narratives pose so that they could engage the latent transformational impact imbedded in the narrative, resulting in their own transformation. Krych drew upon Richard Gardner's work *Therapeutic Communication with Children*, which advocates the use of broken narration in therapy to help children hear and experience alternative endings to their own personal stories. Krych constructed a series of broken narrative versions of biblical stories about Jesus and the stories Jesus told in order to help children implicate themselves in those stories so that deep transformation might occur.

In classroom experiments she told gospel stories to the fifth- and sixth-grade children up to the point where the narration breaks, presenting in essence the existential question (Tillich) implicit in the story. For instance, from her dissertation, she tells of the story of Zacchaeus (Luke 19:1–19) to the children participating in her study, without revealing his name.

> Long ago, in the time when Jesus lived, there was a man whom just about everybody hated. Maybe he wasn't too sure that he liked himself very much. Maybe he wasn't too sure what God thought about him. Maybe he wasn't sure just how much God cared about him.
>
> In those days, the Romans ruled the land of Israel. Imagine if a foreign country sent their soldiers into Philadelphia to rule over us. Imagine if a foreign government told us to pay money called taxes to help support their army! Do you think that you would like that? No, indeed! Well, people in those days didn't like it either.
>
> The man in our story lived in the land of Israel. He was a Jew. He knew how much his people hated the Romans. But do

you know what he did? He went to the Romans and agreed to collect their taxes for them. How do you think the other Jewish people felt about him? (Right, pretty mad.)

Well, this man became very important. He worked for the Romans in the city of Jericho, a city on the main road from Jerusalem. It was an important city and many people passed through it. "Pay up!" ordered the man, and the people angrily paid their tax money.

Soon the man became chief collector of taxes. Now, whenever he and other tax collectors asked the Jews for money, they worked out how much their Roman employers required. Then they added a bit more to the total and charged the Jews that extra amount. Guess what they did with the extra money? (Yes, they kept if for themselves.)

So the man kept the extra money for himself. And he grew richer and richer as time went by. He became very powerful and very important.

But although he had a good job, and although he was rich and important, something was wrong in his life. He knew daily how much people hated him. He also knew that he wasn't the kind of person that he should be. I'm sure that the felt that things weren't right between himself and God. But—he couldn't change. Maybe he didn't even want to change.

Then one day he heard that Jesus would pass through Jericho. No doubt he had heard many things about Jesus. What might some of them have been? (Yes, he had probably heard of Jesus healing and teaching people. He had probably heard that Jesus made their lives new and different. He had probably heard that some people called Jesus the Christ, the one whom people were expecting God to send to help them and make life new and different.) This man thought that he would like to know a little more about Jesus.[6]

At this point Krych broke the sequence and asked the children, "What do you think the ending of the story should be?" The children responded with a variety of written answers. Some ended the story pessimistically; others legalistically; and still others with changes initiated by the tax collector himself. And some children caught an element of grace in their answer. With the narrative broken, the children became self-involved with the story, truly engaged.

---

6. Krych, "Communicating," 468–69.

After the children gave their answers, Krych then completed the story of Zacchaeus, relating the surprising transformational ending in which the tax collector's name was revealed for the first time.

> Jesus knew what everyone else in the crowd didn't know. He knew that Zacchaeus needed him. He knew that Zacchaeus needed to hear the Good News of God's love for him in spite of the kind of person he was. It wasn't that Jesus didn't know what Zacchaeus was like: he could tell from the rich clothes and from the fact that he was perched all alone up in the tree. He knew. But he went ahead and accepted him in a friendly way. He cared about Zacchaeus. He wanted Zacchaeus to know he cared.
>
> Zacchaeus was very, very happy. Why? ("Because he needed to change. Because he had met Jesus.") Yes, Jesus had come to his house in spite of who he was and what he was like. Zacchaeus began to see things in a whole new way. He saw what he had been. And he didn't like what he had been one bit.
>
> But now Jesus was his friend. That made a big difference. Zacchaeus changed. He said to Jesus, "Lord, I will give half of everything I have to poor people, and I will give back four times as much if I have cheated anyone." I guess that he wasn't too rich by the time that he gave away all of that!
>
> Now Zacchaeus' life was changed. His life was new. Not before Jesus came but *because* Jesus came. Jesus said to Zacchaeus, "Salvation has come to this house today," and he also said that he had come to seek and to save the lost. That means, Jesus came with good news to people who were not the kind of people they wanted to be or that God wanted them to be or that other people wanted them to be. He came to people who knew that something was very wrong in their lives. He came to make lives new, to change people, and to help people believe in God's love for them.[7]

Out of their participation in this kind of interrupted storytelling, Krych noticed that children came to realize that this pattern is one Jesus taught and enacted as the mediator. Once they learned the narrative structure, Krych had them write and illustrate their own transformational narratives. What most fascinated Krych was the depth of the children's personal involvement with the stories. One little girl with blond hair and blue eyes drew Saint Paul as a blond-haired, blue-eyed little girl—and no one laughed!

The payoff for us is that as a Lutheran, Dr. Krych was teaching "justification by faith" during a period in their developmental readiness when

7. Ibid, 472.

children, living under the power of socialization, most naturally learned "justification by works." Thus, as we would suspect, transformation in development is stronger than stages. In Krych's work the core of the transformational pattern and process gets transposed into a four-dimensional plot structure in which Christ functions as the Mediator. Perhaps a weakness in her work is that she did not test the learning theory outside a limited age group. But since her dissertation and the release of *Teaching the Gospel Today*, Dr. Krych's theory has certainly been more widely explored.[8]

## (B) Pedagogy of the Oppressed: Paulo Freire's Literacy Project

A second transposition of transformation comes from the work of Paulo Freire. You will recall from our earlier discussion that Freire was a Brazilian educator who was rewarded for implementing migrant worker literacy education in oppressive conditions by being expelled as a revolutionary from both Brazil and Chile. His groundbreaking book was the classic study *Pedagogy of the Oppressed*.[9]

### (1) The Transformational Pattern in Freire's Work

What follows is my reading of Freire's book as a transposition of the transformational logic working change in a context of oppression.

### (A) CONFLICT IN CONTEXT

According to Freire, humanization is our ontological vocation as human beings. But we are hampered from fulfilling this vocation within socioeconomic and educational conditions plagued by acrimonious division between oppressors and the oppressed. In his analysis, the initiative for breaking the power of this oppressor-oppressed condition can only come, and must come, from the side of those oppressed.[10] The power that springs

8. Editor's Note: Margaret Krych's rich tenure at Luther Seminary continues today. When I once asked Dr. Loder which dissertation he supervised which was his favorite, he immediately responded: "Margaret Krych's work teaching 'justification by faith' to grade school children!" For Krych's own assessment of Loder's theories in relation to her Lutheran tradition, see Krych, "Transformational," 279–97.

9. Editor's Note: Freire, *Pedagogy* continues to be one of the most significant books on education ever written. Its thirtieth-anniversary edition in 2000 boasted "over a million copies sold." The book continues to be reprinted almost yearly.

10. Freire, *Pedagogy*, 28. Editor's Note: Freire asserted that "the great humanistic

from weakness alone is sufficient to rectify the situation. And no false charity from the side of the oppressor (which is simply oppression by other means) will do. That is, any initiative from the oppressor ends being nothing more than paternalism, the benign garb of oppression.

Unfortunately, however, the initiatives taken by the oppressed too easily fail because they tend to equate the goal of liberation with adopting their oppressor's dominating lifestyle.[11] Oppressed persons both hate and admire the oppressors, even as they rise up to throw off the oppression. They simply flip the ambivalence, becoming like their oppressors in their efforts to liberate themselves. As long as they live in the duality in which they identify "to be" with "to be like the oppressor," nothing in these contexts substantively changes. Both the oppressor and the oppressed are dehumanized, deprived again of their ontological vocation.[12] For example, I recall a debate in the sixties in which a black respondent, while making what seemed to me to be a legitimate claim for liberation, put himself down at the same time he admired the dehumanizing benefits of white privilege: "I just want a chance to make that mistake."

For developmental reasons, flipping of the ambivalence in oppressive contexts is the inevitable outcome of every attempt at liberation. The search for a positive, strong identity figure that empowers mastery over the other continues the same tragic circumstances as before. The central problem for true liberation, then, can be stated as follows: "How can the oppressed, as divided, disempowered, and forced to live inauthentically by the powerful, participate in a pedagogy that actually liberates them without creating more victims and victimizers in the process?"[13] According to Freire, the oppressed must become the *hosts* of the oppressor, inviting the oppressor to change by joining with the oppressed to forge a new society.[14] The pedagogy of the oppressed then becomes an instrument for the critical discovery that both they and the oppressors are manifestations of dehumanization. Freire showed further that effective educational initiatives taken in this regard can

and historical task of the oppressed" is "to liberate themselves and their oppressors as well."

11. Ibid, 49. Speaking of the oppressed, Freire writes: "In their alienation, the oppressed want at any cost to resemble the oppressor, to imitate him, to follow him."

12. Ibid, 28–30. Editor's Note: Freire writes: "Dehumanization, which marks not only those whose humanity has been stolen, but also (though in a different way) those who have stolen it, is a *distortion* of the vocation of becoming fully human" (ibid., 28; italics original).

13. Ibid., 33. Editor's Note: Loder appears to be elaborating Freire's question a bit. Freire had asked, "How can the oppressed, as divided, unauthentic beings, participate in developing the pedagogy of their liberation?"

14. Ibid.

succeed. Educators seeking liberation "from below" do not have to wait for the oppressed to take action "from above."

One of the greatest obstacles to the achievement of liberation lies in the fact that the oppressive reality absorbs everyone within it, submerging human consciousness in the oppressive milieu.[15] Functionally, oppression domesticates the personal and collective imaginations of oppressed and oppressor, convincing them that there is no other world but the one that presently exists. The oppressors envision themselves as the makers of history in their image, while the oppressed become nameless and faceless pawns in someone else's history. Liberation begins when the oppressed come to a perception that their situation is not inevitable and does not represent history. They come to understand that their situation is not fate, but rather is a limiting situation that they have the power to transform. This perception of the alterability of history becomes then the motivation for liberating action.[16]

Thus, true liberation is difficult because socialization structures the oppressed personality to perceive his/her situation passively and to rationalize it as fate. The fatalism of the oppressed says, "I am just a peasant, what can I do?"[17] Furthermore, the fatalism gets further rationalized and legitimated as the will of God. Fatalism collapses the future, and the resulting depression holds "time" on a dead center. Difficulties continue in the face of this lived ambivalence. The irresistible attraction to the way of life of the oppressor highlights the realization of what one never can have, and thereby subverts any hope for a genuinely owned personal freedom. Difficulties continue because self-deprecation in the oppressed group heightens the magical power of the oppressor group. This self-deprecation continues even as rebellion ensues. And when success follows and things begin to change, those in rebellion begin to feel guilty toward their own group. Furthermore, this experience of lived guilt reveals that the dynamics of oppression are necrophilial—i.e., they manifest the love of death.[18] What needs to be engendered, then, is a love of life, and eventually the realization that rebellion must itself be transformed as an act of love toward the oppressor.

How does Freire approach oppressive contexts transformationally? What process lies at the heart of his liberating pedagogical strategies?

15. Ibid. Editor's Note: Freire argued that the oppressed know they suffer oppression, but what they don't recognize is that their perception of themselves as oppressed is impaired by their submersion in the reality of oppression.

16. Ibid, 110. Editor's Note: Freire writes, "Individuals who were *submerged* in reality, merely *feeling* their needs, *emerge* from reality and perceive the *causes* of their needs" (italics original).

17. Ibid, 48–51.

18. Ibid, 64.

Generally, he argues for a critical and liberating, face-to-face dialogue that enables the oppressed to take charge of their own lives and to fight for their own liberation. He seeks to empower the supposed powerless by enabling them to imagine that what they fight for is not merely freedom from hunger and the like. Rather, he helps them imagine they really fight for the freedom of spirit to see and perceive, to create and to construct, to wonder and to venture, etc.,—all toward an open future they facilitate.[19] He teaches them it is not enough to tell persons they are not slaves. For even those who master the socialization dynamics merely conform their lives to the negation incorporated into the system. Their mastery (freedom) simply manifests the love of death. True freedom is the spiritual freedom to live into the ongoing transformation of experience with the power to construct and compose worlds that continually breathe life into every social construction of reality.[20]

### (b) Interlude for Scanning

Under Freire's leadership, scanning for solutions to oppressive contexts takes the form of a team of educators that immerses itself in and indwells the area of oppression (e.g., a migrant camp). They treat the whole area as an enormous, unique, and living "code" to be deciphered through attentiveness.[21] They attempt to find the hidden order in the conflict or chaos through careful observation, attentive to every aspect of the field, conducting analysis of the parts, discerning major themes and the way the natives of the environment respond to those themes. For example, the workers are shown a picture in which a drunken man stumbles along on the street and three young teenagers converse on the corner. As the workers engage the picture, surprisingly, they are not critical of the drunken man. Instead they say, "He is the only member of the society who is productive. He has worked all day for low wages, so he has to get soused. He's worried that he can't take care of his family."

Thus, as the workers verbalized the connections between their desperately low wages, their feelings of being systematically exploited, and their response in getting drunk, they learn to identify themselves as those caught in this same pattern they observed in the picture. Their verbalization means that some "objectification" of their situation has taken place. They have faced and embraced the hidden conflict and brought it to articulation.

---

19. Ibid, 55. Editor's Note: Freire quotes Fromm, *Heart,* 32, to make this point.
20. Ibid, 31–33.
21. Ibid, 75–118.

## (c) Prototypes—Insight

This step functions as the beginning of "conscientization" in Freire's work, which is accompanied by a literacy program in which generative words, expressive of the themes, are learned. But Freire's educational team carefully chooses words that can also be broken down into syllables, and the syllables can be rearranged to make up new words. First they find words that relate to the problems of food, shelter, clothing, health, and education. For example, the word *favela*, which means, "slum," describes their oppressive context. *Favela* can be broken down in relation to the alphabet as follows:

> FA, FE, FI, FO, FU
> VA, VE, VI, VO, VU
> LA, LE, LI, LO, LU

These learned syllables are then rearranged to create new words:

> VELA = "candle"; VIVO = "I live"

Through this pedagogical process new insights signifying the workers' potential to change the world of the slum on analogy to the way they changed the word *favela* begin to dawn upon them.[22]

## (d) Release of Energy

When the migrants (or others) realize that they can reread and rename their situation and make it new through the power of language and literacy, then they react like Helen Keller did when she learned from Anne Sullivan the sign for "water." This transforming experience opened up in Helen's spirit an epistemic revolution to know and name everything she experienced. In the same way, when it dawns on the migrants they can change their world through language, ecstasy sets in, and a new corporate sense of empowerment and commitment funds the courage to act upon their knowledge. Motivated by a powerful energy that infuses their new sense of themselves, they ask with passion, "What shall we do?"

---

22. Editor's Note: This discussion of the literacy program is not taken from *Pedagogy* but from another book by Freire, *Education*, 77–80. See also, Schipani, *Conscientization*, 9–10.

(e) Repatterning of the Context

Perception and motivation lead directly to action, not a trivialized activism but a powerful reflective action. Freire calls this interplay between reflection and action a liberating form of *praxis*.[23] *Praxis* needs continual and persistent authorization by the awakened human spirit; otherwise corporate self-consciousness collapses back into the oppressor-oppressed stalemate.[24] But from a Christian transformational perspective, liberative *praxis* finds its true power in a four-dimensional context that discerns and gives place to divine action as well as human action. Thus, Letty Russell, in her book *Human Liberation in a Feminist Perspective: A Theology*, argued that what happens in the dynamics of liberation resembles conversion—only the emphasis is different. Conversion places the initiative and the emphasis on God's action and purpose. But humanitarian liberation movements place the emphasis and initiative on autonomous human actions.[25] Humanitarian liberation requires a theological or redemptive transformation in which the negation bound up with socialized existence is negated, and a qualitative complementarity pertains between divine and human action unto liberation.

This last comment leads us to offer a fuller critique of Freire's work.

## (2) Critique of Freire's Work

Daniel Schipani is, I think, quite astute when he notes why Freire's model works from a developmental standpoint.[26] Developmentally there is a close connection between the emergence of initiative in the three-to-five-year-old child and the emergence of the flow of grammatical speech in the child. That is, the excitement about learning to speak as a child motivates the child's capacity to take the initiative and to thrust him- or herself into the world with newfound energy and purpose. This association of language and action was reawakened in adults through Freire's literacy campaign and it accounts in part for why learning to name situations moves persons into liberative action.[27]

---

23. Freire, *Pedagogy*, 119–30.

24. Ibid, 131. Editor's Note: Freire contrasts his "theory of revolutionary action" and a "theory of oppressive action through the rest of chapter 4 (131–86).

25. Russell, *Human*, 121–25, especially 24.

26. Schipani, *Conscientization*, 13–15, 38–46. Editor's Note: Daniel Schipani did his PhD dissertation under Loder's advisement.

27. Ibid, 46–50.

In Freire's work, of course, such motivation comes to the people because the words they learned were emotionally invested and thematic of the solutions they sought. The parallel in child development of this empowering capacity is their passionate sense of euphoria—"omnipotence of intelligence" as Piaget calls it—which accompanies creative action in the child. This emotional investment released in a child's development and in adult literacy demonstrates that the pattern of transformation described in this book inheres in our creaturehood and becomes redemptively transformed in four dimensions through our re-creation in the Spirit as the people of God through convictional experience.

Another important developmental link here is the power of imagination. At the age of three to five the child's imagination runs wild and has tremendous power. Indeed, imagination creates nightmares so real that they quite easily overcome the self. Imagination is also important in liberation because what was awakened in Freire's educational work with the illiterate was the emerging vision of a utopia in which oppression and the oppressed were mutually humanized. Dynamically, the aggressor who was reconnected with imagination through literacy found positive and potentially creative expression in the vision of mutuality. Indeed, creativity became the proper focus for pent-up aggressions that otherwise would have destroyed the vision.

To reiterate, the fundamental failure of Freire's model, which Freire himself later acknowledged, was that the liberated spirit funding imagination and motivation for new action, finally cannot stand as the ground of true freedom. The vocation of humanization requires that persons and communities ground liberation in the presence of God and the life of Christ through the Spirit of Christ. As Schipani noted (and claimed Freire's agreement), the aim and pattern of transformed liberation should be worship.[28]

---

28. Editor's Note: Schipani makes this point but in a rather indirect way. He notes that Freire's theological commitments are the most important factor in understanding his revolutionary pedagogy, but they function in an intuitive and humanistic sense (*Conscientization*, 56). Then he adds, "In spite of Freire's explicitly Christian commitment, however, the *ultimate* character of Christ's mediating-liberating work (rather than the avant-garde's and the oppressed's) is not clearly established in his thought. This distinction between ultimate and proximate mediation and liberation is important in light of what appears to become confusion on the part of the most enthusiastic admirers of Freire" (ibid., 149–50). However, Schipani notes that Freire's pedagogy is a "variation on the creativity model" (ibid., 148) and follows the transformational pattern Loder identified, which includes "release of energy" or "celebration of insight" (ibid., 136). Theologically this dimension concerns the place of Christian worship in redemptive transformation. I could not find any reference to Freire agreeing with this assessment in Schipani's book.

### (3) Freire's Model Transposed to Another Setting: Lynn Gray's Work with Urban Youth

A major example of Freire's implementation of transformation in an American urban setting was Lynn Gray's work in association with New York City's Urban Coalition, which we have already mentioned.[29] The Urban Coalition asked Gray to investigate why some schools in its jurisdiction were collapsing under the urban blight and others were not. He found out that those schools that survived had developed a critical sense of their history and risked telling their stories in conflict-resolving ways, quite self-consciously. With this analysis in mind, Gray visited the schools that were not doing well and taught them, in ways that resembled Freire's literacy program, to name or "historicize" the problem.

Gray later received funding from the Rockefeller Foundation, McDonalds, and other major agencies for the formation of an initiative called "City Kids."[30] Like Freire, he indwelt the lives and schools of young people and established a walk-in location in the city where they were free to just hang out. Essentially, Gray did in a less systematic way what Freire advocated. By indwelling lives and situations of the young people, Gray came up against the same theme of recapitulation. He asked these kids, "Can you change your world?" At first, most said, "No way!" Hence, the fatalism associated with the collapse of time and loss of hope was present. But by the time he finished this initiative, the young people not only said they could change their world—they even sang it! How did Gray achieve these results?

Context was important. Gray and his staff communicated, by how they dressed and by how they exerted energy, that they understood the world in which these kids lived. But more importantly, they encouraged the young people to talk honestly about their lives. Gray used peer pressure in a positive way as a disciplining factor. Kids played a game called Throw the Ball. When the ball was thrown to you, you answered the question that was asked

29. Editor's Note: Lynn Gray was an MDiv student at Princeton Theological Seminary from 1964 to 1967. His work there focused on learning strategies, exploring the theoretical underpinnings for funding innovation in complex organizations. His early professional work was based in New York City, where he created and managed major urban development projects for twenty years. Gray was also senior vice president of the New York Urban Coalition, a partnership of public, private, labor, community, and government agencies, focusing attention and resources on public education and on the development of public-private partnership in underserved communities. Loder misspelled Gray's name in *Logic of the Spirit* and in this manuscript. My thanks to Rev. Mark Koonz, who tracked down this error and sent me on the right path to verify this reference.

30. Lynn Gray confirmed to me by phone the authenticity of this account.

and then threw it back. So, "What do you think of school?" "School sucks." Throw the ball. "What do you want to do in your life?" "Go to Russia." Throw the ball. In time, the kids learned to carry on normal conversations, handle silences, and develop their literacy and job-hunting skills.

The play of imagination was the key to the program. They built a model of New York City in the Jesuit Center and learned from it how the whole city worked. Gray also built up a way of teaching them that empowered them to buy privileges by giving service to needy people in the community. The process focused on the kids learning to reconstruct their world by language and imagination in a way that repelled the temptation for imitation. Gray knew that liberating the human spirit was the key to their learning—the key to changing their world. Gray once showed a videotape in my class of his kids singing at a gala affair hosted by Phil Donahue that featured Jimmy Carter. The title of the program: "You Can Change Your World!"

Lynn Gray came to the seminary because he himself needed to keep in touch with why he was doing this work. Here he learned to put the restoration of the human spirit into the context of his Christian heritage. Again, the freedom of the human spirit is decisive but insufficient for humanization in theological sense. It is powerful, but it is not enough. The human spirit cries out for a commensurate context of meaning that it cannot supply for itself.

## (C) Transforming Young Adults during "the Critical Years": Sharon Daloz Parks

A third transposition comes from Sharon Parks's work on the mentorship needed in the university context in an emerging pluralistic world.[31] What is this mentoring challenge? In her book *The Critical Years*, Parks draws on Alfred North Whitehead's *Symbolism: It's Meaning and Effect* to speak to the imaginative task that must be carefully mentored in each generation.

> A young adult world now depends upon mentorship of those who can embody the promise of a new world culture . . . If the social contract is to be recomposed, there is a need for leadership that will self-consciously participate in formation of a new faith in which to ground it. This will require participation in a new act of imagination, critically reappropriating traditional symbols and giving birth to new images and insight. As Whitehead saw so clearly, "Those societies which cannot combine reverence to their symbols with freedom of revision must

31. Editor's Note: Loder's discussion of Parks here should be read in tandem with Parks's use of Loder in *Critical Years*, 116–32.

ultimately decay either from anarchy, or from the slow atrophy of a life stifled by useless shadows."[32]

With this kind of imaginative vision of the institutional mentoring in mind, Parks set up the pattern of transformation as paradigmatic for the formation of faith and meaning during the young adult years. The pattern resembles the fivefold pattern advocated in this book.

## (1) Conscious Conflict

The university celebrates its primary strength when it "pulls together a livable tension of restless opposites."[33] No matter how threatening their mutual contradiction may at first appear, true conflict seeks a higher order of resolution. As Coleridge put it, "We separate to distinguish, but never so as to divide the one reality there is."[34] This discernment occurs, for example, in interdisciplinary work. The recognition that disciplines have been distinguished and developed separately from other disciplines must not ignore their need to be reintegrated with other disciplines for the sake of the one reality there is. Transformation can occur in investigations of the moral implications of anything—i.e., must psychologists deceive subjects to get to the truth about people? This kind of inquiry can be disconcerting and requires staying power on the part of the teacher, but conflict is decisive

32. Parks, *Critical Years*, 188, quoting from Whitehead, *Symbolism*, 88. Editor's Note: Loder's manuscript quoted from Whitehead's *Aims of Education* here, emphasizing the purpose of the university, and not from Whitehead's *Symbolism*. This quote from the *Aims of Education* was repeated verbatim later in Loder's manuscript in chapter 11, in relation to symbolic learning. I am unsure if Loder intended to repeat the quote, but he did not note that it was being repeated. I struggled whether I should let the repetition stand or not. Then I reread Sharon Daloz Parks's discussion of the mentoring role of universities in the lives of young adults. In her discussion she quotes from Whitehead's *Symbolism*, not *Aims of Education*. This comment seemed to fit Loder's purpose exactly, since Parks emphasized the conflict young people face between affirming the past and being open to the future. So I used Parks's quote from Whitehead and altered sentences before and after the quote to emphasize Parks's point about mentoring young people in a pluralistic setting. I think this quote fits the context at least as well as the Whitehead quote Loder used. In fact, it serves the purpose of Loder's discussion perhaps even more fittingly than the other quote. It also picks up what Parks was saying more specifically than the other quote. And finally, it avoids the repetition.

33. Parks, *Critical Years*, 141.

34. Editor's Note: Loder does not give reference to this quote by Coleridge. However, it is close to the notation of Sharon Daloz Parks in *Critical Years*, 118. Parks, referring to the deep inner conflict that gives rise to new insight, writes: "It is Coleridge's great conviction that his moment of opposition must serve to distinguish but not to divide." She cites Coleridge, *Friend*, vol. 1, cii, as the source.

if the university sustains itself to be a community of the imagination. The pedagogical move must always go against uncritical socialization.

### (2) Pause (Interlude for Scanning)

The modern academy came from the contemplative tradition, but the essence of that heritage has been lost. Congested campuses and schedules make contemplation nearly impossible. But contemplation is of the very essence of true learning. As Parker Palmer suggests, sometimes "silence" needs to be prescribed, not only at the beginning of discussions but in the middle of heated exchanges.[35] True learning takes time.

### (3) Image

Four types of image are of particular importance to young adults, according to Parks. They need access to images that—

- (a) Give fitting form to truth, where the faculty says what they think, and meaning gets composed in the context of real alternatives.
- (b) Resonate with their lived experience. The power of a new image depends upon its fittingness to the truth holding both mind and heart together.
- (c) Capture the "ideal." Images must serve to help young people reach beyond the socialized limits of the constructed world for new possibilities in an open universe.
- (d) Recognize and name the dynamic character of ongoing transformation. Images must be dynamic enough to grasp the composing character of the motion of life, the dynamic of dissolution and recomposition.

### (4) Repatterning and Release of Energy

Students remember a chemistry teacher who continually repatterned their apprehension of the world because "with every fact he also taught a dream." He made the connection between the fact and what it might mean for the

---

35. Editor's Note: Loder is probably referring to chapter 5 of Palmer's book *To Know as We Are Known*. The chapter is called "To Teach Is to Create a Space," and runs from page 69 to page 87. Loder likely refers especially a subsection called "Silence and Speech" (79–83).

world. Step back and marvel, "Isn't God amazing!" The apprehension of implications and integrations of hidden orders is the celebration of learning. Science becomes, implicitly or explicitly, the celebration and praise of God the Creator.

## (5) Interpretation

A "community of confirmation" is needed to complete the act of imagination or indwell the vision that constitutes a new faith. Though desirable, this kind of community is rare. Still, "the university has become, without its being explicated, the transcendental institution in society because it seems to promise the notion of community."[36]

## (IV) A FOURTH TRANSPOSITION: SHARED *PRAXIS* OF THOMAS GROOME

The fourth and final transposition for our consideration is the "Shared *Praxis*" approach to Christian education of Thomas H. Groome, a Roman Catholic associated with Boston College. In the literature, his approach, fully explicated in his *Christian Religious Education*, most closely parallels the approach I am suggesting in this book. To this point, Groome originally wanted to title his book, *Til the Break of Day*.[37] For Groome educational *praxis* is shaped by how persons respond to certain foundational questions of the "reporter source" in light of *praxis*.[38]

36. Ibid, 161. Editor's Note: Loder wrongly attributed this last quote to Sharon Daloz Parks. Parks was discussing what she called "a community . . . of celebratory confirmation" and then cited this quote from Daniel Bell in support of her argument. Bell himself was quoted in Minneman, *Students*, v. See Parks, *Critical Years*, 160–61, 231.

37. Editor's Note: The "Postscript" in *Christian Religious Education*, titled "Until Break of Day" (277–78), focused on Jacob's wrestling with the angel at Jabbok. Loder is apparently thinking here that Groome's image of "daybreak" echoed Loder's own argument about the power of convictional experience in *Transforming Moment*, which came out the same year as Groome's book, under the same publisher.

38. Editor's Note: Groome organizes his text around his version of the "reporter's source." See Groome, *Christian*, xiv. Loder's critique briefly responds to Groome's answers to these questions.

# (A) Groome's Answers to the Reporter Source Questions

## (1) Nature and Purpose

Let me begin this engagement with Groome's theory by briefly summarizing my understanding of his answers to the reporter source questions.

*Question*: What are we doing when we intervene in people's lives to educate religiously on behalf of the Christian faith community? What is the *nature* of Christian religious education?

*Answer*: "*Christian religious education is a political activity with pilgrims in time that deliberately and intentionally attends with them to the activity of God in our present, to the Story of the Christian faith community, and to the Vision of God's Kingdom, the seeds of which are already among us.*"[39]

*Question*: Why do we take up this task? What is the *purpose* of Christian religious education?

*Answer*: "Our *metapurpose* is revealed in 'the Kingdom of God which comes to us as both gift and demand, promise and responsibility, 'already' and 'not yet.'"[40] "Our *immediate* purpose is, by God's grace, to sponsor people toward lived (present) Christian faithfulness." Such faithfulness, as historically expressed, requires the activities of "believing," "trusting," and "doing."[41] The *purpose/consequence* of such lived faith is "human freedom" that begins within history and finds completion in full union with God.[42] Groome is after a transformation of human freedom into freedom in and with God. I would rather speak of *the human spirit*—freedom being a manifestation of spirit, but our views are quite similar.

## (2) Context

*Question*: Where is Christian religious education taking place? What is the *context* of Christian religious education?

*Answer*: "To come to be and remain Christian requires a process of socialization in the midst of a Christian faith community." In addition, "our religious education must promote a critical reflective activity if our faith is truly to be our own and for the sake of the ongoing reform and faithfulness

---

39. Ibid., 25 (italics original). This sentence is repeated on page 140, with no emphasis in the text.

40. Ibid., 35–55.

41. Ibid., 56–81.

42. Ibid., 82–103.

of the whole community."[43] In my judgment, Groome's focus on critical consciousness is not strong enough to transcend the dynamics of socialization he wants to appropriate. Thus, one major weakness of Groome's approach is that he, like C. E. Nelson and others, underestimates the power of socialization to domesticate even the most powerful efforts by human beings to think critically to enable change (see below).

## (3) Timing

*Question*: When are people/congregations ready for Christian religious education? What is the proper *timing* or readiness for learning and teaching?

*Answer*: For coming to critical Christian consciousness and to the *praxis* of the kingdom, Groome avers, "the tree is in the seed." Thus, children from the age of concrete operational thinking (Piaget) onward (i.e., the beginnings of formal education) should be encouraged to think "critically" (grounded in the "concrete") in order to come to a fuller expression of critical consciousness and authentic Christian social engagement in adulthood.[44]

## (4) Personnel

*Question*: Who are we/they who engage events of Christian religious education?" "Who are the *practioners* or copartners?

*Answer*: Groome discusses two partners in the educational task.[45]

(a) *Our Students*: Our students are subjects (not objects) who are called to be and are capable of being makers of history.

(b) *Our Selves*: "*The Christian religious educator is to represent Jesus Christ in service to the community by an 'incarnational' ministry of the Word.*"[46]

Groome believes education is a historical activity that takes place within time.[47] If it exists at all, it exists to be "done" (i.e., "to be" it must find expression beyond the ideational or theoretical levels). This concern for action, he says, is why Aristotle spoke of education as "a practical science"—*not* in the sense of a technique but as a *reflective, intentional activity*. For Groome,

43. Ibid., 108. See also the whole of part 3 (107–34).

44. Ibid., 235–60.

45. Ibid., 261–75.

46. Ibid., 266 (italics original).

47. Ibid., 5–19.

dedicated persons make education happen. These persons continue to live with the kinds of foundational questions summarized here, and they know these questions must come to expression in some particular approach to doing Christian religious education. Further, they know that the "doing" has reformulated and will reformulate reflective responses to the foundational questions. Groome agrees that the old adage, "the most practical thing in the world is a good theory" is true. But he also knows the converse adage: "The most theoretical thing in the world is good practice."

However, from my point of view, while Groome includes the Spirit in his theory, his accounting for the Spirit's action does not appear as the primary factor in Christian education. The Spirit is not conceived as the "Senior Partner," so to say. Still I would grant that Groome's method is open to the Spirit of Christ's initiative. In other words, in my judgment, his method is stronger than the theological rationale adduced to support it.

## (5) Process

*Question*: How do we come to know and use "Shared *Praxis*"? What is the *process* of Christian religious education? This question is central for Groome.

*Answer*: In attempting to articulate a *praxis* approach to Christian religious education, Groome searches for a way of knowing that is capable of bringing us, by God's grace, to know in the biblical sense of *yada'*. Such knowing requires both a knowing *about* and a knowing *of*. But the epistemology of faith must go beyond both knowing *about* and *knowing of* to embrace knowing in the relational sense. Relational knowing engages head, heart, and lifestyle—i.e., one's whole way of being in the world.[48]

Groome closely relates relational knowing to a further concern for a critical epistemology, critical in the dialectical sense. This epistemology cannot be a "debilitating negativism" or a "naïve copying" toward reality and yet must be a knowing that embodies critical consciousness of the social and ideological interests in all our knowing. Critical knowing decodes reality to empower emancipatory *praxis* and maturity for Christian faithfulness. Such a knowing must arise from human *praxis*. While Groome draws his *praxis* epistemology from its roots in Aristotle, his theory is also informed by Hegel, Marx, Habermas, Gadamer (i.e., especially in his critique of Habermas), and Freire. In brief, a *praxis* way of knowing is grounded in critical reflection on, and in the midst of, one's historical engagement in

48. Ibid., 139–51.

the world. Critical reflection engages reason, memory and imagination. As such, it is rational and affective—a holistic way of knowing.[49]

When a *praxis* way of knowing is employed in an intentional educational setting, then the process begins typically with one's own knowing. Groome wants learners to name the knowing that they already know from their own engagement in the world. Critical reflection, employing reason, memory and imagination, is brought to bear on such knowing, and the naming and reflection are shared in dialogue. In such a process the participants come to know at a more critical level, what Groome calls, metaphorically, their own "stories" and "visions."

For the knowing quest that undergirds Christian religious education, however, there is another source of knowing that comes to us as members of this Christian faith community and as stewards of the faith tradition. This knowing is encoded in the narratives inscribed in the Christian tradition that stretch from the patriarchs Abraham, Isaac, and Jacob, and the matriarchs Sarah, Rebekah, and Rachel, to narratives that connect Moses to the rise and fall of Israel, from God's revelation in Jesus Christ and the missionary story of Acts, and to the lived faith of the Christian people over the past two thousand years. This is the Christian community's knowing, the Christian community's "Story" and "Vision," according to Groome.

This "Story" and "Vision" must also be made accessible in the context of Christian religious education. But these two sources of knowing cannot simply be placed alongside of each other. Nor can they be applied to each other in a simple correlation, nor imposed upon each other in an act of authoritarian power. That is, Groome does not intend a simple application of the Bible to life experience. He advocates for a critical correlation of the twin sources of knowing. Groome calls the hermeneutical principle involved in critical correlation "present dialectical hermeneutics."[50] By this principle one's own knowing and the community's knowing are held together in a dialectical tension in which the "Story"/"stories" and "Vision"/"visions" become mutual sources of truth, correlation, critical assessment, and creativity for each other.[51]

The typical movements of the shared *praxis* hermeneutic within intentional settings of Christian religious education begin with the participant's own knowing and with critical reflection upon how they name their own engagement in the world. Next, the Christian community's "Story"/"Vision" is made accessible by placing these two sources of knowing in a dialectical

49. Ibid., 152–83.
50. Ibid., 195.
51. Ibid., 184–206.

hermeneutic with each other. This process leads to a new quality of knowing that, in fact, is a *decision*. Thus, the approach begins with our own present *praxis*, becomes informed by the knowing that comes out of the faith *praxis* of Christians in different times and places, and ultimately returns to further enable Christian *praxis*, which is Christian faithfulness as a lived reality.[52]

## (B) Critical Issues in Shared *Praxis* and Education in the Logic of the Spirit

Groome's work goes a long way toward an educational articulation of the major concerns of this book. However, key issues remain. So let me use my critical assessment of Groome's theory in preparation for the conclusion of this study. In doing so I hope to make more clear my overriding concern that Christian education in the theological sense requires a much stronger accounting for the work of *Spiritus Creator* than Groome and others give. Let me highlight four lingering concerns about Groome's theory.

(1) Where Groome places critical reflection over against socialization and argues in essence that we are socialized into the church, we should be skeptical. Groome, like C. E. Nelson, vastly underestimates the power of socialization to quash transformation and overestimates the power of critical reflection to liberate socialized communities.

(2) In this connection, Groome's Shared *Praxis* approach does not sufficiently account for the dynamics of authoritarianism (as well as other humanly generated lifestyles) working in many religious contexts. Groome's own Roman Catholic context is especially vulnerable in this regard. Groome should acknowledge more fully how extremely difficult it is for anyone to seek and to enable lasting and true transformation that goes against the word of the church on so many matters.

(3) Groome's emphasis on critical thinking does not pay sufficient enough attention to the constructive power of word and language that other approaches emphasize. Groome's theory calls out, in my judgment, for a greater and more explicit emphasis on creativity as central to transformational process. Groome acknowledged in a later article that he underemphasized the significance of *poiesis* for enabling imagination and for empowering the church's appropriation of her Story and Vision.[53]

---

52. Ibid., 207–34.

53. Editor's Note: Loder does not give the reference here for this later article. After looking for it without success, I contacted Dr. Groome to see if he could help me locate

(4) Finally, the unacknowledged Teacher in Groome's theory is the Holy Spirit. Since the Spirit is not acknowledged as such, one is led to believe that Christian religious education is the work of human agency. But human agency, as we have discussed it, can only facilitate adaptation to the status quo, subsumed under the power of socialization. But if, as we have argued, the Holy Spirit's action is the central dynamism and integrity of Christian education, this pneumatological source should not only be much more firmly acknowledged but also made thoroughly explicit and integrated into any theory or activity called Christian.

## (V) CONCLUSION

In light of my concern for the Spirit, let me conclude with some additional critical comments on Groome's approach that might lead to further discussion about the Spirit's action in Christian education.

(a) *The Spirit in Four Dimensions.* Attention needs to be given to the human spirit's redemptive transformation by the Holy Spirit as the power behind personal storytelling and the telling of the Christian "Story." The human spirit must be awakened to know the Christian "Story" and the person and/or the community's own story in the theological dimensions the Holy Spirit communicates. Christ's "Story" and "Vision" are four-dimensional, and this four-dimensionality can only be known in the Spirit. Only the Spirit has the power to communicate theological reality as it impinges on the two-dimensional reality socialization claims to govern.

(b) *Testimony and Prayer.* The church's "Story" must include not merely its past and future, but its present. Acts of prayer and self-implicated testimony of the reality of Christ should be intrinsic to the presentation of the church's "Story" or "Vision" if they are to make existential sense. Therefore, teachers as well as learners should be invited to witness to their present experience of the church's "Story" and "Vision." Only through personal witness and passionate prayer will the community experience the present dynamism of the logic of the Spirit at work in their midst.

(c) *Continuity of Purpose.* The order of the moments of Shared *Praxis* may be mixed and turned in and around, so the bases may be covered in any number of ways. But for the sake of preserving the integrity of the transformative process, Groome needs a stronger emphasis on the continuity of

---

it. He did not recall writing an essay on *poiesis*.

the human spirit's creative power to engage the shared *praxis* hermeneutics passionately toward its intended result.

(d) Shared *Praxis* moves toward decision, which is necessary. But this movement toward decision finds its true and liberating context in worship. The church's "Story" and "Vision" are not just points of view to be incorporated somehow for one's personal benefit or comfort. Worship provides the only context in which the larger orders of the meaning and intelligibility of human existence, narrated and imagined in the church's "Story" and "Vision," can be properly disclosed. Worship is the context in which the church tells its own "Story" and envisions its own destiny.

We have emphasized throughout this study that the source of the human spirit's creativity and freedom lies in its transparent relationship to the presence of Christ through the Holy Spirit. All human action begins and ends in the unredeemed human spirit unless and until it is redeemed and transformed according to the logic of the Spirit. We now turn to elaborate why worship is the only fitting context in which the redemptive transformation of human existence by the Spirit of God can be known.

# 11

# Theory

## Climax in Worship

## (I) INTRODUCTION: A SHORT REVIEW OF KEY CONCEPTS AND WORDS

THE BOOK OF HEBREWS portrays Jesus's life as an act of worship in which he is both priest and the sacrificial lamb. Accordingly, the aim of Christian education is for every human life to become an act of worship through the Spirit of Christ working in and beyond us. But between our present life and this aim falls the shadow of uncertainty. How do we come to participate in Christ's Spirit and follow the pattern of his life as an act of worship? Whatever means we find to this end must be in keeping with the nature of Spirit. The appropriate means are in fact a foretaste of the ultimate end. Teaching requires that we recognize that the high calling *to* teach can never be considered apart from the question of *how* we teach—i.e., what is the proper spirit through which we exercise this high calling?

We have emphasized throughout this study that Christian education takes place in the dynamic rationality between two conflicting forces—*socialization* and *transformation*. Basically, the purpose of socialization is equilibrium, so that the process of education governed by socialization preserves at all costs the desire to reduce tension and maintain predetermined adaptational patterns in human existence. The purpose of transformation, as the word suggests, is the emergence of new essential forms. The process of transformation is governed by the desire to discover hidden orders of meaning within a given frame of reference that has the power to redefine and/or reconstruct that frame of reference. Instead of adapting to dehumanizing patterns of society, we have attempted to explicate how *Spiritus Creator* works within the socialization-transformation conflicts (a form of oppression) to disclose to us new insights, releasing the creative energy of the human spirit, and firing us back into the world as bearers of a redeemed creation.

Thus, although transformation and socialization differ qualitatively in principle and move towards radically different ends, the interplay between these two forces can be dynamically creative, yielding new insights for Christian teaching and for the development of a Christian lifestyle. Clearly an encounter with the Holy Spirit engenders redemptive transformation in persons and communities. Yet the argument of this book is that all transformation, including redemptive transformation, never exists in a separate realm where socialization is not present or is completely obliterated. Transformational understanding of human existence can never discard socialization, as if that were even possible, but must always presuppose it. In this study we have presupposed and elaborated the imposing power of socialization so that the interplay between socialization and transformation comes into focus as a four-dimensional conflict generative of four-dimensional insights and actions. Theologically speaking, transformation exercises marginal control over socialization in the creation of a redemptive lifestyle only when the Spirit upholds the transformational potential of human existence, personal and corporate, according to the logic of the Spirit.

Part of our endeavor in the book has been to discern what certain words mean. For example, *transformation* has become quite popular in Christian education theorizing. Yet paradoxically, this usage often shows up in the proposals by proponents defending the redemptive power of socialization.[1] In these proposals, *transformation* refers simply to change in a positive direction. But our development of a theological understanding of transformation means much more than any positive change. We illustrate this *more* by referring to the Greek meaning of two different words for change. The first word, *morphe*, refers to a substantive change in the essential nature of something. The second word, *schema*, refers to changes in the aesthetic or perceptual form of something. As we might expect, the transforming work of the Holy Spirit moves us toward deep change, giving

---

1. Editor's Note: This sense that the word *transformation* had been co-opted by proponents of socialization lay behind Loder's encouragement to add the adjective "redemptive" to the title of his Festschrift. See Wright and Kuentzel, *Redemptive*, 9, note 11.

us a new identity and re-creating every aspect of human action—biological, psychological, social, and cultural—a change of *morphe*.

*Creativity* is another word we have sought to understand. Unaided human ingenuity can propagate significant changes, as we have seen, for instance, in the explosion of technological innovation that marks our time. In many ways, the human spirit is a loose cannon of creativity. But mere creativity is a two-edged sword. We can invent vaccines to cure diseases, or methods of germ warfare to spread them. While creative transformations of the human spirit are abundant, the purpose of Christian education is to engender *redemptive* transformations in which the human spirit cooperates with the Holy Spirit to create new forms of life. Thus we have spoken of a "transformation of transformations" in which the transformational capacities of the human spirit become vivified, enlarged, and reconstituted in relation to the Holy Spirit. In the school of the Spirit, all our creativity is offered to God, and thus worship becomes a way of life. Our human spirits testify with the Holy Spirit that we are children of God (Rom. 8:16).

## (II) WORSHIP AS PARADIGM FOR TRANSFORMATIONAL CHRISTIAN EDUCATION

In conclusion, then, as the climatic claim of our theory, its "organizing principle" in which all parts work together in the Spirit, we focus on worship. Worship serves as the paradigmatic form of an education that is four-dimensional, transformational, and christocentric—i.e., a form of education whose purpose is to create and exemplify a Christian style of life that becomes and ongoing act of worship. To move us into this discussion, since no educational theory would be complete without an understanding of learning theory, I will begin the discussion with a brief introduction to three types of learning. This exposition culminates with a discussion of a fourth type of learning that includes all others and that is uniquely fostered by the liturgy of the Word. This approach affirms the ancient Latin tradition *lex orandi, lex credendi*—in which a necessary reciprocity exists between how we pray (*lex orandi*) and how we believe (*lex credendi*). Thus, in worship what we believe is learned and appropriated in a way that both replicates the basic pattern of belief and brings it to a culminating celebration.[2]

---

2. There is no attempt here to settle the long-standing issue of whether prayer or belief is the norm for the other. It is to say that educationally they cannot properly be separated or in contradiction with each other.

## (A) The Four Types of Learning Theory

I present here a summary of four types of learning theory: classical conditioning, operant conditioning, symbolic learning, and paradigm shift.

### (1) Classical conditioning

Regarding *classical conditioning*, everyone knows about Pavlov's dog. But only certain beginning psychology students know about Zimbardo in the dorm shower. Standing in the dorm shower Zimbardo quickly learned by classical conditioning to get out of the shower quickly when he heard the conditioned stimulus. The conditioned stimulus was not a bell, as in the case of Pavlov's dog, but the sound of the toilet flushing upstairs. One or two scalding changes in the water temperature were sufficient to condition an automatic alert reaction to the sound of the distant flushing. Dogs conditioned to salivate and Zimbardo conditioned to go on automatic alert are just two examples of this lower order of learning through which we acquire many of our prereflective reactions to the world.[3] Social psychologist Roger Brown hypothesizes that given certain instinctual endowments (fight, flight, eat, sleep, excrete), we learn most of our autonomic emotional responses in this manner. Consequently, to some extent we all depend on this kind of learning to survive. Classical conditioning can be diagrammed as follows:

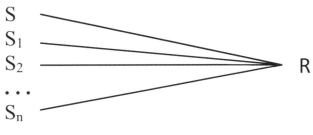

*Classic Conditioning (Pavlov, Zimbardo)*

### (2) Operant or respondent conditioning

The second kind of learning is *operant conditioning*, which B. F. Skinner made famous and in some ways notorious. The principle is that rewarded

---

3. Editor's Note: This example of classical condition is found in Zimbardo, *Psychology*, 95–96.

behavior is repeated. More specifically, if a new desired behavior is rewarded on a certain schedule, which includes appropriate times of nonreward, then this new pattern of action will become entrenched and old patterns discarded. By this method pigeons can be taught to play ping-pong, chimpanzees can learn to use symbols in a limited fashion, and some kinds of psychopathology (like hyperactivity in children) can be brought under control.

Working in Skinner's laboratories at Harvard, I was amazed at the power and mystique of this learning theory in operation. Many of his laboratory assistants actually believed that Dr. Skinner could, with his theory, solve all of the problems of war. I heard many testify to the effect: "If we can just condition everybody into peaceful activity and peaceful responses, there will be no more war." He wrote a book titled *Walden II* in which the design for a community controlled by classical conditioning could be constructed—and indeed, such a community does exist! But the demeaning of human nature implicit in this system makes it unsatisfactory as a total explanation of life as Skinner would want it. The following vignette may illustrate the point.

One fellow I knew in Skinner's lab was so completely devoted (conditioned!) to behaviorism that he interacted with his wife in accord with the theory's principles. He owned a Volkswagen Beetle. As you know, the little bugs were so tightly constructed that to get the door shut, you had to roll down the window. Every time this man's wife got into the car on the passenger's side, she forgot to roll down the window before shutting the door. Consequently, she would have to shut the door twice. One day, however, she did remember to open the window. When she "acted right," her Skinner-trained husband responded quickly with a tangible reinforcement by tossing her a quarter. How's that for a formula for a happy marriage!

As a further illustration, a student of mine once confessed that he sometimes used behavior modification in his church school by giving out candy for memorized Scripture verses. He didn't realize, as Skinner often doesn't, that we learn as much from *how* we teach as from *what* we teach. Still operant conditioning is a powerful learning device. We do learn this way, even though it must not be allowed to dominate or absorb all learning, as Skinner wants to have it. But we accept Roger Brown's hypothesis that given certain innate behavioral tendencies (grasping, sucking, etc.), we learn most of our habits of action and behavior, usually under the direction of the central nervous system, through operant conditioning. We diagram this type of learning as follows:

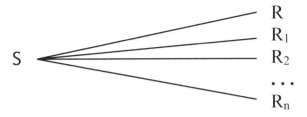

***Operant Conditioning (B. F. Skinner)***

## (3) Symbolic Learning

A third type of learning is what the Dutch philosopher Cornelius van Peursen, who helped Harvey Cox write *The Secular City* and who gave the Warfield Lectures at Princeton in 1976, calls *symbolic learning*. In essence, symbolic learning refers to our ability to construct and appropriate meaningful *gestalts* or whole constellations of things.[4] Included in this form of learning are sign-*gestalt* learning, imitation, identification, and other types of social learning. In symbolic learning, one grasps whole configurations of meaning from a single part or single stimulus. One may sense the implicate order of the whole in the particular specimen, like, for example, in holograms that contain the whole in the parts. *Gestalt* learning moves from the part to the whole, and the whole in turn reciprocates, calling up the parts and giving them meaning in relation to the whole. What is most exciting about this sort of learning occurs when someone realizes that s/he learns this way. For example, in the famous Helen Keller episode cited earlier, in which she learned the sign for water, what excited Helen the most was not that she learned the sign. What excited her most was that in learning the sign for water she could now symbolically construct her entire world. In other words, her power to learn as human spirit burst into the open and thrust her into a meaningful world.

Learning symbolically—and learning that one learns this way—is a unique human phenomenon. As we noted earlier, Pannenberg points out

4. Editor's Note: Loder wrongly wrote that van Peursen gave "the Stone Lectures a few years ago." He actually gave the Warfield Lectures, in 1976. C. A. van Peursen (1920–1996) was an eminent Dutch philosopher who wrote extensively on creativity and the learning process. His five Warfield Lectures were called *Creative Capitulations*. See Princeton Theological Seminary's listening library (http://diglib.ptsem.edu/). Loder apparently also read van Peursen's essay "Creativity as Learning Process," 157–85. Even his diagrams in this section seem to have been inspired, at least in part, by this essay (159–61).

that human nature is born deficiently programmed for its environment, but is endowed with an extraordinary mass of cerebral cortex and its synapses for constructing one's own environment and ways of relating to it. By contrast, a Sphex wasp is programmed for action in a given environment and only *appears* to be thinking. The preprogrammed wasp lays its eggs, then flies off to sting and paralyze a grasshopper. It brings its victim to the threshold of the hole, goes in and checks the eggs, returns and brings the grasshopper inside for the newly hatched wasps to eat later. If, however, a researcher moves the grasshopper while the wasp is checking the eggs, the wasp upon discovering the grasshopper lying at the side of the hole does not *think* to simply push the grasshopper into the hole and leave. No, the wasp mechanically repeats the programmed procedure. She drags the grasshopper to the threshold, goes in and repeats the process.

By contrast, symbolic learning is *ecstasis*. The symbolic learner stands outside the self in such a way as to allow recognition of the lived world as a symbolically constructed human invention. Symbolic learning becomes the spirited and risky act of representing the world to ourselves and responding to those representations. When we realize that we can and are involved in this process, learning becomes a challenging, exciting, and sometimes frightening undertaking. For example, as I have already mentioned, when Paulo Freire taught the migrant workers of Chile to read and write, it dawned on them that they could symbolically construct their lived world. They gave ecstatic expression to their new sense of empowerment when they asked, "Now what will we do?" Of course, this realization that the world is changeable underlies all hopes for revolution and, almost inevitably, Freire indeed was exiled from Chile for his initiatives involving symbolic learning.

On a more strictly classroom level, Eleanor Duckworth of the Piagetian tradition, in a memorable essay titled "The Having of Wonderful Ideas," argued how important it is to allow children to accept their own ideas and to work them through. We must not give children a set of intellectual ideas and tasks already formulated and self-contained, to be used like a bag of contentless tools. Rather, once they discover something real to think about, we must encourage them to play out the transformational potential in them that wants to know "whole." Moreover, wonderful ideas do not have to look wonderful to the outside world in order to engender creative acts of intelligence. The subjectivity of the learner generates the awareness that intelligence is for the creation and composition of one's world.

Alfred North Whitehead calls the realization that we symbolically construct the world "the supreme human possibility." Commenting on the university (comments that I believe could as easily apply to any school at almost any level of literacy), Whitehead wrote:

The justification for a university (or any institution designed for distinctively human learning) is that it preserves the connection between knowledge and the zest for life, by uniting the young and the old in the imaginative consideration of learning. The university imparts information, but it imparts it imaginatively. At least this is the function it should perform for society. A university which fails in this respect has no reason for existence. This atmosphere of excitement, arising from imaginative considerations, transforms knowledge. A fact is no longer a bare fact; it is invested with all the possibilities. It is no longer a burden on the memory; it is energizing as the poet of our dreams, and as the architect of our purposes.[5]

That powerful statement articulates the promise of implicate, *gestalt,* or symbolic learning, that quality of learning in which it becomes clear to us that all knowledge exists for the imaginative construction and reconstruction of the world. The *gestalt* approach to learning—our distinctly human capacity for knowing that we learn in this way, and our intention that it happens this way in educational settings—diagrams as follows:

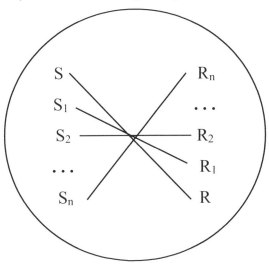

**Symbolic Learning (van Pearsen)**

Note briefly that symbol and symbol system combine all sorts of stimuli and responses into a unified *gestalt.* For example, in a child's identification with a parent, both autonomic and central system responses are involved—conditioning and reinforcement in a larger whole. Of course the

5. Whitehead, *Aims of Education,* 93.

imperialists of the conditioning schools try to break all this down into stimulus-response bonds, but the *gestalt* learner counters that stimulus-response is already a *gestalt*. Eventually the debate leads to a kind of standoff. As a consequence, the controversy is not worth our time here.

## (4) Learning as Paradigm Shift

Instead, let us go on to the fourth type of learning also singled out by van Peursen, but more popularly articulated for psychology by Jean Piaget in his study of cognitive growth and the stage transition process, and for the history of science by Thomas Kuhn in his famous study *The Structure of Scientific Revolutions*. We characterize this form of learning as a *paradigm shift* because when this form of holistic learning takes hold, a whole new constellation of meaning emerges within a field of study, usually from the mind of a key investigator. As a consequence, the data within any given field that had been organized under some previously accepted structure of meaning (paradigm) is not falsified but given new significance and meaning. Einstein's revolutionary understanding of relativity with its famous $E=mc^2$ formula is a prime example of paradigm shift. The new paradigm of relativity replaced the Newtonian paradigm of classic physics. Of course, since Newton's observations retain their validity in our slow-moving day-to-day existence, most of us still live with a Newtonian worldview. Be that as it may, the meaning of that validity has changed, and vast new fields of research have opened up because the paradigm has shifted.

Paradigmatic learning occurs through the spontaneous emergence of a new grammar or logic by which every previous symbol and symbol system is simultaneously reconstructed. In personality transformation, for example, Jungian analysis seeks to induce paradigmatic change. The ego (considered prior to analysis the center of the personality) is replaced by an archetype of the Self. The ego retains its reality-testing function, but now it does so as an agent of the Self, not merely as an agency in the service of adaptation.

A similar shift happens in the Christian transformation of personality, when Christ becomes the center of the personality displacing but not eliminating the ego. Christ-centered personhood reconstellates the entire personality and its relation to reality. Devoted Jungians argue that Christ is a symbol of the Self, but in doing so they confuse the orders of knowing and being. If anything the Jungian view of the Self may serve as a transcendental and archetypical symbol of the ontological reality of Christ. No one learns Christ by means of the archetype unless Christ transforms the archetype itself into an iconic vehicle for the communication of his nature and personal presence. Thus one claims the dialectical identity of which we spoke earlier. One says with Saint Paul, "*I, yet not I, but Christ.*" Dialectical identity is a familiar hallmark of the convicted person. Jesus said, "*I, yet not I, but the Father.*" The prophets said, in essence, "*I, yet not I, but Yahweh*" is speaking to you. This paradigmatic form of learning transforms all previous, as well as all subsequent, learning. It may be diagrammed as follows:

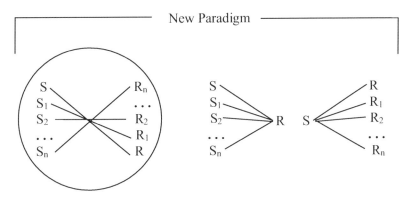

***Paradigm Shift (T. Kuhn, M. Polanyi)***

These then are the four basic types of learning: (1) classical conditioning, (2) respondent or operant conditioning, (3) symbolic construction, and (4) paradigm shift. I suggest that this last type of learning, paradigm shift, is of paramount importance for our consideration of transformation in Christian education, even though it is probably the least understood.

Some of you may have recognized that a theological transposition of paradigm shift inheres in the Reformed tradition's thinking and practice of the worship of God, particularly in the liturgy of the Word. Unfortunately, we oftentimes design and experience the worship service as the embodiment of the other types of learning. We may design worship to make persons feel better at the autonomic level of awareness. We may design worship to make them feel worse if they need to cry and come to terms with their guilt. We may design worship, if we are skillful enough, to manage many emotional sides of persons to accomplish certain outcomes. In doing so, however, we think of and practice the liturgy as if it were a form of classical conditioning.

We treat worship as a form of respondent conditioning when we condition regular church attendance with rewards, like pleasant socialization opportunities at coffee hours. The idea here is to make church attendance a habit. Now we may affirm these kinds of motives for habituating worship at one level. But they have little to do with what we as the church are distinctively created to be. Even if worship becomes a skillful manipulation of Christian symbolism, such ways of habituating the faith remain unsatisfactory theologically. Such efforts may give rise to repeated liturgical "revivals" without any idea of what constitutes progress in the revival of Christian faithfulness. Congregations may switch from learning organ to learning guitar, but the significance of the liturgy must go deeper if all this activity avoids degenerating into matters of taste and power. I am reminded of Søren Kierkegaard's ironic account of the geese that waddled to church on Sunday morning. During the service, they heard the goose preacher proclaim in eloquent oratory that they could fly, even soar! After the service they all waddled home. The conditioning approach to worship not only remains impotent but makes God into a fool whose Word simply gaggles on about something all of us well-socialized geese know can never happen.

An act of worship, like any other transformational pattern, will indeed include all these forms of learning. But the church at its most profound designs the liturgy to let the hidden order of meaning—ultimate meaning in this case—emerge to challenge all previous frames of knowledge or contexts or explanations or conditioning. In order to help this to happen—to prepare the way of the Lord—worship must be structured so as to allow God to speak God's Word to us for our redemption and for the redemption of the world. This redemptive aim is exactly what the liturgy of the Word is designed to do in the Reformed tradition.

## (B) The Liturgy of the Word as the Context for Learning Theological Language

In the Reformed liturgy of the Word, we employ symbols that are uniquely theological. That is, they are designed to point to a four-dimensional reality. We also design and employ a structure of worship to bring the church into a listening posture before the Word of God. Recall our discussion in chapter 8 of theological symbols as doubly intentional, embracing an inherent negation of the ordinary world so as to point to a heightened sense of meaning that implicitly reaches beyond imagination. Thus, there is love, yet not like any ordinary love but *agape* love, that comes from God. There is grace, yet not like any ordinary but the grace that God bestows. There is peace, yet not as the world gives peace but *"the peace that passes understanding."*

This theological language is also self-involving language, enthymemic in nature. An enthymeme is a syllogism in which a major premise is missing. You must add your own participation to make it work. For example, *"If you know how to give good gifts . . ."* You participate in theological language by allowing it to point beyond the specific referent to an ultimate referent. Thus, faith becomes the major premise for learning and speaking four-dimensional faith language meaningfully.[6]

We must realize that theological language does not derive from marketplace language. When the profane fellow, newly converted, "felt so damned blessed," his testimony points to its source beyond the marketplace. Here the knower is partly dependent on a tacit awareness that the theological language he used, "blessed," bears a four-dimensional depth from beyond all social constructions of reality. Theological language points to a different world from that which socialized patterns lets us recognize. However, by itself theological language may not be enough to create the reality of the world it signifies, especially when used out of context, so to speak. The context in which theological language finds its true meaning is worship. Worship, as a four-dimensional context for the *koinonia*, is the paradigm case for the use of theological language.

To be sure, theological language may be used to argue out issues in the classroom, to write a church dogmatics, to engage in educational catechesis, as well as many other places. But in many of these contexts theology does not get a hearing. As professor Richard Fenn pointed out in his book *Liturgies and Trials*, theological or doxological language is not trial language. So wherever a trial is taking place—in courts or in schoolrooms—theological language cannot be heard. Contexts of trial and testing remain tone deaf to theological language. But, of course, it is not impossible that the deaf may indeed hear. At times the society and culture *will* hear—as when Martin Luther King Jr. inspired our culture to listen to theological language during the civil rights movement. Nevertheless, the paradigm case for theological language is worship, or more specifically, the liturgy of the Word. And the power of that liturgy is to evoke in us an awareness of God's spiritual presence and the hearing of God's Word among us.

## (C) Four Phases of the Liturgy of the Word

How does this form of worship supply the context for appropriate use of theological language? In his unpublished dissertation, John McClure describes four basic phases in the classical form of the "liturgy of the Word."[7]

---

6. Editor's Note: We should keep in mind here that for Loder, the convictional pattern of redemptive transformation in human experience that he discussed in chapter 5 engenders in the convicted worshiper a redemptive transformation of theological language and symbol. See Loder, "Fashioning," especially 194–203.

7. McClure, "Preaching."

He discerned these four phases through his exhaustive historical and structural analysis of eighteen forms of the liturgy of the Word in church history. Thus, these four enduring structural components in some respect express the historical wisdom of the worshiping people of God. In the liturgy, God's Word exposes the unreality of our everyday speech in which the language of testing, trial, and temptation prevail, while drawing the people into a revelation of their identity as a *koinonia* community. This movement involves four radical linguistic shifts, according to McClure.

(1) *First*, the liturgy draws worshipers out of the marketplace language of the world into the presence of divine language, a language that speaks from God to people and to God from people. The "call to worship," "confession," and "absolution" are familiar expressions of this first and basic linguistic phase. The minister or priest mediates this movement. That is, the minister mediates the move from the language of the market place to the language of worship by speaking in theological symbols. S/he articulates those liturgical acts, which, in theological substance, move worshipers from the two-dimensional reality of the marketplace into the four-dimensional reality of the worship of God.

That this linguistic world is very different from our daily world was born in on me by an experience I had at the YMCA when I was still playing squash. I happened to mention to my friend in the locker room that I wanted to know "what God was doing." Suddenly, the place stopped, the lockers no longer banged, and everything became still. It was like I had said, "E. F. Hutton is my broker . . ."[8] So this sense of God's speaking is the linguistic impact of the first liturgical move. But this first liturgical move, its mediator and mediation, must yield to another.

(2) Building on the first movement, the *second* brings the worshipers into the linguistic world of the Scripture from which, remarkably, we hear not second-order divine language but the Word of God spoken directly. The mediator here is the Bible and its capacity under the power of the Holy Spirit to become the faithful bearer of the Word of God. The essential shift in this movement takes place when the written text becomes the spoken Word, not of the reader but of God. When a person speaks disclosing him-/ herself toward you, you are brought into the whole realm of their mind and consciousness. Similarly, when the Bible becomes speech, the Word of God written becomes the iconic bearer of living Word. Thus, we enter a strange and wonderful realm—the mind of Christ through the Bible.

8. Editor's Note: The reference here is to a popular television advertisement for EF Hutton financial services, in which one person in conversation with another in a public place began, "My broker is E. F. Hutton . . ."—and all of the people in the room leaned in to listen to an oracle from on high.

(3) The *third* movement, most scandalous of all, makes ordinary language—the very language one presumably left behind in the marketplace—the bearer of God's Word. The mediator here is the sermon, the Word of God preached. Here, God reclaims the marketplace as the arena of God's action through God's own Word mediated in common human language. As the tradition testifies, "The preaching of the Word of God is the Word of God."[9]

(4) *Fourth*, the reception of the Word of God in ordinary speech gives the forms of ordinary life a new capacity to become the bearers of the extraordinary claim of God's Word. People gain the capacity to see their ordinary existence as bearers of an extraordinary identity and mission. The community becomes a four-dimensional people. We have called this people the *koinonia*, the corporate version of the four dimensions inherent in the language of theology used in worship.

At this point in the classical tradition of the liturgy a unique move was made (one which we have lost), by which the *koinonia* began its mission to the world. That is, the worshipers dismissed all noncommunicants and began intercession and prayer for the world. In effect, the newly identified people become mediators in an effort to reinstate the original movement in the liturgy from two-dimensional to four-dimensional reality—but now for the whole world. Acting as ministers or priests for the whole world, *koinonia* becomes the mediator signifying new life is possible. Thus, the liturgy of the Word implicitly and paradigmatically signifies a movement of the whole world into worshipful conformity to the Word of God.

The liturgy does not signify and embody the learning of new life, however, because it followed a certain form, or because the service was well performed, or because the pastor delivered a well-constructed, three-point sermon. As marks of a learning event, these concerns signify superficial and deficient learning. The liturgy works redemptively when it discloses and celebrates the hidden order of all creation and redemption into which we are baptized, which is the pattern of Christ. Indeed, the liturgy of the Word is a definitive expression of the pattern of Christ. Geoffrey Wainwright and other liturgical theologians have identified this pattern as the irreducible *sui generis* core of worship.[10] Let us look more closely at this pattern to see how it works.

---

9. Editor's Note: I added this phrase from the Second Helvetic Confession, 1.5004, 77, to affirm Loder's point.

10. See for example, Wainwright, *Doxology*, 69–79.

## (III) THE PATTERN OF CHRIST
## AS THE LIVING GRAMMAR OF THE LITURGY

The pattern is developed extensively in the book of Hebrews, but summarily in Phil 2:5–11, the so-called *kenosis* passage. This passage reads in part:

> *Have this mind among yourselves, which is yours in Christ Jesus, who, though he was in the form of God, did not count equality with God a thing to be grasped, but emptied himself, taking the form of a servant, being born in the likeness of men. And being found in human form he humbled himself and became obedient unto death, even death on a cross. Therefore God has highly exalted him and bestowed on him the name which is above every name, that at the name of Jesus every knee should bow, in heaven and on earth and under the earth, and every tongue confess that Jesus Christ is Lord to the glory of God the Father.* (RSV)

The church at Philippi was much beloved, but it was not without some difficulties. Thus, in chapter 2, Paul urges them to have the mind of Christ. To encourage them, he borrows (or perhaps writes) an ancient hymn, the *Carmen Christi* ("Hymn of Christ"). I believe an examination of certain aspects of this text will illuminate the pattern of Christ essential to worship. For this examination I will use of Ralph Martin's book *Carmen Christi*, an exhaustive history of the interpretation of this text.

*First,* note that the text sets down a pattern. The hymn celebrates little or nothing about the content of Jesus's ministry, who Jesus was, what he did, or what he taught. All this content comes from the four gospel accounts. The hymn sets forth only the essential pattern, setting forth a basic grammar of the Christian life revealed in Christ. As in speech, nouns and verbs are essential, and you can write volumes so long as you don't break out of the grammatical patterns. True, some *avant-garde* poetry may break rules, but even this poetry has to presuppose rules to get the desired effect. In music, there is a basic melody out of which a whole range of variations may be derived. I once read in the *New York Times* that someone had extracted by factor analysis the essence of Bach. Philosopher Susanne Langer claims that there is a basic structure to music from which all compositions come.[11] In Christianity, the basic pattern is the pattern of Christ, and all creation is its context—from creation out of nothing, to redemption via the cross and

---

11. Editor's Note: Loder does not give the specific reference to Langer's claim. He may have had in mind chapter 8 of *Philosophy in a New Key*, 204–45, or her treatise on the systematic theory of art titled *Feeling and Form*.

through the harrowing of hell to the final consummation. The pattern of Christ is the grammar of God's action upon and within creation.

*Second*, the pattern is already in you, already a part of each one of us who make up the *koinonia*. It is the pattern you already have in Christ Jesus. The grammar of Christ brings ultimate meaning for our lives. Paul's letter, addressed to the beloved church of Philippi, reminds them of this pattern as they sang this hymn, presumably as a part of their baptismal rites. So Paul admonishes, as the King James Version translates it, "*Let this mind be in you . . .*" That is, let this mind, which is already in you, be formative for the way you are before God and toward one another. Notice further in the same connections that this pattern is not merely something we sing, not just something we say or do, but it describes who we essentially *are* in Christ. If baptism gives us our identity in Christ, then in baptism we die with Christ, and we are raised with him. The same Spirit who brought you to faith in Christ conforms your existence to the pattern of his existence.

*Third*, this pattern also describes, by implication, who we are *not*. The structural opposite or antithesis recognizes this pattern as an intentional reversal of the Adamic disaster. Adam tried to raise himself, but fell! Christ by contrast rose by first falling. This contrast between Adam and Christ can be diagrammed as follows:

| *Adam* | *Christ* |
|---|---|
| Made in the Divine Image | Being the image of God |
| thought it a prize to be grasped at to be as God; | thought it *not* a prize to be grasped at to be as God; |
| and aspired to a reputation; | and made himself of no reputation; |
| and *spurned* being God's servant | and *took upon* him the form of a servant |
| seeking to be in the likeness of *God*; | and was made in the likeness of *men*; |
| and being found in fashion as a man (of dust, now doomed) | God (Jesus) being found in fashion as a man (Rom 8:3) |
| he *exalted* himself and became *disobedient* unto death | He *humbled* himself and became *obedient* unto death |
| he was condemned and *disgraced* | God highly *exalted* him and gave him the name and rank of Lord. |

**Adam and Christ**[12]

12. Martin, *Carmen Christi*, 163-64

Thus, the pattern of Christ is here set over against a pattern of self-deception and self-destruction. Here we can see the essential negation of God implicit in the pattern of socialization– obsession with achievement, authoritarian control, protean evasion, or oppressive acquiescence—that was discussed at some length in previous chapters. Implicitly, obedience to the one nullifies the other.

*Fourth*, the crux of this pattern of Christ involves a double twist, which can be discerned and focused by looking at two key Greek words used in this text. Earlier interpreters such as C. H. Dodd made more of this twist than later ones, but structural hermeneutics helps us to revive this important distinction. The words are *morphe* and *schema*.

| | | |
|---|---|---|
| Morphe | = | essential form |
| Schema | = | schematic form, the false perception of the true form |

### *Morphe/Schema Relation*

In the *Carmen Christi*, Christ is *morphe*, but he is perceived to be made in the likeness (*schema*) of humankind. This misperception leads to his crucifixion.

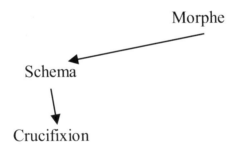

### *Christ Perceived as Schema*

We already illustrated the power of false perception (*schema*) in our discussion of the material of Don Barnhouse and the schematic world of television. Recall that Barnhouse worked with a famous television news personality. People came to the television station specifically to see this newscaster in person. But they always ended up watching the monitor, not the real man during the show's taping. Thus, we create worlds to our liking and for our use, but they inevitably generate self-destructive lifestyles such as those identified in previous chapters. Of course, we always have. What is new in our technoinformational age is the facility and power that television and other media give us to construct these schematic worlds. Yet Christ submitted himself to this schematic world then and he continues to do so now, so that we might discover the true difference between appearance and reality and choose for the latter over the former.

*Fifth*, the corresponding twist on the other side is that in raising Jesus Christ from the dead God definitively reversed the *morphe-schema* relationship. His ascension and glorification reveals that his name (nature) reigns over all.

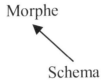

Morphe

Schema

### *Morphe/Schema Reversed*

Note here that the schematic false perception that distorts and crucifies Christ also becomes the source of death to the self, so its reversal is simultaneously freedom to see Christ as he is and to experience the release of his new life in us. Torn free from our distorted perception, Christ can now be seen for who he really is, even by those who are *"under the earth."* The astounding implication here is that Christ has reversed all history in the so-called harrowing of hell. We are liberated to live out the pattern of Christ, secure in the knowledge that no past bondage can hold us. No kinship ties, or developmental or genetic schema can determine the essential form our relationship to God takes. In turn, our intimate relationship with God changes all the rest of our human experience. The result, therefore, is a complete transformation in which all things made through Christ are returned to him. This transformation can be drawn as follows:

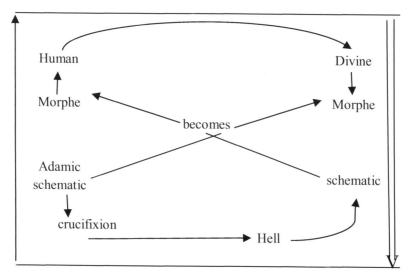

***Transformation Completed***

The conflictual convergence between *morphe* and *schema* reinstates the crux of Christian education, and calls us to "*work out our salvation with fear and trembling.*" According to the pattern of Christ, this redemptive reversal of the *morphe/schema* relation is the decisive condition for transformation through faith that is unfolding in us through the Spirit.

Note then that the pattern of Christ functions as the underlying grammar of the liturgy. The liturgy is designed to break down schematic assumptions of the marketplace and transform them via an ever-deepening participation in our conformation to Christ and his pattern for the redemption of the world. As such, Christ compels us to embrace the limits of our existence at the margins of our ego-structured behavior. The claims of the liturgy against our two-dimensional worlds enact the merciful judgment of God at the center of our confession. This confession cannot become habit. We must learn to see the pattern in all the depth that it implies. Then, the forgiveness can be as holy as it is supposed to be.

Likewise the Word of God is not just the word of human beings, because it is Holy. Only by recognizing this holiness does the miracle of preaching take hold of us and accomplish in us the astonishing thing it seeks to do. Moving through the extremities of the four dimensions, from Void to Holy, we are thrust by the Spirit into a liminal state—the threshold of the ego boundaries—where we may be informed and transformed by the Word of God to us. To worship as these theological symbols provoke us to do presses us to the four-dimensional limits of our existence again and again in order to recover and embody our identity in Christ, which is "new every morning." The Spirit works through this pattern to create in us and among us a Christian style of life because, given this pattern, each act of worship reenacts the life of Christ, whose whole life, as tradition has it, was an act of worship.

As McClure points out, the basic pattern of transformation is embedded in the liturgy of each of the four movements. Four times during the liturgy, the pattern is enacted. Thus, each movement is a transformation of the preceding condition or conditions, where the whole is designed to bring the worshipers into the position in which they can intercede for the world. In effect, by the liturgy of the Word, the grammar of Christ emerges for the people of God, putting everything else, even the whole world, "*under his feet.*"

## (IV) CONCLUSION: WORKING OUT OUR SALVATION

The pattern we have described here is not primarily socialization, but primarily transformation. The holistic pattern of Christ, which is embedded in us through our baptism into his nature, emerges for the worshiper as the configurations of a photograph image emerge from the negative exposure by being repeatedly immersed in an appropriate chemical process. Socialization and related forms of learning are all involved, but they are all gathered up under the larger pattern of Christ, which transforms us, and all creation, into the life of God. All learning is designed to give rise to the new grammar in the liturgy. In turn, then, all such learning needs reinterpretation in light of the vision of Christ, according to whose nature all things are destined for redemptive transformation into the glory of God.

The ultimate point about this transformation is not that we go out and live better lives. Rather, the people of the liturgy discover who they are as the *koinonia* of God and continue to intercede for the world against the world's proclivities toward self-delusion and self-destruction. Such transformation in the Spirit is not an automatic process, reducible to a technique. But if faithfully celebrated in the hearts and minds of the people, the underlying pattern of Christ as *Logos* (Word) made flesh increasingly becomes the key to the ultimate intelligibility of the universe and our place in it. In and through this pattern we worship the very One "*according to whom all things have been made,*" who continues to transform and re-create all things.

Grounded in this ultimate intelligibility, individuals learn to break from their socialization milieus and to act according to ultimate Truth, the *morphe* of Christ, rather than according to proximately socialized expectations and idolatrous schematic misperceptions of his nature. Transformed communities and individuals will learn to return good for evil. They will learn go a second mile when asked to go one. They will learn to forgive even before the other has repented. They will learn to love the stranger, the outcast, and even the enemy. Why? Certainly not because living this way works for them or because it rewards their behavior. Indeed, disciples rarely see the outcome of such redemptive actions. In the Spirit they learn through this pattern to live convictionally, moving out through personal or corporate transformations in anticipation toward the transformation of all things.

Educationally, we *"work out our salvation with fear and trembling"* as we learn to speak the unspeakable and learn to live the miracle—but only with fear and trembling.

# Bibliography

Adorno, Theodore W., et al. *The Authoritarian Personality.* The American Jewish Committee. Social Studies Series 3. New York: Harper, 1950.

Anderson, Bernhard W. *From Creation to New Creation: Old Testament Perspectives.* OBT. Minneapolis: Fortress, 1994.

Ardrey, Robert. *The Territorial Imperative: A Personal Inquiry into the Animal Origins of Property and Nations.* New York: Atheneum, 1966.

Arendt, Hannah. *On Revolution.* New York: Viking, 1963.

Atlas, James. "What Is Fukuyama Saying? And To Whom Is He Saying It?" *New York Times Magazine* 131 (October 22, 1989) 38–40.

Axel, Gabriel, dir. *Babette's Feast.* DVD. Copenhagen: Nordisk Films, 1987.

Barth, Karl. *Church Dogmatics* IV/3.2. Translated by Geoffrey Bromiley. Edinburgh: T. & T. Clark, 1962.

————. *Dogmatics in Outline.* New York: Harper & Row, 1959.

————. *Epistle to the Romans.* Translated by Edwin C. Hoskyns. 6th ed New York: Oxford University Press, 1968.

————. *Der Romerbrief.* Munich: Kaiser, 1924.

————. *The Word of God and the Word of Man.* Translated by Douglas Horton. 1928. Reprint, Gloucester, MA: Smith, 1978.

Bell, Daniel. *The End of Ideology: On the Exhaustion of Political Ideas in the Fifties.* Rev. ed. New York: Free Press, 1965.

Bellah, Robert N. "Civil Religion in America." *Daedalus* 96/1 (Winter 1967) 1–21. Reprinted in *Religion in America,* edited by William C. McLoughlin and Robert N. Bellah, 3–23. The Daedalus Library 12. Boston: Beacon, 1968; and in *Rethinking Education: Selected Readings in the Educational Ideologies,* edited by William F. O'Neill, 32–45. Dubuque: Kendall/Hunt, 1983.

Bellah, Robert N., et al. *Habits of the Heart: Individualism and Commitment in American Life.* Perennial Library. New York: Harper & Row, 1986.

Berger, Peter, and Thomas Luckmann. *The Social Construction of Reality: A Treatise on the Sociology of Knowledge.* Garden City, NY: Doubleday, 1966.

Bettelheim, Bruno. *Symbolic Wounds: Puberty Rites and the Envious Male.* Glencoe, IL: Free Press, 1954.

Bloom, Allan. *The Closing of the American Mind: How Higher Education Has Failed Democracy and Impoverished the Souls of Today's Students.* New York: Simon & Schuster, 1987.

Bloom, Allan et al. "Responses to Fukuyama." *National Interest* 16 (Summer 1989) 19–35.

Bonhoeffer, Dietrich. *Creation and Fall: A Theological Interpretation of Genesis 1–3*. Translated by John C. Fletcher. London: SCM, 1959.

Boys, Mary C. *Educating in Faith: Maps and Visions*. San Francisco: Harper & Row, 1989.

Bronfenbrenner, Urie. "The Effects of Social and Cultural Change on Personality." In *Personality and Social Systems*, edited by Neil J. Smelser and William T. Smelser, 347–56. New York: Wiley, 1963.

Brown, Roger. "The Achievement Motive." In *Social Psychology*, 423–76. New York: Free Press, 1965.

———. "The Authoritarian Personality and the Organization of Attitudes." In *Social Psychology*, 477–546. New York: Free Press, 1965.

———. *Social Psychology*. New York: Free Press, 1965.

Browning, Don S. *A Fundamental Practical Theology: Descriptive and Strategic Proposals*. Minneapolis: Fortress, 1991.

Brunner, Emil. *The Scandal of Christianity*. Robertson Lectures 1948. Philadelphia: Westminster, 1951.

Burrell, David. *Analogy and Philosophical Language*. New Haven: Yale University Press, 1973.

Bushnell, Horace. *Christian Nurture*. 1861. Reprint, Twin Brooks Series. Grand Rapids: Baker, 1979.

Buxton, William. *Talcott Parsons and the Capitalist Nation-State: Political Sociology as a Strategic Vocation*. Toronto: University of Toronto Press, 1985.

Calvin, John. *Institutes of the Christian Religion*. 2 vols. Edited by John T. McNeill. Translated by Ford Lewis Battles. Library of Christian Classics. Philadelphia: Westminster, 1960.

Coleridge, Samuel Taylor. *The Friend*, Vol 1. In *Collected Works of Samuel Taylor Coleridge*. Edited by Barbara Rooke. London: Routledge Kegan Paul, 1969.

Cox, Harvey. *Religion in the Secular City: Toward a Postmodern Theology*. New York: Simon & Schuster, 1984.

Crossan, John Dominic. *The Dark Interval: Towards a Theology of Story*. 1975. Reprint, Sonoma, CA: Polebridge, 1988.

Cully, Iris V. "Christian Education: Instruction and Nurture." *Religious Education* 61/1 (1966) 8–10.

Dahrendorf, Ralf. "Out of Utopia: Toward a Reorientation." In *System, Change, and Conflict: A Reader on Contemporary Sociological Theory and the Debate over Functionalism*, edited by N. J. Demerath and Richard A. Peterson, 465–80. New York: Free Press, 1967.

Davies, W. D. *The Gospel and the Land*. 1974. Reprint, Biblical Seminar 25. Sheffield: JSOT Press, 1994.

De Beausobre, Iulia. *Creative Suffering*. Westminster: Dacre, 1956.

———. *The Woman Who Could Not Die*. London: Gollancz, 1948.

Demerath, N. J., and Richard A. Peterson. *System, Change, and Conflict: A Reader on Contemporary Sociological Theory and the Debate over Functionalism*. New York: Free Press, 1967.

Diem, Hermann. *Kierkegaard's Dialectic of Existence*. Translated by Harold Knight. Edinburgh: Oliver & Boyd, 1959.

Duckworth, Eleanor. "The Having of Wonderful Ideas." In *The Having of Wonderful Ideas, and Other Essays on Teaching and Learning*, 1–14. New York: Teachers College, 1987. First published in *Harvard Educational Review* 42/2 (Summer, 1972) 217–31. Reprinted in *Piaget in the Classroom*, edited by Milton Schwebel and Jane Beasley Ralph, 258–77. New York: Basic Books, 1973.

Dykstra, Craig. *Growing in the Life of Faith: Education and Christian Practices*. Louisville: Geneva, 1999.

Ebeling, Gerhard. *Word and Faith*. Translated by James W. Leitch. Philadelphia: Fortress, 1963.

Elliot, Harrison S. *Can Religious Education Be Christian?* New York: Macmillan, 1940.

Erikson, Erik H. *Insight and Responsibility: Lectures on the Ethical Implications of Psychoanalytic Insight*. New York: Norton, 1964.

———. *Toys and Reasons: Stages in the Ritualization of Experience*. Godkin Lectures at Harvard University 1972. New York: Norton, 1977.

Fairchild, Roy. "Spiritual Technology and Prophetic Word." In Issues in Contemporary Spirituality, Warfield Lectures, 1987. diglib.ptsem.edu/.

Falwell, Jerry. "Freedom's Heritage and Education." In *Rethinking Education: Selected Readings in the Educational Ideologies*, edited by William F. O'Neill, 63–65. Dubuque: Kendall/Hunt, 1983.

Farley, Edward. "Does Christian Education Need the Holy Spirit? Part I: The Strange History of Christian *Paideia*." *Religious Education* 60/5 (1965) 339–46.

———. "Does Christian Education Need the Holy Spirit? Part II: The Work of the Holy Spirit in Christian Education." *Religious Education* 60/6 (1965) 427–36, 479.

———. *Ecclesial Man: A Social Phenomenology of Faith and Reality*. Minneapolis: Augsburg, 1975.

———. "'Rigid Instruction' versus Brahman: A Reply." *Religious Education* 66/3 (1966) 229–41.

Farrar, Austin. *Finite and Infinite: A Philosophical Essay*. 2nd ed. London: Dacre, 1959.

Fenn, Richard. *Liturgies and Trials: Secularization of Religious Language*. Oxford: Blackwell, 1982.

Fowler, James W. *Stages of Faith: The Psychology of Human Development and the Quest for Meaning*. San Francisco: Harper & Row, 1981.

Fowler, James W., and James E. Loder Jr. "Conversations on Fowler's *Stages of Faith* and Loder's *The Transforming Moment*." *Religious Education* 77/2 (1982) 133–48.

Freud, Sigmund. "Negation." In *Organization and Pathology of Thought: Selected Sources*, edited by David Rapaport, 338–48. Austen Riggs Foundation Monograph 1. New York: Columbia University Press, 1951.

Friedman, Meyer, and Ray H. Rosenman. *Type A Behavior and Your Heart*. New York: Knopf, 1974.

Friere, Paulo. *Conscientization*. CCPD Documents: Justice and Development 7. Geneva: World Council of Churches, 1975.

———. *Education for Critical Consciousness*. A Continuum Book. New York: Seabury, 1973.

———. *Pedagogy of the Oppressed*. Translated by Myra Bergman Ramos. New York: Herder & Herder, 1970.

Fromm, Eric. *The Heart of Man: It's Genius for Good and Evil*. Religious Perspectives 12. New York: Harper, 1964.

Fukuyama, Francis. "The End of History?" *National Interest* 16 (Summer 1989) 3–18.

———. *The End of History and the Last Man*. New York: Free Press, 1992.

Gadamer, Hans Georg. *Truth and Method*. Translated by Garrett Barden and John Cumming. A Continuum Book. New York: Seabury, 1975.

Gardner, Richard. *Therapeutic Communication with Children: The Mutual Storytelling Technique*. New York: Science House, 1971.

Garfinkel, Harold. *Studies in Ethnomethodology*. Englewood Cliffs, NJ: Prentice-Hall, 1967

Gilkey, Langton. *Naming the Whirlwind: The Renewal of God-Language*. Indianapolis: Bobbs-Merrill, 1976.

Gilligan, Carol. *In a Different Voice: Psychological Theory and Women's Development*. Cambridge: Harvard University Press, 1982.

———. "In a Different Voice: Women's Conceptions of Self and Morality." Cambridge: *Harvard Educational Review* 47/4 (1977) 481–517.

Gordon, Chad, and Kenneth J. Gergen, eds. *Classic and Contemporary Perspectives*, 259–66. The Self in Social Interaction 1. New York: Wiley, 1968.

Grandfield, Robert. *Making Elite Lawyers: Visions of Law at Harvard and Beyond*. Critical Social Thought Series. New York: Routledge, 1992.

Greely, Andrew. *Sociology of the Paranormal*. Beverly Hills, CA: Sage, 1975.

Green, Roger Lancelyn, and Walter Hooper. *C. S. Lewis: A Biography*. New York: Harcourt Brace Jovanovich, 1974.

Groome, Thomas. *Christian Religious Education: Sharing Our Story and Vision*. San Francisco: Harper & Row, 1982.

Gunton, Colin. *A Brief Theology of Revelation*. 1993 Warfield Lectures. Edinburgh: T. & T. Clark, 1995.

Habermas, Jürgen. *Knowledge and Human Interests*. Translated by Jeremy J. Shapiro. Boston: Beacon, 1971.

Haitch, Russell. "A Summary of James E. Loder's Theory of Christian Education." In *Redemptive Transformation in Practical Theology: Essays in Honor of James E. Loder Jr.*, edited by Dana R. Wright and John D. Kuentzel, 298–324. Grand Rapids: Eerdmans, 2004.

Hamilton, Peter. *Talcott Parsons*. Key Sociologists. London: Routledge, 1983.

Hampden-Turner, Charles. *Radical Man: The Process of Psycho-Social Development*. Cambridge: Schenkman, 1970.

Hardy, Alister. *The Spiritual Nature of Man: A Study of Contemporary Religious Experience*. Oxford: Clarendon, 1979.

Harlow, Harry F. *Learning to Love*. San Francisco: Albion, 1971.

Harris, Thomas A. *I'm OK—You're OK: A Practical Guide to Transactional Analysis*. New York: Harper & Row, 1967.

*Harvard Magazine* (unnamed reviewer). "Endpapers." Review of *Making Elite Lawyers: Visions of Law and Beyond*, by Robert Granfield. *Harvard Magazine* 95/3 (January-February, 1993) 112.

Heilbroner, Robert L. *An Inquiry into the Human Prospect*. New York: Norton, 1974.

Heisenberg, Werner. *Physics and Beyond: Encounters and Conversations*. World Perspectives 42. New York: Harper & Row, 1971.

Hendry, George S. "The Human Spirit and the Holy Spirit." In Hendry, *The Holy Spirit in Christian Theology*, 96–117. Rev. and enl. ed. Philadelphia: Westminster, 1965.

Hiltner, Seward. *Religion and Health*. New York: Macmillan, 1943.

Hofstadter, Douglas R., and Daniel C. Dennett, eds. *The Mind's I: Fantasies and Reflections on Self and Soul*. New York: Basic Books, 1981.

Homans, George C. "Structural, Functional and Psychological Theories." In *System, Change, and Conflict: A Reader on Contemporary Sociological Theory and the Debate over Functionalism*, edited by N. J. Demerath and Richard A. Peterson, 347–66. New York: Free Press, 1967.

Hunter, David R. "The Box Theory of Christian Education." *Religious Education* 61/1 (January–February, 1966) 5–8.

Illich, Ivan. *Deschooling Society*. World Perspectives 44. New York: Harper & Row, 1970.

———. "The Ritualization of Progress." In *Rethinking Education: Selected Readings in the Educational Ideologies*, edited by William F. O'Neill, 464–72. Dubuque: Kendall/Hunt, 1983.

———. *Tools for Conviviality*. World Perspectives 47. New York: Harper & Row, 1973.

Jorstad, Erling. "The Politics of Doomsday." In *Rethinking Education: Selected Readings in the Educational Ideologies*, edited by William F. O'Neill. 66–76. Dubuque, IA: Kendall/Hunt, 1983.

Kardner, Abram, and Lionel Ovesey. "On the Psychodynamics of the Negro Personality In *The Self in Social Interaction*. Vol. 1, *Classic and Contemporary Perspectives*, edited by Chad Gordon and Kenneth J. Gergen, 259–66. New York: Wiley, 1968.

Keller, Evelyn Fox. *A Feeling for the Organism: The Life and Work of Barbara McClintock*. San Francisco: Freeman, 1983.

Kermode, Frank. *The Sense of an Ending: Studies in the Theory of Fiction*. The Mary Flexner Lectures 1965. London: Oxford University Press, 1967.

Kierkegaard, Søren. *Attack upon "Christendom."* Translated, with an introduction, by Walter Lowrie. Princeton: Princeton University Press, 1944.

———. *Concluding Unscientific Postscript to Philosophical Fragments*, vol. 1. Edited and translated by Howard V. Hong and Edna H. Hong. Kierkegaard's Writings 12. Princeton: Princeton University Press, 1992.

———. *Søren Kierkegaard's Journals and Papers*, Vol. 2, *F–K*. Edited and translated by Howard and Edna Hong. Bloomington: Indiana University Press, 1970.

———. *Søren Kierkegaard's Papirer*, vol. 2. 11 vols. in 20. 2nd ed. Edited by P. A. Heilberg et al. Copenhagen: Gyldendal, 1909.

Kirmmse, Bruce. *Kierkegaard in Golden Age Denmark*. The Indiana Series in the Philosophy of Religion. Bloomington: Indiana University Press, 1990.

Koestler, Arthur. *The Act of Creation*. New York: Macmillan, 1964.

———. *Insight and Outlook: An Inquiry into the Common Foundations of Science, Art, and Social Ethics*. A Bison Book. Lincoln: University of Nebraska Press, 1949.

Kohlberg, Lawrence. *The Philosophy of Moral Development*. Essays on Moral Development 1. San Francisco: Harper & Row, 1981.

Kraemer, Hendrik. "Foreword." In *Christianity in World History: The Meeting of the Faiths of East and West*, by Arendt Theodor van Leeuwen, ix–xi. Translated by H. H. Hoskins. Edinburgh: Edinburgh House, 1964.

———. *A Theology of the Laity*. Philadelphia: Westminster, 1958.

Krych, Margaret A. "Communicating 'Justification' to Elementary-Aged Children: A Study in Tillich's Correlation Method and Transformational Narrative for Christian Education." PhD diss., Princeton Theological Seminary, 1985.

———. *Teaching the Gospel Today: A Guide for Education in the Congregation*. Minneapolis: Augsburg, 1988.

———. "Transformational Narrative in a Non-Transformational Tradition." In *Redemptive Transformation in Practical Theology: Essays in Honor of James E. Loder Jr.*, edited by Dana R. Wright and John D. Kuentzel, 279–97. Grand Rapids: Eerdmans, 2004.

Kuhn, Thomas. *The Structure of Scientific Revolutions*. Chicago: University of Chicago Press, 1962.

Langer, Susan. *Feeling and Form: A Theory of Art Developed from Philosophy in a New Key*. New York: Scribner, 1953.

———. *Philosophy in a New Key: A Study in the Symbolism of Reason, Rite and Art*. Cambridge: Harvard University Press, 1942.

Lawson, Kevin, ed. *Christian Educators of the 20th Century*. La Mirada, CA: Talbot School of Theology, n.d. http://www.talbot.edu/ce20/.

Leeuwen, Arend Theodor van. *Christianity in World History: The Meeting of the Faiths of East and West*. Translated by H. H. Hoskins. Edinburgh: Edinburgh House, 1964.

Lehmann, Paul. *Ethics in a Christian Context*. New York: Harper & Row, 1963.

———. *The Transfiguration of Politics*. New York: Harper & Row, 1975.

Lifton, Robert. "Adaptation and Value Development: Self-Process in Protean Man." In *The Acquisition and Development of Values: Perspectives on Research*. 38–51. Bethesda, MD: National Institute of Child Health and Human Development, 1969.

———. "Protean Man." In *Archives of General Psychology* 24/4 (1971) 298–304.

———. *The Protean Self: Human Resilience in an Age of Fragmentation*. New York: Basic Books, 1993.

Lindbeck, George A. *The Nature of Doctrine: Religion and Theology in a Postliberal Age*. Philadelphia: Westminster, 1984.

Lockwood, David. "Some Remarks on 'The Social System.'" In *System, Change, and Conflict: A Reader on Contemporary Sociological Theory and the Debate over Functionalism*, edited by N. J. Demerath and Richard A. Peterson, 281–92. New York: Free Press, 1967.

Loder, James E. "Developmental Foundations for Christian Education." In *Foundations for Christian Education in an Era of Change*, edited by Marvin J. Taylor, 54–67. Nashville: Abingdon, 1976.

———. "Educational Ministry" (ED 105 Class Lectures). Princeton Seminary, Speer Library, Princeton. Loder Archive.

———. *Education Ministry in the Logic of the Spirit* (Unpublished manuscript). Princeton Theological Seminary, Speer Library, Loder archive.

———. "The Fashioning of Power: A Christian Perspective on the Life-Style Phenomenon." In *The Context of Contemporary Theology: Essays in Honor of Paul Lehmann*, edited by Alexander J. McKelway and E. David Willis, 187–208. Atlanta: John Knox, 1974.

———. *The Logic of the Spirit: Human Development in Theological Perspective*. San Francisco: Jossey-Bass, 1998.

———. "Normativity and Context in Practical Theology: The 'Interdisciplinary Issue.'" In *Practical Theology: International Perspectives*, edited by F. Schweizer and J. A. van der Ven, 359–81. Erfahrung und Theologie 34. New York: Lang, 1999.

———. "The Place of Science in Practical Theology: The Human Factor." *International Journal of Practical Theology* 4 (2000) 22–41.

———. *Religious Pathology and Christian Faith*. Philadelphia: Westminster, 1966.

―――. "Sociocultural Foundations for Christian Education." In *Introduction to Christian Education*, edited by Marvin J. Taylor, 71–84. Nashville: Abingdon, 1966.

―――. *The Transforming Moment.* 2nd ed. Colorado Springs: Helmers & Howard, 1989.

―――. *The Transforming Moment: Understanding Convictional Experiences.* San Francisco: Harper & Row, 1981.

Loder, James E., Jr., and W. Jim Neidhardt. "Barth, Bohr and Dialectic." In *Religion and Science: History, Method, Dialogue*, edited by W. Richardson and Wesley J. Wildman, 271–98. New York: Routledge, 1996

―――. *The Knight's Move: The Relational Logic of the Spirit in Theology and Science.* Colorado Springs: Helmers & Howard, 1992.

Lonergan, Bernard. "Elements of Metaphysics." In *Insight: A Study of Human Understanding*, 431–87. San Francisco: Harper & Row, 1978.

Lorenz, Konrad. *Evolution and Modification of Behavior.* Chicago: University of Chicago Press, 1965.

―――. *Studies in Animal and Human Behaviour.* 2 vols. Translated by Robert Martin. Cambridge: Harvard University Press, 1970–1971.

Lynch, James J. *The Broken Heart: The Medical Consequences of Loneliness.* New York: Basic Books, 1977.

Lynn, Robert W., and Elliott Wright. *The Big Little School: Two Hundred Years of the Sunday School.* Birmingham: Religious Education, 1980.

Maccoby, Michael. *The Gamesman: The New Corporate Leaders.* New York: Simon & Schuster, 1977.

Maltz, Maxwell. *Psycho-Cybernetics.* A Fireside Book. New York: Simon & Schuster, 1960.

Martin, Ralph. *Carmen Christi: Philippians 2:5–11 in Recent Interpretation and in the Setting of Early Christian Worship.* SNTSMS 4. London: Cambridge University Press, 1967.

Marx, Karl. *Articles on India.* Bombay: People's, 1951.

Mayr, Marlene, ed. *Modern Masters of Religious Education.* Mishawaka, IN: Religious Education, 1983.

McClure, John. "Preaching and the Pragmatics of Human/Divine Communication in the Liturgy of the Word in the Western Church: A Semiotic and Practical Theological Study." PhD diss., Princeton Theological Seminary, 1984.

McIntyre, Alasdair. *After Virtue: A Study in Moral Theory.* 2nd ed. Notre Dame, IN: Notre Dame University Press, 1984.

McNeill, David. *The Acquisition of Language: The Study of Developmental Psycholinguistics.* New York: Harper & Row, 1970.

Mead, George Herbert. *Mind, Self & Society: From the Standpoint of a Social Behavior.* Edited, with an introduction, by Charles W. Morris. Chicago: University of Chicago Press, 1934.

Mead, Margaret, and James Baldwin. *A Rap on Race.* Philadelphia: Lippincott, 1971.

Milbank, John. *Theology and Social Theory: Beyond Secular Reason.* Signposts in Theology. Oxford: Blackwell, 1990.

Milbank, John et al., eds. *Radical Orthodoxy.* London: Routledge, 1999.

Milgram, Stanley. "Behavioral Study of Obedience." *Journal of Abnormal and Social Psychology* 67/4 (1963) 371–78.

———. "Dynamics of Obedience: Experiments in Social Psychology." Mimeographed report. National Science Foundation, Jan. 25, 1961.

———. *Obedience*. DVD, available from the Stanley Milgram Films on Social Psychology. Distributed by Alexander Street, Alexandra, VA. Alexanderstreet. com/.

———. *Obedience to Authority: An Experimental View*. New York: Harper & Row, 1974.

———. "Some Conditions of Obedience and Disobedience to Authority." In *Human Relations* 18/1 (1965) 57–76.

Miller, Randolf Crump. *Christian Nurture and the Church*. New York: Scribner, 1961.

———. *The Clue to Christian Education*. New York: Scribner, 1950.

Mills, C. Wright. "Grand Theory." In *System, Change, and Conflict: A Reader on Contemporary Sociological Theory and the Debate over Functionalism*, edited by N. J. Demerath and Richard A. Peterson, 171–84. New York: Free Press, 1967.

———. *The Sociological Imagination*. Oxford: Oxford University Press, 1959.

Minneman, Charles E., ed. *Students, Religion, and the Contemporary University*. Yipsilanti: Eastern Michigan University Press, 1970.

Montagu, Ashley. *On Being Human*. 2nd ed. New York: Hawthorn, 1966.

———. *Touching: The Human Significance of the Skin*. New York: Columbia University Press, 1971.

Moore, Allen J., ed. *Religious Education as Social Transformation*. Birmingham: Religious Education, 1989.

Nagel, Thomas. "What Is It Like to Be a Bat?" In *The Mind's I: Fantasies and Reflections on Self and Soul*, edited by D. R. Hofstadter and Daniel C. Dennett, 391–414. New York: Basic Books, 1981.

Nelson, C. Ellis, ed. *Congregations: Their Power to Form and Transform*. Atlanta: John Knox, 1988.

———. *How Faith Matures*. Louisville: Westminster John Knox, 1989.

———. "Toward Accountable Selfhood." In *Modern Masters of Religious Education*, edited by Marlene Mayr, 160–173. Birmingham: Religious Education, 1983.

———. *Where Faith Begins*. The James Sprunt Lectures 1965. Richmond: John Knox, 1967.

Nelson, James M. *Psychology, Religion, and Spirituality*. New York: Springer, 2009.

Niebuhr, H. Richard. *Christ and Culture*. New York: Harper, 1951.

Njoya, Timothy. "Dynamics of Change in African Christianity: African Theology through Historical and Sociopolitical Change." PhD diss., Princeton Theological Seminary, 1971

O'Neill, William F. ed. *Rethinking Education: Selected Readings in the Educational Ideologies*. Dubuque: Kendall/Hunt, 1983.

Osmer, Richard. "James W. Fowler and the Reformed Tradition: An Exercise in Theological Reflection in Religious Education." *Religious Education* 85/1 (1990) 51–68.

Otto, Rudolf. *The Idea of the Holy: An Inquiry into the Non-Rational Factor in the Idea of the Divine and Its Relation to the Rational*. Translated by J. W. Harvey, 1958. Reprint. New York: Oxford University Press, 1977.

Palmer, Parker. *To Know as We Are Known: A Spirituality of Education*. San Francisco: Harper & Row, 1983.

Pannenberg, Wolfhart. *Anthropology in Theological Perspective*. Translated by Matthew J. O'Connell. Philadelphia: Westminster, 1985.

———. *Jesus, God and Man*. Translated by Lewis L. Wilkins and Duane A. Priebe. Philadelphia: Westminster, 1968.

———, ed. *Revelation as History*. Translated by David Granskou. New York: Macmillan, 1968.

Parks, Sharon Daloz. *Big Questions, Worthy Dreams: Mentoring Young Adults in Their Search for Meaning, Purpose, and Faith*. Rev. ed. San Francisco: Jossey-Bass, 2011.

———. *The Critical Years: Young Adults and the Search for Meaning, Faith and Commitment*. San Francisco: Harper & Row, 1986. Reprinted as *Big Questions, Worthy Dreams: Mentoring Young Adults in Their Search for Meaning, Purpose, and Faith*. San Francisco: Jossey-Bass, 2000.

Parsons, Talcott et al. *Family: Socialization and Interaction Process*. Glencoe, IL: Free Press, 1955.

Penfield, Wilder *The Mystery of the Mind: A Critical Study of Consciousness and the Human Brain*. Princeton: Princeton University Press, 1975.

Peter, Laurence J., and Raymond Hull. *The Peter Principle: Why Things Always Go Wrong*. New York: Morrow, 1969.

Pettigrew, Thomas F., and Patricia J. Pajonas. "The Social Psychology of Heterogeneous Schools." In *Cultural Challenges to Education: The Influence of Cultural Factors in School Learning*, edited by Cole S. Brembeck and Walker H. Hill, 87–106. Lexington, MA: Heath, 1973.

Peursen, C. A. van. "Creative Capitulations: An Approach to Human Thought." Warfield Lecture Series 1976. Princeton Theological Seminary. diglib.ptsem.edu/.

———. "Creativity as the Learning Process." In The Concept of Creativity in Science and Art, edited by Denis Dutton and Michael Krausz, 157–85. Martinus Nijhoff Philosophical Library 6. The Hague: Nijhoff, 1981, distributed by Kluwer Academic.

Piaget, Jean. *The Construction of Reality in the Child*. Translated by Margaret Cook. New York: Basic Books, 1954.

———. *Genetic Epistemology*. Translated by Eleanor Duckworth. New York: Columbia University Press, 1970.

———. *The Origins of Intelligence in Children*. New York: International University Press, 1952.

———. *The Principles of Genetic Epistemology*. New York: Basic Books, 1972.

Piaget, Jean, and Rolando Garcia. *Psychogenesis and the History of Science*. Translated by Helga Felder. New York: Columbia University Press, 1989.

Pinker, Steven. *The Language Instinct: How the Mind Creates Language*. New York: HarperPerennial, 1994.

Polanyi, Michael. *Personal Knowledge: Towards a Post-Critical Philosophy*. Harper Torchbooks/Academy Library. New York: Harper & Row, 1964.

Pope, Liston. *Millhands & Preachers: A Study of Gastonia*. Yale Studies in Religious Education 15. New Haven: Yale University Press, 1942.

Popper, Karl R. and John C. Eccles. *The Self and Its Brain*. New York: Springer,1977.

Prenter, Regin. *Spiritus Creator*. Translated by John M. Jensen. Philadelphia: Muhlenberg, 1953.

Presbyterian Church, Office of the General Assembly. "The Second Helvetic Confession." In *The Constitution of the Presbyterian Church (U.S.A): Part I, Book of Confessions*, 75–143. Louisville: Presbyterian Distribution Service, 2014.

Presbyterian Panel. *The March: 1978 Questionnaire on Prayer, Religious Practices, and Sources for Christian Growth*. New York: Research Division of the Support Agency, United Presbyterian Church in the U.S.A., August, 1978.

Prigogine, Illya, and Isabelle Stengers. *Order out of Chaos: Man's New Dialogue with Nature*. New York: Bantam, 1984.

Princeton Theological Seminary. *The Listening Library: Speech Studios Catalogue of Recordings*. Princeton: n.d.

Rad, Gerhard von. *Genesis: A Commentary*. Translated by John H. Marks. Rev. ed. OTL. Philadelphia: Westminster, 1961.

Ramsey, Ian T. *Religious Language: An Empirical Placing of Theological Phrases*. New York: Macmillan, 1963.

Rapoport, Judith L. *The Boy Who Couldn't Stop Washing: The Experience & Treatment of Obsessive-Compulsive Disorder*. New York: Signet, 1991.

Ricoeur, Paul. "Toward a Hermeneutic of the Idea of Revelation." *HTR* 70 (1977) 1–37.

Rizzuto, Ana-Maria. *The Birth of the Living God: A Psychoanalytic Study*. Chicago: University of Chicago Press, 1979.

Rogers, Carl. *Freedom to Learn: A View of What Education Might Become*. Columbus, OH: Merrill, 1969.

Root, Andrew, with Blair Bertrand. "Postscript: Reflections on Method—Youth Ministry as Practical Theology." In *The Theological Turn in Youth Ministry*, by Andrew Root and Kenda Creasy Dean, 218–36. Downers Grove, IL: IVP Books, 2011.

Russell, Letty. *Human Liberation in a Feminist Perspective: A Theology*. Philadelphia: Westminster, 1974.

Sanford, Nevitt. *Self & Society: Social Change and Individual Development*. New York: Atherton, 1966.

Sartre, Jean-Paul. *The Words*. Translated by Bernard Frechtman. New York: Braziller, 1964.

Sawicki, Marianne. *The Gospel in History: Portrait of a Teaching Church; The Origins of Christian Education*. New York: Paulist, 1988.

Schipani, Daniel S. *Conscientization and Creativity: Paulo Freire and Christian Education*. Lanham, MD: University Press of America, 1984.

Skinner, B. F. *Walden Two*. Indianapolis: Hackett. 1948. Rev. ed., 1976.

Smart, James D. "The Holy Spirit—Superfluous to Education or Essential?" *Religious Education* 61/3 (1966) 223–29.

———. *The Teaching Ministry of the Church: An Examination of the Basic Principles of Christian Education*. Philadelphia: Westminster, 1954.

Smith, Constance Babington. *Iulia de Beausobre: A Russian Christian in the West*. London: Darton, Longman & Todd, 1983.

Smith, H. Shelton. *Faith and Nurture*. New York: Scribner, 1941.

———. "Let Religious Educators Reckon with Barthians." *Religious Education* 24/1 (1934) 45–51.

Sperry, Roger. *Science and Moral Priority: Merging Mind, Brain, and Human Values*. Convergence. New York: Columbia University Press, 1983.

Spitz, Rene. *The First Year of Life: A Psychoanalytic Study of Normal and Deviant Development of Object Relations*. New York: International Universities, 1965.

———. *No and Yes: On the Genesis of Human Communication*. New York: International Universities Press, 1957.

Swidler, Ann. "In Groups We Trust." Review of *Sharing the Journey: Support Groups and America's Search for Community*, by Robert Wuthnow. *New York Times Book Review* 13 (March 20) 1994. http://search.proquest.com/docview/109295078?acc ountid=14784/.

Taylor, Marvin J., ed. *Foundations for Christian Education in an Era of Change*. Nashville: Abingdon, 1976.

Tenner, Edward. "The Revenge Effect." *Harvard Magazine* 93/4 (March/April, 1991) 27–31.

Thomas, George F. *Spirit and Its Freedom*. Chapel Hill: University of North Carolina Press, 1939.

Tomkins, Silvan S. *Affect, Imagery, Consciousness*. Vol. 1, *The Positive Affects*. New York: Springer, 1962.

Torrence, Thomas F. *Space, Time and Resurrection*. Grand Rapids: Eerdmans, 1976.

———. *Theological Science*. London: Oxford University Press, 1969.

Turnbull, Colin. *The Forest People*. New York: Simon & Schuster, 1961.

Wainwright, Geoffrey. *Doxology: The Praise of God in Worship, Doctrine, and Life*. New York: Oxford University Press, 1980.

Wallace, Anthony F. C. *Culture and Personality*. Studies in Anthropology. New York: Random House, 1961.

Weber, Max. *The Protestant Ethic and the Spirit of Capitalism*. Translated by Talcott Parsons. Scribner Library. New York: Scribner, 1958.

Weir, Peter, dir. *Dead Poets Society*. DVD. Los Angeles: Touchstone Pictures, 1989.

Whitehead, Alfred North. *The Aims of Education, and Other Essays*. A Mentor Book. New York: New American Library, 1964.

———. *Symbolism: Its Meaning and Effect*. Barbour-Page Lectures, University of Virginia, 1927. New York: Macmillan, 1927.

Windelband, Wilhelm. *A History of Philosophy*. New York: Macmillan, 1893.

Wink, Walter. *The Bible in Human Transformation*. Philadelphia: Fortress, 1973.

Winter, Gibson. *Elements for a Social Ethic: Scientific and Ethical Perspectives on Social Process*. New York: Macmillan, 1966.

———. *Liberating Creation: Foundations of Religious Social Ethics*. New York: Crossroad, 1981.

Wolfson, Harry A. *The Philosophy of the Church Fathers*. Structure and Growth of Philosophic Systems from Plato to Spinoza 3. Cambridge: Harvard University Press, 1956.

Wright, Dana R. "Are You There? Comedic Interrogation in the Life and Witness of James E. Loder Jr." In *Redemptive Transformation in Practical Theology: Essays in Honor of James E. Loder Jr.*, edited by Dana R. Wright and John D. Kuentzel, 1–40. Grand Rapids: Eerdmans, 2004.

———. "Babylonian Mythology in the Genesis Record." Research file. Compiled for James Loder, 1994. Held by Dana Wright.

———. "*Educational Ministry in the Logic of the Spirit*: A Loder Legacy?" In *The Logic of the Spirit in Human Thought and Experience: Exploring the Vision*, edited by

Dana R. Wright and Keith White, 155–201. Eugene, OR: Pickwick Publications, 2014.

———. "*Homo Testans*: The Life, Work, and Witness of James E. Loder Jr." In *The Logic of the Spirit in Human Thought and Experience: Exploring the Vision of James E. Loder Jr.*, edited by Dana R. Wright and Keith White, 1–30. Eugene, OR: Pickwick Publications, 2014.

———. "James E. Loder Jr." In *Christian Educators of the 20th Century Project* (hard copy), edited by Kevin Lawson. La Mirada, CA: Talbot Seminary, n.d. http://www.talbot.edu/ce20/.

———. "Personal Knowledge Transformed: James Loder's Neo-Chalcedonian Science of Practical Theology." In *Tradition & Discovery* 42/2 (2015–2016) 34–51.

Wright, Dana R. and John D. Kuentzel, eds. *Redemptive Transformation in Practical Theology: Essays in Honor of James E. Loder Jr.* Grand Rapids: Eerdmans, 2004.

Wright, Dana R., and Keith White, eds. *The Logic of the Spirit in Human Thought and Experience: Exploring the Vision of James E. Loder Jr.* Eugene, OR: Pickwick Publications, 2014.

Wuthnow, Robert. *Sharing the Journey: Support Groups and America's Quest for Community.* New York: Free Press, 1994.

Wyckoff, D. Campbell. "Instruction, the Person, and the Group." *Religious Education* 61/1 (1966) 10–12.

———. *Theory and Design of Christian Education Curriculum.* Philadelphia: Westminster, 1961.

———. "Understanding Your Church's Curriculum." *Princeton Seminary Bulletin* 63/1 (1970) 77–84.

Zimbardo, Philip G., in consultation with Floyd L. Ruch. *Psychology and Life.* 9th ed. Glenview, IL: Scott, Foresman, 1975.

# Index